D0609522

6/26/12
$60.00

Posthumous Interests

Daniel Sperling discusses the legal status of posthumous interests and their possible defeat by actions performed following the death of a person. The author first explores the following questions: Do the dead have interests and/or rights, the defeat of which may constitute harm? What does posthumous harm consist of and when does it occur, if at all? This is followed by a more detailed analysis of three categories of posthumous interests arising in the medico-legal context: the proprietary interest in the body of the deceased, the testamentary interest in determining the disposal of one's body after death and the interest in post-mortem medical confidentiality. Sperling concludes that if we acknowledge the interest in one's symbolic existence and legally protect it, not only do some interests survive a person's death but we should also enjoy a peremptory legal power to shape in advance our symbolic existence after death.

Daniel Sperling teaches philosophy of law and bioethics at Netanya Academic College.

Cambridge Law, Medicine and Ethics

This series of books was founded by Cambridge University Press with Alexander McCall Smith as its first editor in 2003. It focuses on the law's complex and troubled relationship with medicine across both the developed and the developing world. In the past twenty years, we have seen in many countries increasing resort to the courts by dissatisfied patients and a growing use of the courts to attempt to resolve intractable ethical dilemmas. At the same time, legislatures across the world have struggled to address the questions posed by both the successes and the failures of modern medicine, while international organizations such as the WHO and UNESCO now regularly address issues of medical law.

It follows that we would expect ethical and policy questions to be integral to the analysis of the legal issues discussed in this series. The series responds to the high profile of medical law in universities, in legal and medical practice, as well as in public and political affairs. We seek to reflect the evidence that many major health-related policy debates in the UK, Europe and the international community over the past two decades have involved a strong medical law dimension. Organ retention, embryonic stem cell research, physician assisted suicide and the allocation of resources to fund health care are but a few examples among many. The emphasis of this series is thus on matters of public concern and/or practical significance. We look for books that could make a difference to the development of medical law and enhance the role of medico-legal debate in policy circles. That is not to say that we lack interest in the important theoretical dimensions of the subject, but we aim to ensure that theoretical debate is grounded in the realities of how the law does and should interact with medicine and health care.

General Editors
Professor Margaret Brazier, *University of Manchester*
Professor Graeme Laurie, *University of Edinburgh*

Editorial Advisory Board
Professor Richard Ashcroft, *Queen Mary, University of London*
Professor Martin Bobrow, *University of Cambridge*
Dr Alexander Morgan Capron, *Director, Ethics and Health, World Health Organization, Geneva*
Professor Jim Childress, *University of Virginia*
Professor Ruth Chadwick, *Cardiff Law School*
Dame Ruth Deech, *University of Oxford*
Professor John Keown, *Georgetown University, Washington, D.C.*
Dr Kathy Liddell, *University of Cambridge*
Professor Alexander McCall Smith, *University of Edinburgh*
Professor Dr Mónica Navarro-Michel, *University of Barcelona*

Posthumous Interests

Legal and Ethical Perspectives

Daniel Sperling

SJD, BA (Philosophy)

CAMBRIDGE
UNIVERSITY PRESS

CAMBRIDGE UNIVERSITY PRESS
Cambridge, New York, Melbourne, Madrid, Cape Town, Singapore,
São Paulo, Delhi, Dubai, Tokyo, Mexico City

Cambridge University Press
The Edinburgh Building, Cambridge CB2 8RU, UK

Published in the United States of America by Cambridge University Press, New York

www.cambridge.org
Information on this title: www.cambridge.org/9780521187664

First published 2008
First paperback edition 2010

A catalogue record for this publication is available from the British Library

Library of Congress Cataloguing in Publication data
Sperling, Daniel.
Posthumous interests : legal and ethical perspectives / by Daniel Sperling.
p.   cm. – (Cambridge law, medicine and ethics)
ISBN 978-0-521-87784-8
1. Dead bodies (Law)   2. Interest (Ownership rights)   3. Body, Human –
Law and legislation.   4. Autopsy – Law and legislation.   5. Donation of organs,
tissues, etc. – Law and legislation.   6. Body, Human – Moral and ethical aspects.
7. Privacy, Right of.   8. Wills.   1. Title.   11. Series.
K564.H8S64   2008
344.04´194–dc22
2007050179

ISBN 978-0-521-87784-8 Hardback
ISBN 978-0-521-18766-4 Paperback

For my beloved parents,
Rina and Adrian Sperling

Contents

Contents

Acknowledgements

This book is a development of the ideas explored in my SJD thesis, written for the University of Toronto, and its production took almost four years. I am grateful and indebted to my SJD supervisor, Bernard Dickens, who guided and supported me as much as possible, making the experience of writing this book lively and stimulating. Special thanks and much appreciation are also owed to Wayne Sumner and Trudo Lemmens for reviewing my work in progress and contributing significantly to its development.

Further gratitude is owed to Matthew Kramer, who invited me to the University of Cambridge and supported me while I was there. Matthew also read a considerable part of my book and contributed extensively to its enrichment and flourishing.

Throughout the work on my book I discussed my ideas with many people, some of whom also read and reviewed parts of my manuscript. I wish to thank John Broome, Hanoch Dagan, Abraham Drassinower, David Enoch, Martin Friedland, Ruth Gavison, Alon Harel, Halvard Lillehammer, Onora O'Neill, Guy Pessach, Denise Réaume, Arthur Ripstein, Julian Savulescu, Dominic Scott, Shmuel Shilo, James Warren and Joshua Weisman.

The financial support I received in the last four years enabled me to concentrate on my work and devote myself to its progress. I am grateful for receiving such support and would like to thank the Faculty of Law and the School of Graduate Studies at the University of Toronto, the Lucille Norris Graduate Fellowship, Strauss Fellowship in Law and Biotechnology, Bell University Laboratories Graduate Fellowship and the Lady Davis Fellowship. Special thanks are owed to Canada Institutes for Health Research Fellowship for providing three years of financial support and organizing annual colloquiums to present my work in progress. I wish to thank Colleen Flood, Jocelyn Downie, Tim Caulfield and Chrystal Gray for all their support and help in this regard.

Finally, I wish to show gratitude to my parents who provided endless love, support and encouragement all the way through, and to Aryeh with whom I shared my personal experiences while writing this book.

Table of cases

Table of national provisions

United States

Introduction

'There are three things', writes Salmond, 'in respect of which the anxieties of living men extend beyond the period of their deaths in such sort that the law will take notice of them. These are a man's body, his reputation and his estate.'[1] This book deals with all three. The following chapters discuss the notion of posthumous interests, namely interests whose advancement or fulfilment occurs after a person's death, and the representation of these interests in three legal areas: property, estate and privacy law. Special emphasis is given to the medical context. The examination focuses on various actions, procedures and decisions relating to the state of affairs occurring soon after a person's death. As such, the book is mainly concerned with the 'newly-dead' as opposed to the 'long-dead'. Examples of such actions include the performance of autopsies, organ donations and research on the body or its parts after death, the enforcement of a testament expressing the testator's wishes concerning the disposal of her body, and the disclosure of personal health information relating to a patient who has just died.

There are five major reasons why the book focuses on the idea of interest. First, medical procedures performed on dead patients provide an intersection of interests. The different standpoints and perspectives from which one can regard each of the situations described in the book are best understood by an appeal to the idea of interest. Consider, for instance, the procedure of taking an organ from the deceased without her express consent. In this situation, there are multiple conflicting interests. There is the interest of the deceased in having her organs harvested only following her prior wishes or the consent given by a substitute decision maker; society has an interest in overcoming the shortage of organs and providing dying patients with an accessible and affordable cure; the recipient may also have an interest in being cured and helped, especially when such medical aid does not physically harm any other person; and

---

[1] Glanville Williams, *Salmond on Jurisprudence* (London: Sweet & Maxwell, 1966), 12th edn, 301.

relatives of the decedent may have an interest in having their emotional stability preserved at the time of the death of a beloved one. While the language of 'interests' is common to all parties involved, little has been discussed in the legal literature as to whether the dead have interests of their own and, if so, what the content of these interests is and what theoretical basis supports them.

A second reason for the discussion of the idea of interest lies in the fact that examinination of the patient's interests is often advanced as a way to decide the proper medical treatment for a patient lacking mental capacity. A newly-dead patient who is subjected to various medical procedures from which no personal benefit is gained resembles in many aspects an incompetent patient for whom health-related decisions are being made by others. In the medical-law context, there exist two major mechanisms for reaching a healthcare decision for the incompetent. The dominant mechanism characterizing the English law involves the 'best interests' test. According to this test, initially established in *F* v. *West Berkshire Health Authority*[2] and reaffirmed in the case of *Anthony Bland*[3] and more recently under the Mental Capacity Act,[4] the administration of the proposed medical treatment or procedure should be in the patient's best interests.[5] In order to know what is in the patient's best interests one has to inquire about the nature of these interests in the first place. A counter-approach to the 'best interests' test is substituted decision making. This approach, specifically articulated by the majority opinion in *Cruzan*,[6] seeks to replicate the decision the patient would have made had she been competent by an appeal to the patient's substitute decision maker. Under this mechanism, the patient's subjective perspective as to the administration of the proposed medical treatment is being sought. Nevertheless, this perspective is learnt from another person, namely the patient's substitute decision maker. It follows that, according to both mechanisms, the interests of the incompetent patient play a major role in shaping and determining the medical procedure performed on her. This may suggest a parallel examination of posthumous interests as well.

A third reason why discussion of the concept of interest is necessary concerns the notion of harm. Advancement in medical technology and

[2] *F* v. *West Berkshire Health Authority* [1989] 2 All ER 545.
[3] *Airedale NHS Trust* v. *Bland* [1993] 1 All ER 821.
[4] Mental Capacity Act 2005, especially ss. 4, 5(b).
[5] A similar approach, though not as wide as the English one, was taken in the US by Justice Stevens in *Cruzan* v. *Director, Missouri Department of Health* 497 US 261 (1990) [*Cruzan*] and in Canada by the Law Reform Commission of Canada, *Euthanasia, Aiding Suicide and Cessation of Treatment*, working paper 28 (Ottawa: Ministry of Supply and Services: 1982).
[6] *Cruzan, ibid.*

scientific knowledge in recent years has created enormous possibilities to 'use' the body of the deceased or the medical information relating to it for purposes external to the deceased who is obviously beyond recovery. These various possible uses are sometimes misuses of power and reflect exploitation of the circumstances of death. A major concern accompanying posthumous use in the medical context involves the idea that the deceased is being harmed or wronged. To explore more on this idea one needs first to adopt a concept of harm or wrong. When applied to an insentient person, the more useful approach to harm or wrong would be one that connects the subject harmed to the interests she may have and their defeat by the harmful event. In this regard, harm is explained as the setting back or defeat of a person's interests. Exploring the question of whether the dead can have interests the defeat of which may constitute posthumous harm is beneficial to the development of this latter concept as well.

Fourth, interests are possible bases for a theory of rights. The law usually speaks in a language of rights and duties. Frequently, a legal entity may have rights, so that some rights of the same person may be competing with each other, or those rights may be in conflict with the rights of another legal entity or the rights of society as a whole. The language of rights carries with it political and social meaning that is both unique and powerful. This is why it is perhaps difficult to argue from the start that the dead have rights. The legal aspects of medical procedures performed post-mortem, the need to decide in relation to them and the potential harm caused by them all evoke the jurisprudential question of whether the dead who are subject to these procedures have legal rights the breach of which may constitute a legal wrong. In contrast to the choice theory of rights, which emphasizes the exercise of control by the right-holder, the interest theory of rights holds that the purpose of rights is to protect and promote some of the right-holder's interests. The discussion of interests rather than control seems more apposite when considering the dead as potential right-holders. Exploring the question of whether the dead have interests deserving legal protection strategically promotes the discussion of posthumous rights, and may raise fewer objections to such an idea due to the more neutral way in which interests are regarded in comparison to rights.

A fifth reason for the discussion of posthumous interests concerns the serious philosophical problems raised by this issue. In the introduction to his anthology, Desmond Manderson writes, 'on the one hand death seeks to control every aspect of our lives, including the manner of our passing; while death is precisely that element which lies outside of our control. On the other hand, the legal order is constructed around individual action and responsibility, yet death is precisely the moment at which this "*I*" ceases to be.'[7] Events pursued after a person's death continue to relate to that person as if she were alive, but nonetheless are treated as incidents which cannot affect the person subjected to them. This paradoxical situation may be explained by the (assumed) annihilation of the person and the cessation of her capacity to experience or be aware of actions to which she is subject. The only way to resolve this paradox is to ascribe the dead some moral and legal attribute which is weaker than the one characterizing a living person and yet sufficient not to be violated or ignored by others. The concept of human interest is a good candidate for conveying such an idea, mainly because it is both flexible and morally significant to form legal protections for the values which are in the background of these posthumous events.

A great deal has been written in the philosophical literature on the distinction between a person and a thing. A person is a creature who usually has capacity for rationality, is a social being consisting of part of a specific culture, and usually uses a language to communicate with other persons. A person also maintains the ability to experience things and to hold different mental states with regard to their external surroundings as well as their internal state of affairs. The concept of person is in Strawson's words 'the concept of a type of entity such that both predicates ascribing states of consciousness and predicates ascribing corporeal characteristics . . . are equally applicable to a single individual of that single type'.[8] Things, on the other hand, do not have value in their own right. Rather, their value consists entirely in their being objects of other beings' interests.[9] Mere things 'have no conative life; no conscious wishes, desires and hopes; or urges and impulses; or unconscious drives, aims and goals; or latent tendencies, direction of growth, and natural fulfillments'.[10] Because mere things can have no good of their own, it is argued that they do not have interests.[11]

The newly-dead may be an interim category between a person and a thing. It is difficult to regard the newly-dead only as a mere corpse, a decaying organic matter, a mere 'thing'. The dead retain their value after death and are distinguishable one from another due to specific

---

[7] Desmond Manderson, 'Introduction' in Desmond Manderson ed., *Courting Death* (London: Pluto, 1999) 1–16, at 2.

[8] P. F. Strawson, *Individuals* (London: Methuen, 1959) 101–2. See also A. J. Ayer, *The Concept of a Person* (New York: St Martin's, 1963) 82.

[9] Joel Feinberg, 'The Rights of Animals and Unborn Generations' in Joel Feinberg ed., *Rights, Justice and the Bounds of Liberty* (Princeton, N.J.: Princeton University Press, 1980) 159, 166.

[10] *Ibid.*   [11] *Ibid.*

characteristics representing the persons they were. On the other hand, to hold that the dead are still 'persons' demands substantial revisions for this concept which may detract from its undisputed meaning. A new concept must be invoked to capture the nature of this 'creature' and highlight its moral and legal significance. The following chapters search for that concept, exploring the tension between the 'personhood' and 'thinghood' approaches, both of which are implicit in different areas of the law. As will be addressed in these chapters, judges, legislators and lawyers are in conflict about whether to follow their gut feelings and stand for the dead by regarding them as the persons they were, or stick to existing legal doctrines and hold that the dead are no longer persons in the eyes of the law. The result of this internal conflict would be hard to accept.

It is striking that although death has existed since the beginning of life, our understanding of the dead has received such little attention and still suffers from serious lacunas. There may be psychological, biological or cultural explanations for such a phenomenon and yet one should wonder why the law has surrendered to it as well. Is there something inherent in the law itself that does not make it possible to overcome people's fear of death? Historical review of the regulation of the dead suggests that the law has always suffered from low confidence in its treatment of the dead, characterized by shaky responses ranging from irrational assertiveness to complete emotionalism.

In 1752, the Murder Act of England established that the corpse of the murderer was further to be punished, allegedly suggesting that the Act's concern had to do more with the infliction of punishment than with benefit to society.[12] According to this law, 'the body of any such murderer shall ... be immediately conveyed ... to the hall of the Surgeons' Company ... and the body so delivered ... shall be dissected and anatomised by the said surgeons ... in no case whatsoever the body of any murderer shall be suffered to be buried, unless after such body shall have been dissected and anatomised as aforesaid'.[13] It is reported that in England doctors were granted around ten corpses of executed criminals every year.[14]

With the rising demand for cadavers for dissections beginning in the eighteenth century, corpses gained commercial value, and as a result were

---

[12] Ruth Richardson, *Death, Dissection and the Destitute* (London: Routledge & Kegan Paul, 1987) 36.

[13] Ngaire Naffine, '"But a Lump of Earth"? The Legal Status of the Corpse' in Desmond Manderson ed., *Courting Death* (London: Pluto, 1999) 95–110, 96 (quoting Clare Gittings, *Death, Burial and the Individual in Early Modern England*, London: Croom Helm, 1984, at 74) [Naffine].

[14] *Ibid.*, at 98 (referring to Gittings, at 74).

subject to snatching.[15] There were two reasons for this: there was not much willingness, let alone awareness, to leave one's body to medicine, and Christianity itself promoted the idea of decent burial.[16] Body snatching was a serious social concern. In a report of an English committee on this subject established in 1828, it was evidenced that 1,211 adults and 179 small children were dug up and sold in London between 1809 to 1813.[17] In May 1828, a surgeon, a medical student and an apprentice were convicted and fined for having 'in their possession a body knowing it to be disinterred'. Not only was this the first time that health practitioners were criminalized, but the fine they had to pay was 150 times more than the normal weekly wage.[18] The trial provoked tremendous attention and resulted in a statutory enactment, the Anatomy Act 1832, which regulated the giving of corpses to medicine. The statute provided a legal mechanism by which a person could direct while alive the disposing of her body to be used by medicine. It similarly also empowered relatives of the deceased when such an advance directive was not issued by the deceased.

The Anatomy Act abolished the compulsory dissection of executees, but the motivation behind it was to legalize use of unclaimed bodies, and gradually to regulate the donation of bodies to medicine. No specific concern for the interests of the decedent was reflected in the Act. The same motivation is encountered with the redefinition of death towards the end of the previous century. Countries in most Western societies have now included the irreversible cessation of whole brain functions (including brain-stem functions) known as brain-death in their legislation, acknowledging this form of death as legal death. By overcoming the need to require consent from living donors or patients, the major incentive behind this initiative was to have more transplants, and to use the human body more frequently for research and training purposes. The interests of the dead patient, especially her right to determine the fate of her body and remains, did not receive proper weight. These interests were not compelling and at most were only suggestions or mere recommendations.[19]

---

[15] Scott cites a famous surgeon who gave evidence to a British Parliamentary Select Committee in 1828 saying 'there was no newly buried person whose body he could not obtain, let his situation in life be what it may'. Russell Scott, *The Body as Property* (London: Allen Lane, 1981) 6 [Scott].

[16] Naffine, above n 13, at 98.

[17] *Ibid.*, at 99 (citing Scott, above n 15, at 8).

[18] Scott, above n 15, at 8.

[19] Margaret Brazier, 'Retained Organs: Ethics and Humanity' (2002) 22 *Legal Studies* 550.

The analysis provided in the following chapters fills the void concerning the interests of the dead. This analysis comprises two major parts: theoretical and practical. In the theoretical part, which consists of the first two chapters, there is an examination of whether the dead can have interests and whether as a conceptual matter they can be harmed. Following the argument for posthumous interests, it is further queried whether all or some of these posthumous interests should be advanced and protected as legal rights. The practical part of the book consists of chapters 3–5. In these chapters, the particular examination of posthumous interests is made in regard to three major questions: Is there and should there be a proprietary interest in the body of the deceased? Should the testamentary interest pertaining to the disposal of one's body after death be compelling and legally binding? And should medical confidentiality be extended after death? The difficulties explored in the practical part, together with the theoretical concepts of posthumous interest, posthumous harm and posthumous rights, lead to the formation of a unified concept of a human interest, entitled the *interest in the recognition of one's symbolic existence*, explaining but also justifying the legal outcomes reached in each of the chapters in the book.

Death as a concept evokes questions and problems from various perspectives. Because of its obvious limitations, this book will only provide a legal and philosophical examination of the issues raised. It will not deal with religious aspects that are strongly associated with the concept of death. Nor will it discuss cultural or anthropological variations in death. The main purpose of the book is to investigate the legal regulation of posthumous interests reflected in different areas of law, and to offer not only a better understanding of the issues described but also a coherent and original conception of the notion of posthumous interests. More significantly, by exploring the notion of posthumous interests one is called to reflect upon one's nature as a human being and the implications of one's death. It is hoped that the following analysis will achieve these goals.

1   Posthumous harm, posthumous interests and symbolic existence

Many of the medical procedures performed on brain-dead patients are driven by the motivation to promote the public good. These procedures aim to enhance scientific and medical knowledge relating to the human body, protect the public well-being or save other people's lives. While arguing for the importance of such practices, especially the extraction of organs from the dead, John Harris writes:

> Indeed, it seems clear that the benefits from cadaver transplants are so great and the reasons for objecting so transparently selfish or superstitious, that we should remove altogether the habit of seeking the consent of either the deceased or relatives.[1]

Are the reasons for objecting to such procedures when performed without prior consent from the dead indeed selfish or superstitious? And is the requirement of obtaining consent a mere practice of ours? It seems to be strongly intuitive that these procedures when performed secretly or without due care or dignity to the dead patient are terribly wrong and may also harm the patient. They raise the following concerns: When subjected to these non-consenting procedures are the dead being harmed? Are they wronged? And if so, in what sense? Assuming that there is such harm would entail not only that the dead, who are now being harmed, *exist* as subjects to be harmed, but also that they are *the same* persons or subjects they were before death. But is this a convincing argument?

In this chapter, I will deal with these questions merely from the philosophical and jurisprudential perspectives. I will not attempt to discuss them by providing a descriptive analysis of the legal position nor will I argue for prescriptive legal regulations of this issue. Such an analysis will be postponed to later chapters. My main goal in this chapter is to provide an analytical account for the possibility of harming the dead and to argue for a specific human interest the defeat of which may result

---

[1] John Harris, *Wonderwoman and Superman: The Ethics of Human Biotechnology* (Oxford: Oxford University Press, 1992) 102 [*Wonderwoman*].

in that harm, namely the interest in the recognition of one's symbolic existence.

Harm

General

Let me begin with the general concept of harm.[2] In the usual sense, to harm X is to do something bad to X. But in what sense should the harm be bad for X? Should it be bad *per se* so that the harmful action will be examined regardless of its actual effects on the subject harmed? Or should we require it also to be bad for X (the subject harmed) or to deprive that person of potential good (welfare) they would have gained had the harm not been done to them? If the latter is what interests us in the notion of harm, must X experience and also know or at least be aware of the bad action and its outcomes, or is it sufficient for the action to be 'objectively bad', regardless of X's awareness of its occurrence, its extent, or its origin? We may further ask whether the harmful event should be directed to X only, or whether a derivative harm to X's property or to X's family members can still count as a direct harm to X.[3]

Interests

The concept of harm can be fully conceptualized if it is interconnected with the idea of interest.[4] An interest is a kind of stake in the well-being of an object or state. It is the fact or relation of being concerned in

[2] Throughout the discussion of this chapter I will interconnect the notion of harm with the notion of interest. Assuming that the concept of wrong may involve 'the unjustifiable and inexcusable (indefensible) conduct to violate one's *rights*' (my emphasis), and given that I will not discuss the concept of right until the next chapter, the idea of wrong will not be dealt with in this chapter. For further discussion, see Joel Feinberg, *Harm to Others* (New York: Oxford University Press, 1984) 34 [*Harm*].

[3] For the distinction between direct, derivative and non-derivative harm, see *ibid.*, at 32–3.

[4] Barbara Levenbook, however, relates the concept of harm to *loss of functions* necessary to one's existence. Barbara Baum Levenbook, 'Harming Someone After His Death' (1984) 94 *Ethics* 407 [Levenbook]. This book will not follow Levenbook's definition of harm since, while such definition may be applied to the question of whether death is harm to its subject (discussed by Levenbook in great length), it may not be applicable to many other forms of harm such as the violation of one's interest in maintaining a good reputation or in protecting the integrity of one's body after death. These latter interests are not purely functional in one's life, yet they can constitute an important part of one's life. Walter Glannon proposes a different formula to the concept of harm. In his view, only events or states of affairs which directly or indirectly affect the intrinsic properties of the body *or* the mind of a person can harm her. Glannon's concept of well-being is based on the requirement of actual and potential experience. Hence, capacity for well-being requires an ability

something, which usually benefits or otherwise improves the prosperity of the interest-holder's state of affairs. This is not to say that all interests that are legally safeguarded are identical to legal rights. The interest in the absence of emotional distress is, for example, protected by tort law. However a person does not have a legal right not to be emotionally distressed. Indeed, in many cases a claim for compensation for such distress is denied. The same applies to interests in 'domestic relations', such as the interests in family solidarity and marital fidelity. The latter interests are usually protected by family law. Although these interests are protected by family law, they are not necessarily recognized as legal rights.

A distinction needs to be made between having an interest in the realization of a certain state of affairs and having a legal or moral claim to the realization of that state of affairs. The justification for the latter may derive from the interest-holder's moral or legal status, or, as argued by Joel Feinberg, from her personal investment, involvement or participation in an activity or condition for the promotion or the advancement of an interest.

In this book, I wish to propose a different account for the legal significance of interests. I will argue that the legal importance of an interest derives from the social value attached to the content of the interest and its contribution to the well-being of its holder. As such, the significance of an interest is objectively determined and evaluated.

When tied to the concept of interest, harm is conceived as the thwarting, setting back, or defeating of an interest.[5] X is harmed if her interest in an object or a state is in a worse condition than it would otherwise have been in, had the harmful event not occurred at all. A harmful event is one that frustrates the realization of an outcome the existence of which would have improved the interest-holder's state of affairs or the way such a state of affairs would have been described by an outside observer.

---

to experience the outcome resulting in the state of well-being. Glannon distinguishes between effects on one's *life* and effects on one as a *person*. While facts about X that do not affect X's body or mind may affect how *X's life* goes, they do not affect X. Hence, because there is no experiencing mind and, as a result, there is no person having the capacity for well-being after death, a person cannot be harmed posthumously according to Glannon. Yet, Glannon's conclusion may still be that while the deceased cannot be harmed as a person, the way her life goes may still be affected by events occurring after her death. See Walter Glannon, 'Persons, Lives and Posthumous Harms' (2001) 32(2) *Journal of Social Philosophy* 127 [Glannon].

[5] Feinberg, *Harm*, above n 2, at 33. For the definitions of these different terminologies, see *ibid.*, at 53. Common to all these terms is the *relativistic* notion of harm: whether a person is harmed by an event is determined by reference to where she was before, and whether her position has improved or regressed.

As implied earlier, the concept of interest can be regarded subjectively or objectively. One could hold an objective theory of well-being, according to which some things are just good or bad for a person, regardless of whether one enjoys, experiences or wants them. At the other extreme, one could hold a mental-state theory of well-being. Under this theory, a person's well-being is dependent upon the person's subjective state of affairs akin to actions and outcomes leading to change in their well-being.

In addition, it is possible to interrelate the idea of an interest to the subjective meaning of a want or desire and also to the awareness or knowledge of that interest. Thus, it is reasonable to believe that when X has an interest in Y, X also wants, desires or merely prefers the outcome Y.[6] In any event, X must be familiar with her entitlement to Y (exemplified by her interest) or be aware of it. Under a contrasting interpretation, it is not necessary to ask for the occurrence of any mental state to be attached to the concept of interest. Hence, a person may have an interest even without her wanting or preferring a specific outcome, let alone being aware of it.

Within these two competing approaches, an objective perspective for the concept of interest is more powerful. While under the subjective approach people determine – as much as it is up to them – their objects of desire or enjoyment, and therefore have a wide discretion over their sources of well-being, the subjective account cannot address situations where the making of such discretion is lacking, for example with regard to the mentally ill, children or animals, so that opting for an objective approach may provide a more substantive protection for these categories of creatures. Support for this approach may be found in the matter of Anthony Bland, where the House of Lords held:

Counsel for the Official Solicitor argued that ... being unconscious, he felt no pain or humiliation and therefore had no interests which suffered from his being kept alive. Anthony Bland was in fact indifferent to whether he lived or died and there was nothing to put in the balance against the intrinsic value of his life. I think that the fallacy in this argument is that it assumes that we have no interests except in those things of which we have conscious experience. But this does not accord with most people's intuitive feelings about their lives and deaths ... counsel for the Official Solicitor offers a seriously incomplete picture of Anthony Bland's interests when he confines them to animal feelings of pain or pleasure. It is demeaning to the human spirit to say that, being unconscious, he can have no interest in his personal privacy and dignity, in how he lives or dies.[7]

---

[6] I assume here that X is a mentally capacitated and rational person.
[7] *Airedale NHS Trust v. Bland* [1993] 1 All ER 821, 853–4 (per Hoffmann LJ).

Moreover, reliance on mental states as manifestations for and sources of interests may be doubtful, since for each set of interests there could be few correlating mental states. If X is in my interest I can *want* X, *desire* it, *prefer* it to other outcomes, *know* it, *be aware* of it or perhaps *be emphatic* about it. How are the different mental states linked together? On the other hand, what is the difference between them? Is there a hierarchy or a specific order in which their importance should be organized? A subjective approach cannot tell.

Furthermore, mental states are vague and obscure. They may be erroneous or illusionary as well. It is also difficult to observe or identify them from the outside, and to measure the degree of their occurrence, and these obstacles add to their dubious reliability.

By regarding interests from an objective perspective, the concept of interest takes into consideration the overall well-being of creatures living in a society, so that one's conception of well-being is shaped not only by one's level of welfare but also by an appeal to consider the well-being of other persons. On a more personal level, it seems correct to say that what we care deeply about is the *realization* of the ends for which we act and not solely the *feelings* that may accompany their realization.[8] Furthermore, there are cases in which X possesses an interest in Y though she does not want it nor is she aware of it.[9] Other cases involve a situation in which a person desires something that would not be good for her to fulfil. Loren

---

[8] A relevant distinction mentioned by Feinberg (following Brian Barry) is between 'want-regarding' and 'ideal-regarding' concepts. A concept is want-regarding if it can be analysed *entirely* in terms of the wants which people happen to have, whereas it is ideal-regarding if reference is *also* made to what would be ideal, or best for people, their wants notwithstanding, or to the wants they ought to have whether they in fact have them or not. Feinberg, *Harm*, above n 2, at 67. Feinberg applies here Ross's distinction between want-fulfilment and want-satisfaction. The *fulfilment* of a want is simply the coming into existence of that which is desired. The *satisfaction* of a want is the pleasant experience of contentment or gratification that normally occurs in the mind of the desirer when she believes that her desire has been fulfilled. Feinberg successfully shows how the occurrence of subjective satisfaction is an unreliable phenomenon, and concludes that harm is better defined on an objective level. *Ibid.*, at 84. Desire-satisfaction theory is different from both objective and subjective perspectives of well-being. In one sense it is subjective, because what is good for me on this view depends on what I want and differs from what is good for you. In another sense it is objective, because on a desire-satisfaction theory what matters is whether my desires are actually satisfied or not, not whether I know that they are, enjoy that they are, etc.

[9] According to Feinberg, whenever a person has an interest, she 'to some degree' wants the outcome for which the interest stands. Feinberg, *Harm*, above n 2, at 38. However, Feinberg seems to offer a contrasting view to his own when he later asserts that 'an interest in, and desire for, some development Y does not imply an interest in or desire for a *satisfied state of mind*, or for the *avoidance of a disappointed state of mind* in respect to Y' (my emphasis). *Ibid.*, at 43. I believe his later view is more correct.

Lomasky, for example, follows this view by correctly arguing that there is no necessary connection between satisfaction of a *desire* and satisfaction of the *agent*.[10] Of course, even if the fulfilment of an interest is what counts in assessing one's welfare, it still should be closely related to the holder of such interests. Douglas Portmore makes the same point, arguing that since one's desires can take as their object states of affairs that have nothing whatsoever to do with one, the fulfilment of such desires can have nothing to do with one's welfare.[11]

Having established the argument that we need to conceptualize the idea of interest from an objective perspective, I wish to divide the whole group of interests into four categories.[12] The first category will be named '*pre-birth*' interests. Interests in this category refer to a period prior to the birth of the person whose interests they are, so that their fulfilment depends on the person's coming into actual existence, and hence is examined retroactively. The content of these interests relates to the conditions upon which the person whose pre-birth interests they are is brought into the world. Interests in this category include, for example, the interest in not being delivered with severe physical impairments that could otherwise be fixed or prevented, the interest in coming into a non-polluted or not physically dangerous environment, and the interest in being brought up by a family which is mentally and financially capable of caring for that person. As this book is concerned with interests relevant to the post-mortem context, I shall not deal with interests from this category. It is thus sufficient to mention this category as part of the scale of interests I wish to draw in this chapter.

---

[10] Loren E. Lomasky, *Persons, Rights and the Moral Community* (New York: Oxford University Press, 1987) 215 [Lomasky].

[11] Douglas W. Portmore, 'Desire Fulfillment and Posthumous Harm' (2007) 44(1) *American Philosophical Quarterly* 27.

[12] It is possible to divide the group of interests into categories other than the ones suggested here. Compare, for example, Walter Glannon, who offers two categories of interests: personal or person-affecting and impersonal or non-person-affecting interests. In the first category, a person has interests in a state of affairs which will affect her, and therefore presupposes that she will continue to exist when that state of affairs obtains. In the second category, a person has interests in a state of affairs that she knows will not affect her. The content of these interests does not depend upon the existence or experience of their subject. The problem with Glannon's distinction is that it begs the metaphysical question of whether the deceased as subject of these interests exists or not. Glannon, above n 4, at 137–8. For another division of the group of interests, see Ronald Dworkin's distinction between experiential and critical interests. While experiential interests are things we have interest in because we like the experience of doing them, critical interests are those interests the satisfaction of which makes life genuinely better. Ronald Dworkin, *Life's Dominion* (New York: Alfred Knopf, 1993) 201.

In the second category of interests there exist '*life interests*', if there are any such interests. The importance of most interests included in this category derives from the experience or awareness of their fulfilment and is dependent upon the existence of the person, whose interests they are, and the mere fact that this person is a living person. Both the fulfilment and the satisfaction of these interests play an important role here. This category includes, for example, the interest in survival and financial security, the interest in maintaining one's physical health and functioning of one's body and the interest in the absence of severe pain and suffering. It is clear that, by their very nature, interests in this category can no longer be helped or harmed by posthumous events.

The third category of interests consists of '*after-life interests*', if there are any such interests. These are posthumous interests in the strict sense so that they apply *only* to states or events that happen after a person's death. Interests in this category include the interest in being posthumously respected in decisions regarding the disposal of one's body and estate, the interest in remaining and being remembered after death as a human being with specific characteristics, etc. Legal and social institutions such as wills, life-insurance policies, donor cards, the bequeathing of one's body to medical research and the like are mechanisms to protect interests from this category.[13]

In the fourth category of interests, the '*far-lifelong*' interests, there exist interests that, if there were any such interests, would apply to one's life but also to episodes after one's death. This group of interests does not have any necessary characteristics whose contents may be affected by their temporal application. Included in this category are interests in being the object of an affection or esteem of others, the interest that one's promises not be broken, the interest that one's loved ones flourish within and beyond one's life, the interest in the integrity of one's body[14] and the interest in respecting one's privacy and good reputation.

---

[13] Joel Feinberg addresses interests from this category – although he does not call them the same thing – in his 'The Rights of Animals and Unborn Generations' in Joel Feinberg ed., *Rights, Justice and the Bounds of Liberty* (Princeton, N.J.: Princeton University Press, 1980) 159, 173–4.

[14] Compare, however, John Harris's exceptional view that our body succumbs to an inevitable disintegration so that there is no such thing as bodily integrity, at least after death. John Harris, 'Organ Procurement: Dead Interests, Living Needs' (2003) 29(3) *Journal of Medical Ethics* 130 ['Organ']. Undoubtedly, Harris's interpretation of bodily integrity narrowly focuses on the physical aspect or component of the concept of integrity rather than on one's feeling and one's being perceived as being integrated with one's body. I believe the latter meaning is more common in understanding the idea of bodily integrity.

Some of the far-lifelong interests are what Steven Luper calls 'both personally and impersonally defined projects', namely projects we want to fulfil by ourselves, but if we fail to undertake them, we want them fulfilled by someone else.[15] With regard to most of these interests, their holder invests or has invested a desire so strongly and durably that she has an independent personal stake in them herself. Hence, thwarting these interests by posthumous events affects 'whether people are the kinds of people they take pains to be'.[16] As John Martin Fischer explains when he discusses these categorical desires, 'it is not that one merely desires to raise a family, *if* one should continue to live; rather, one wishes to continue to live (in part) because one desires to raise a family'.[17]

Posthumous harm: the real puzzles

The concept of posthumous harm, that is harm caused after the victim has died, raises two difficult puzzles. First, how can one be harmed when one does not know or experience the evil of harm? (the 'experience problem');[18] and, second, if a dead person no longer exists, who is the subject of posthumous harm, or, in other words, who is being posthumously harmed? (the 'problem of the subject'). Since both puzzles occur when a person is said to be harmed by her own death, I shall deal first with the arguments discussed in the literature concerning the issue of death as harm.

The experience problem

The 'experience problem' takes us back to our discussion of the distinction between objective and subjective perspectives of the concept of interest, since the requirement of experience is an extended demand for a mental state to be associated with the harm condition. This is the demand that in order to be constituted, the harmful event must be experienced by the subject of harm. Beside the inaccuracy that lies in the idea that an experience is a necessary condition for a bad thing to occur, the very concepts of after-life interests and far-lifelong interests,

---

[15] Steven Luper, 'Posthumous Harm' (2004) 41(1) *American Philosophical Quarterly* 63 [Luper].

[16] Dorothy Grover, 'Posthumous Harm' (1989) 39 *Philosophical Quarterly* 334, 351 [Grover].

[17] John Martin Fischer, 'Introduction: Death, Metaphysics, and Morality' [Fischer Introduction] in John Martin Fischer ed., *The Metaphysics of Death* (Stanford: Stanford University Press, 1993) at 17 [Fischer].

[18] Summed up by the common remark: 'What you don't know can't hurt you.'

should they exist, may reflect the fact that a significant portion of our interests is unconditioned with mental states of want, desire or experience. Rather, the objects of a person's interests are usually wanted or aimed-at events that occur outside her immediate experience and at some future time.[19] Thus, a person's experiential state is relatively unimportant for the fulfilment of such interests.

But even if one does not seek a mental state of wanting or desiring the interest at stake, one may still require the knowledge or awareness of such an interest. Of course, the dead are permanently unconscious. But people in a persistent vegetative state or with severe mental disabilities are not aware of their environment nor do they know what their interests are. Is it questionable that they still have interests?

It seems clear, as Feinberg asserts, that some of our interests are protected *as such*, and can be violated without our being aware of it. This is the case, for example, in what he calls our 'possessory interests', such as a landowner's interest in the exclusive possession and enjoyment of his land, or our 'interests in domestic relations', for example the interest that one's spouse will not engage in *secret* adulterous activity with a lover.[20] Note that what provides the harm is not necessarily the action itself but the fact that it is done behind one's back. Our interest in maintaining a good reputation, not being betrayed by our friends or ridiculed behind our back can serve as other examples of the fact that a person can be harmed by what she does not know.[21] People dislike the thought of being insulted or despised not only to their face but also behind their back. The case of harming the dead is not different from any other situation in which harm is possible without knowledge or awareness of its subject. As observed by Aristotle:

For a dead man is popularly believed to be capable of having both good and ill fortune – honor and dishonor and prosperity and the loss of it among his children and descendants generally – in *exactly the same way as if he were alive but unaware or unobservant of what was happening.*[22]

---

[19] Feinberg, *Harm*, at 86.   [20] *Ibid.*, at 87.

[21] However, one can argue that in all of these examples, although the person whose interests are set back does not *in fact* know or is aware of the harm, she has a *potential to learn about it* at some point in the future. Of course, an action by law for the protection of such interests is made possible only after the harm has been learnt, especially by its sufferer. Thomas Nagel provides a good response to this argument when he writes: 'For the natural view is that the discovery of betrayal makes us unhappy because it is bad to be betrayed – not that betrayal is bad because its discovery makes us unhappy.' Thomas Nagel, 'Death' in Thomas Nagel ed., *Mortal Questions* (New York: Cambridge University Press, 1979) 1, 5 [Nagel].

[22] Aristotle, *Nicomachean Ethics*, trans. J. A. K. Thomson (Baltimore: Penguin Books, 1953), I.10 para. 1 (my emphasis).

Thwarting after-life and far-lifelong interests is in Palle Yourgrau's words, 'a relational evil'.[23] Under this kind of evil, we are harmed because of what happens *in relation to us*, not because of a felt condition of our present state. The nature of the harmful condition needs to be examined more carefully.

Death as harm

It is obvious, so I presume, that death is commonly perceived to be harm – perhaps the most serious harm a person can suffer. The large majority of us fear death or circumstances that may hasten its arrival. We would rather not talk about death or directly engage ourselves in morbid discussions about it. We cry at funerals. We grieve *for* the deceased. On an immediate level, death is awful. The view that death is dreadful is what Jeff McMahan calls a 'fixed point' or 'starting point' in ethics, namely a conviction that would require extremely convincing reasons to overturn, if it could be overturned at all.[24]

There are many ways in which we can conceptualize the harm of death. Death deprives us of life which is assumed to be good.[25] The idea of 'death as deprivation' evokes the difficulty deriving from our asymmetric attitudes toward prenatal non-existence and death: we think it is reasonable to regard death as a bad thing in a way which prenatal non-existence is not. But just as death deprives us of good experiences we would have had, had we died later, our actual date of birth deprives us of good we would have experienced had we been born earlier.[26] Death is the loss of being alive, doing certain things, and having certain experiences that we consider good. More generally, it is a loss of action. Death is the frustration of a 'higher order project of the most fundamental kind: the

---

[23] Palle Yourgrau, 'The Dead' (1987) 86(2) *Journal of Philosophy* 84, reprinted (with some modifications) in Fischer, above n 17, at 140.

[24] Jeff McMahan, *The Ethics of Killing: Problems at the Margins of Life* (New York: Oxford University Press, 2002) 104.

[25] This assumption applies to cases of good health and reasonable circumstances of living and not, for example, to living in famine-ravaged countries.

[26] I will not discuss this problem, which was originally associated with Lucretius. For a detailed discussion, see Anthony L. Brueckner and John Martin Fischer, 'Why is Death Bad?' (1986) 50 *Philosophical Studies* 213, reprinted in Fischer, above n 17, at 22; Stephen Rosenbaum, 'How to Be Dead and Not Care: A Defense of Epicurus' (1986) 23(2) *American Philosophical Quarterly* 217 [Rosenbaum], reprinted in Fischer, above n 17. at 128–9; Frances A. Kamm, *Morality, Mortality – Death and Whom to Save from It*, vol. I (New York: Oxford University Press, 1993) at 25–55; and Tim Bayne, 'On Death and Being Dead' (unpublished), available at www.phil.mq.edu.au/staff/tbayne/death.doc, last visited on 12 December 2007 [Bayne].

project of living a valuable and fulfilling human life'.[27] It is both what Steven Luper calls a 'destruction harm' and a 'preclusion harm', namely it involves the destruction of good conditions present in us, such as knowledge or abilities, and it also presents us with harms, which prevent us from acquiring goods.[28]

Perhaps the most frightening thing about death is that it annihilates us, thereby completely extinguishing our existence. It brings about the irreversible loss of our ability to experience, and thwarts our desires by their complete removal. The fear of death can be explained psychologically. Death is perhaps the only thing on which we do not and cannot have empirical first-hand knowledge. It seems that no one has any information on what really happens when we die, and this lack of knowledge is a constant threat to our apparent securities in life. Woody Allen nicely articulates this special fear:

> The thing to remember is that each time of life has its appropriate rewards, whereas when you're dead it's hard to find the light switch. The chief problem about death, incidentally, is the fear that there may be no afterlife – a depressing thought, particularly for those who have bothered to shave. Also, there is the fear that there is an afterlife but no one will know where it's being held. On the plus side, death is one of the few things that can be done as easily lying down.[29]

More importantly, death evokes the difficulty in thinking of ourselves distinct from our bodies. Since we so habitually identify ourselves with our bodies, we think that if bad things can happen to *our bodies* after death, bad things can happen to *us*. Compare Fred Feldman, who asserts that a person *is* her body. Feldman writes: 'No one would dream of saying that when a tree dies, it goes out of existence. Why should we treat people otherwise? My own view is that a person is just a living human body. In typical cases, when the body dies, it continues to exist as a corpse. So the thing that formerly was a person still exists, although it is no longer alive (and perhaps no longer a person).'[30] Of course, death sets back our universal interest in not dying (or in survival), which is 'an indispensable condition for the advancement of most, if not all, of the ulterior interests that constitute our good'.[31]

By defeating life, death then prevents us from achieving all of our ultimate goals that actually give life a meaning. The strong and common

---

[27] Geoffrey Scarre, 'Should We Fear Death?' (1997) 5(3) *European Journal of Philosophy* 269, 279.

[28] Luper, above n 15.

[29] Woody Allen, *Without Feathers*, mentioned in Fischer, above n 17, at 267.

[30] Fred Feldman, 'Some Puzzles About the Evil of Death' (1991) 100(2) *Philosophical Review* 205 [Feldman, 'Puzzles'], reprinted in Fischer, above n 17, at 313.

[31] Feinberg, *Harm*, above n 2, at 81–2.

beliefs about death seem to reflect the fact that there is a way to conceive death even though there is no experiencing subject to whom the harm of death can be referred. As illuminated by Feinberg, support for such a proposition is seen in our grieving process. When we mourn the death of a young and successful person, we mourn *for them*, whereas when we mourn the death of a terminally ill patient or the unhappy and miserable person we usually mourn *for their dependants and loved ones*. This shows that when we care for the person's life, and regard its deprivation as a great loss for her, we see the *person* who was alive as the immediate sufferer of the harm caused by death, even though she may not 'actually' exist to be harmed.

The Epicurean argument

Perhaps our well-grounded psychological reactions to death are totally wrong and completely irrational. Epicurus and Lucretius thought this way. It is worthwhile having here the entire Epicurean argument:

> So death, the most terrifying of ills, is nothing to us, since so long as we exist, death is not with us; but when death comes, then we do not exist. It does not concern either the living or the dead, since for the former it is not, and the latter are no more.[32]

Stephen Rosenbaum, a contemporary Epicurean, provides a logical structure for this argument. Since

(i) something can be bad for a person only if the person can be *affected* by it, and since

(ii) a person cannot be affected by something after she ceases to be, hence

(iii) a person's being dead cannot be bad for her and one should not fear it.[33]

John Harris follows this line of Rosenbaum, arguing that posthumous interests are never 'person affecting', namely they are neither good nor bad for a person who no longer exists.[34] Another reading of the Epicurean

---

[32] Epicurus, *Letter to Menoeceus*, mentioned in Harry S. Silverstein, 'The Evil of Death' (1980) 77(7) *Journal of Philosophy* 401 [Silverstein], reprinted in Fischer, above n 17, at 95.

[33] Stephen Rosenbaum, 'Epicurus and Annihilation' (1989) 39 *Philosophical Quarterly* 81, reprinted in Fischer, above n 17, at 295. In another place, Rosenbaum holds the assumption that 'one experiences a state of affairs only if it can affect one in some way'. Rosenbaum, above n 26, at 124. Rosenbaum is right to claim that the dead cannot experience any states of affairs (at 123). But he is wrong to conclude that the dead cannot be affected, as such a conclusion does not *logically* derive from his assumption.

[34] Harris, 'Organ', above n 14. Interestingly, Harris later argues that there is a sense in which what happens to one's body after death *is* person affecting. It affects the actual *living person* who will benefit from the organs or tissue harvested from the dead. But

thesis would be the claim that death is instantaneous. It cannot find a time to harm us, since after we no longer exist it is too late to harm us, whereas while we are alive it is too early.[35]

Indeed, the Epicurean argument rests on the so-called 'existence condition' according to which nothing either good or bad can happen to a subject s at time t unless s exists at t. Of course, the awfulness of harmful events can be demonstrated in what McMahan calls 'a fully impersonal way', that is for reasons that are independent of considerations of effects on particular people.[36] While the 'existence condition' may be helpful for the Epicurean argument, it has a less convincing power in the context of posthumous harm. It is reasonable to argue that things that happen after one's death can adversely affect the evaluation of one's welfare level in the world. A person's life-work, for example, could be unjustly despised or neglected just as it could be acknowledged and respected far beyond that person's lifetime. As Feldman points out, 'A state of affairs can be bad for a person whether it occurs before he exists, while he exists, or after he exists. The only requirement is that his welfare level at the nearest world where it occurs is lower than his welfare level at the nearest world where it does not occur.'[37] Indeed, the harm of death does not deprive us of all possibilities for good. It deprives us only of possibilities for good *of an active or experiential* kind,[38] most of which is represented by the category of life interests. Hence, after death the frustration of interests belonging to other categories may still be possible. Such a frustration amounts to posthumous harm.

Surviving interests

How can we adhere to our evident response to death and still face the puzzles of death as harm and posthumous harm, especially the 'problem of the subject'? One way would be to assert that even though a person may

Harris cannot tell why one's interest in bodily integrity after death is dependent upon the potential benefit derived from one's body. Furthermore, Harris's thesis may not apply to all cases. For example, in the case of a fetus whose dead mother's body will be maintained on 'life support' for its successful delivery, it is doubtful whether the fetus would be considered a 'living person' for the purposes of Harris's argument. Likewise, Harris's approach may not apply to medical procedures benefiting *future and indefinite persons*, such as practising resuscitation procedures on dead patients or using their bodies to gain scientific knowledge. Under these practices there is no specific and immediately living *person* to be affected by the fulfilment or non-fulfilment of such an interest.

[35] Luper, above n 15.

[36] Jeff McMahan, 'Death and the Value of Life' (1988) 99 *Ethics* 32 [McMahan], reprinted in Fischer, above n 17, at 240 (note 8).

[37] Feldman, 'Puzzles', above n 30, at 319. See also W. J. Waluchow, 'Feinberg's Theory of "Preposthumous" Harm' (1986) 25 *Dialogue* 727, 734 [Waluchow].

[38] McMahan, above n 36, at 242 (note 11).

not survive her death, some of her interests do.[39] Focusing on the effect the harm has on *surviving interests* rather than the *person* whose interests they were may support the argument for posthumous harm despite the belief that this person may no longer exist to be harmed.

Even if the solution of surviving interests is good, it is still partial since it only shifts our attention from the question of the subject of *harm* to the question of the subject of a *surviving interest*. Still, we may want to ask: who is this subject? I shall not discuss here Feinberg's first answer to this problem, according to which the surviving interests themselves are the true subjects of harm,[40] for Feinberg himself refused to continue to hold this view.[41] Certainly, a surviving interest, like any other interest, needs to be ascribed to someone, whom we can identify, refer to or name at the time of their survival. To say that X is X is always true, but does not provide any significant information about the world. The argument that an object (interests) is the subject of itself does not resolve the problem of the subject and was rightly abandoned by Feinberg.

It seems that there are two possible solutions for the problem of the subject. The subject of surviving interests is *the deceased herself*, which at the time of the harmful event is a mere physical thing commonly called 'a corpse'. Alternatively, it is *the living person who no longer exists* at the moment of posthumous harm. But neither of these options is reasonable. For how can physical and inanimate things such as a corpse have interests? On the other hand, how can an event from the present (posthumous harm) be retroactively responsible for the harm of a subject, which existed in the past (prior to the harming event) but no longer exists at the moment of harm?

George Pitcher and Joel Feinberg preferred the view that the interests harmed by posthumous events, including the harm of death itself, are not interests of the remaining body ('the *post-mortem* person'); rather they are interests of the living person who no longer exists ('the

---

[39] Feinberg, *Harm*, above n 2, at 83; George Pitcher, 'The Misfortunes of the Dead' (1984) 21(2) *American Philosophical Quarterly* 183, 184 [Pitcher]; Tim Mulgan, 'The Place of the Dead in Liberal Political Philosophy' (1999) 7(1) *Journal of Political Philosophy* 52, 61–2; Allen E. Buchanan and Dan W. Brock, *Deciding for Others – The Ethics of Surrogate Decision Making* (New York: Cambridge University Press, 1989) 162–4. T. M. Wilkinson prefers to argue that there is a partial or complete *overlap* between the interests of the living and the dead. T. M. Wilkinson, 'Last Rights: The Ethics of Research on the Dead' (2002) 19(1) *Journal of Applied Philosophy* 31, at 35 [Wilkinson]. In this chapter, I prefer the idea of *surviving* interests rather than *overlapping* interests, as it is difficult to identify which interests overlap and to what degree.

[40] Joel Feinberg, 'Harm and Self-Interest' in P. M. S. Hacker and J. Raz eds., *Law, Morality and Society* (Oxford: Clarendon Press, 1977) 308.

[41] Feinberg, *Harm*, above n 2, at 83. For a critique on his former view, see Ernest Partridge, 'Posthumous Interests and Posthumous Respect' (1981) 91 *Ethics* 243, 247 [Partridge].

ante-mortem person').[42] T. M. Wilkinson helps us understand the categories of *ante-mortem* and *post-mortem* person through our memories. 'When I remember my dead grandmother,' says Wilkinson, 'I remember not the grandmother *as she is now* but the *living woman in the past*.'[43]

The problem of retroactivity

There is a conceptual difference between remembering a dead person and harming her. A harmful event to the dead has, like any other harm, its effects. It follows from the Pitcher–Feinberg thesis that these effects apply retroactively to the living. Under the first understanding of this formula, although the harm occurs *now* it is ascribed to a subject who existed *before*.

However, one can argue that there is no retroactivity problem involved in posthumous harm just as there is no such problem in relation to thinking about the deceased. If one, for example, thinks at t_1 of Socrates, Socrates did not have the property of 'being thought of by one' until t_1, while at t_1 he does have such property. The act of thinking of Socrates, it can be rightly argued, does not involve backward causation. Can we say the same of posthumous harm? I believe we cannot. In thinking of Socrates, one is not *causing* a change in Socrates. Any change occurring in Socrates is not an *effect* of our thinking of him; instead, our thinking of him is *constitutive* of that change. Harming someone is different from thinking of that someone. Harm involves the causation of harm to the subject harmed. Harm is a *relativistic* notion. Whether someone is harmed by an event is determined by reference to what she was before, and whether her position has improved or regressed. The harmful event is not only constitutive of the change caused in the subject harmed. It is an effect of that event.

Pitcher and Feinberg reject the problem of backward causation by arguing that the harming event does not *cause* something bad to happen to the *ante-mortem* person (the living person who she was *before she died*). Rather the shadow of it '*reaches back across the chasm even of a person's death and darkens his ante-mortem life*'.[44] Thus, it '*makes it true*' that the *ante-mortem* person is harmed, and in a sense it is responsible for that harm.[45]

---

[42] Pitcher, above n 39, at 184; Feinberg, *Harm*, above n 2, at 89. See also Geoffrey Scarre, 'Archaeology and Respect for the Dead' (2003) 20(3) *Journal of Applied Philosophy* 237, 244 [Scarre].

[43] Wilkinson, above n 39, at 34. But can one not also remember the dead woman as she is *after* her death?

[44] Pitcher, above n 39, at 187 (my emphasis).

[45] *Ibid.*, at 187–8; Feinberg, *Harm*, above n 2, at 90–1.

Feinberg and Pitcher's terminologies are nicely put, but how does the logical connection between the harmful event and the state of being harmed really work? It seems, as Steven Luper puts it, that on the Pitcher–Feinberg thesis posthumous events can only be *indirect* harms.[46] The harmful event does not *cause* a 'real' harm, but *makes it true* that a person who existed previously to the harmful event is harmed. It follows that if posthumous events do not *cause* their effects, then the effects cannot be 'real' effects, just as our thinking of Socrates today does not have a 'real' effect on Socrates.[47] However, the problem of posthumous events is not that they are not real. Rather, the problem lies in the difficulty of determining whether a causal relationship between the event and the subject harmed exists, for such causal relationship is necessary for any concept of harm, including posthumous harm.

But if Feinberg and Pitcher are right to claim that 'reaching back', 'making true' or being 'responsible for' an event is not a relation of physical causation at all, what is it then? Feinberg further explains:

The ante-mortem person was harmed in being the subject of interests *that were going to be defeated* whether he knew it or not. It does not become 'retroactively true' that as the subject of doomed interests he is in a harmed state; rather it was true *all along*.[48]

The moment of harm

However, if the harm occurred before death why is Feinberg's account one of posthumous harm? Strictly speaking it is not. Consider another dimension of Feinberg's response to the problem of backward causation. It follows from Feinberg that whenever one of the projects of a living person fails, she is harmed all along rather than only at the point of failure. More disturbing is the idea that a person is harmed by the *future defeat* of her interest. Being mortals, are we not all now harmed by our *future* and inevitable defeat of our interest in staying alive? And if we say such harm was true *all along*, how far back in time do we go to say that a person is in a harmed condition? Feinberg's answer to this problem does not seem to be better than his previous ones:

It does not suddenly 'become true' that the ante-mortem Smith was harmed. Rather it becomes apparent to us for the first time that it was all along – that *from the time Smith invested enough in his cause to make it one of his interests*, he was playing a losing game.[49]

---

[46] Luper, above n 15.   [47] Grover, above n 16, at 335.
[48] Feinberg, *Harm*, above n 2, at 91 (my emphasis).   [49] *Ibid.*, at 91 (my emphasis).

Feinberg's requirement of investing in an interest is puzzling. Let us call the moment Feinberg suggests as the beginning of the harm, 't_1'. Of course, a financial collapse of a life-insurance company through which someone has protected her dependants can constitute harm for that person from the time that she started paying her insurance (t_1). What about the violation of one's reputation after death or the mutilation of one's corpse without notification of next-of-kin? When does the moment of harm (t_1) start with regard to these interests? In other words, when do people invest in their interest in good reputation or bodily integrity? Moreover, are people really expected to invest *actively* in such interests in order for them to be fulfilled or defeated?

Yet, Feinberg seems to propose another criterion for determining the moment of harm. According to this criterion, 'The harmed condition began *at the moment he first acquired the interests that death defeats.*'[50] This is indeed a refreshing argument. When considering, for example, the interest in remaining alive, we will have to conclude unreasonably that a person has been harmed by her own death since birth or maybe before, and that throughout her whole life she has actually been in a harmed condition.[51] It follows from his theory that I am harmed now by what will occur later. Contrary to our intuitions, the harmed condition exists well *before* the harmful event. Feinberg's view may sound fatalistic. Under his conception of harm, the future is fixed and determinate. Our lives, including their good and evil aspects, are already complete. All the effects would already be included and there is no way to change them. Joan Callahan properly explains the flaws of such an argument:

For what now shall we say of a person who will later perform an action productive of posthumous harm? It seems that we must say that he is, long before *doing* something, already responsible for placing the ante-mortem Smith or A in a harmed state. Even worse, it can surely turn out on this view that our would-be agent is responsible for harming another even before he is born, just as long as it is now true that he will perform the act.[52]

---

[50] *Ibid.*, at 92 (my emphasis).

[51] Later, Feinberg softens his approach by arguing that the degree of harmfulness depends on how premature it is. According to this view, the death of a person at the age of thirty is a greater harm to that person than in the case of the death of an eighty-year-old, since the latter has fewer interests to be defeated by death. Feinberg, *Harm*, above n 2, at 92–3.

[52] Joan C. Callahan, 'On Harming the Dead' (1987) 97 *Ethics* 341, 345 [Callahan]. Compare Steinbock, who argues that to be more plausible the Pitcher–Feinberg account should be interpreted not as if one is being harmed 'all along', but that 'all along' one has the property of being harmed at a particular time. Bonnie Steinbock, *Life Before Birth – The Moral and Legal Status of Embryos and Fetuses* (New York: Oxford University Press, 1992) 26 [Steinbock]. Still, even under this interpretation, if the harm occurs after a person's death, how can it not apply in backward causation to the ante-mortem person?

Furthermore, Feinberg seems to have no way to distinguish between different points in time when one is harmed and when one is not in a harmed condition. W. J. Waluchow brings an additional example to show how Feinberg's requirement cannot stand:

> At a time T1, subsequent to my death, S1 harms me by undermining my reputation. At a later time, T2, however, S2 repairs the damage, thus bringing it about that from T2 onwards, I am no longer harmed . . . Are we to say that I am at this moment harmed because of S1's actions – and that I am *not* at this moment harmed owing to S2's actions? If so, then it seems to follow that I am at one and the same time both in and not in a state of harm, which seems flatly contradictory. So perhaps we must say that at one point prior to my death I am in a harmed state, because of S1's actions, while at some other point I am not, owing to S2's actions? Taking this option would of course force a serious modification in Feinberg's theory. He could no longer cite, as the moment when the harmed state begins, that point in time when the relevant interest is acquired.[53]

Aside from the flaws associated with the relation between the *ante-mortem* person and the posthumous event, as well as its timing, what seems to be the main problem in Feinberg and Pitcher's suggestions is that by presenting the *ante-mortem* person as the subject of harm, Feinberg and Pitcher are supporting an opposite view to their own. Their solution actually proves that the dead *cannot* be harmed. Instead, it is the ante-mortem person, the *living* person as she was, who is the subject of harm, including posthumous harm.

Solving the problem of posthumous (non-)existence

Indeed, the assumption under which the deceased does not exist from the moment of death ('*the existence assumption*') creates the many puzzles discussed above. One needs to deal with the metaphysical problem concerning the nature of posthumous existence to solve these puzzles. Before I suggest my own solution to the question of whether the 'deceased' exists as a subject of harm, four alternatives to the existence assumption will be briefly discussed.

Existence as a possibility

According to the first alternative, there is always a logical possibility that the deceased would have existed in this world – or indeed the deceased 'exists' in some other worlds – so that it is sufficient to argue that the deceased still exists to be harmed. Barbara Baum Levenbook, for

[53] Waluchow, above n 37, at 733.

example, holds that losses – the concept by which she analyses the idea of harm – can be attributed to someone as *her* loss even if the event of her losing does not occur within the time of her existence.[54] Levenbook further argues that the ordinary concept of loss does not demand an existing loser in the way that the ordinary concept of interests does.[55] She supports this argument by asserting that there is always a logically possible state of affairs in which that person would have existed at the time of the harming event.[56] Similar reasoning is evidenced in the writings of Jeff McMahan. He argues that there is an appropriate antecedent-world as the closest possible world to the actual world in which the deceased still exists, and if to exist in such a possible world is really to exist, then the deceased really exists.[57]

Even if one accepts Levenbook's view that someone can lose something at the moment she ceases to exist (or no longer exists), Levenbook does not seem to avoid the problem of the subject discussed above. In her view, it is also required that the occurring event (when someone does not exist) be bad for that someone. But who must that someone really be? Furthermore, both the Levenbook and McMahan suggestions raise the difficulty of properly defining alternative possibilities. One can hold, as Hide Ishiguro does, that possible worlds or a near world are ideal entities. They are abstract entities, whose existence is invoked as part of our imaginative thought. As constructs of thought, they are not the kind of things to which actual things and the actual world can stand in any relation.[58] Hence, the fact that the dead may still exist in these worlds does not entail any necessary relation to their existence in the actual world. The premise in Levenbook and McMahan's theses that to exist in 'some possible world' is to exist *as* in the actual world may be doubtful.[59]

---

[54] Levenbook, above n 4, at 414. Compare Levenbook with Rosenbaum, who argues that 'Typical losses that are bad for persons seem to instantiate the following principle: A person *P* loses good *g* only if there is a time at which *P* has *g* and there is a later time at which *P* does not have *g*. If *P* ceases to exist when *P* dies, then being dead cannot be considered a loss of this typical sort in which losses are bad for persons, for in typical cases *P* exists after the loss and is able to experience it.' Rosenbaum, above n 26, at 127. But a person can lose a thing by *being deprived of it*, without having had it earlier (and not having it later) and without experiencing the loss, for there is nothing to experience. It is apparent that the definition proposed by Rosenbaum for 'loss' is not exhaustive.

[55] Barbara Baum Levenbook, 'Harming the Dead, Once Again' (1985) 96 *Ethics* 162, 163.

[56] Levenbook, above n 4, at 415.

[57] McMahan, above n 36, at 249.

[58] Hide Ishiguro, 'Possibility' (1980) 54 *Proceedings of the Aristotelian Society* 73.

[59] Of course, one can reply by questioning whether there is only *one* actual world and asking how one can be sure that there could not be an actual world for which possible or near worlds would not be constructs of thoughts. I shall not discuss these problems here.

Existence in after-life

Belief in after-life could refute the 'existence assumption'. If there were life after death, one would not cease to exist, and for that reason one would not cease to be a possible subject of harm occurring after one's death.[60] There are several versions of after-life and I shall not elaborate on them here.[61] I will, however, briefly discuss Fred Feldman's materialistic version of after-life. By being a 'survivalist', Feldman rejects what he calls 'the termination thesis', according to which people cease to exist when they die.[62] Feldman illuminates an interesting point on the termination thesis by showing that this very same metaphysical principle is invoked on both sides of the debate about the evil of death. The termination thesis is brought as an argument in order to conclude that death is nothing to be feared. On the other hand, it explains the horror of death as responsible for our annihilation.[63] Based on a dualist approach, the termination thesis holds that a person is a compound entity, composed of body and soul, and that at death these components are separated, thereby bringing about the extinction of a person. In Feldman's view, when we die we do not *simply* cease to exist. Rather, we cease to exist *as (psychological) persons*, but continue to exist *as corpses*. It follows that our *biological personality*, namely the assertion that we are members of the biological species *Homo sapiens*, is maintained even after we die. Feldman analogizes this to the case of a Jewish boy who reaches the age of thirteen. This boy, he writes, ceases to exist *as a boy*, but continues to exist *as a man*.[64]

[60] Among other problems, one may wonder how, if people survive in heaven, we can harm them.

[61] See Keith Augustine, 'The Case Against Immortality' (unpublished draft), available at www.infidels.org/library/modern/keith_augustine/immortality.html, last visited on 13 February 2007. It is not clear at all that after-life is desirable. Bernard Williams, for example, argues that immortal life would consist of boredom, indifference and anomie. For his thought-provoking piece, see Bernard Williams, 'The Makropulos Case: Reflections on the Tedium of Immortality' in Bernard Williams ed., *Problems of the Self* (Cambridge: Cambridge University Press, 1973).

[62] Fred Feldman, *Confrontations with the Reaper – A Philosophical Study of the Nature and Value of Death* (New York: Oxford University Press, 1992) 89 and onward [Feldman, *Confrontations*]. A representative of this thesis is L. W. Sumner, who writes: 'The death of a person is the end of that person; before death he *is* and after death he *is not*. To die is therefore to cease to exist.' L. W. Sumner, 'A Matter of Life and Death' (1976) 10 *Nous* 145, 153.

[63] Fred Feldman, 'The Termination Thesis' (2000) 24 *Midwest Studies in Philosophy* 98, 99 [Feldman, 'Termination'].

[64] But see Chisholm, who criticizes the confusion between the alteration of a thing and its ceasing to be: Roderick M. Chisholm, 'Coming into Being and Passing Away: Can the Metaphysician Help?' in John Donnelly ed., *Language, Metaphysics and Death* (New York: Fordham University Press, 1978) 13.

Feldman assumes that 'if you exist as a corpse, then you exist'.[65] But to be sure that it is the same person that existed before death and after it (as a corpse), one needs to identify oneself with one's body completely. This may be highly problematic. Additionally, the materialistic view held by Feldman equates human beings to other organisms. When a tree is dead, writes Feldman, we do not say it goes out of existence. Likewise we should regard people as not ceasing to exist. Such a view may be disputed and may not be easily acknowledged.

Indeed, Feldman's theory is not unproblematic. If a person exists after her death by turning into something *else* (a corpse), does it mean that she maintains her personal identity? Feldman seems to be committed to the change from a state of affairs A (body + soul) to another state B (corpse), but he does not address the inevitable question whether what becomes a (mere) corpse is the *same* living person as it was before its death ($A = B$?). It is also not clear what happens 100 years or so after a person becomes a corpse. After all, a corpse does not persist through change eternally. Biologically, the corpse turns into ashes and completely vanishes. Feldman appears to admit this fact when he writes that formerly living objects deteriorate and finally go out of existence.[66] By this, he surely acknowledges the limits of his theory. Furthermore, even by Feldman's own account it is difficult to pin down the exact moment when the corpse ceases to exist. When is the first moment in which a corpse ceases to be and from which there exists no more subject to be harmed? Feldman cannot tell. Overall, Feldman's theory may explain why death is harm to its subject (the corpse), but does not successfully deal with events occurring *after* a person has died, and its application to posthumous harm has evident limitations.

Harm and change without existence

The third alternative[67] analyses harm from a linguistic perspective, thereby referring to it as a property of our language. Under such an alternative, the property of 'being harmed' can be applied without the necessary existence of a subject bearing this property. Following David Lewis, we may distinguish between intrinsic and extrinsic properties.[68] Some of the properties we have in our language are in virtue of what we

---

[65] Feldman, 'Termination', above n 63, at 101.
[66] Feldman, *Confrontations*, above n 62, at 106. 'The formerly living, complex material object, however, continues to exist *for some other time* after death' (my emphasis), *ibid.*, at 112; see also his 'Termination', above n 63, at 102.
[67] I am greatly indebted to Matthew Kramer for making me consider this alternative.
[68] David Lewis, 'Extrinsic Properties' (1983) 44 *Philosophical Studies* 197, at 197. See also his *On the Plurality of Worlds* (Oxford: Blackwell, 1986) 62.

are: for example 'being round'. These are termed 'intrinsic properties' since an object may have or lack them regardless of what is going on outside it. Other properties we have are in virtue of the way we *interact with the world*: for example 'being almost round', 'being a father', 'being 7 miles from Cambridge'. These latter properties depend upon the existence of other objects in the world ('roundness'; 'father'; 'Cambridge') and assume some kind of relation between the property at stake and properties held by external objects. Properties in this category are called 'extrinsic properties'.

Another important distinction, initially made by Peter Geach, concerns two forms of change occurring in a subject: 'real' and 'Cambridge'.[69] To explain this distinction better, take, for example, the event of X's death. This event creates a *real* change in X. X in reality no longer exists after his death. On the other hand, X's death does not constitute any real change with regard to X's wife. X's wife becomes a 'widow' from the moment of X's death. Thus, X's death leads to some change in X's wife. This is not a real change as her real existence is not changed by such an event. Rather, it is a *mere Cambridge* change. It is a change that enables one to argue that at t_1 (prior to X's death) the statement 'X's wife is a widow' was false, whereas at t_2 (after X's death) this statement is true.[70]

It is agreed in the literature that an object undergoes a *real* change in an event if, and only if, there is some *intrinsic* property it satisfied before the event but not afterwards.[71] The property of '*being harmed*' is an extrinsic property. This property is dependent upon a subject causing the harmful condition so that it is shaped by some kind of *relation* between the subject of harm and its doer. Hence, from a philosophy of language perspective, a person who is being harmed can undergo only a *Cambridge* change.

It seems plausible that a subject, which does not necessarily exist in the actual world, can undergo a Cambridge change in its extrinsic properties. It is possible that this subject did not exist either before the change or after it. The following exampes will make this point plainer:

(1) '*Being born*' – X, who is now being born (an extrinsic property as it is dependent on someone else giving birth to X), undergoes a Cambridge change (from not being born to being born) whilst X did not exist at all *before* the event.

---

[69] P. T. Geach, *God and the Soul* (Indiana: St Augustine's Press, 1969) 71–2 [Geach]. The latter form is called 'Cambridge change' since it keeps on occurring in philosophers like Russell and McTaggart who worked at the University of Cambridge.

[70] This line of argument reminds us of Fred Feldman's argument on existence as a corpse (above). The argument illuminates Feldman's mistake. Feldman did not distinguish between these two forms of change, thereby arguing that the dead continue to exist.

[71] Geach, above n 69.

(2) *'Being invented'* – X is a new invention. X's property of 'not being invented' underwent a Cambridge change to the property of 'being invented'.

(3) *'Being remembered'* – Y is dead. She is now being remembered by T. Y, though she does not exist, undergoes a Cambridge change from 'not being remembered' to 'being remembered'. Hence, one can argue that the sentence 'Y is remembered (as dead)' was false prior to her death and is true after her death.

(4) *'Being erased'* – S is writing a paragraph in his essay and then decides to erase it. The paragraph that existed before the erasure no longer exists after it. Nevertheless, this paragraph undergoes a Cambridge change of being erased.

If a subject which does not necessarily exist can undergo a Cambridge change, and if 'being harmed' is a property that can undergo only a Cambridge change, then one can harm a non-existing subject and so arguing for posthumous harm may be sound. When harm is construed as the defeat of interests, there is no conceptual difficulty in claiming that X was harmed, or in other words that X underwent a Cambridge change from 'not being harmed' to 'being harmed', though X does not exist at all when the effect of the harm occurs. David Hillel-Ruben holds this view. He argues that all posthumous changes are possible as Cambridge changes.[72]

However, such a conclusion may be problematic. Recall the original example of a Cambridge change. X's wife, a living person, undergoes a Cambridge change from 'not being a widow' to 'being a widow' following the death of her husband. The idea of a Cambridge change assumes two necessary conditions for undergoing such a change. First, one has to hold properties in two different points in time. In the original example, X's wife has to have both the property of *not being a widow* and the property of *being a widow*. Second, it is necessary that these two properties (before and after the Cambridge change) be carried by the *same* subject. In the original example, it is the same X's wife, the woman who married X before his death, who undergoes a Cambridge change and who has properties of both 'being a widow' and 'not being a widow'.

When applied to the dead, or more generally to a subject that at the time of the Cambridge change does not exist in the actual world, both

---

[72] David Hillel-Ruben, *Action and its Explanation* (New York: Oxford University Press, 2003) 27 [Hillel-Ruben]. It is possible that Peter Geach also takes this view when he mentions the case of posthumous change as an example of a Cambridge change. Nevertheless, the notion of posthumous change is not expounded in Geach's writings. Geach, above n 69, at 70.

conditions may not be met. The dead cannot be said to have any properties at all. For, as David Hillel-Ruben himself argues, 'if a property is true of some object at t, then surely the object of which the property is true at t must itself exist at t, just in order to display or exemplify that property at that time'.[73] It follows that, according to Hillel-Ruben's own account, a subject cannot have properties if she does not exist in reality. Hillel-Ruben's argument on the possibility of Cambridge changes in the post-mortem context is inconsistent with his own general theory of properties or with Geach's theory under which the idea of Cambridge change was originally established.

Furthermore, Hillel-Ruben claims that X's change is 'Cambridge' if and only if X changes and there is some *possible world* in which X changes from having to lacking P at t and X undergoes no non-relational change at all at t.[74] Since under Hillel-Ruben's account the dead can still exist in some possible world, they can exist (in general) and therefore they can hold properties as well. Additionally, since 'X's being harmed is or can be a Cambridge change in X then there is no reason in principle why one cannot sometimes do things which do harm the dead'.[75] As explained above, an appeal to possible worlds can be unhelpful and unconvincing. If Hillel-Ruben's account of posthumous harm rests on such an appeal, we have another reason not to follow it and the conclusions deriving from it.

Finally, if the dead are mere corpses stripped of their own personalities, it is not clear whether the dead are identical to the living person who no longer exists, namely the ante-mortem person. So, even if it were possible to argue that the living person who no longer exists holds the property of 'not being harmed' (before the harmful event), it would still not be clear whether they could have undergone any Cambridge change to hold the property of 'being harmed'. This is because the second condition for such a change, namely the requirement that the subject undergoing the change be the *same* subject who held the opposite property prior to the alleged change, may not be fulfilled. It follows that the third alternative to the 'existence condition' should be rejected as well.

Harm in no particular time

According to this fourth alternative, which is inspired by the writings of Thomas Nagel, Harry Silverstein and John Broome, harm can occur or be referred to in no particular time. Hence, it is irrelevant whether the subject who is being harmed exists at the moment of harm because this

---

[73] Hillet-Ruben, above n 72, at 11.   [74] *Ibid.*, at 27.   [75] *Ibid.*, at 28.

moment is not important, if it can be identified at all. Therefore, the argument concludes, a person is in a harmed condition irrespective of whether the moment of harm occurred during or after her life.

In a remarkable article on death, Thomas Nagel refutes the view that our fear of, and objection to, death derives from the belief that when we die, we cease to exist.[76] Nagel suggests two indications to support this conclusion. First, we do not regard the *temporary* suspension of life, even for substantial intervals, as *in itself* a misfortune. Second, we did not exist before we were born or conceived, and yet few of us regard that as a misfortune.

Nagel holds the position that most good or ill fortune has as its subject a person identified by her *history and possibilities*, rather than merely by her categorical state of the moment. The idea that there necessarily is a temporal relation between the subject of harm and the circumstances constituting it is unconvincing for Nagel:

> There are goods and evils which are irreducibly relational: they are features of the relations between a person, with spatial and temporal boundaries of the usual sort, and circumstances which may not coincide with him either in space or in time. *A man's life includes much that does not take place within the boundaries of his body and his mind, and what happens to him can include much that does not take place within the boundaries of his life.*[77]

Nagel's idea that certain good or bad things attach to *human* subjects without a necessary reference to time reaffirms the classification of interests suggested above, specifically the categories of after-life and far-lifelong interests. In order for such interests to be fulfilled, it is justifiable to argue that the value of one's life extends beyond one's lifespan and that some interests that belong to the person continue to have effect after her death.

John Broome follows this line of Nagel, arguing that we must recognize that some good may be caused by an event which is not simultaneous with the existence of that good, and he goes on to argue that some goods ('pattern goods') may not exist at any specific time at all, although they may be caused by an event that occurs at a particular time.[78] Following this reasoning, Broome holds that some types of good for a person seem not to require the person to be alive when they are caused, for example the good of being famous or having one's desires about what happens after one is dead satisfied. These goods, writes Broome, may be fulfilled only after death.[79] The same analysis may apply to the concept of harm. According to Broome, an event may harm a person without harming her at any time. The example provided for such a phenomenon is the harm of

---

[76] Nagel, above n 21.   [77] *Ibid.*, at 6 (my emphasis).
[78] John Broome, *Weighing Lives* (New York: Oxford University Press, 2004) 46.
[79] *Ibid.*, at 47.

shortening one's life. Broome writes: 'At first it might be surprising that you can be harmed without being harmed at any time. If we compare T1 with T2, we can see that the person's lifetime wellbeing g may be less in T1 than it is in T2. Yet, there is no time when she is worse off in T1 than she is in T2.'[80]

However, the problem that may follow from Nagel and Broome's theses is that it would be difficult to conceptualize, let alone identify, the temporal relation between the harm (or the benefit) induced and its circumstances.[81] This seems unreasonable. Our understanding of events and their effects presumes some kind of relation in time. In order for this relation to hold at all, we must say it exists at some time and we must also refer to the moment it exists, although both relata may not necessarily exist at *the same time*.[82] The relation between posthumous harm and its circumstances should exist in time (after the person is dead) and be referred to at that very moment.

A somewhat different version of Nagel's and Broome's theses is expressed by Harry Silverstein in an article on the relation between time and space.[83] Silverstein argues that posthumous events (states, objects, etc.) can coherently be accorded the same status as spatially distant events.[84] Therefore, the argument goes, just as spatially distant events, such as the death of A's son on a remote island that harms A, exist even though they do not exist *here*, so do temporally distant, including posthumous, events exist even though they do not exist *now*.[85] While Nagel argues that posthumous events occur in time the reference of which may

---

[80] *Ibid.*, at 237–8.

[81] Julian Lamont, 'A Solution to the Puzzle When Death Harms Its Victims' (1998) 76(2) *Australian Journal of Philosophy* 198, 205 and onward. For a critique of the interpretation of Nagel's theory, see William Grey, 'Epicurus and the Harm of Death' (1999) 77(3) *Australian Journal of Philosophy* 358.

[82] See Ben Bradley, 'When Is Death Bad for the One Who Dies?' (2004) 38(1) *Noûs* 1, 6 [Bradley].

[83] Silverstein, above n 32, at 109–16.

[84] Compare Steven Luper-Foy, who writes: 'Just as I can have properties by virtue of what goes on outside my spatial boundaries (for example being attacked by a cat), so I can have properties by virtue of what is going on outside my temporal boundaries. Thus it is partly due to events that occurred before I came into existence that "having been conceived" and "born after Aristotle" are both true of me. And it is partly due to events that will take place after I die that "will have his will read" and "will die" are true of me.' Luper-Foy, 'Annihilation' (1987) *Philosophical Quarterly* 233, reprinted in Fischer, above n 17, at 271, 274 (note 9).

[85] In his critique of Silverstein, Rosenbaum argues that if (according to Silverstein) *events* occurred and existed atemporally, there would be no difference between past and future events. Hence, one may still hold that all events *exist* atemporally but that, among the existing events, some have already occurred (past events) and some have not yet occurred (future events). Rosenbaum, above n 26, at 131.

be unnecessary (if possible), according to Silverstein posthumous events occur in no time. Silverstein's theory is inspired by W. V. Quine's book, from which the following quote is taken in its original form:

We say Elsa Lanchester is the widow of Charles Laughton; but there is no Charles Laughton for her to be the widow of, and there never was any, either as long as she was his widow. We say that Charles Laughton married Elsa Lanchester, more-over, and yet we refuse to conclude that he married his own widow . . .
    . . . The simplest way of putting all this mess in order is by viewing *people and other physical objects as deployed in four-dimensional space-time and all as coexisting in an eternal or timeless sense of the word. Temporal segments or stages of physical objects are physical objects in turn, temporally shorter ones.*[86]

Under the Quine–Silverstein theory, time is a characteristic of *objects* and the ability to ascribe objects with predication is seen to be timelessly true. A's existence in the past tells us where (in time) she exists, not *whether* she exists, just as A's existence in Toronto tells us where she is (in space) and not *whether* she is (at all). Thus, since A is timelessly existent, she can have X or be Y even when she is dead and not with us either *now* or *here*. It follows that posthumous events can exist, and, if they do, they exist in no particular time.

As elucidated earlier, this view is very problematic and goes against our intuition and understanding of harm as an event that exists in time, the significance of which one should be able to discern from the change occurring in the subject harmed. Moreover, it forces us to accept the disputed and highly criticized Quinean view of objects as a major premise in Silverstein's theory. This is an analytical move I do not wish to make and, as will be illustrated by my proposal, is certainly not necessary for ascribing harm to the dead.

Persistent existence of the Human Subject

My proposal

I wish to propose an analytical solution to the problem of posthumous harm derived from the 'existence assumption'. My proposal is premised on the notion according to which there are different forms under which one can exist. I can exist materially as a physical being in the form of an 'aggregate of cells', and/or in a non-material way as a 'man', a 'person', a 'human being', etc. It will be argued that some of the ways in which one exists – like human being or person – are fictions, that is their creation is

---

[86] Quine, 'Physical Objects', mentioned in Silverstein, above n 32, at 111 (my emphasis).

an imaginative construction or a pretence that does not represent *actuality*, but has been invented in order to symbolize some kind of moral or legal status their owner is endowed with. Hence, for example, the concept of 'person' is the creation of that which symbolizes a subject who usually has cognitive capacities and self-awareness, and is accorded with legal rights. We use the concept of personhood as a convenient way to provide this or that subject, whose body is usually present with us, with some characteristics, but surely such a 'person' does not exist in reality. What exists in reality is the body of a man or a woman with their unique combination of mental and physical states. In contrast, when we see a dog, we do not refer to it as a 'person'. We do not have any *motivation* to attribute this subject with the qualities and properties associated with the concept of personhood.[87]

With the death of a man or a woman the concept of personhood is no longer applicable to them (unless we are willing to apply it to them). Hence, we usually say, 'the deceased is not a person' or 'the dead person does not exist'. However, as the concept of personhood was not the only one by which we could categorize the existence of that man or woman while alive, there could be other forms of existence, some of which also have moral and legal significance like personhood, applicable to them even after their biological death. One such form is existence as a Human Subject. The Human Subject is the subject *holding* all human interests *belonging* to the person whose interests they are.

The problems associated with posthumous harm arise because of our tendency to identify the man or woman that exists in the actual world exclusively with the 'person' – a mere construct of ours that exists in some other way. They stem from a mistaken belief that the concept of personhood is the only possible concept that could and should apply to this or that man or woman, and that even if there could be other forms or concepts by which it is possible to refer to this or that man or woman while alive, the 'death' of a person necessarily results in the death of other possible attributes of that person.

The concept of personhood may be broader than the life of the man or woman to whom it refers. A significant discussion in this area, for example, attempts – sometimes, with not much success – to apply the concept of personhood to fetuses and even to embryos. Likewise, a rich debate in the literature concerns the question of whether the concept of 'human being' is one that can be attributed to the dead. I am not concerned now

---

[87] Of course, this is a contingent matter as our motivation to attribute a thing with the concept of personhood can be changed. An example of this would be the entity of corporation. Such an entity has been declared 'person' for legal purposes in recent years.

with either of these discussions. However, I take the position that these discussions show that the view according to which the existence of a human being can be referred to only in a binary classification as 'person' and 'non-person' is problematic. These debates also echo the fact that we do, and should, have concepts which can apply far beyond a man or woman's actual lifespan, whether before or after it.

Since I believe the concept of personhood is strongly rooted in our daily thinking, I do not suggest revising our understanding of that concept to apply also posthumously. Instead, I would like to suggest a new way to conceptualize the human existence. This is the existence as a subject holding interests, which, due to its uniqueness and membership in the human moral community, will be termed the 'Human Subject'. This subject, I will argue, has a persistent existence in time. To be precise, this subject always exists and its existence is temporal. Like other existing subjects, the 'Human Subject' (HS) does not exist in a physical or material way. Instead, its existence is logical or non-material.

The nature of the Human Subject

What is this 'Human Subject'? Recall my four categories of interests discussed above: pre-birth interests, life interests, after-life interests and far-lifelong interests. I argue that these interests, should they exist, are held by one subject whose existence persists over time. The idea of the HS represents a subject whose existence has three main characteristics. First, it is *persistent* over time: that is, there is no point in time where its existence ceases. A question may be raised as to how long after the death of a person there still exist interests relating to this person (held by the HS). My answer to this query is simple: although the existence of the HS is persistent over time, the effect of the interests held by it may be limited in time. I discuss this and other possibilities in the concluding chapter of the book. A second characteristic of the HS is that it is *in time*, namely that it has a temporal definition; and a third is that it is *non-material*. By this latter characteristic I mean that the HS existence is not physical or material. Instead, the HS exists in a non-material form like any other concept in our language or thought.[88] The diagram on the opposite page demonstrates the existence of the HS in time and the relation between its existence and the holding of human interests.

---

[88] By this, I do not follow the belief in after-life or in other form of physical existence post-mortem.

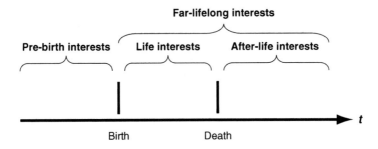

The relation between the Human Subject and the person

A question may arise regarding the relationship between the subject holding interests and the 'person'. Is there a relationship between the two? Do they refer to the same thing or are they distinguishable one from another? Some similarity exists between the 'person' and the 'Human Subject'. Both ideas refer to a subject which does not exist in reality as a physical being and which, due to its moral significance, is accorded with special moral and legal entitlements. The subject of the 'person' (or the person) is endowed with psychological and intellectual capacities that provide it with the holding of legal rights. In addition, the person is the 'owner' of the interests held by the Human Subject. The Human Subject holds these interests *for* the person and they are the latter's interests. The Human Subject, on the other hand, is not associated with having any mental traits and its significance lies in the fact that this subject belongs to the moral community of humans. Members (subjects) of that community are bestowed with an entitlement merely to hold interests for the person whose interests they are, the defeat of which may constitute legal harm.

As will be elaborated in chapter 2, the group of human interests is larger than the group of legal rights, and, as has been argued above, some of the human interests should apply to periods before and after a person's actual life. Correspondingly, the existence of the Human Subject extends to a longer period of time than the existence of the person whose interests they are. However, when the subject holding interests (the 'Human Subject') exists from birth to death, namely when the man or woman whose interests they are is alive, there is a logical identification between the live man or woman, the 'person' and the 'Human Subject'.

The relationship between the 'subject holding interests' (the 'Human Subject') and the 'person' has four aspects. First, the subject holding interests has a moral and legal status, deriving from its membership in the moral group of humans. Most notably, the Human Subject is also capable of holding rights that refer to and protect some of the life interests and far-lifelong interests of the person. This idea will be developed in chapter 2. Second, the subject holding interests holds not just any interests but the interests of *that* person whose interests they are. There is specificity attached to each Human Subject, which allows us not only to identify it but also to distinguish it from another Human Subject. Third, the person has a legal *right* that his or her overall interests (namely interests from all four categories) will not be defeated without proper justification, namely a right not to be harmed. The subject holding interests is the logical construct by which such a right may be fulfilled. Lastly, by exercising its moral and legal powers the person affects the content, scope and extent of the interests held by the subject holding interests. The person, for example, may have children or produce a work of art while alive. This may create new interests and affect the content and scope of the interests held by the Human Subject, and the extent to which other interests of that person may be protected.

Strengths of the Human Subject model

Although death is an event that ends one's life, it does not extinguish most of one's interests, which are essential to, and constitute a large part of, one's life. As Loren Lomasky nicely puts it, 'Like a projectile that has attained escape velocity, we leave our home behind but remain within the pull of its gravitational attraction for some time.'[89] Conceptualizing our existence only in terms of the concept of personhood is too narrow an approach and leaves many important human interests unprotected at times when such legal safeguards are necessary. The surviving of our interests in the future can only be guaranteed by a subject whose existence persists over time. The moral and legal significance of the institution of interests is thus maintained by the proposal to conceptualize the human existence through the idea of the Human Subject. We should therefore dispense with our habit of regarding and referring to ourselves exclusively as persons.

Not only is the persistent existence of the HS not counter intuitive to us, but it is also an *inherent* part of life itself. Some support for this phenomenon may be seen in our language.[90] For example, in the phrase

---

[89] Lomasky, above n 10, at 218.
[90] Compare Leonard Nelson, who discusses the connection between language and interests: Leonard Nelson, *System of Ethics*, (H. J. Paton trans.) (New Haven: Yale University Press, 1956) 138–9. See also David Hillel-Ruben, who offers three possible posthumous uses in our language. Hillet-Ruben, above n 72, at 10.

'Napoleon is now being eulogized', reference is made *now* to Napoleon who no longer exists as a person. Napoleon is posthumously being ascribed with a *property* ('being eulogized') in the present tense. In sentences like this, we clearly have a particular subject in mind to refer to or to attribute with some properties or concepts. Although this subject may no longer exist in the actual world, it is used in our thought and language in a very specific and concrete fashion.

Moreover, when we now say 'we love Socrates', we presume in a way that Socrates still exists to be loved so that the human subject bearing the interests of 'Socrates' (the person who died long ago) still exists, and holds an interest in being loved and appreciated after death.[91] We still maintain the *relationship* of love (to Socrates) even when one relata has ceased to exist as a person. But the relationship of the living to the dead is maintained not only by our remembering or thinking of the dead. It continues, for example, through the actions of the living as they carry out the wishes of the dead. This will be elaborated in chapter 4, where a discussion of the testamentary interest in determining the disposal of one's body will be carried out.

Of course, the occurrence of a non-material subject in our language, thought or memories is not something restricted to the dead or to any subject whose person does not exist in reality. We say, 'God is good', 'love is great' or 'red is a royal colour' even though we do not know if God, love or red exist at all. Likewise, for the purpose of our talking, thinking and ascribing properties to the dead or the subject whose person is no longer 'alive' (including the property of holding certain interests), it is sufficient to argue for the existence of a non-material subject holding interests for that person.

The advantage of my proposal concerning the Human Subject, who holds – among others – after-life and far-lifelong interests after the death of the person, is that such proposal avoids the critique associated with comparing an existing state and a non-existing state. Any attempt to solve the problem of experience and the problem of the subject caused by posthumous harm without arguing that the deceased still exists to hold certain interests is exposed to the same critique as in harmful-birth cases. In these cases, it is meaningless to argue that non-existence, for example by aborting a fetus, could be a better condition for one to be in, for it is no condition of anyone at all.[92] If we hold, as I do, that the subject holding after-life and far-lifelong interests continues to exist after the death of the

---

[91] For the limitation of the content of this interest due to remoteness in time, see above n 90.
[92] This problem is also known as the 'Non-Identity' problem, extensively discussed by Derek Parfit in his *Reasons and Persons* (New York: Oxford University Press, 1984).

person whose interests they are, we will not have to engage ourselves in such an impossible and unconvincing comparison.

The subject bearing after-life and far-lifelong interests continues to exist after the death of the person whose interests they are. Since to hold interests one need not necessarily have mental traits (unlike the concept of holding rights applying to the 'person'), no difficulty arises with regard to the preservation of 'personal identity' of that subject when the owner of interests, namely the person, loses her mental capacities upon death. After the death of the person, it is the same Human Subject holding interests of that person as it was prior to death.

For all of these reasons, it seems adequate to argue for an additional form by which human existence should be perceived, namely existence as 'Human Subject'. This subject belongs to the human community and holds all four categories of human interests presented at the beginning of this chapter. Although some relations are maintained between the Human Subject and the person whose interests are held by the former, there are periods of time (prior to and after a person's life) in which the former exists despite the latter's coming into existence or cessation to exist. The Human Subject does not *have* rights or interests, for the only subject who has rights or interests is the person. The person and the Human Subject are two distinct subjects sharing some common characteristics and having an interesting connection between them, the most important of which is that the Human Subject *holds* the interests of the same person before the person is born, while he or she is alive, and after he or she is dead.

The existence of the Human Subject after the death of the person enables it to continue to hold certain human interests important to that person. The defeat of these interests after the death of the person may constitute legal harm occurring at the moment of the harmful event. In such a scenario, posthumous harm is possible through the thwarting or setting back of these interests. The harmful condition occurs simultaneously with the harmful act, and the subject harmed is the Human Subject and not the *ante-mortem* person who no longer exists after death.

Symbolic existence

The concept of the Human Subject, argued for in the last section, not only solves the problem of the subject, thereby allowing the proposition that dead humans may still be harmed, but also enriches our general understanding of holding interests and existing in various and multiple forms other than as persons. Before we go on to the next chapters, it is important to argue at the outset of this book for a human interest the conceptualization of which may be easily made having established the concept of the Human Subject.

Following the idea that human beings may exist in different forms, and that their interests may still have effect before they are born and after they die, the acknowledgement of a human interest, which I will call the *interest in the recognition of one's symbolic existence*, will be argued for. This interest is premised on the notion described above, according to which there are different forms in which one can exist in the world. Some of these forms are material or physical: for example, existence as an aggregate of cells, tissues and organs functioning together in a sophisticated way governed by the nervous system. Other forms include existence in a non-material way, that is existence in the abstract form: for example, existence as 'a person', 'a man', 'a member of the human community', a 'Human Subject', etc.

Symbolic existence is a non-material second-order existence of abstract existence or material existence usually taking place in the minds, thoughts and language of other existing creatures or in the actions, possessions and the like of the first-order existing creatures. An example of symbolic existence in the first category is the existence of a person X in the thought of her husband, or in the memory of her daughter. An example of symbolic existence in the second category is the existence of the person I am in (or through) my writings, or in the house I own. Hence, symbolic existence is a form of existence representing and standing for the real or abstract existence of the person whose existence it is/was. By the interest in the recognition of 'one's symbolic existence', I therefore refer to the interest held by the Human Subject, within a person's life or after it, surviving the death of the *person* whose interest in symbolic existence it is.

It is possible to conceptualize symbolic existence from three different aspects: temporal, dimensional and spatial. From a temporal perspective, symbolic existence extends to a longer period of time than material or physical existence. This is a form of existence that commences prior to material or physical existence of that person and ends long after the cessation of it. While symbolic existence represents a form of existence which is different from material or physical existence, its duration is dependent upon the specific type by which the Human Subject symbolically exists. Hence, the Human Subject may exists 'as a human' for a longer period of time than its existence as 'a loving parent', and this latter form of existence may last for longer than existence as 'a person'.

The dimensional aspect of symbolic existence emphasizes the flexibility characterizing this form of existence to encompass various non-material forms of existence of the same subject. In material or physical existence, the existing subject must fulfil certain physical criteria for existence. It must be identified by its weight, volume and height; it must be tangible and trigger animal instincts and senses; and it can be subject to decay, deformation and physical change. On the other hand, a subject existing symbolically need not fulfil these criteria. Nor is symbolic existence bounded by any physical dimensions limiting its possible subjects. The only criterion for symbolic existence is that its existing subject must belong to the human community. As expressed above, the association with the human community is not restricted by time so that both subjects who will join this community and those who have departed from it may be potential subjects for symbolic existence.

The spatial aspect of the symbolic existence infers that, in contrast to material or physical existence that has evident spatial characteristics by which its subject may be identified, symbolic existence may occur in the same 'place' whereby its subject exists materially, but can also take place in other 'settings', some of which cannot be articulated physically or geographically, for example in the minds, thoughts and memories of living people.

Because creatures that can exist symbolically belong to the human community, symbolic existence is not neutrally valued. In advocating symbolic existence two major ideas are advanced: the idea of wholeness and the idea of distinctiveness. Symbolic existence emphasizes the idea that a person has an interest in being regarded as a whole and that such wholeness should be maintained as much as possible. 'Wholeness' refers to a state of affairs in which the existing subject's physical or mental/evaluative integrity are being preserved. Acknowledgement of this interest safeguards the appearance of the subject's body as complete and inviolable, and keeps her reputation as a specific person with certain values, attitudes, and good and bad characteristics undisturbed.

A second idea promoted by the interest in the recognition of one's symbolic existence concerns the subject's distinctiveness from another subject. The subject's distinctiveness and uniqueness as an individual human being are being secured, inter alia by broadening the perspectives upon which she may be referred to and perceived as an existing subject. Due to its flexible conditions, symbolic existence enriches the ways in which a subject may exist (temporarily, dimensionally and in space), and so provides it with significant moral attributes emphasizing its special place in the universe.

The idea of symbolic existence reflects the proposition that a person's individual image and legacy and recollections of them by others consist and should consist of more than the visual images of the flourishing or deteriorating body of a person. They also should include the person's human relationships with others and her seeking to advance those relationships, inter alia through her symbolic existence, even during post-competency as a living or dead person. This idea is premised on a concept of a social self and is inspired by the philosophies of George Herbert Mead and Charles Cooley.

The concept of social self

The idea of symbolic existence is influenced by the symbolic interactionist view outlined by George Herbert Mead. This view holds that developing a sense of identity stems from the human activity for self-reflexivity, or in Mead's terminology viewing oneself from the perspective of the other. The idea is that the self originates in a social context and becomes aware of itself only after communication with another is enabled. By communicating to another one places oneself in the position of the other and is able to ascertain the attitude the recipient takes in respect to one's gesture. In Mead's language:

The individual experiences himself as such, not directly, but only indirectly, from the particular standpoints of other individual members of the same social group, or from the generalized standpoint of the social group as a whole to which he belongs. For he enters his own experience as a self or individual, not directly or immediately, not by becoming subject to himself, but only in so far as he first becomes an object to himself just as other individuals are objects to him or in his experience; and he becomes an object to himself only by taking the attitudes of other individuals toward himself within a social environment or context of experience and behavior in which both he and they are involved.[93]

A similar view to Mead's is held by Charles Cooley. While exploring the idea of the social self and the reference someone makes to other persons to distinguish and make particular his or her own self, Cooley illuminates another aspect of that self, which is the reflected or looking-glass self. Cooley writes:

In a very large and interesting class of cases the social reference takes the form of a somewhat definite imagination of how one's self – that is any idea he appropriates – appears in a particular mind, and the kind of self-feeling one has is determined by the attitude toward this attributed to that other mind. A social self of this sort might be called the reflected or looking-glass self:

> Each to each a looking-glass
> Reflects the other that doth pass

[93] George H. Mead, *Mind, Self and Society* (Chicago: University of Chicago Press, 1934) 138.

As we see our figure and dress in the glass and are interested in them because they are ours, and pleased or otherwise with them according as they do or do not answer to what we should like them to be; so in imagination we perceive in another's mind some thought of our appearance, manners, aims, deeds, character, friends, and so on, and are variously affected by it.[94]

The idea of the reflected or looking-glass self consists of the following three principal elements: the imagination of our appearance to the other person, the imagination of this other person's judgement of that appearance, and some sort of self-feeling, such as pride or embarrassment. As Cooley himself writes, 'the character and weight of that other, in whose mind we see ourselves, makes all the difference with our feeling'.[95]

Both Mead and Cooley emphasize the importance and significance one attaches to the appearance of one's character and good name in the mind of another. Mead also attaches a constitutive function to regarding oneself from the perspective of others. By taking the role of another and being able to set upon oneself the attitudes of others, one is turning from *I* to a sophisticated *me*.[96] However, neither Mead nor Cooley pays much attention to the fact that the meaning one ascribes to the reflection of one's persona as seen in other persons does not diminish – and perhaps even increases – when one is not around to defend or correct it. The idea of symbolic existence put forward in this chapter successfully captures this fact. Thus, I wish to follow Mead's symbolic interactionist view and Cooley's idea of the reflected self, and substitute Cooley's three elements described above with the following elements: the imagination of our appearance to another person *in the present or the future*; the *actual or hypothetical* imagination of this person's judgement of that appearance and the *actual or hypothetical* self-feeling in response to such imagination. It should be noticed that while I argue that the interest in the recognition of one's symbolic existence must be secured objectively, the *evaluation* of the degree by which a breach of that interest is being made is assessed subjectively so that the *hypothetical* response of the specific person whose interest was breached is being tested. By revising Cooley's conditions for the reflected self, a better protection for his and Mead's very idea is being secured. This protection allows us to defend on behalf of the person who can no longer defend for herself what she values and cares much about.

The interest in the recognition of one's symbolic existence is not a novel notion. Discussion of it goes back to 44 BC when Cicero wrote that

---

[94] Charles Horton Cooley, *Human Nature and the Social Order* (New York: Charles Scribner's Sons, 1922) 183–4.
[95] *Ibid.*, at 184.
[96] Ronald G. Alexander, *The Self, Supervenience and Personal Identity* (Aldershot: Ashgate, 1997) 92.

'For the life of the dead consists in the recollection cherished of them by the living',[97] and it extends into this century where internet websites may be considered as an additional or alternative space to memorialize the dead.[98] The idea of symbolic existence can also find support in other legal conceptions.

Legal support for the interest in symbolic existence

The interest in the recognition of others in one's symbolic existence is acknowledged by case law, especially legal decisions dealing with end-of-life issues. In *Bland*, the House of Lords ruled that a mentally incompetent patient retains 'the right to be well regarded by others, and to be well *remembered* by his family. That right is *separate* from that of his family to remember him and to have the opportunity to grieve for him when he is dead.'[99] The Lords applied that right or interest also to situations occurring after death, and explained:

At least a part of the reason why we honour the wishes of the dead about the distribution of their property is that we think it would wrong *them* not to do so, despite the fact that we believe that they will never know that their will has been ignored. Most people would like an honourable and dignified death and we think it wrong to dishonour their deaths, even when they are unconscious that this is happening. We pay respect to their dead bodies *and to their memory* because we think it an offence against *the dead* themselves if we do not. Once again I am not concerned to analyse the rationality of these feelings. It is enough that they are deeply rooted in our ways of thinking and that the law cannot possibly ignore them.[100]

In *Cruzan*, Justice Stevens recognized a person's interest in not having her memories dishonoured by a prolonged and undignified dying process, and he extended that interest to apply also after a person's death. Justice Stevens held that 'Nancy's interest in life . . . includes an interest in how she will be thought of after her death by those whose opinions matter to her . . . How she dies will affect how that life is remembered.'[101]

---

[97] Marcus Tullius Cicero, *The Ninth Oration Against Marcus Antonius*, (44 BC) Charles D. Yonge trans., available at www.4literature.net/Cicero/Ninth_Oration_Against_Marcus_Antonius/2.html, accessed on 13 February 2007.

[98] See the fascinating article by Kylie Veale, 'Online Memorialisation: The Web as a Collective Memorial Landscape for Remembering the Dead' (2004) 3 *Fibreculture*, available at http://journal.fibreculture.org/ issue3/issue3_veale.html, accessed on 6 March 2006.

[99] *Airedale NHS Trust* v. *Bland* [1993] 1 All ER 821, 848 (per Butler-Sloss LJ) (my emphasis).

[100] *Ibid.*, at 853–4 (per Hoffmann LJ) (my emphasis).

[101] *Cruzan* v. *Director, Missouri Department of Health* 110 S Ct 2841, 2885–6, 2892.

The wholeness of a person's existence observed symbolically through her body may also find support in case law. Legal decisions in the USA validating the constitutionality of legislation that permits taking corneas from the dead without notifying families emphasize that cornea removal does not affect the deceased's *appearance*.[102] Preserving the deceased's physical appearance and returning organs and tissues extracted from the body to families to be disposed of together with the whole body are other examples of the protection of a person's symbolic existence.

In addition to these legal cases, there are some legal areas in which one can find support for the idea of the interest in the recognition of one's symbolic existence. With regard to the living, and in some jurisdictions also to the dead, defamation law and the law of privacy protect a person's interest in maintaining her good name and reputation and having her image (within other living creatures) fixed when violated. This interest protects the way a person's 'story of life' is being told by and to others, and as long as this story is distorted or substantially incorrect, its retelling is encouraged. Under cases of this kind, it is clear that there is something additional to the person's physical existence that the law seeks to protect which by its nature is akin to the interest in the recognition of one's symbolic existence.[103]

The legal protection of 'moral rights' that authors have in the work they create is another example of a legal area where the interest in the recognition of one's symbolic existence may find support.[104] Moral rights consist of two main protections: the right to be identified as the author of the work and the right to protect the work from alterations that would be harmful to the author's reputation. In some jurisdictions, moral rights also consist of the right to decide when and under what circumstances to divulge the work and the right to withdraw all published copies of the work if it no longer represents the author's views or is detrimental to the author's reputation.[105] The idea behind moral rights is that a person's artistic and literary creation emanates from, and is representative of, the

---

[102] See e.g. *State* v. *Powell* 497 So. 2d 1188, 1191 (Fla. 1986), cert. denied, 481 US 1059 (1987).

[103] Immanuel Kant argued that the right to a good name must survive the death of the person because 'it is at least ungenerous to spread reproaches against one who is absent and cannot defend himself, unless one is quite certain of them'. Immanuel Kant, *The Metaphysics of Morals*, Mary Gregor ed. and trans. (Cambridge: Cambridge University Press, 1996) 76.

[104] Moral rights are recognized mainly in Europe, especially in Germany and France, but also in other countries including Canada. See e.g. Copyright Act, RSC 1985, c. C-42, s. 14.1.

[105] Pamela Samuelson, 'Privacy and Intellectual Property' (2000) 52(5) *Stanford Law Review* 1125, 1147.

personality of its creator even when the work has been commercialized and transferred to other parties. The work is one of the means by which the personality and identity of its creator are communicated to the world. As expressed by Neil Netanel, 'Although a work may be commercially exploited, it is not simply a commodity and many commentators would say that it is not a commodity at all. Instead, the work is seen, partially or wholly, as an extension of the author's personality, the means by which he seeks to communicate to the public.'[106] This is why moral rights are not assignable to others and continue after a person's death.[107]

A third area in which one can find support for the interest in the recognition of one's symbolic existence is the criminal law. Some states in the USA make it a crime to express by printing, writing, signs, pictures or the like an opinion 'tending to blacken the memory of the dead'.[108] The purpose of this prohibition is to deter potential criminals from violating the way a person is represented in the minds of others. The interest in recognition of the memory of the deceased receives direct protection under these statutes.

If the argument for acknowledging the interest in the recognition of one's symbolic existence is sound, then such an interest may strongly apply to situations after death, so that we would be tempted to explain our attitudes to the dead by an appeal to that interest. I will postpone such temptation to later analysis and instead turn to discuss in the next chapters three main areas where one's symbolic existence may be acknowledged. These areas include the control of others and oneself of one's body after death and the control of others and oneself of one's health information and medical confidentiality post-mortem.

Conclusion

The main question addressed in this chapter was whether posthumous events could harm the dead. In order to answer this question, the concept of harm was first analysed as the defeat or thwarting of human interests. A distinction was made between the satisfaction of an interest and the

[106] Neil Netanel, 'Alienability Restrictions and the Enhancement of Author Autonomy in United States and Continental Copyright Law' (1994) 12 *Cardozo Arts and Entertainment Law Journal* 1, 7; see also Martin A. Roeder, 'The Doctrine of Moral Rights: A Study in the Law of Artists, Authors and Creators' (1940) 53 *Harvard Law Review* 554, 557.
[107] See e.g. Copyright Act, RSC 1985, c. C-42, ss. 14.1(2), 14.2(2) (Can.); Copyright, Designs and Patents Act 1998, c. 48, ss. 94–5 (Eng.).
[108] See e.g. Nevada Rev. Stat. Ann. s. 200.510 (Thomson/West 2005); Idaho Stat. s. 18-4801 (2005); Col. Rev. Stat. Ann. s. 18-13-105 (Thomson/West 2007); Ga. Code s. 16-11-40 (Thomson/West 2005); Okl. Stat. Ann. s. 1441 (Thomson/West 2005).

fulfilment of it, and an argument for the conceptualization of the idea of interest from an objective perspective was called for. Following a brief introduction on the concept of harm, the group of human interests was divided into four sub-categories: pre-birth interests, life interests, after-life interests and far-lifelong interests. Subsequently, two main puzzles concerning the concept of posthumous harm were discussed, namely 'the experience problem' and the 'problem of the subject'. Examining Feinberg's solution to these problems, specifically the idea of surviving interests, revealed that its application to the *ante-mortem* person raises difficulties that have not been successfully resolved by the Pitcher–Feinberg formula. Four alternatives to the problem of the subject were then discussed and rejected: existence as a possibility; existence in after-life; the occurrence of harm without the existence of the subject harmed; and the occurrence of harm in no time.

Consequently, a suggestion has been made to expand our view regarding the applicable concepts describing our existence as humans. A call for a new subject, holding human interests from all four categories and entitled the 'Human Subject', was made. This new subject should be construed as one whose existence persists over time and extends over the life of the person whose interests they are. When interests held by the Human Subject are defeated after the death of the person, whose surviving interests it is, the Human Subject is being harmed at the moment of the harmful event. The strengths of the idea of the Human Subject were presented, thereby leading to the conclusion that the deceased, or the 'Human Subject' holding after-life and far-lifelong interests, can be harmed by events occurring after death.

In the last part of this chapter, the acknowledgement of a new human interest, namely the interest in the recognition of others in one's symbolic existence, was argued for. This interest, should it exist, may be highly applicable to the dead, the existence of whom we may refer to as merely symbolic. Even if one can refer to the deceased or the Human Subject as existing symbolically, the status of its surviving interests still remains to be examined. Specifically, we may ask whether all or some of the surviving interests of the deceased, which are held by Human Subject, amount to the protection of legal rights. This question will be discussed in the next chapter.

2   Posthumous rights

Having established the theoretical grounds for posthumous interests and the possibility of their defeat after one's death, it will now be investigated whether some of these interests may also be protected as posthumous rights, or, put differently, does the Human Subject in its capacity of holding the surviving interests of a dead person also hold the rights of the person whose interests they are? This question is important not because an affirmative answer to it necessarily leads to different moral treatment of the dead than does a negative response. As Matthew Kramer points out, 'to rule out attributions of legal rights is not to rule out legal protections for the creatures who are incapable of holding rights'.[1] Indeed, from moral and legal perspectives one can owe duties to another creature without the necessary holding of rights by the latter. For example, a requirement to be vegetarian or to avoid fox-hunting[2] can still be sound even if animals have interests but do not have rights, just as the moral and legal obligation not to take organs from the dead when their wishes are unknown can be established without determining whether the dead have posthumous rights.[3] The question raised in this chapter is important because it examines the characterization of the safeguards against harming the dead without prescribing what these safeguards

---

[1] Matthew H. Kramer, 'Getting Rights Right' in Matthew Kramer ed., *Rights, Wrongs and Responsibilities* (Basingstoke: Palgrave, 2001) 28–95, 29 [GRR].

[2] See the UK Hunting Act 2004 (c. 37) s. 1, making it an offence to hunt wild mammals with a dog. The Act terminates a well-established tradition of the English people on the grounds of preventing animals' suffering. Likewise, the Supreme Court of Israel decided on 11 August 2003 that the artificial fattening of geese by insertiong of a feeding tube in their oesophagus so that their liver is fat and tasty (*foie gras*) should be prohibited. Bagatz 9232/01 *Noach, the Israeli Association of the Organizations for Animal Protection* v. *The General Attorney* et al., available at http://62.90.71.124/files/01/320/092/s14/01092320.s14.HTM, accessed on 2 January 2005 (in Hebrew).

[3] Compare Kramer, who argues that if we adhere to Hohfeld's definitions of 'duty' and 'right', our acknowledgement that we have duties toward the dead is tantamount to acknowledgement that they have rights against us. Matthew H. Kramer, 'Rights Without Trimmings' in Matthew H. Kramer, N. E. Simmonds and Hillel Steiner eds., *A Debate Over Rights* (Oxford: Clarendon Press, 1998) 7–111, 31–2 [RWT].

should necessarily look like. By this, it enables one to regard the duties owed to the dead from the perspective of their recipients, thereby suggesting far-reaching moral and legal repercussions.[4]

One way to examine if a creature is a right-holder is to ask whether it has moral standing, namely to explore its moral status. The assumption behind such an examination is that the language of rights is identical – or almost identical – to the language of morals, and vice versa.[5] But this assumption is controversial, let alone problematic, and needs further discussion that is beyond the scope of this chapter.[6] Although the Human Subject has some moral standing in so far as it belongs to the human moral community, this chapter will focus on its jurisprudential rather than moral status. The chapter will directly analyse and discuss various theories of rights and their possible application to that subject as potential right-holder. It should be emphasized at the outset that the question examined in this chapter is whether, in its capacity of holding the surviving interests of the person, the Human Subject can also *hold* rights belonging to that person. No question arises as to the *owner* of these rights, should they exist. The owner of these rights is the *living* person who no longer exists at the time of the query. The suggestion made in this chapter is that a person may *have* legal rights relating to her surviving interests, although they may not be held by her after death. Instead, these posthumous rights may be held by the Human Subject, holding the surviving interests of that person.

It is reasonable to argue that the problem of the subject discussed in the previous chapter ('who is the subject holding interests whose defeat constitutes posthumous harm?'), is common to concepts of both posthumous interests and posthumous rights. Once the possibility of ascribing a subject with posthumous interests has been resolved, such a solution may equally apply to the context of posthumous rights. Joel Feinberg holds such a view. After establishing that the *ante-mortem* person is the subject of surviving interests defeated by death or other posthumous events, Feinberg argues that duties toward the dead have corresponding rights which can also be violated after death. It is implied in this argument that posthumous rights are held by the same subject, namely the

[4] Kramer, GRR, above n 1, at 31.
[5] L. W. Sumner, *The Moral Foundation of Rights* (Oxford: Clarendon Press, 1987) 16 [Sumner].
[6] See Joseph Raz, 'Right-Based Moralities' in J. Waldron ed., *Theories of Rights* (Oxford: Oxford University Press, 1984) 182–200; H. L. A. Hart, 'Are There Any Natural Rights?' in Jeremy Waldron ed., *Theories of Rights* (Oxford: Oxford University Press, 1984) 77–90 ['Natural Rights'].

ante-mortem person.[7] It follows that if one accepts that there is a subject holding interests whose existence persists over time (the Human Subject), and that this subject may hold interests the extent of which goes beyond the lifespan of the person whose interests they are, there should be no prima facie conceptual difficulty in holding that this subject can also be a *potential* right-holder.

However, what needs to be further explored is whether the holding of rights by the subject whose existence persists over time is legally and morally justifiable: that is, whether this subject should also be an *actual* right-holder. A related question would be whether this subject is 'qualified' enough to have rights derived from, or related to, some of the interests held by it. In order to answer these questions, one needs to explore the concept of right further.

Surprisingly, the concept of right is relatively modern. It is not found either in the works of the Greek philosophers or in Roman law.[8] Despite the short history of this concept, there is a wide consensus that rights are requirements with great importance. Although rights have individualistic character, they can only be conceptualized in a society. By reference to the individual's worth, dignity or freedom, rights usually protect the individual from uninhibited pursuit of collective or social goods.[9] Ronald Dworkin, for example, argued that rights are 'trumps over some background justification for political decisions that states a goal for the community as a whole'.[10] Dworkin further maintained that 'we need rights only when some decision that injures some people nevertheless finds prima-facie support in the claim that it will make the community as a whole better off on some plausible account of where the community's general welfare lies'.[11]

Many of the medical procedures performed on the dead have significant and substantial importance to practices by which health, knowledge and scientific skills of members of the society are or can be benefited. Overall, these practices contribute enormously to the community as a whole. According to Jeremy Bentham, the corpse may be regarded as a utilitarian object. If preserved, exhibited and studied, the corpse could

---

[7] Joel Feinberg, *Harm to Others* (New York: Oxford University Press, 1984) 94–5.

[8] H. L. A. Hart, 'Legal Rights' in H. L. A. Hart, *Essays on Bentham* (Oxford: Clarendon Press, 1982) 162–93, 163 ['Legal Rights'].

[9] Alon Harel, 'Theories of Rights' in Martin P. Golding and William Edmundson eds., *Blackwell's Guide to the Philosophy of Law and Legal Theory* (2005) 191–206 [Harel].

[10] Ronald Dworkin, 'Rights as Trumps' in J. Waldron ed., *Theories of Rights* (Oxford: Oxford University Press, 1984) 153–67, 153. Dworkin assumes that the background justification for rights is in the form of utilitarianism which aims to achieve as many of people's goals as possible. *Ibid.*

[11] *Ibid.*, at 166.

serve 'moral, political, honorific, dehonorific, money-saving, money getting, commemorative, genealogical, architectural, theatrical and phreno-
logical ends'.[12]

On an individual level, to assert that one has rights entails the justification for a certain action with regard to such rights.[13] To have a right is
to have a claim to something or against someone.[14] It follows that 'legal
claim-rights are *defined* in terms of other people's duties',[15] although, as
Philip Montague correctly argues, even if a statement concerning one
individual's obligation to another implies a statement about the second
individual's rights against the first, it does not follow that the rights-
statement can serve as either a justification or an explanation of the
obligation-statement because both statements are logically equivalent.[16]
Under a Hohfeldian analysis, a right or a claim is 'the legal position
created through the imposing of duty on someone else'.[17] What distinguishes a right from any other claim is that the first is enforceable,
although the power to enforce a right need not necessarily vest in the
hands of the right-holder. In the post-mortem context, there are some
who maintain that in our ordinary discourse we speak of the dead as
having claims on the living.[18]

Two dominant approaches to the concept of rights are discussed in the
literature. The first argues that rights protect, promote and benefit (some
of) the right-holder's interests (the 'benefit theory' or, more commonly,
the 'interest theory'). The second holds that rights advance the right-
holder's ability to control her own freedom to choose by waiving or
enforcing other people's duties owed to the right-holder (the 'will theory'

---

[12] Dorothy Nelkin and Lori Andrews, 'Do the Dead Have Interests? Policy Issues for
Research After Life' (1998) 24 *American Journal of Law and Medicine* 261–91, 261.
[13] Nevertheless, it is plausible to argue under some theories that rights could exist even
when there is no duty-bearer. See MacCormick's example of the Succession Act 1964
(Scotland) acknowledging the rights of an intestate estate prior to the nomination of an
executor. D. N. MacCormick, 'Rights in Legislation' in P. M. S. Hacker and J. Raz eds.,
Law, Morality and Society – Essays in Honour of H. L. A. Hart (Oxford: Clarendon, 1977)
189–209, 200 [MacCormick].
[14] Joel Feinberg, 'The Rights of Animals and Unborn Generations' in Joel Feinberg ed.,
Rights, Justice and the Bounds of Liberty (Princeton: Princeton University Press, 1980)
159–83, 159 ['Animals and Unborn Generations']. See also his 'Duties, Rights and
Claims' (1966) 4 *American Philosophical Quarterly* 137–44 and 'The Nature and Value
of Right' in his *Rights, Justice and the Bounds of Liberty* (Princeton: Princeton University
Press, 1980) 143–58, 150. In this latter piece, Feinberg further distinguishes between
'claiming to', 'claiming that' and 'having a claim'. *Ibid.*, at 149–51.
[15] Joel Feinberg, *Social Philosophy* (Englewood Cliffs, N.J.: Prentice-Hall, 1973) 62.
[16] Philip Montague, 'Two Concepts of Rights' (1980) 9(3) *Philosophy and Public Affairs*
372–84, 375.
[17] *Ibid.*, at 9.   [18] Kramer, RWT, above n 3, at 32.

or the 'choice theory').[19] Both theories analyse rights in terms of their purpose: that is, they purport to answer the question of what rights aim to achieve. This teleological examination of rights consists of two stages. In the first, an argument is brought to characterize the general purpose of a legal right defined as broadly as possible. In the second stage, the applicability of a possible candidate for the purpose of right to the general definition obtained in the first stage is examined.

This chapter explores the possibility of a new category of rights, posthumous rights. In this context, it is desirable to focus on the general purposes of rights discussed by the major theories of rights. However, such a general inquiry will follow the discussion of different theories specifically addressing the idea of posthumous rights, should this latter group of rights exist.

Specific theories of posthumous rights

Hillel Steiner

The concept of posthumous rights is part of Hillel Steiner's general discussion of persons and times.[20] Steiner holds the view that we undoubtedly have serious moral duties to the dead, but these duties nevertheless do not have correlative rights. In his book, he examines the right to leave a bequest, which he regards as the paradigm case of posthumous rights, although he also maintains that the right to dispose of one's bodily remains is vulnerable to the same criticism as leaving a bequest.

At the outset of his analysis, Steiner shows that he does not rule out the possibility of justifying the practice of leaving a bequest under utilitarian or interest-based theories by the argument that allowing persons a power to dispose of their property after death increases people's incentives to develop and conserve resources, contributing to the well-being of contemporaries and successors alike. Nevertheless, he contends that the testamentary power is impossible, as the testator fails to transfer real property to its recipients, whoever they may be. According to Steiner, there are only four ways for a person to acquire title to things: by appropriation of unowned things; by transformation of other self-owned things into the things newly owned; by voluntary transfer of things from their

---

[19] A more recent approach combines elements from both theories, creating a 'hybrid theory' of rights. See Gopal Sreenivasan, 'A Hybrid Theory of Claim-Rights' (2005) 25(2) *Oxford Journal of Legal Studies* 257–74 [Sreenivasan].

[20] Hillel Steiner, *An Essay on Rights* (Oxford: Blackwell, 1994) 249–61 [Steiner].

owners; and by having the titles to those things transferred from owners in redress for the violation of one's rights.[21] Ownership acquired by bequeathal is an extension of gift-giving and belongs to the above third category. In Steiner's view, transferring property by leaving a bequest is different from any other transfer in that, until the moment of death, there is no certified heir, and the testator can alter her will as she chooses. Hence, the testator incurs no duty not to interfere with the recipient's possession of the object at stake.[22] According to Steiner, bequests only 'supply a form of *insurance* for the bequeather: it ensures him against the fate of King Lear, against the ingratitude and cupidity of prospective heirs upon whom the bequeather is unwilling to rely up to the moment of his death. At most, it's a lever by which the bequeather can, during his lifetime, strongly influence the current behaviour of aspiring heirs.'[23]

Steiner's main argument is that it is impossible to describe leaving a bequest in Hohfeldian terms. Consequently, he turns to examine the nature of transferring ownership through the act of leaving a bequest. Steiner claims that such legal transfer can be a *duty* neither to the heirs nor to the testator. It is not the first since the heirs acquire title only after the transfer of such property is completed. On the other hand, to argue that it is the latter entails that such a duty is owed by the executor who is appointed by the deceased. But, according to Steiner, if the executor owes a duty to the testator, the latter must have a corresponding right, and (according to Steiner) this would entail that the testator would have been able to waive or demand the enforcement of that duty.[24] Surely, the power to waive or enforce that duty does not vest in the heir, for if the deceased could transfer the property and the power related to its corresponding duty directly to the heirs, the executor's duty would be superfluous.

Rejecting this first legal possibility, Steiner turns to examine an alternative proposition, according to which the bequest confers a *power* upon the executor. Clearly, before death the executor lacks the power to dispose of the property. Does she have a power to dispose of the property after the death of the testator? Arguing that she does have such power must assume, in Steiner's view, that the deceased conferred upon her the same power. But if the deceased could have transferred the power to the executor after her death, then she could have also transferred her property directly to the heirs. Under this explanation, the power vesting in the executor is unnecessary. Moreover, simply arguing that the executor has a

---

[21] *Ibid.*, at 251–2.   [22] *Ibid.*, at 254.   [23] *Ibid.*, at 254.

[24] Steiner's understanding of the concept of rights corresponds with the choice theory which will be discussed below.

power to dispose of the property does not imply that the disposition need be in favour of the heir. This raises once again the question concerning the power to demand compliance with the bequest: who maintains such power?[25] Steiner's conclusion is that rights, duties and powers involved in testamentary succession are founded upon a fiction.[26] The major effect of this fiction is to imply that the deceased's property, which otherwise became *res nullius*, namely the title of which could have been acquired by anyone, remains uninterrupted.[27] Steiner concludes that there could be no moral counterpart to the legal power of leaving a bequest. Therefore, the justification for leaving a bequest, if there is any, lies in the demands of justice.[28]

Steiner's analysis is intellectually inspiring but has some problems. First, it is open to question whether the right to leave a bequest is indeed the paradigmatic case of a posthumous right. Surely, such a right, if it exists, belongs to the *ante-mortem* person rather than the *post-mortem* person or to the Human Subject, existing before and after the death of the person whose interests they are. The action of leaving a bequest has its starting point when the person was alive, and its legal validity could also be explained if it is regarded as a form of contract or promise made within a person's lifetime. However, the notion of posthumous rights should mainly be examined in light of situations commencing after the death of the person and not during her life. Steiner acknowledges the second type of right commonly ascribed to the dead, namely the right against posthumous defamation, but he prefers not to discuss this specific right in its post-mortem context since it relies upon the interest theory.[29]

However, a person's right to a good name can also be explained by the choice theory. Steiner does not discuss this alternative, but instead focuses on a more problematic type of posthumous right, namely the right to bequeath. More importantly, and as will be elucidated below, the choice theory may find it difficult to account for any right that is exercised after the death of the right-holder unless the right-holder exercised her advance power with regard to it. Under this general conceptual difficulty, no posthumous right may be justified regardless of whether leaving a bequest makes sense or not. Steiner's whole discussion of the different forms of the right to bequeath appears inevitably unnecessary in light of his general theory of rights.

---

[25] Steiner holds that the state holds such power in theory but also in practice. *Ibid.*, at 255–6. Hence, the executor's duty to dispose of the property of the deceased in favour of the heir is owed to the state. *Ibid.*, at 257.
[26] *Ibid.*, at 256.   [27] *Ibid.*, at 257.   [28] *Ibid.*, at 258.   [29] *Ibid.*, at 250 (note 29).

In addition to these preliminary objections, Steiner's argument concerning the right to bequeath creates further problems. Steiner assumes that since the transfer of property can only occur after the death of the testator, it must be performed by the executor, who is obviously a living person. This is, as Cecile Fabre argues, not a necessary conclusion.[30] Fabre examines two alternatives to regard a bequest as other than the transfer of property. The first alternative seeks to analyse the right to bequeath as a form of *promise*. By writing a will, the decedent transfers a right to the heir that when she is dead, a third party will let the heir control what was then the deceased's property. However, Fabre successfully shows the flaws of such an argument. First, the testator can change her mind and decide not to transfer her property to the heir. This would still be legitimate under the law of succession. Second, although the testator can waive the performance of an executor, the heir cannot put the executor under a duty. It follows that the heir could not have had a right transferred by the deceased.[31]

Fabre's second alternative suggests that the right to bequeath is a form of *contract* for future performance. Under this option, a contract is made between the testator and the heir to the effect that the deceased's property will belong to the heir after the testator dies. Fabre argues that the heir can be a party to this contract only by virtue of the deceased having agreed to the heir's receiving the property, or, in other words, only if the deceased has a right that her wishes with respect to the property be respected after she is dead. Since, as will be seen, according to the choice theory the deceased cannot waive or demand the performance of such a right, it does not exist, and so the heir cannot be a party to such a contract.[32]

However, it is unclear why, under Fabre's account, being a party to the contract depends on the deceased's agreement (after death) that the heir will receive the property, and why the latter necessarily derives from our acknowledgement of posthumous rights. Moreover, it follows from Fabre's analysis that under this contract the deceased has a duty to perform but not a right to exercise. Although I find Fabre's explanation with regard to the contract model unconvincing, I believe she makes a strong claim when she argues that under the choice theory it is difficult to argue that the deceased has any rights. In any event, it shows that the heir acquires property from the deceased by virtue of the will and the death of the testator. The role of the executor is to make sure that such rights transfer to the heir nominated in the will, but it is not concerned with the actual transfer of the property.

---

[30] Cecile Fabre, 'The Choice-Based Right to Bequeath' (2001) 61(1) *Analysis* 60–5, 61.
[31] *Ibid.*, at 62–3.   [32] *Ibid.*, at 63–4.

Moreover, if the purpose of the bequest fiction is, like Steiner asserts, to prevent the appropriation of property that otherwise would have been abandoned and become *res nullius*, one still needs to inquire why death is an exception to the general rule regarding such form of property. Why does the general rule concerning *res nullius* not apply to property abandoned by the deceased? Steiner raises this question in his discussion but does not reply to it. Instead, he examines legal fictions in general and their possible background. Steiner asks: 'Why should property of the deceased persons *not* be regarded as abandoned? Upon what grounds can all other persons be said to lack appropriative entitlements to it? ... Can this power of promulgating fictions be derived from a set of just rights?' Nevertheless, while attempting to answer these questions he cites Bentham and Fuller on legal fictions and does not provide any satisfactory answer to his many queries.[33]

In conclusion, as a choice theorist Steiner assumes that to have rights is to be in the possession of powers to waive or demand and enforce compliance with the correlative duties of these rights. Such an assumption leads Steiner to an inevitable conclusion that the right to bequeath, which he regards as the paradigmatic case of posthumous rights, makes no sense and does not accord with any systematic understanding of rights, claims, duties and powers. According to Steiner, this right is based on a legal fiction, and finds no support in the law. While Steiner illuminates the conceptual difficulties echoing from the notion of posthumous rights, he is not successful in showing the collapse of such notion.

Annette Baier

In her essay, 'The Rights of Past and Future Persons',[34] Annette Baier argues that there is no theoretical problem in speaking of the rights of past or future persons. Baier maintains that the dead can and do hold moral rights and that living people have corresponding duties toward them. She supports her argument by claiming that the dead are members of *our* moral community. Baier writes:

The crucial role we feel, as moral beings, is as members of cross-generational community, a community of beings who look before and after, who interpret the past in light of the present, who see the future as growing out of the past, who see themselves as members of enduring families, nations, cultures, traditions.

---

[33] Steiner, above n 20, at 257–8.

[34] Annette C. Baier, 'The Rights of Past and Future Persons' in Ernest Partridge ed., *Responsibilities to Future Generations* (Buffalo, N.Y.: Prometheus Books, 1980) 177 [Baier].

Perhaps we could even use Kant's language and say that it is because persons are
noumenal beings that obligations to past persons and future persons reinforce one
another, that every obligation is owed by, to and towards persons as participants in
a continuing process of the generation and regeneration of shared values.[35]

Baier's theory supports the 'reciprocity thesis', according to which only
members of the same moral community can have rights.[36] According to
Baier, it is membership in the same moral community that guarantees the
possession of posthumous rights. Baier proposes two criteria for holding
rights. First, there should be at least one other person to carry out the duty
owed to the right-holder. Second, there is or should be a 'socially recognized means' for the right-holder or her proxy to 'take appropriate action'
with regard to that duty.[37] Baier maintains that because the dead – like
other members of the moral community – have social roles which persist
over time, they can hold rights, and that reliance on these roles creates
dependency which gives rise to obligations within an interdependent
community.[38] To give her idea a more concrete meaning, one could
appeal to Martin Golding's theory of moral communities. Under such a
theory, moral communities can be formed by explicit contract between
their members, namely a social arrangement within which each member
benefits from the efforts of other members and out of altruism.[39]

    The idea that existing in a society is a sufficient condition for holding
rights is disputable. As Carl Wellman argues, some members of a society,
like slaves, may be denied the power to exercise any actions concerning
duties owed to them, if there are any.[40] But more importantly, Baier
provides no account for posthumous rights. Instead, she establishes the
moral ground for our duties toward the dead. Baier's language of 'social
role', 'dependency/interdependency' and 'reliance' and her invoking of
Kant's theory of obligations reflect her main concern to offer some
justifications for our moral obligations to members from our moral community, including the dead. Baier is not genuinely concerned with establishing a theory or an idea of posthumous rights.

    Moreover, one can doubt whether Baier's assumptions concerning her
argument on posthumous obligations hold at all. First, it is possible to
argue that the dead (and other future persons) do not belong to our moral
community under Baier's own account. Surely, the dead cannot 'feel',

---

[35] *Ibid.*, at 177.
[36] Joseph Raz, *The Morality of Freedom* (Oxford: Clarendon Press, 1986) 176 [*Morality of Freedom*].
[37] Baier, above n 34, at 171–2.   [38] *Ibid.*, at 179.
[39] Martin Golding, 'Obligations to Future Generations' (1972) 56(1) *The Monist* 85–99, 91 [Golding].
[40] Carl Wellman, *Real Rights* (New York: Oxford University Press, 1995) 147 [Wellman].

'look before and after their time', 'interpret the past', 'see the future' or 'see themselves' – all terms used by Baier to identify members of a moral community. Baier provides members in the moral community with some cognitive capacities which are all absent among the dead. If one is to give an account for posthumous rights on the basis of membership in a moral community whose members are characterized by the performance of actions that cannot be shared by the dead, one is led to an unconvincing argument.

Why do the dead belong then to the same moral community according to Baier? Perhaps it is because the dead are part of the future in which they (in the past) or we, the living persons (in the present), consider that they have rights. But should the fact that someone is considered by others as having rights (whether within or not within their own moral community) morally and legally matter to the question of whether that someone should *in fact* have and hold these rights in the first place? I believe it should not. Furthermore, if what makes the dead and the living part of the same moral community is the mere fact that the dead exist in some future anticipated by them before and experienced by the living now, then this is likely to be too narrow an explanation for posthumous rights, let alone rights which come into effect only after a person's death.

Carl Wellman

While analysing Baier's idea of moral community described above, Wellman argues that 'the dead are incapable of being members in any community defined in terms of the capacities of making and responding to claims',[41] and that a mere membership in our forensic community is not a sufficient condition for being a moral right-holder.[42] According to Wellman, membership in any 'ideal community' cannot survive one's death, for such membership assumes that there are good and bad things for their member and this is inapplicable to the dead. In Wellman's view, crucial to the idea of posthumous rights is the showing of surviving interests whose advancement or defeat can benefit or harm the dead respectively.[43] Wellman maintains that although projects desired in life can be good after one's death, they are still not good *for* the deceased.[44] He further argues that even if surviving interests did have any influence on the dead, as a general principle interests in and of themselves lack those special aspects required to explain both the bindingness of the duties implied by rights and the moral powers associated with them.[45]

---

[41] *Ibid.*, at 150.   [42] *Ibid.*, at 151.   [43] *Ibid.*, at 153.   [44] *Ibid.*   [45] *Ibid.*, at 154.

Another problem with the concept of posthumous rights observed by
Wellman lies in the ascription of surviving interests (if there are any) to a
subject that no longer exists: if there could be no subject holding interests
surviving the death of the person, there could be no subject holding rights
as well.[46] But Wellman does not conclude his analysis by ruling out the
possibility of posthumous rights. He proposes another argument that may
avoid the problems discussed earlier. Wellman argues that the living
persons who survive the deceased have posthumous *duties*, e.g. to keep
a deathbed promise or not to damage the reputation of the dead, and he
goes on to say that these surviving duties are 'real'.[47] What are the
grounds for these duties? Wellman explains:

[Surviving duties] are duties *implied by the rights of the individuals who have died.*
But this need not be to ascribe rights to the dead; it can and should be to assert that
*the rights of the living continue to impose duties even after the persons who possessed those
rights have ceased to exist.* I do not imagine that their rights continue to exist
without subjects. I suggest that *surviving duties are implied by proactive rights –
rights that impose future duties.*[48]

Wellman maintains that there is a problem identifying the subject who
holds rights, the latter of which imply posthumous duties. However, he
does not deal with this problem at all. Reading Wellman seems to convey
the idea that it is the living person who no longer exists – the *ante-mortem*
person – who holds these rights. But when, for example, Wellman discusses the duty to keep promises made to the deceased, he writes
'although that right and that person no longer exists, the moral reasons
do still exist *because they are essentially social reasons relevant not only to the
individual right holder who has died but to the surviving duty-bearer and all
those who continue to be in society with him or her*'.[49] So, according to
Wellman, the existence of the right-holder (whether living or dead) is
not important to, and has no bearing on, posthumous duties. Wellman's
main concern is to acknowledge that these duties exist because of their
relevance to the *ante-mortem* person, to the living person who owes them
and to society in general.

If the rights of the *ante-mortem* person imply 'real' duties (whatever they
are) after the death of a person, is it not equally true that the rights of the
ante-mortem person survive her death? Not according to Wellman. In his
view, since death destroys the capacity for agency and the essential
qualifications for being a moral right-holder, we cannot give an affirmative answer to this question.[50] Peculiarly, the deceased retains her moral

---

[46] *Ibid.*, at 155.   [47] *Ibid.*, at 155.   [48] *Ibid.*, at 156 (author's emphasis).
[49] *Ibid.*, at 157.   [50] *Ibid.*, at 156.

characteristics to serve as an object of posthumous obligations because there are surviving persons capable of owing such obligations, but she does not have the same (or other) qualifications to hold rights (corresponding to these obligations) after death.[51]

Wellman's theory seeks to give an account for a strong belief or intuition that we still owe duties to the dead, perhaps ones which are based on their symbolic existence. But although we owe these duties in the present, and although some of these duties can be created after the death of their recipient, Wellman calls them 'surviving duties'. By this, Wellman wants to connect the duties owed to the deceased with their recipients and still not argue that the latter are right-holders. Whether Wellman is convincing or not, like other theorists writing on this issue he successfully establishes the idea that we owe duties to the dead, although their recipients may not have corresponding rights at the time of the fulfilment of those duties. Wellman may successfully argue for posthumous duties, but he does not show why the reasons justifying the existence of such posthumous duties might not actually imply the holding of posthumous rights by the dead.

Raymond Belliotti

One of the prominent advocates of posthumous rights is Raymond Belliotti. In an article written in 1979, Belliotti claims that human beings have interests that can be satisfied after they are dead, and that they have rights which can be violated or respected once they are dead.[52] In this article, Belliotti examines what he calls the 'transference argument', according to which, since the interests/rights of a person are transferred to relatives and survivors upon the person's death, any transgression of these interests/rights is not a violation of the interests/rights of the deceased, but rather of the living.[53] Belliotti correctly maintains that there would be situations to which such an argument would not apply, e.g. when the dead person has no surviving relatives, when surviving relatives do not care if the dead person is maligned or his corpse mutilated, or when the relatives themselves malign or mutilate him.[54] Therefore, he concludes that it is not merely our aversion to insulting the surviving relatives of the dead that accounts for our thinking that

---

[51] *Ibid.*, at 157.
[52] Raymond A. Belliotti, 'Do Dead Human Beings Have Rights?' (1979) *The Personalist* 201–10 [Belliotti].
[53] *Ibid.*, at 203.   [54] *Ibid.*

certain acts performed by the living against the dead are morally wrong. Belliotti searches for that additional explanation.[55]

A first alternative would be that the wrongs performed on the dead are bad not because they defeat the interests or rights of the deceased but because they are wrong by themselves, that is they are inherently wrong. Belliotti examines this possibility when he discusses the phenomenon of telling falsehoods about the dead. It is always morally wrong to tell falsehoods, writes Belliotti, regardless of whether the deceased or indeed anyone else has been harmed. But still no one will condemn telling falsehoods about cartoon characters, and the reason for that lies in the fact that cartoon characters, like other things, cannot be harmed. Belliotti assumes that the dead are different from cartoon characters in that they can be harmed. However, the assumption that the dead can be harmed is disputable and the cartoon example does not mitigate the existing controversy concerning such an assumption. Still, according to Belliotti, there must be another reason justifying the claim that telling falsehoods about the dead harms them.[56]

In Belliotti's view, it makes good sense to speak of the rights of the dead.[57] Two accumulative justifications are implied in his argument. First, the dead have interests that can be defeated by the living. It seems prima facie wrong to deny certain things to dead humans because such a denial involves their interests in these things, e.g. their interest in a good reputation, proper disposal of their possessions, and considerate handling of their corpse. The second justification for posthumous rights is that there are third parties who can act on behalf of the dead and claim that these interests and desires be respected or that the violation of these interests be prevented. Finally, Belliotti dismisses the claim that the dead cannot hold rights because they are not moral agents, pointing to the fact that infants, the mentally incapacitated and animals have acknowledged rights.[58]

In addition to arguing for the existence of posthumous rights, Belliotti claims that there is a contractual reciprocity element built into such rights. By this he maintains that we may all contractually agree to respect the interests of the dead, and in return expect that those who are living when we are dead will respect our interests. But even if Belliotti is correct

---

[55] *Ibid.*   [56] *Ibid.*, at 203–4.

[57] Although Belliotti argues that this is not an exhaustive list, he mentions four types of posthumous rights: the right to dispose of property; the right to the reputation which is merited by deeds performed when alive; the right to any posthumous award to which a claim of entitlement can justifiably be lodged; and the right to specify the burial procedures and handling of one's corpse. *Ibid.*, at 209.

[58] *Ibid.*, at 208.

in describing such contractual relations, this may not yet establish that the dead have rights. At most, his argument shows that we may have duties to respect posthumous interests and that we also have good reasons to do so. Hence, the only justification for posthumous rights that may be discerned from Belliotti's arguments is that the dead have rights because their interests can be defeated and there is someone who can claim for them. While the first part of this argument does not necessarily lead to such a conclusion without expounding more on the normative relation between interests and rights, the latter part of it does not explain why the dead hold posthumous rights. Why is it not the claimant representing the decedent who is the right-holder in this case? Belliotti does not provide any general theory of rights to support his first assumption and to refute the possibility raised in light of his second assumption, and, by failing to do so, his thesis is substantially lacking.

In conclusion, each of the specific theories of posthumous rights aims to analyse the holding of rights by the dead. Instead, these theories actually explain why it is reasonable to hold that living persons owe duties to the dead without any commitment to the argument that these duties have corresponding rights. The question of whether there may be rights after death, especially rights for which the correlative duties are also constituted after death, should be analysed by the discussion of general theories of rights and their possible application to the dead as potential right-holders.

General theories of rights

The choice theory

While criticizing Bentham's interest theory of rights (which will be discussed below), H. L. A. Hart develops an alternative idea to Bentham's – that of the choice theory of rights. According to Hart:

This idea is that of one individual being given by the law the exclusive control, more or less extensive, over another person's duty so that in the area of conduct covered by that duty the individual who has the right is a small-scale sovereign to whom the duty is owed.[59]

---

[59] Hart, 'Legal Rights', above n 8, at 183. In another place, Hart explains that the right-holder has a justification for limiting the freedom of another and that 'he has this justification not because the action he is entitled to require of another has some moral quality but simply because in the circumstances a certain distribution of human freedom will be maintained if he by his choice is allowed to determine how that other shall act'. Hart, 'Natural Rights' above n 6, at 80.

But what is it like to be a 'small-scale sovereign' with regard to the person who owes the duty? Hart further claims:

> The fullest measure of control comprises three distinguishable elements: (1) the right holder may waive or extinguish the duty or leave it inexistent; (2) after breach or threatened breach of a duty he may leave it 'unenforced' or may enforce it by suing for compensation or, in certain cases, for an injunction or mandatory order to restrain the continued or further breach of duty; and (3) he may waive or extinguish the obligation to pay compensation to which the breach gives rise. It is obvious that not all who benefit or are intended to benefit by another's legal obligation are in this unique sovereign position in relation to the duty.[60]

As can be seen, control and choice are extremely dominant in Hart's theory. By allowing the right-holder to waive the duty in the first place, the choice theory gives more weight to the idea of control than to the right-holder's entitlement to certain benefits. It also appears to under-estimate the right-holder's entitlement to be compensated when a duty owed to her has already been breached by allowing her to waive, perhaps under public policy concerns, the action against the duty-bearer or nullify the latter's duty to compensate her once the duty-bearer has already been held responsible.

Critique of the choice theory From a general perspective, Hart's idea of control and choice is narrowly focused. Indeed, duties formed under contracts or property law are ones over which the right-holder can exercise a full measure of control. But duties under the public law, e.g. duties formed under the criminal or constitutional law, are ones in respect of which the person who benefits from their compliance usually does not have *any control* whatsoever. It follows that the idea of exercising control is not applicable to all legal rights. The motivation to emphasize the idea of control may be political.[61] Choice theorists glorify the importance of individual discretion and self-determination but only in specific settings. The choice or will of the right-holder is paramount in a given legal relationship where the two parties involved are equally empowered. Choice cannot be fully exercised in other legal settings.

Moreover, the requirement of control and choice entails three additional components to the choice theory. First, under this theory, it should be sufficient and necessary for holding a right that the right-holder is competent and authorized to demand or waive the enforcement of that right.[62] The potential right-holder should be able to exercise powers conferred on her by legal or moral norms. If she cannot exercise these

---

[60] Hart, 'Legal Rights', above n 8.   [61] Kramer, RWT, above n 3, at 75.   [62] *Ibid.*, at 62.

powers due to her medical condition or other physical or mental restrictions, or if no such powers are conferred in a given legal system, she is not qualified to be a right-holder. Second, the holding of a right does not necessarily involve the protection of one or more of the right-holder's interests.[63] The interests a person may have can be irrelevant to the establishment of her legal rights.[64] Consequently, a person can have a right that is against her interests. She can also have interests which cannot be protected by her legal rights. Third, and following the previous requirement of this theory, the potential of a person's right to protect one or more of the right-holder's interests is not sufficient *per se* for the assertion that this person is an actual right-holder.[65] To make such an assertion, she needs also to exercise her legal power over the duty-bearer.

It follows from the choice theory that 'the essence of a right consists in opportunities for the right holder to make normatively significant choices relating to the behavior of someone else'.[66] The choice theory glorifies the choices a person may have with regard to a certain behaviour rather than emphasizing the behaviour itself and the important consequences deriving from it. The choice theory attaches moral or legally significant value to the right-holder in so far as, and only if, it derives from the right-holder's control or choice. The contribution of the right-holder's behaviour and its effects is contingent and depends upon the ability of the right-holder to control them.

The requirement of control, which is at the heart of the choice theory, makes it difficult to explain many existing rights when control is possible but is lacking or inappropriate, such as with the right to receive proper medical care, to be paid unemployment relief or to be compensated by strict liability policies. Hart's answer to this criticism is that these cases represent two sufficient features: the duty to supply the benefit is conditional upon the request of it, and the beneficiary of the duty is free to demand it or not.[67] Instead of referring to a standard power to waive or extinguish the duty, Hart refers to a 'weaker' form of power ('some measure of control'). In another place, Hart implies that it is the person who makes the beneficial service rather than the beneficiary who is the right-holder:

---

[63] *Ibid.*

[64] Hart and other choice theorists did not rule out the idea of benefit to the right-holder. This idea should be incorporated, according to Hart, to supplement the notion of individual choice. In his view, freedoms but also benefits are essential for the maintenance of life, security, development and dignity of the individual. Hart, 'Legal Rights', above n 8, at 189.

[65] Kramer, RWT, above n 3, at 62.   [66] Kramer, GRR, above n 1, at 28.

[67] Hart, 'Legal Rights', above n 8, at 186.

[Rights] … may be accorded by a person consenting or authorizing another to interfere in matters which but for his consent or authorization he would be free to determine for himself. If I consent to your taking precautions for my health and happiness or authorize you to look after my interests, then you have a right which others have not, and I cannot complain of your interference if it is within the sphere of your authority.[68]

This latter view seems not only impractical in cases where no such authorization is made, but also completely unreasonable.

The requirement of control is also problematic in justifying cases where *control is inherently impossible*, such as with regard to children's rights or the rights of the permanently mentally disabled. Moreover, according to the choice theory, a right-holder must have some wish or desire that her right be fulfilled. The theory assumes some kind of a mental state that not only allows for the awareness of the existing right but also presupposes a psychological inclination toward it. However, there are many rights for which such a mental state is unnecessary. The rights to be provided with education and healthcare establish duties to guarantee these services regardless of the right-holder's wishes or desires.

Furthermore, the choice theory cannot account for the conceptual possibility of inalienable rights, namely rights that cannot, by their very nature, be waived at all.[69] In this respect, the constraint comes not from the right-holder's lack of capacities, but from the nature of the rights at issue. While some of these rights are mostly important to human existence, such as the right to life and liberty, they cannot be classified as rights in the first place according to the choice theory. Other rights, which are far less important, would be considered as legal rights under the choice theory.[70]

Likewise, the choice theory cannot justify rights that are not enforceable, like moral rights. The theory assumes that all rights entail duties that can and should be enforced by law and whose control by the right-holder is a necessary requirement for holding rights. Rights, according to this view, should be recognized by society as such, and once they are claimed, their claim is valid. But this is not a necessary understanding of a system of rights, for rights could also be socially unacknowledged and unenforced.

---

[68] Hart, 'Natural Rights', above n 6, at 85.   [69] Harel, above n 9.
[70] *Ibid.* Gopal Sreenivasan adds two more examples (derived from the right to liberty) for such inalienable rights: the right not to be enslaved and the right not to be operated upon without informed consent. Sreenivasan, above n 19. However, Sreenivasan's second example seems inappropriate as the right to be operated on with informed consent can be easily waived by authorization of proxies and therefore is not inherently inalienable.

Moreover, by arguing that the right-holder must have control over the duty of another, it is assumed that rights are correlative to duties. However, it is not sufficient to assume such correlativity since it is possible to argue for the existence of rights for which there are no duties, e.g. a parent's right to punish her child, just as it would be possible to argue for duties with no correlative rights, e.g. a duty to report on danger.

The exclusion of right-holders The exclusion of certain groups from holding rights, resulting from the requirement of control, has been a major concern for choice theorists. Hart's response to this problem is worth mentioning. In his essay, Hart discusses the problem of children's rights. Hart provides two reasons why it is still possible under the choice theory to argue that acts of enforcement and/or waiver with regard to children's welfare imply children's rights and not the rights of the persons controlling them. He writes:

> Where infants or other persons not *sui juris* have rights, such powers [i.e. power of enforcement/waiver] … are exercised on their behalf by appointed representatives and their exercise may be subject to approval by a court. But since (a) what such representatives can and cannot do by way of exercise of such power is determined by what those whom they represent could have done if *sui juris* and (b) when the latter become *sui juris* they can exercise those powers without any transfer or fresh assignment; the powers are regarded as belonging throughout to them and not to their representatives, though they are only exercisable by the latter during the period of disability.[71]

Note that people who have been mentally disabled since birth do not meet Hart's first condition since there is no possible (let alone imaginative) way for them to determine and control duties of others. Also note that the dead or the permanently mentally incapacitated who will never become *sui juris* do not meet Hart's second requirement.

Consider now the two reasons suggested by Hart to justify the argument that children are right-holders although they cannot exercise control. Under the first, one is being asked to imagine a hypothetical situation in which the child at issue is *sui juris*; the child is exercising some powers; and these powers determine the actual exercise of power by the child's representatives in reality. This move seems to be impossible, totally unrealistic and unfortunately pointless. Moreover, if the choice theory is concerned not with actual power that is being exercised by the right-holder but with *hypothetical power* that the candidate for holding rights could have exercised, why does Hart's explanation apply only to children?

---

[71] Hart, 'Legal Rights', above n 8, at 184 (note 86).

It is plausible to think of other creatures who could have exercised powers, had they been *sui juris*. What is unique in the case of a child that makes it an exception to the general requirement of control under the choice theory of rights? Hart does not tell us.

Perhaps the second reason is more helpful. According to this explanation, since the child, when she becomes *sui juris*, can exercise powers without being appointed or qualified to do so and without any transfer of powers from the representative back to the child, Hart wants us to regard the power exercised by the representative as if it belonged to the child originally. It is clear that such a reasoning is a mere fiction constructed by Hart to maintain his requirement of control and exercise of powers on the one hand, and still be able to provide an account for children's rights on the other hand. As such, it is a weak and unconvincing explanation. This explanation is also not necessarily true, as one can successfully hold that the child did not have original powers when she was a child and that she has been legally qualified to exercise powers only from the moment she became an adult. Alternatively, contrary to Hart, one can hold that the representative implicitly transferred her powers to the child when the first terminated her role as a legal representative, and that only from this moment onwards did the child (already an adult) have the capacity to exercise legal powers, resulting in her having rights according to the choice theory.

Nigel Simmonds defends Hart's theory of children's rights.[72] He argues that Hart's set of reasons for ascribing rights to children even when they cannot exercise powers of waiver and enforcement is persuasive, and that there are also moral considerations that can be taken into account, specifically our moral concern for children based on an interest in promoting their welfare quite independently of their choices. As they grow older, writes Simmonds, some of our duties toward children come to be contingent upon their will.

But why would the choice theory accept such an exception to the requirement of control? If there are other moral concerns that choice theorists like Simmonds would want to consider, and if these concerns constitute the establishment of rights, as Simmonds argues, then we are introduced to a revised notion of right under the choice theory. It does not seem straightforward that such a revision to the choice theory is something Hart would have wanted to pursue while making his exception to children's rights.

---

[72] Nigel E. Simmonds, 'Rights at the Cutting Edge' in Matthew H. Kramer, N. E. Simmonds and Hillel Steiner eds., *A Debate Over Rights* (Oxford: Clarendon Press, 1998) 113–232, 226 (note 138) [Simmonds].

The dead as right-holders Leaving aside the general difficulties inherent in the control requirement discussed above, it remains to be asked whether the dead have rights according to the choice theory. It seems intuitively correct that the dead cannot have control or power to enforce or waive duties that relate to their well-being. The dead are neither competent nor authorized to act. They cannot make motions to court or initiate any legal proceeding, nor can they be aware of the violation of their rights. But while alive the dead (or the *ante-mortem* person) can exercise powers and choices pertaining to duties owed to them after death. Moreover, the dead may choose to enforce or waive the enforcement of these duties following death. In principle, there should be no conceptual difficulty for the choice theory to acknowledge the exercise of such powers, thereby validating the holding of rights by the dead.

An alternative possibility according to which the dead may hold rights under the choice theory would be in situations where, while alive, the dead assign the living to represent their interests after they die, or serve as an executor or an administrator and take actions for and on behalf of the dead. Other scenarios may include the appointment of a guardian for the dead person by court. Moreover, the proposed situations are all legally feasible, and do not require special arrangements. For example, section 38 to the Ontario Trustee Act provides that '. . . the executor and administrator of any deceased person may maintain an action for all torts or injuries to the person or the property of a deceased *in the same manner and with the same rights and remedies as the deceased would, if living, have been entitled to do*'.[73] A question that remains to be asked is whether, according to the choice theory, it is necessary that the right-holder *herself* exercise control over the duty owed to her, or whether it is sufficient that some control *on behalf of the right-holder* be exercised.

Few scholars attribute to choice theorists the view that it is *either* the right-holder *or* some other person acting on behalf of the right-holder who has the relevant powers over the duty-bearer in respect of the

---

[73] Ontario Trustee Act, RSO 1990, c. T. 23, s. 38. A relevant distinction here would be Martin Golding's distinction between *having claims* and *making claims*. The *making of a claim* is the mere fact of claiming something whereas the *having of claims* is the entitlement one has relative to the other to make a claim whether or not one chooses to make the claim, or is even able to make it. Golding, above n 39, at 89. According to Golding, there are two criteria for determining whether one can make a claim. First, the content of the claim needs to fit what he calls a 'social ideal', that is the conception of the good life for individuals under some general characterization and which can be maintained by them as good for them in virtue of this characterization. *Ibid.*, at 93. Second, the claimant and the claimee have to be members of the same *moral community*. Golding maintains that these two criteria establish the notion of claim rather than any actual demand. *Ibid.*, at 89–90. I shall elaborate on these criteria below.

right-holder.[74] However, such an attribution is not obvious, for there is no specific reference to this issue in the writings of choice theorists. Moreover, the opposite view may seem plausible as well. Choice theorists may want to argue that in cases where there is an indirect control over a duty via a representative, the representative and not the creature for whom the representation is being made is the right-holder.

Let us call the right a representative has *qua* representative a 'secondary right' as opposed to a 'primary right' held by the creature or person capable of exercising her powers with regard to duties owed to her. Arguing that the representative is the right-holder is not problematic unless there is a conflict between the representative's own primary rights derived from the exercise of control over her duty and the representative's secondary rights. A similar conflict may arise between the representative's secondary rights and her duties to the person for whom she acts. An example of such a scenario would be the right of next-of-kin to give consent for donating an organ from the deceased when there is no advance directive from the latter which may be in conflict with the indirect right of next-of-kin – as representative of the deceased – to refuse any physical interference with the body of the deceased without the deceased's prior consent. The choice theory would find it difficult to provide solutions for such conflicts, and the notion of control or choice cannot help decide which of the conflicting rights or duties prevails. On the one hand, there should be no reason to believe that when a representative acts to control (by enforcing or waiving) the duty owed to another whom she represents, she – and not the beneficiary for whom control is being exercised – is the right-holder. On the other hand, one can perfectly hold that a representative of the decedent can have control and make choices for and on behalf of the dead person, and that in this situation the latter is the holder of a legal right.

It follows thus far that, according to the choice theory, the dead person may hold rights when, while alive, some choice had been expressed by her as to the exercise of future duties. What if the dead person did not exercise such powers and/or did not appoint any representative to protect her interests after death? In the medico-legal context there exist two mechanisms of decision making for incompetent patients when no express wishes can be found. Under the English and Canadian models, any health-related decision for an incompetent patient (whether mentally incapacitated, a minor, or a patient in PVS) is being made according to

---

[74] Neil MacCormick, 'Children's Rights: A Test-Case for Theories of Right' in Neil MacCormick, *Legal Right and Social Democracy – Essays in Legal and Political Philosophy* (Oxford: Clarendon Press, 1982) 154–66, 156 ['Children's Rights'].

the 'best interests' criterion.[75] This objective criterion examines what the best interests are for the incompetent patient, and whether the proposed action or health-related decision accords with these interests. The 'best interests' criterion is objective because it aims to decide whether to pursue the proposed action regardless of the personal circumstances of the patient at stake. Under the American model, on the other hand, a subjective criterion is sought, according to which the following hypothetical question is being asked: Would the incompetent patient have agreed to the proposed action or health-related decision, had she been able to do so? This question is being decided by an appeal to the patient's personal religious and cultural background, her expressed or implied wishes and actions taken by her in the past.[76]

In the medical context, when a 'newly deceased' patient continues to lie in the hospital for further medical procedures, e.g. organ transplantation, medical research and training, management of pregnancy, the performance of an autopsy, etc., it is possible to regard such a patient like any other incompetent living patient. Hence, it is plausible to argue that under this situation the choice theory of rights may acknowledge the existence of posthumous rights within legal systems adhering to a subjective model of decision making for incompetent patients. When the deceased's choices and wishes are being presumed and followed accordingly, the requirement to control another person's duties toward oneself can be fulfilled. However, the choice theory cannot accommodate the existence of posthumous rights in cases where the criterion for decision making for an incompetent patient is objective. Nor can it justify such rights in contexts other than the medical one. The interest theory of rights, however, fills these crucial gaps.

The interest theory

According to the interest theory of rights, legal rules conferring rights promote the right-holder's well-being represented by her legal interests.[77] It is the well-being of a right-holder that justifies the imposition of a duty on another person.[78] Under this theory, the right-holder is perceived as

---

[75] *Airedale NHS Trust* v. *Bland* [1993] 1 All ER 821; *Child and Family Services of Manitoba* v. *L. and H* [1997] 123 Man. R (2d) 135 (CA).

[76] *Cruzan* v. *Director, Missouri Department of Health* 497 US 261 (1990) (majority opinion).

[77] This is not to say that the *weight* of a right necessarily corresponds to the weight of the interest it serves, for there may be interests of other parties involved. See Joseph Raz, 'Rights and Individual Well-Being' in his *Ethics in the Public Domain* (Oxford: Clarendon, 1994) 44–59, especially 45–51.

[78] Joseph Raz, 'Legal Rights' (1984) 4(1) *Oxford Journal of Legal Studies* 1–21, 5 ['Legal Rights'].

the passive beneficiary of a network of protective and supportive duties shared by others,[79] although, as MacCormick rightly suggests, it is not necessarily the case that all rights benefit the right-holder and that acquiring rights at the individual level cannot also harm the right-holder.[80]

The idea that rights promote and protect existing interests was first expressed by Leonard Nelson in his *System of Ethics*.[81] Discussion of a similar idea is seen in the writings of Bentham, analysed by Hart. Bentham's theory of rights consists of the view that almost all obligations, civil or criminal, have correlative rights held by those intended to *benefit* from their performance.[82] A 'beneficiary' is not necessarily one who is *actually* benefited from the performance of the obligation. Instead, it is one who *can* benefit from it, should it occur.[83] Additionally, benefiting from an action should not automatically be regarded positively like gaining or profiting from an action, but can also be described in a negative form, e.g. by not losing or not being harmed.

Hart extracts three ideas from Bentham's theory of rights: the notion of benefit or detriment, the distinction between assignable and unassignable persons[84] and the idea of a person intended by the law to benefit.[85] Under the interest theory, right-holders are not just the beneficiaries of the law conferring rights to them but they are the *directly* intended beneficiaries. Hence, for example, statutes prohibiting cruelty to animals would be considered under this theory as intended not to benefit animals' interests directly. Instead, they would be seen as ways to protect human beings who are sensitive to animals' suffering.[86]

[79] Sumner, above n 5, at 47.   [80] MacCormick, above n 13, at 202.

[81] Leonard Nelson, *System of Ethics*, mentioned in R. G. Frey, *Interests and Rights – The Case Against Animals* (Oxford: Clarendon Press, 1980) 5 [Frey]. It is not clear, however, if Nelson and Frey discuss the same concept of right. With regard to Nelson, the term 'right' is equivalent to the claim to respect one's own interests as a human being, whereas in Frey's writings it serves to express a greater and more general claim. *Ibid.*, at 99.

[82] Hart, 'Legal Rights', above n 8, at 174.   [83] Sumner, above n 5, at 40.

[84] Bentham distinguishes between obligations toward assignable persons (by name or any description which sufficiently distinguishes one individual from another) and obligations beneficial or detrimental to unassignable individuals, e.g. obligations toward a whole community or a state or toward classes of persons within a community. Hart, 'Legal Rights', above n 8, at 175, 178. While obligations from the first group benefit directly the assignable individuals, obligations from the second group constitute an indirect benefit to members of a class or society. *Ibid.*

[85] *Ibid.*, at 175.

[86] But see Feinberg, who nevertheless excludes such an interpretation of the interest theory, arguing that it would be difficult to account for feeling sensitive to animals' suffering without the belief that animals deserve protection in their own right. Feinberg, 'Animals and Unborn Generations', above n 14, at 161–2.

Bentham does not identify the idea of benefit with pleasure or avoidance of pain, as would have been expected from his general utilitarianism. Instead, his idea of benefit includes 'the provision or maintenance of *conditions* of treatment which are regarded by human beings generally, or in a particular society, as desirable or "in their interests" and so to be sought *from others*'.[87] Hence, according to Bentham, benefit is not interpreted subjectively from the perspective of the interest-holder whose benefit is being examined. It is also not sought by an appeal to the cognitive (e.g. awareness, knowledge) or emotional (e.g. desire, wish, belief) state accompanying it. Instead, it is valued objectively from the perspective of creatures 'other' than the potential right-holder.

But the idea of benefit is not sufficient for our understanding of the concept of right. Think about the act of walking a dog in a park. Would it be intelligible to say that from the mere fact that the dog is being benefited by the walk (which will no doubt be regarded in the dog's interest), it has a right to be walked in the park? What if I promised my close friend to walk her dog while she is away? Here, what stands at the centre of the proposed action is *the promise* I made to my friend and *her* interest in having this promise kept rather than the *dog's* interest in being walked in the park. Does it matter that my walking of the dog derives from my promise and not from the dog's benefit from it?

Versions of the interest theory Let us look at some more complicated versions of the interest theory. Inspired by Bentham's beneficiary theory of rights, Joseph Raz turns to define a right in the following way:

'X has a right' if and only if X can have rights, and other things being equal, an aspect of X's well-being (his interest) is a sufficient reason for holding some other person(s) to be under a duty.[88]

Raz's definition provides that the justification for making another person under a duty lies in some aspect of the right-holder's well-being. But it is not clear from this definition what is the moral basis for the relation between the well-being of a person and the imposition of a duty to perform an act or to refrain from it. Nor is it explainable how broad the 'aspect' of someone's well-being should be for her to hold rights, and who, if anyone at all, should determine this. As Nigel Simmonds argues, in treating rights as

---

[87] Hart, 'Legal Rights', above n 8, at 176 (my emphasis). A correlative view would regard harm as the loss of such benefit generally seen as undesirable. *Ibid.*

[88] Raz, *Morality of Freedom*, above n 36, at 166; Joseph Raz, 'Right-Based Moralities' in J. Waldron ed., *Theories of Rights* (Oxford: Oxford University Press, 1984) 182–200, at 183 ['Right-Based Moralities'].

reasons that will justify the imposition of duties, the interest theory abandons the idea of rights as possessing peremptory force.[89]

Consider another version of the interest theory, that of Matthew Kramer. Kramer introduces two theses for this theory. First, it is necessary but insufficient for the actual holding of a right that the right protects one or more of the right-holder's interests. Second, the right-holder's being competent and authorized to demand or waive the enforcement of a right is neither sufficient nor necessary for the right-holder to be endowed with that right.[90] In contrast to Raz, who emphasizes what the right-holder *receives* from the holding of a right, under Kramer's version of the interest theory the focus is on what the right *does* to the right-holder, namely the focus is on the *right* rather than on the *right-holder*. However, both versions are morally neutral with regard to determining which interests should be protected as legal rights. As Kramer points out, '[the interest theory] is not advancing any criterion or set of criteria for what should count as the "worthiness" of an interest'.[91]

A more complicated version of the interest theory is offered by Neil MacCormick. He suggests three features for the characterization of any legal rules conferring rights.[92] First, such rules should concern 'goods' (or advantages/benefit/interests) that are usually (but not necessarily always) good for human beings. Second, the benefit that the right is about to secure is designed for each individual. Consequently, legal rules conferring rights should concern the enjoyment of goods by individuals separately and not as members of a collective. Lastly, these rules should provide what he calls 'normative protection' for individuals enjoying rights. By this, he means legal protection broad enough to include any or all forms of 'rights' identified by Hohfeld, namely rights in the strict sense, liberty, power and immunity.[93]

---

[89] Simmonds, above n 72, at 215. Alon Harel makes a distinction between reasons which are *intrinsic* with respect to a right, namely reasons by virtue of which a certain demand is classified as a right, and reasons which are *extrinsic* with respect to a right, i.e. reasons which may justify protection of the object protected by a right but not its inclusion within the scope of the right. Animals' suffering, for example, may be an intrinsic reason for an animals' right, whereas the prevention of an inhumane behaviour in general can be classified as an extrinsic reason for that right. Harel, above n 9, at 201. It seems that Simmonds confuses these two types of reasons. His critique is directed against *extrinsic reasons*, whereas under the interest theory reasons have an *intrinsic* role.

[90] Kramer, RWT, above n 3, at 62.   [91] *Ibid.*, at 79.

[92] MacCormick, above n 13, at 204–5.

[93] For Hohfeld's famous work, see Wesley Hohfeld, 'Some Fundamental Legal Conceptions as Applied in Juridical Reasoning' in W. Cook ed., *Fundamental Legal Conceptions as Applied in Juridical Reasoning* (New Haven: Yale University Press, 1923) 23–64.

Yet, in another place MacCormick sets two conditions for the ascription of rights.[94] To ascribe to all members of a class of right-holder (e.g. the dead, children, animals, etc.) a right to treatment X is to presuppose first, that X is, in all normal circumstances, a good for every member of the class, and, second, that X is a good of such importance that it would be wrong to deny it to, or withhold it from, any member of this class.[95]

MacCormick's version of the interest theory adds some new aspects to the earlier discussion, but seems questionable. First, it is not clear what is the moral significance of legal rules conferring rights if there are other normative protections in the form of a duty or immunity owed to or held by the right-holder. What distinguishes then between all four Hohfeldian forms of rights and how can one infer the correct form of right conferred by the very same legal rule? Second, MacCormick's requirement that legal rules conferring rights should apply to an individual rather than a member of a collective is interesting. However, it raises concerns with regard to some important rights the existence of which is conditioned upon social membership, e.g. the freedom of assembly, the right to vote, the right to enter, remain in and leave one's country of citizenship, the right to use the official language of a country, etc. MacCormick would find it difficult to justify the existence of these rights. Finally, according to MacCormick, the good one seeks to promote is of such importance that it would be wrong to deny it to the right-holder. Still, one can ensure that there are other ways not to deny certain goods without conferring any rights on the beneficiary. One such way would be the establishment of duties to protect these goods. If MacCormick is concerned with the protection of the good as such, why is his account concerned with legal rights? It seems more plausible to argue that MacCormick can explain the existence of legal or moral obligations, but not more than that.

In conclusion, the main difference between the interest theory and the choice theory is that while according to the former a right-holder is the beneficiary of a correlative duty,[96] in the view of the latter it is the controller of that duty and not merely one who benefits from it. The interest theory holds that the power to enforce or waive any particular right does not necessarily have to vest in the person or creature holding the right (although it is usually held by her in the paradigmatic cases), whereas according to the choice theory a person who does not have a power of enforcement/waiver cannot be eligible to hold rights in the first place.

---

[94] MacCormick, 'Children's Rights', above n 74, at 160.   [95] *Ibid.*
[96] Although proponents of the interest theory do not argue that every beneficiary of a correlative duty is a right-holder.

The idea of interest Before inquiring whether the dead or the Human Subject may have interests the advancement of which justifies holding rights, it is necessary to explore further the notion of interest. According to the interest theory, in order to hold rights one also needs to be able to hold interests. Two major reasons are supplied for this line of argument. First, a right-holder must be capable of being represented and it is impossible to represent a being that has no interests. Second, a right-holder must be capable of being a beneficiary. A being without interests is incapable of being harmed or benefited, having no 'good' or 'sake' of its own.[97] Joseph Raz does not discuss what it means to hold interests, although in his view holding interests is a sufficient condition for holding rights. Instead, he argues that 'an individual is capable of having rights if and only if either his well-being is of ultimate value or he is an "artificial person", (e.g. a corporation)'.[98] Since the dead cannot be considered 'artificial persons', Raz's first condition needs to be further explored.

Raz defines 'being of ultimate value' as being 'intrinsically valuable, i.e. being valuable independently of one's instrumental value'.[99] Something is of an 'instrumental value' if it 'derives its value from the value of its consequences, or from the value of the consequences it is likely to have, or from the value of the consequences it can be used to produce'.[100] An example brought by Raz for a thing which has an instrumental value is the *experience* concerned with a work of art. The value of a work of art is derivative as it derives from the work's contribution to the well-being of persons who appreciate it.[101] Nevertheless the *existence* of works of art is an intrinsic good, as one cannot experience them unless they exist. The experience is explained by reference to a belief in the existence of this object.[102]

Consider again the walking of the dog example. In the scenario mentioned above, the dog's benefit from the walk is important to the extent that it guarantees the keeping of my promise. The direct and valued beneficiary from walking the dog is my friend but not the dog. Why is it

---

[97] Feinberg, 'Animals and Unborn Generations', above n 14, at 167. But see Tom Regan's critique of Feinberg's argument in his 'Feinberg on What Sorts of Beings Can Have Rights?' (1976) 14(4) *Southern Journal of Philosophy* 584–98. Regan reads Feinberg as postulating another principle, according to which for a being to hold interests, it has to have a capacity to be a beneficiary in its own person, and that the only beings who can be beneficiaries in their own persons are those who can have a good of their own. Regan shows that such a principle contradicts Feinberg's own requirement that in order for a being to hold rights it should also be capable of having interests (understood as the performance of cognitive abilities such as forming desires, wishes, beliefs, etc.).

[98] Raz, 'Morality of Freedom', above n 36, at 166.   [99] *Ibid.*, at 177.   [100] *Ibid.*, at 177.

[101] *Ibid.*, at 178.   [102] Raz, 'Right-Based Moralities', above n 88, at 189.

not possible to argue that in my example *both* my friend and her dog can be benefited *independently* from the same act?[103] Does the fact that my friend is a beneficiary necessarily exclude the conferral of benefit upon her dog as a result of its walk in the park?

Think about another example in which I promised my friend that I would deposit some money I owe her in her account while she is away. No doubt, in this example, my friend is being benefited when I deposit the money. It also seems clear that my money (which becomes the title of my friend upon the deposit) is not being benefited from my act. What is the difference between this example and the walking of the dog example? Treating both examples the same provokes some resistance and uneasiness. I would suggest that the reason for such a response stems from our belief that there exists an independent benefit and intrinsic value conferred to and vested in the dog under the first example which are absent in the money example. The attribution of benefit to the dog derives from an act initially aimed to promote and protect another potential interest-holder, but also results in a benefit to a third party, the dog.

The requirement that only those creatures whose well-being is of ultimate value can have rights does not entail that rights are based only on interests which are of ultimate value. Rights can protect interests that are not intrinsically valuable.[104] Indeed, as suggested by Raz, it is also possible to base rights on interests, held by the right-holder, whose value is instrumental. An example of such rights is the right to protect the confidentiality of a client which is based on a societal interest, namely an interest whose value derives from the well-being of society in general.

What is then the relation between the interests of a person and her rights? Must rights always match one's interests? What does it take for an interest to 'become' a right? Raz's reply to this query seems more confusing than helpful and will not be discussed here. Raz writes:

An interest is sufficient to base a right on if and only if there is sound argument of which the conclusion is that a certain right exists and among its non-redundant premises is a statement of some interests of the right holder, the other premises supplying grounds for attributing to it the required importance, or for holding it to be relevant to a particular person or class of persons so that they rather than others are obligated to the right holder. These premises must be sufficient by themselves to entail that if there are contrary considerations then the individuals concerned have the right. To these premises one needs to add others stating or establishing

---

[103] Raz seems not to rule out this possibility when he writes that 'having an intrinsic value is being valuable *even apart* from one's instrumental value' (my emphasis): Raz, 'Morality of Freedom', above n 36, at 177.

[104] *Ibid.*, at 178; Raz, 'Legal Rights', above n 78, at 20.

that these grounds are not altogether defeated by conflicting reasons. Together they establish the existence of the right.[105]

An alternative suggestion put forward by Raz holds that rights do not protect all interests a person may have but only those in being free to choose, do and live as one likes. Under this alternative approach to rights, rights are not based on interests but on the concept of respect to persons as persons. According to this line of thinking, 'the capacity to be free, to decide freely the course of their own lives, is what makes a person ... Respect for people consists in respecting their interest to enjoy personal autonomy.'[106] This latter view supports Raz's assertion that people's well-being is promoted by having an autonomous life and that it is in their interest not to be subjected to someone's else decision with regard to their own lives.[107]

In some cases, an individual has rights which are against some of her interests. I have a right to commit suicide now, though it is against my interest in living. Perhaps I do not have such an interest when my life goes bad. However, if I do not have such an interest, how does my right protect any of my interests at all? And how are we to decide which of our interests are worth protecting by legal rights and which of them should just be ignored or protected through other forms? (What will the latter be?) Take, for example, the prohibition to walk on the grass in a public park. Does it follow that lawns have interests protected by rights which are conferred by this norm?[108] And if not, why not?

The problems occurring as a result of the idea that interests are the basis for rights are intensified when interests of remote parties, whom the legal norm did not intend to benefit, are involved. Consider the following example. A promises B to pay C $100. C, according to the interest theory, is a beneficiary vis-à-vis A who has a duty to pay $100. Now, suppose also that C owes $100 to D and that C plans to pay his debt to D once A gives him the money. Apparently, under the interest theory, D is also a beneficiary. D benefits from A's promise to B. Now, suppose further that D is going to buy her daughter a present once she gets the money from C. D's daughter is also a beneficiary and as such is a potential right-holder. Being beneficiaries, C and D should be regarded as having rights vis-à-vis A, but this seems rather absurd. How then are we to exclude C, D and other remote parties from holding rights under the interest theory?

The problem of holding rights by remote parties has occupied many interest theorists. Bentham, for example, suggested that we ask what

---

[105] Raz, 'Morality of Freedom', above n 36, at 183.
[106] *Ibid.*, at 190.   [107] *Ibid.*, at 191.
[108] I have used Matthew Kramer's example in GRR, above n 1, at 32.

findings are *sufficient* to establish that a breach of contract or norm has occurred. Put differently, X is holding a right under a contract or a norm if and only if a violation of a duty under the contract or norm can be established by simply showing that the person who owes the duty has withheld a benefit from X or has harmed X.[109] Still, as Gopal Sreenivasan points out, this test fails for being too broad. Many parties who suffer detriment due to the breach of a duty may easily pass this test.[110] In the previous example, D can show she suffered a serious detriment from A's not paying the money to B. Although there is no direct contract or norm between A and D, the payment to D is dependent upon the performance of A's duty to B.

Sreenivasan himself prefers the solution taken implicitly by Raz's definition of rights mentioned above, and believes it is a good solution to the problem of the remoteness of parties discussed here, although he argues that this definition instrumentalizes the individual's status as right-holder by using the individual to enable others to grace their cause according to the weight of their interests with the banner of right-holding.[111] According to that definition, we should ask whether D's aspect of well-being (D's interest in the $100) is sufficient reason to *impose* a duty on A (vis-à-vis D) to pay B the $100. Another way to ask this question would be whether D is the sort of person whom a legal norm is 'intended', 'designed', 'supposed' or 'meant' to protect against the violation of A's duty.[112] It is plausible to give a negative answer to this question as D's interest in the $100 could be fulfilled by controlling the duty C already owes to D, or by asking A to pay $100 directly to D. No duty should be imposed on A (with regard to D), if A does not wish to be involved in the legal relations between C and D.

Applying the interest theory to the dead As emphasized above, many theoretical problems arise with the requirement that rights protect and promote some of the right-holder's interests. Regardless of these problems, does such a requirement apply to the case of posthumous rights? In the previous chapter, it was established that there could be interests the existence of which extends the lifespan of the person whose interests they are. There seems to be no conceptual difficulty in claiming that the bearer of these interests may also hold rights which promote and protect some or all of these interests. As argued above, this is especially true within legal systems where the criterion for decision making for incompetent patients is objective ('best interests' criterion). It is not clear, however, how the

---

[109] Kramer, RWT, above n 3, at 81.   [110] Sreenivasan, above n 19.
[111] *Ibid.*   [112] This is David Lyons's view described in Kramer, RWT, above n 3, at 85.

interest theory of rights would regard cases arising in systems where such a rule is subjective. On the one hand, the question at stake would be what course of action the specific patient would have wanted had she been asked. On the other hand, according to the interest theory, if a person's hypothetical wishes are contrary to her interests, the first may be defeated by the latter.

However, although the argument for posthumous rights can be logically valid, it needs to be justified and premised on some moral theory. Specifically, it needs to be shown that we do have a strong motivation to expand the group of right-holders also to include the dead person or the Human Subject in its capacity of holding surviving interests of the dead person. We need to ask not only if the dead person or the Human Subject *can* be a potential right-holder, but also whether she *should be* an actual one.

Should the dead be actual right-holders? The idea that creatures other than a living human being are capable of holding rights is a recent one, and it was only in the 1960s and '70s that much attention was given to such a question.[113] What are the accepted moral criteria for creatures who hold rights? Alan White maintains that only the animate and perhaps also the intelligent can have interests.[114] However, the class of beings for which certain things could be of an interest is much larger. Light, for example, is in the interest of the flower for growth, although the flower can have no interest in itself. But ineligibility to hold interests does not, in White's view, entail ineligibility to hold rights. In White's example, children hold the right to higher education although they are incapable of having an interest in it. Similarly, an ability to hold interests does not necessarily result in holding a right to which the interest applies. For in White's view there is no necessary connection between the idea of an interest and the concept of right.[115]

Applying White's theory to the dead will lead to the conclusion that the question of whether the dead can or cannot have interests, developed in the first chapter of this book, is not necessarily relevant to the question of whether they can have rights. Having discussed and advocated the interest theory of rights, we shall assume that there *is* a connection between one's interests and one's rights. We are concerned now with the moral theory that will enable one to explain such a connection better, and to examine the concept of posthumous rights accordingly.

---

[113] Alan R. White, *Rights* (Oxford: Clarendon, 1984) 75.   [114] *Ibid.*, at 80.
[115] *Ibid.*, at 81–2.

One such theory may be inferred from White's writings. White specifies the many predications attached to the term 'right': to be 'exercised', 'earned', 'enjoyed', 'which can be claimed', etc. He argues that a possessor of rights is whatever can properly be spoken of in such language, namely a person.[116] However, White maintains that if we do speak of the dead as being persons, then the dead are logically possible subjects of rights.[117] But *should* we speak of the dead as being persons? White does not tell us. White's concern is not with the normative question of how we should speak of the dead. Rather it is with the question of whether – as a descriptive matter – we predicate the dead with properties and names usually associated with a person holding rights. As such, the answer to this question is trivially negative.

A more substantive approach to posthumous rights is expressed by Matthew Kramer. He suggests we implicitly or explicitly take into consideration the moral status of the being to whom the attribution of rights is being examined, and inquire about the moral significance of the similarities and differences between that being and the paradigmatic case of a right-holder, namely a mentally competent adult human being.[118] Following Kramer's advice will lead to undecided outcomes. On the one hand, unlike a mentally competent human adult, the dead are neither animate nor sentient.[119] They have departed from the cycle of life and, when their holding of rights is being examined, they do not feel and/or are not aware of their surroundings. The dead are out of consciousness permanently. Unlike animals, the dead cannot experience any pain, suffering or physical harm.[120]

---

[116] *Ibid.*, at 90.   [117] *Ibid.*   [118] Kramer, GRR, above n 1, at 33.

[119] Frey mentions four different meanings of the term 'sentiency': reaction to stimuli; reaction to sensory stimuli; capacity to feel pain; and the possession of a nervous system remarkably similar to our own. Frey, above n 81, at 34–7. The dead are insentient according to the first three meanings. However, the dead may still be sentient under the fourth meaning by possessing a human nervous system, although this system will have permanently lost its ability to function.

[120] But see Frey's general critique of the criterion of feeling pain and being sentient: 'An individual has rights on this construal of a sentiency criterion up to the moment, for example, when he lapses into a coma and can no longer feel pain, at which time his rights go out of existence; should he later emerge from the coma, however, his rights presumably pop back into existence again, the moment he can feel pain ... is it plausible to suggest, for example, that the right many have wanted to claim for human beings to be treated as an end and not as a means pops in and out of existence like this? After all, what has the dignity and respect of my being an end in itself to do with my ability to feel pain?' Frey, above n 81, at 35–6. Later on, Frey undermines the assumption that the ability to feel pain has intrinsic value and should be singled out as a criterion for holding rights from all other experiences a person/creature may have. *Ibid.*, at 47–50. See also Descartes' holding that only a being who can use a language can experience pain, and the discussion of this argument in Tom Regan, 'The Moral Basis of Vegetarianism' (1975) 5(2) *Canadian Journal of Philosophy* 181–214, especially at 184 and onwards.

However, in contrast to fetuses the dead have already lived in this world and emerged into fully fledged human beings. Significantly, the dead were once persons, the paradigmatic right-holders. In contrast to mere things such as rocks they showed capacity to experience and respond to environmental stimuli surrounding them. Unlike plants, their reaction and response to the outside world was not just a physiological reflex but involved a reflection, that is a process characterized by a mental state of self-consciousness and self-awareness.

More importantly, the dead are identifiable. They can be recognized by their name, physical look and the memories that surround them specifically. The dead (and especially the 'newly-dead') are familiarized by their unique smell, shape and colour. To use the terminology argued for in the previous chapter, the dead continue to exist symbolically through their specific characteristics. They continue to be psychologically personalized even after their death. They are still the subject of affection, love, hate, mercy, joy, satisfaction and gratitude held by others. Their similarity to mentally capacitated persons in such respects is profound.[121] More significantly, the dead still belong to the moral community of humans. The dead are dead *people*. Their affiliation with this moral group does not end upon their death.

Not only are the dead part of a moral group, they are part of our *moral community*.[122] In contrast to Annette Baier, I do not hold that members of the same moral community must exercise some cognitive actions to be aware of or to acknowledge their membership in that group. It is sufficient that by their moral classification as *humans*, present or past (identifiable) persons be part of such a moral community. To use Martin Golding's terminology, the dead reserve the same social ideal.[123] Golding mentions two main ways by which moral communities are generated: through an explicit contract between their members or through a social arrangement in which each member is benefited by the efforts of other members.[124] Wills, advance directives, donor cards and promises to and from the dead are special forms of explicit contracts. The requirement of respect to

---

[121] I use here what Frey calls 'the similarity argument', usually raised in the context of severely mentally incapacitated persons. According to this argument, these persons 'betray strong physical similarities in their appearance to the remainder of our species and it would and does offend our species horribly not to provide such similar creatures with rights'. Frey, above n 81, at 31.

[122] Golding, above n 39, at 91. For a discussion of moral communities see my section on Annette Baier's theory, above n 34, and accompanying text.

[123] Golding, above n 39, at 96.

[124] *Ibid.*, at 91. Golding emphasizes that the entrance to and participation in these communities are fundamentally a matter of self-interest and not altruism and fellow-feeling.

persons within life and after death is an implicit social arrangement by which past, present and future generations are benefited.

The idea that the dead are still part of a cultural and moral community is best expressed by Bob Brecher, who, following Avner De-Shalit's conception of transgenerational communities,[125] writes, 'for although dead, we do not cease entirely to be members of a particular community; and it is on that account that the dead can be said to have interests'.[126] Brecher concludes that 'in some ways you do not cease to be a person after you are dead; and to the extent that you remain (if you do) part of a community, you remain a person, even though a dead person'.[127]

Remaining in the community has its best manifestation in the fact that we leave behind us a legacy, whether material (by bequeathing our property), psychological (by being remembered, thought about and referred to), or both. Moreover, as Raymond Belliotti argues, much of our behaviour while we are alive is motivated by a desire to leave some kind of legacy to those who remain after we die.[128] Belliotti goes further to argue that our being remembered after death is something we deserve due to our past performances and deeds.[129] In his view, we want to be remembered, or in my line of argument to continue to exist symbolically, in light of what we accomplished and the kind of person we were. Our desire to be remembered after death is a demand 'that a principle of justice be applied properly when evaluating the life we have led'.[130] Under such reasoning, posthumous events that harm the dead are bad because they violate the demands of justice.[131] This is, in Bellioti's view, the justification for granting rights to the dead. For all of the above reasons, it seems fair to conclude that the moral attributes of the dead person (or the Human Subject) make this subject a potential but also an actual right-holder.

Content of posthumous rights How do the above moral attributes of the dead influence the content of posthumous rights? It is reasonable to assert that the dead should deserve more protection than creatures who did not and never will live, experience, feel or be conscious. It is also plausible to argue that the dead should be accorded with rights which logically relate to their past experiences, the mere fact of their living in the past or to circumstances following their being conscious. It is to be argued

---

[125] Under this conception, one's notion of one's identity extends into the future, including those times subsequent to one's death: Avner De-Shalit, *Why Posterity Matters* (London: Routledge, 1995) 34.

[126] Bob Brecher, 'Our Obligation to the Dead' (2002) 19(2) *Journal of Applied Philosophy* 109–19, 113 [Brecher].

[127] *Ibid.*, at 115. [128] Belliotti, above n 52, at 206. [129] *Ibid.* [130] *Ibid.* [131] *Ibid.*

that only posthumous interests which will accord with some significant moral attributes characterizing the dead may be protected and promoted as legal rights. Posthumous rights should therefore fall into the following categories. Posthumous rights should be rights that relate to actions made by the deceased while alive or to promises made to or by the deceased. Also included in this group are rights whose fulfilment was anticipated or hoped for by the deceased even if he or she did not take any active steps to pursue their implementation while alive. Finally, the dead person or the Human Subject can hold rights which are consistent with their being identifiable persons and members of the human moral group. Rights in this category enable the person's symbolic existence after death. These rights may include the right that one's body and character be remembered positively after death, the right to be treated with respect, the right to legal protection as a member of a religious, political or ethnic community, and the right to respect within an intimate or familial context.

It does not follow from these conclusions that the dead have rights as extensive as those held by the living. All that can be inferred from the analysis of this chapter is that it is possible to give an account for post-humous rights in so far as the content of these rights is deduced from the moral attributes that are significantly important for holding posthumous rights, namely the past experiences and cognitive capacities of the persons they were, and their continuous membership in the human moral com-munity and symbolic existence which we can easily identify.

Duration of posthumous rights A complementary component of our analysis concerns the duration of posthumous rights, should they exist. In this context we may want to ask how long the dead person or the Human Subject holds the rights of the person. Matthew Kramer argues that, in order to accord the dead with rights, an interest theorist has to subsume the aftermath of the dead person's life within the overall course of her existence.[132] Kramer explains:

By highlighting the sundry constituents of that aftermath – for example, the continuing influence of the dead person on other people and on the development of various events, the memories of him that reside in the minds of people who knew him or knew of him, and the array of possessions which he accumulated and then bequeathed or failed to bequeath – we can highlight the ways in which the dead person still exists ... for a certain period, then, he can be morally assimilated after his death to the person he was during his lifetime.[133]

---

[132] Kramer, GRR, above n 1, at 49. See also Matthew H. Kramer, 'Do Animals and Dead People Have Legal Rights?' (2001) 14 *Canadian Journal of Law and Jurisprudence* 29–54.
[133] *Ibid.*, at 49–50.

So, according to Kramer, the dead can hold rights for a limited period of time – one which depends upon the existence of the dead mainly (if not exclusively) as they are perceived by others through memories, the continuing effect of past actions or accomplishments of the deceased. According legal rights to the dead under this view varies from one person to another and hinges on the durability of this person's presence in other people's lives. Personal reasons (whether this specific person was a well-known and sociable person or not) or cultural explanations (whether this person belonged to a culture which regards it ancestors highly) will determine the duration of this prolonged existence.

Kramer's suggestion has much charm but many potential problems, the most serious of which is the continuing attribution of legal rights to heinous tyrants such as Saddam Hussein or Adolf Hitler. Although this type of problem has been acknowledged by Kramer, the solution offered to it, namely withdrawing the designation of holding rights from a person whose strong posthumous presence in people's lives is due to his evil,[134] seems unsatisfactory for there is no logical reason to support such a solution.[135] If Kramer holds that the tyrant held legal rights while alive, it is not clear why the tyrant's presence in the memories of others (symbolic existence) after death contributes less to his holding of rights than it did while he was alive. On the other hand, if Kramer holds that the tyrant did not have legal rights while alive, he needs to support such a view with a moral account. Such an account is missing in his theory.

Later on, Kramer seems to abandon his earlier argument by claiming that the tyrant keeps holding legal rights so long as he is assimilated to the person he was before his death. The tyrant's evil influences not his logical holding of rights but the extent of the legal safeguards set up around his interests.[136] But if Kramer's concern is with these legal safeguards, and if these safeguards do not necessarily correspond to the tyrant's logical holding of rights, how does Kramer's account help distinguish between the duration of posthumous rights held by an evil person and the duration of those held by a non-evil person?

Moreover, as Bob Brecher argues:

are the dead really no more than items in our memory? If that really is all they are, all that the dead amount to, then any obligations we may be said to have to the

---

[134] Kramer, GRR, above n 1, at 51.

[135] Kramer makes a stronger claim when he writes that we should decline to assimilate the tyrant's moral status after death with that which he occupied during his lifetime, notwithstanding that people's memories of him are intense.

[136] Kramer, GRR, above n 1, at 51–2.

dead are in fact a particular sort of obligations to ourselves and/or to other people. Memories may matter but they are not themselves objects of obligations.[137]

Brecher confuses the claim that the dead are *present* in our memories with the claim that the dead *are* memories, and so he is led to make a logical mistake according to which duties owed to the dead are in fact duties to one's self (memory). Regardless of this mistake, it follows from Brecher's thesis that determining the duration by which posthumous rights have effect only by the presence of the deceased in our memories or their being referred to by others is too narrow an account for such a fundamental issue.

Although Kramer's theory brings about important ideas in light of which the duration of posthumous rights can be established, much work needs to be done in this respect. A preferable view may be to determine the duration of posthumous rights by the content of those rights. According to this view, rights derived from actions made by the deceased or from promises made by or to her while alive will have legal effect deriving from the specific act or promise at issue. On the other hand, rights relating to the deceased's interests in being identifiable as a specific person with his or her unique character will be valid as long as the deceased's personal characteristics, e.g. the special shape of her body, her general appearance, her good or bad character, etc., are easily recognized or acknowledged by others. Finally, rights relating to the deceased's mere membership in the human moral community will have legal effect derived from our motivation to continue to include the deceased in that moral group. Such rights may last much longer than previous posthumous rights.

Conclusion

In this chapter the question of whether the dead person or the Human Subject should hold rights was examined. As shown, specific theories of posthumous rights do not provide serious justifications for the existence of rights coming into effect after death, but at most offer an explanation as to our legal obligations owed to the dead. The application of the general theories of rights to the case of the dead suggests more promising results. The choice theory of rights may justify the holding of rights by the deceased when, while alive, some choice has been expressed by her as to the exercise of future duties. It may also justify the imposition of posthumous rights in the medical context within legal systems adhering to a subjective model of decision making for incompetent patients. The

---

[137] Brecher, above n 126, at 114.

interest theory of rights, on the other hand, may support the argument for posthumous rights in a larger number of cases than the choice theory. In light of the significant moral attributes of the dead, it is argued that the dead can have rights whose content relates to the past experiences and cognitive capacities of the persons they were and their continuous membership in our human moral community. Additionally, the dead may hold rights relating to their being identified as the persons they were while alive, or, put differently, to their symbolic existence. These rights may exist for at least as long as the deceased are still 'present' among the living, but may exist for longer or shorter periods of time depending on the content of the rights at stake.

3 Proprietary interest in the body of the deceased

The question of whether there exists a proprietary interest in the body of the deceased was dealt with in law as early as in 1614, and ever since it has received a somewhat automatic and reflexive reply, according to which there is no property in the body of the deceased (hereinafter the 'no property' rule). The exclusion of any proprietary interest applying to the body of the deceased resulted in the following three propositions. First, the 'no property' rule applies to the dead person herself, so that the deceased cannot have property in her own body.[1] Second, since interests concerning one's body after death are not part of one's property, it follows that one cannot direct, in a will or otherwise, the disposal of one's own body after death.[2] Lastly, as an object not having the status of property, a corpse cannot be subjected to theft.[3]

---

[1] *Haynes's Case* 77 ER 1389 (1614) (Eng.) [*Haynes*].
[2] *Williams* v. *Williams* (1882) 20 Ch. D 659 [*Williams*]; *Hunter* v. *Hunter* (1930) 65 OLR 586, [1930] 4 DLR 255 (Ontario High Ct) [*Hunter*]; *Kassem Saleh* v. *Andreas Reichert* (1993) 50 ETR 143, 104 DLR (4th) 384 (Ontario Ct Jus.) [*Saleh*]. The relation between the 'no property' rule and the proposition that there is no testamentary interest pertaining to one's body may be uncalled for. Peter Skegg argues, 'a legal system could refuse to recognize property in a corpse, but recognizes a power to give binding directions as to what is to be done with it. Conversely, a legal system could recognize property in a corpse (so that, for example, the law of theft and the possessory actions applied to it), but have a rule that property vests in, say, the executors, who would have a discretion as to what they did with it.' P. D. G. Skegg, 'Human Corpses, Medical Specimens and the Law of Property' (1975) *Anglo-American Law Review* 412, 416 [Skegg]. Nevertheless, for the sake of the analysis suggested in this chapter, it will be assumed that such a relation is indispensable.
[3] *Doodeward* v. *Spence* (1908) 6 CLR 406, 419 (per Judge Higgins) (Australia) [*Doodeward*]. The relation between property and the prohibition of theft is necessary, at least in jurisdictions where the definition of theft comprises the term 'property'. For example, the English Theft Act 1968 defines theft as (inter alia) the 'appropriation of property belonging to another'. *Ibid.*, at section 1. But compare, for example, the Canadian criminal law defining the intent of the person who commits theft as 'to deprive ... a person who has a special property *or interest* in it [the object of the theft]'. Criminal Code, RSC 1985, c. C-46, s. 322(1)(a). This section may be interpreted to include an interest which in itself is not proprietary. Compare also the Israeli Criminal Act establishing that a theft constitutes the taking of a thing 'which can be stolen', defined as a 'valuable thing

Since its establishment by the ecclesiastical laws of England, the 'no property' rule and its major outcomes have been challenged. Moreover, other rules purporting to be exceptions to the original 'no property' rule have emerged. Overall, although courts up until now have begun their legal analysis with a clear statement that there is no proprietary interest in the body of the deceased, it is apparent that not much substance is left out of this anachronistic and, as will be shown, doubtfully established rule.

Is there a proprietary interest in the body of the deceased?

The 'no property' rule

Historically, three important developments have contributed to the discussion about whether there exists a proprietary interest in the body of the deceased.[4] First, as familial ties loosened and families grew apart, cases emerged where the widow and the next-of-kin contested control of the body. Such control was articulated in a language which included ideas of property, e.g. possession and custody. Second, with the rise of medical schools and medical science, the need for bodies on which to experiment and gain knowledge increased. Anatomy departments paid between $10 and $35 for a body, more than the weekly wage of skilled workers at that time.[5] Body snatching and unauthorized autopsies became common among funeral home personnel, coroners, university clinics, anatomists and the like. Survivors sought legal remedies in these circumstances, justifying their standing in courts with a proprietary interest in the body of the deceased. Third, with the rise of other forms of disposal of the body, e.g. cremation, family members opposing such forms challenged the testamentary right of the deceased to determine the manner of disposition of her body or the right of others in respect of it. One way to challenge the testator's right to determine the fate of her body was to argue that she did not have any proprietary interest in it.

In addition to these specific developments, the language of property has always conveyed an impression of a solid and complete form of legal

which is the asset of a person': Criminal Act 1977, s. 383(c)(4). Interestingly, it was formerly a felony in England to steal bodies for the purposes of witchcraft, under the statute 1 Jac. 1, c. 12, s. 2, but this was abolished by the Witchcraft Act 1735 (9 Geo. 2, c. 5), s. 1. Paul Matthews, 'Whose Body? People as Property' (1983) 36 *Current Legal Problems* 193–239, 231 (note 43) [Matthews].

[4] Jennifer E. Horan, '"When Sleep At Last Has Come": Controlling the Disposition of Dead Bodies for Same-Sex Couples' (1999) 2 *Journal of Gender, Race and Justice* 423–60, 426–7.

[5] Dorothy Nelkin and Lori Andrews, '*Homo Economicus*: Commercialization of the Body Tissue in the Age of Biotechnology' (1998) 28(5) *Hastings Center Report* 30–9, 32 [Nelkin and Andrews].

protection – one that appeared extremely suitable to the situation of
dealing with the body after death. This phenomenon seemed to fit well
with the common law where the legal system is based primarily on
property and inheritance, and where, as Bernard Dickens argues, 'less
attention is paid to the inherent qualities or rights of people than to their
property: people are a means by which property is owned, possessed,
protected and transferred'.[6] Explaining any legal relation with respect to
the body of the deceased by way of articulating the inherent qualities of
that body (or the person whom it represented) was almost impossible. An
appeal to the idea of property seemed promising.

Although common law courts constantly hold the 'no property' rule
(unlike the civil law courts),[7] it is imperative to bear in mind that the rule
was originally established under the ecclesiastical law, as all maters pertaining to consecrated burial grounds and the management of dead
bodies were under such jurisdiction in early England. The ecclesiastical
jurisdiction reflected dominant religious beliefs about God, men and
death.[8] This historical fact may affect the appropriateness of the rule's
application to the common law, especially within legal systems which did
not include the ecclesiastical court system in their foundations, for example the American, Canadian and Australian legal systems.[9] Regardless of
this historical factor, the authority of the rule remains doubtful. Four
major sources are cited to support the rule: (1) *Haynes's Case*; (2) Sir
Edward Coke's commentary; (3) *R* v. *Sharpe*; and (4) *Exelby* v. *Handyside*.

Haynes's Case[10] William Haynes dug up the graves of three men
and one woman, took their winding sheets and reburied them. The
English Report states that this case was resolved by the decision that the
property in the sheets remains in their original owners, namely in those

---

[6] Bernard M. Dickens, 'Legal and Judicial Aspects of Post-Mortem Organ Donation' in
G. M. Collins, J. M. Dubernard, W. Land and G. G. Persijn eds., *Procurement,
Preservation and Allocation of Vascularized Organs* (Dordrecht: Kluwer, 1997) 343–57,
343 [Dickens, 'Legal and Judicial Aspects'].

[7] See, for example, the Quebecois case of *Phillips*, where the court held that in the civil law,
in the absence of personal directions, the remains are the property of the family of the
deceased, just as is the body of an animal. Referring to the French law, the court cited
Pandectes Belges: 'Le cadavre d'une personne, qui n'a rien prescrit elle-même en ce qui
concerne sa dépouille, appartient donc à la famille, comme le cadavre d'un animal et la
propriété de celui qui était propriétaire de ce animal en vie.' *Phillips* v. *Montreal General
Hospital* 4 ELR 477, 33 Que. SC 483 (1908) at para. 19 [*Phillips*]. The analysis in this
chapter will refer to the common law only.

[8] *In re Johnson's Estate* 7 NYS 2d 81, 84 (Sup. Ct N.Y. 1938).

[9] *Darcy* v. *Presbyterian Hospital in the City of New York* 202 NY 259, 261 (Ct App. N.Y.
1911).

[10] *Haynes*, above n 1.

who had property in the sheets when they wrapped the dead body, for '*the dead body is not capable of it*', or in other words, for 'a dead body being but a lump of earth hath no capacity'.[11]

The inclusion of this case as one of the sources of the no property rule is very problematic. It is clear that what the court means here is not that the dead body cannot be subject to property, but instead that the dead do not have the capacity for holding property in the sheets. Moreover, the court states, 'A man cannot relinquish the property he hath to his goods, unless they be vested in another.' It follows from this principle that if the dead cannot hold property, the sheets must remain the property of their original owner prior to wrapping the dead body.

Coke's commentary[12] In the third part of his *Institutes of the Laws of England*, at chapter 97, entitled 'Of Buildings', Sir Edward Coke begins his discussion of building or creating tombs, sepulchres and monuments for the deceased. Coke explains why it is lawful to erect such buildings, and states that after death the heir has a common law right to bring action for their defacing.[13] He then makes observations concerning the importance and the historical role of buildings, monuments and pyramids, thereby suggesting four reasons for constructing such buildings. At the end of this discussion, Coke comments:

It is to be observed that in every sepulcher, that hath a monument, two things are to be considered, *viz.* the monument, and the sepultre or buriall of the dead. The buriall of the cadaver (that is, *caro data vermibus*) is *nullius in bonis*, and belongs to Ecclesiastical cognizance, but as to the monument, action is given (as hath been said) at the common law for defacing therof.[14]

Coke's comment is regarded as one of the major authorities to support the 'no property' rule. It is apparent, however, that the context in which this comment was made cannot suggest that Coke was concerned with property in the body of the deceased. It is evident that Coke's comment refers to a situation in which the dead person has already been buried. This becomes plain from his Latin sentence 'caro data vermibus', which can be translated as 'flesh given to worms'. The passage is taken from a discussion on real property concerning buildings, monuments and tombs. It follows a previous analysis of the prohibition to build without licence[15] and is part of a more general discussion 'of buildings' as suggested by its title. Coke's main concern here is to provide a legal remedy in the common law for the violation (by means of defacing) of such buildings.

---

[11] *Ibid.*, at 1389.
[12] Sir Edward Coke, *Institutes of the Laws of England*, Part 3, 203 (1797).
[13] *Ibid.*, at 202.   [14] *Ibid.*, at 203.   [15] *Ibid.*, at 201.

He wants to argue that such a remedy is possible despite the ecclesiastical jurisdiction on the dead. Coke has nothing to do here with maltreating the body of the deceased which has been buried in unconsecrated ground or which is awaiting burial (or other modes of disposal), both of which are not subject to the ecclesiastical jurisdiction.

Indeed, as Judge Mitchell reflected on Coke's proposition in the *Larson* case:

> If the proposition that a dead body is not property rests on no better foundation than this etymology of the word 'cadaver', its correctness would be more than doubtful. But while this dictum, severed from its context, has been repeatedly quoted as authority for the proposition, yet it will be observed that it is not asserted that no individual can have any legal interest in a corpse, but merely that the burial is nullius in bonis, which was legally true at common law at that time, as the whole matter of sepulture and custody of the body after burial was within the exclusive cognizance of the church and the ecclesiastical courts.[16]

R *v.* Sharpe[17] A criminal charge was brought against Sharpe, who disinterred his mother's body which was buried in a burial ground belonging to a congregation of Protestant dissenters. Sharpe, whose father had recently died, broke into the grave of his mother so that he could estimate whether his father's coffin would fit the size of the grave. However, the accused took both corpses of his parents a few miles away to another churchyard where he eventually intended to bury them. Sharpe was convicted for the 'unlawful, willful and indecent' opening of the grave and removal of a body. His conviction was affirmed in the Court of Appeal.

In his brief decision, Judge Erle wrote that Sharpe's action was wrong 'for the licence which he obtained to enter and open, from the person who had the care of the place, was not given or intended for the purpose to which he applied it, and was, as to that purpose, no licence at all'.[18] It was held that, regardless of Sharpe's motives for removing the body, his act was still a misdemeanour.[19] Judge Erle stated that a child does not have a right

---

[16] *Larson v. Chase* 47 Minn. 307, 310 (Sup. Ct Minn. 1891) [*Larson*].

[17] *R v. Sharpe* 169 ER 959 (1856–7) [*Sharpe*]. Occasionally, the case of *Williams v. Williams* (above n 2) is regarded as another authority for the 'no property' rule. However, since the *Williams* case cites *Sharpe* as support for the same rule, I will refer to the *Sharpe* case only.

[18] *Sharpe*, above n 17, at 960.

[19] The court added that removing a body for the purpose of an 'anatomical science' is also not excusable for such a conviction. *Ibid*. The court referred in its *obiter dictum* to the case of *R v. Lynn* 100 ER 394 (1788). In *Lynn*, the defendant was charged with entering into a burial ground and taking a body for the purpose of dissecting it. Pointing to *Haynes's Case* and Coke's commentary discussed above, the defendant argued that his action was not cognizable by the common law. Rejecting his argument, the court held that common decency required that such practice should be put to an end, and that the offence was

to the corpse of his or her parents, and that the law does not recognize property in a corpse, so that the 'protection of the grave at common law, as contradistinguished from ecclesiastical protection to consecrated ground, depends upon this form of indictment' and that this latter protection is 'the only protection the law affords in respect of the burials of dissenters'.[20]

It is clear that the court in *Sharpe* did not substantiate its ruling that there exists no property in a corpse, if such a ruling was necessary for its decision at all. If it had any meaning, the no property rule established in *Sharpe* must have served as a justification for the court to use its common law jurisdiction on the matter, thereby affirming Sharpe's conviction. Although formally the court did not take into consideration the motives for Sharpe's actions, it nevertheless gave him a nominal fine of one shilling.

Exelby *v.* Handyside[21] This is a case which is not reported in any of the English law reports, and is noted in a textbook by East, in his *Pleas of the Crown*, published in 1803. It appears that an action of trover was brought by the father of two dead female infants against an eminent male midwife for taking away the deceased infants after their delivery. Newspaper reports from that time seem to indicate that the case was resolved by compromise, thereby making the midwife return the infants to their father.[22] East comments that Lord Willes (who in fact never was a Lord),[23] Chief Justice of the Court of Common Pleas, held that 'the action would not lie, as no person had any property in corpses'. Paul Matthews, who researched this case, argues that Lord Willes died in 1761, whereas East was born not before 1764. Hence, it is not clear where East obtained the information about the case from.[24] It is also not clear whether the corpses had ever been buried, nor is there any indication whether the parties in this case made reference to the idea of property in the body. Another argument made by Matthews is that even if the dictum reported by East formed part of the decision in the case, it cannot form part of the *ratio decidendi*, as this case was settled by compromise and not actually decided.[25] It follows that *Exelby* v. *Handyside* cannot be regarded as a case upon which the 'no property' rule should be based.

cognizable in a criminal court 'as being highly indecent, and contra bonos mores: at the bare idea alone of which nature revolted'. *Ibid.*, at 395. However, it is clear that the notion of property in the body of the deceased was not discussed in *Lynn*. It was therefore erroneously held in a later case, reflecting on *Lynn*, that 'the act done would have been a peculiarly indecent theft if it had not been for the technical reason that a dead body is not the subject of property'. *Queen* v. *Price* (1884) 12 QBD 247, 252 [*Price*]. The *Price* case is mistakenly cited to support the 'no property' rule.
20 *Sharpe*, above n 17, at 960.   21 *Exelby* v. *Handyside* [1749] 2 East PC 652.
22 Matthews, above n 3, at 210.   23 Skegg, above n 2, at 421 (note 9).
24 Matthews, above n 3, at 208.   25 *Ibid.*, at 210.

The discussion thus far reveals that all major authorities for the 'no property' rule are unambiguously suspicious.[26] Whatever the case may be, all sources refer to situations dealing with the whole body of a buried decedent and their application to present legal cases is doubtful.[27]

Common law exceptions to the 'no property' rule

In addition to its dubious sources, the 'no property' rule has been undermined by the establishment of three major common law principles purporting to be exceptions to the original rule.

Possession with regard to the duty to bury Soon after its establishment, common law courts suggested a major exception to the 'no property' rule. This was the proposition that there exists a possessory or a custodial interest in the body of the decedent for purposes of burying (or otherwise disposing of the body of) the deceased.[28] The right to possess the body provides next-of-kin with an interest in possessing the remains for burial purposes, opposing disinterment, refusing autopsies, medical examinations and non-consensual organ donations, and seeking damages for mutilating or intervening with the body without consent. Whether such an interest amounts to full property, a 'quasi-property' or a privacy right in the disguise of property[29] will be discussed shortly.

As early as in 1840, courts acknowledged that there is a duty to bring the dead to a decent interment.[30] In *R* v. *Stewart*, following the death of a poor woman whose family could not pay for burial, the hospital sought a

---

[26] See also J. K. Mason and G. T. Laurie, 'Consent or Property? Dealing with the Body and its Parts in the Shadow of Bristol and Alder Hey' (2001) 64(5) *Modern Law Review* 710–29, 713–14 [Mason and Laurie].

[27] There are three cases which discuss unburied corpses in this context. As noted earlier, the court's holding in *Exelby* v. *Handyside* cannot be regarded as *ratio decidendi*. Also, the case of *Williams* v. *Williams* (above n 2), which refers back to the *Sharpe* decision dealing with a buried corpse, is sceptical and in any event provides the 'no property' proposition in an *obiter dicta*. Matthews, above n 3, at 211–12. The third case which discusses unburied corpses is *Doodeward*, above n 3. However, even in this case Judge Griffith's decision holding that there could be no property in the dead body unless work and skill have been performed with regard to it seems not to enjoy the support of other judges. Judge Barton joined Judge Griffith in so far as maintained by the first that a stillborn fetus is not an unburied corpse within the general no property rule. *Ibid.*, at 417. Judge Higgins, who explicitly held that 'no one can have under British law, property in another human being – alive or dead', dissented.

[28] *Williams*, above n 2, at 665; *Pettigrew* et al. v. *Pettigrew* et al. [1904] 207 Pa. 313, 315 [*Pettigrew*].

[29] *State* v. *Powell* 497 So. 2d 1188, 1196 (Fla. 1986), cert. denied, 481 US 1059 (1987) [*Powell*].

[30] *R* v. *Stewart* (1840) 113 ER 1007 [*Stewart*].

writ to have the overseers of the woman pay for the burial. The court
declared that every person has a right to Christian burial, which implies
the right to be carried from the place where the body is located to the
parish cemetery.[31] Although this duty was first established by the ecclesiastical law, it was later declared as a common law obligation.[32]
However, the exact character of this duty remains uncertain. First, it is
not clear who bears this duty and correlatively who holds the possessory
interest in the body of the deceased. While in the English[33] and
Canadian[34] jurisdictions this duty is owed by the executor, the administrator or the personal representative of the deceased, in the USA[35] it is
the relatives of the deceased or next-of-kin who must carry out this
obligation.[36] Nor is the content of the duty clear enough. It is not firmly
established whether the duty reflects a public-health concern according to
which bodies must be disposed of promptly,[37] or if it derives from a
concern relating to treating the body with dignity,[38] or if it perhaps

[31] See *Price*, above n 19 (applying the duty of Christian burial to other methods of disposing
of the body). For a discussion of the duty to provide Christian burial, see Stephen White,
'The Law Relating to Dealing with Dead Bodies' (2000) 4 *Medical Law International*
145–81, 149–53 [White].

[32] *Doodeward*, above n 3, at 422 (per Judge Higgins).

[33] *Williams*, above n 2; *Buchanan* v. *Milton* [1999] 2 FLR 844; White, above n 31, at 156.
White further maintains that in English law, though the executor holds a duty of dealing
with the dead body, relatives of the deceased may also have a *privilege* of doing so. *Ibid.*
But see Kennedy and Grubb, who suggest that it is more likely that the relevant persons
who owe this duty are the next-of-kin: Ian Kennedy and Andrew Grubb, *Medical Law*,
3rd edn (London: Butterworths, 2000) 2243.

[34] *Saleh*, above n 2; *Aida Abeziz* v. *Benjamin Harris Estate* 3 WDCP (2d) 499, [1992] OJ No.
1271 (Ont. Gen. Div.) [*Abeziz*]; *Hunter*, above n 2; *Sopinka* et al. v. *Sopinka* et al. [2001]
55 OR (3d) 529 (Ont. Super. Ct Jus.) [*Sopinka*]. But see *Miner* v. *Canadian Pacific
Railway* 3 Alta. LR 408, 18 WLR 476 (1911) (recognizing a right of the decedent's
mother to possess the body for purposes of burial) [*Miner*].

[35] *Nathaniel Weld* v. *Gideon Walker* et al. 130 Mass. 422, 423 (Sup. Jud. Ct Mass. 1881)
[*Weld*]; *Larson*, above n 16; *Enos* v. *Snyder* 131 Cal. 68, 71 (Sup. Ct Calif. 1900) [*Enos*];
David Cohen et al. v. *Groman Mortuary Inc.* et al. 231 Cal. App. 2d 1, 5 (Ct App. Calif.
1964) [*Cohen*]. But see *Welch* v. *Welch* 269 Ga. 742, 743 (Sup. Ct Ga. 1998): 'We hold
that if an executor has any duty or authority relating to burial or disposition of a body, that
duty or authority terminates after initially discharging any such obligation in accordance
with the testamentary direction. Thereafter, disinterment and reburial may be sought by
the surviving spouse, or by the next of kin in the absence of a surviving spouse.'

[36] For a combination between these different legal positions, see *Sopinka*, above n 34, where
the Ontario Superior Court of Justice held that although the duty to dispose of the body
vests in the executor or the personal representative of the deceased, this person has a duty,
upon reasonable request, to provide particulars to next-of-kin regarding disposition of
the body. With regard to dead infants, the duty to bury lies jointly on their parents, and in
respect of unclaimed bodies, the duty falls on the local authority with control over the
place in which the body was found. Heather Conway, 'Dead, But Not Buried: Bodies,
Burial and Family Conflicts' (2003) 23(3) *Legal Studies* 423–52, 426–7 [Conway].

[37] This can be suggested by *Queen* v. *Fox* [1841] 114 ER 95.

[38] *Stewart*, above n 30, at 1009. See also *Saleh*, above n 2, and *Abeziz*, above n 34.

reflects both ideas.[39] Uncertainty also exists in relation to the consequences of violating the duty to dispose of the body of the deceased. Some cases suggest that breach of that duty results in criminal responsibility,[40] whereas others hold that it amounts to civil liability only.[41]

Not only is there confusion with respect to the nature of the duty to dispose of the body of the deceased, but there is also doubt as to the relation between such duty and a possessory or custodial interest in the body of the deceased. Jurisprudential analysis of the duty to dispose of the body, as it is portrayed in case law, results in the observation that the duty-bearer is the same legal entity as the right-holder. In contrast to a standard duty–right analysis, according to which X's duty to perform an action toward Y entails that Y has a right that such action be performed by X, in the post-mortem context we are introduced to a new notion: X has *both* rights and duties toward and in respect of Y. However, a closer examination of this situation reveals that what is at issue is not X's rights, but rather X's *claims* vis-à-vis third parties such as the state, physicians or the coroner not to interfere with the duty that X owes to Y. Hence, when X is making a claim against third parties with regard to his or her duty to dispose of the body of Y, X is not demanding that which *is* his or hers. Nor is X claiming that which he or she *will* be entitled to have as his or hers. At most, X is demanding that Y's interest in having X's duty performed be legally protected.

Another obscure matter relating to the right to possess the body of the deceased derived from the duty to dispose of the body involves the timing by which such a right or duty has legal effect. Courts have ruled that the right to possess and control the body of the deceased continues *after* the body is interred.[42] Additionally, courts have recognized the retrospective interference with the right to possess and control the dead, and awarded damages to a family who had been informed that the deceased had already been buried.[43] If the right to possess the body is related to the

---

[39] Conway, above n 36, at 426.
[40] R v. *Vann* 169 ER 523 (1851); *In the Matter of the Estate of Benjamin B. Eichner* (1940) 173 Misc. 644 (Surrogate's Ct N.Y.) [*Eichner's Estate*].
[41] *Waldman* v. *Melville (City)* [1990] SJ No. 13 (Sask. Ct Queen's Bench) [*Waldman*].
[42] *Ibid.* But compare *Elizabeth Dougherty* v. *Mercantile Safe-Deposit & Trust Co.* 282 Md. 617, 620 (Ct App. Md. 1978) ('When the duty to furnish proper burial has been discharged, the right of custody ceases and the body is thereafter in the custody of the law and disinterment and disturbance of the body is subject to the control of a court of equity').
[43] *Mackey* v. *US* (1993) 8 F 3d 826 (Ct App. D.C. Cir.), discussed in Ian Kennedy, 'Negligence: Interference with Right to Possession of a Body' (1995) 3 *Medical Law Review* 233.

duty to bring the decedent to a decent burial, an alternative theoretical background needs to support these legal decisions.

Regardless of the relation between the duty to dispose of the body and the possessory interest in it, existing legislation may also imply possessory and custodial interests in the body of the deceased. The English Human Tissue Act and Canadian legislation dealing with post-mortem donations for therapeutic, scientific or medical research mention the 'person lawfully in possession of the body' as one of the legal entities who may authorize post-mortem organ removal.[44] Possessory rights are statutorily recognized by the legal requirement to give the ashes of a decedent to the person who requested cremation.[45] They are also acknowledged in the context of performing an autopsy. A coroner has possession over a body for conducting an inquest of the cause of death. The coroner enjoys a prior right to possession even if he or she was not informed of the incident or has not yet decided whether to require a post-mortem examination.[46] So long as the medical examination has not been exhausted, it is the coroner who has the right to possess the body, and not the person who performs the medical examination. Once the coroner's jurisdiction is over, any body parts retained by him must be returned to the executor or dealt with in accordance with the executor's instructions.[47] The vast regulation of this area suggests that the idea that one may possess the body for specific purposes is not alien to legal thinking.

Most importantly, even assuming that possessory and custodial rights pertaining to the body of the deceased constitute property, these rights seem to enjoy a very weak protection – definitely not representative of a full property right – at least in the following five categories. Common to the situations discussed below is the idea – already held by courts – that

[44] Human Tissue Act 1961, c. 54, s. 1 (Eng.). See also the new Human Tissue Act 2004, c. 30, ss. 5(4)(b), 10(4)(a) (Eng.); Human Tissue Act, RSNB 1973, c. H-12, s. 3 (Can.); Human Tissue Gift Act, RSBC 1996, c. 211, s. 5 (Can.); Trillium Gift of Life Network Act, RSO 1990, c. H. 20, s. 5(2) (Can.). Interestingly, the Uniform Anatomical Gift Act 1987 (US), regulating, among others, post-mortem gifts in the USA, does not use a proprietary terminology when specifying the persons who may give consent to a post-mortem gift. *Ibid.*, at s. 3. The Act, however, mentions the 'person in possession' of the body as an authority to provide the examination or copying of a document connected with such a gift. *Ibid.*, at s. 7(b). But see Matthews, who argues that the expression 'lawfully in possession' refers to factual rather than legal possession. Matthews, above n 3, at 228.
[45] Cremation Regulations 1930 (SR & O 1930 No. 1016), reg. 16 (Eng.), mentioned in Matthews, above n 3, at 207.
[46] *R v. Bristol Coroner, ex parte Kerr* [1974] 1 QB 652, 658–9.
[47] White, above n 31, at 163. See also Loane Skene, 'Proprietary Rights in Human Bodies, Body Parts and Tissue: Regulatory Context and Proposals for New Laws' (2002) 22 *Legal Studies* 102–27, 112.

the rights to custody and possession of the body of the deceased for purposes of burial should be subordinated to the demands of justice or public good.[48]

EXISTING LEGISLATION CONCERNING ORGAN DONATION Whatever the possessory and custodial interest in the body of the deceased may be, it does not enjoy constitutional protection.[49] Hence, courts in the USA upheld the constitutionality of state legislation allowing the removal of corneas from the dead without notifying families.[50] Additionally, courts interpreted the 'good faith' immunity clause in the Uniform Anatomical Gift Act broadly enough to release healthcare providers from civil liability with respect to organ donation pursuant to this act, even when the decedent or relatives expressed their intent not to donate organs or tissues extracted from the deceased.[51]

PUBLIC INTEREST IN BURIAL GROUND Courts have ruled that an interred body belongs to the owner of the land wherein it is buried,[52] and that interference with that right can result in an action of trespass

---

[48] *Edmonds* v. *Armstrong Funeral Home Ltd* [1931] 1 DLR 676 (Ala. Sup. Ct) para. 18 [*Edmonds*].

[49] *Georgia Lions Eye Bank Inc.* v. *Lavant* 335 SE 2d 127, 128 (Ga. 1985); *Tillman* v. *Detroit Receiving Hospital* 360 NW 2d 275, 277–8 (Mich. Ct App. 1984).

[50] *Powell*, above n 29. But see *Brotherton* v. *Cleveland* 923 F 2d 477, 482 (6th Cir. Ohio 1991) [*Brotherton*], where the court held that the interest of the state 'is not substantial enough to allow the state to consciously disregard those property rights which it has granted'. See *Whaley* v. *County of Tuscola* 58 F 3d 1111 (Ct App. 6th Cir. 1995) and *Robert Newman* et al. v. *L. Sathyavaglswaran* 287 F 3d 786 (Ct App. 9th Cir. 2002). The constitutional challenge usually involves three arguments: the statute permitting the taking of corneas from the deceased without notifying next-of-kin is unconstitutional as it (1) deprives survivors of their fundamental personal and property right to dispose of the deceased; (2) creates an invidious classification which deprives survivors of their right to equal protection; and (3) permits a taking of private property by state action for a non-public purpose.

[51] *Donald Nicoletta* v. *Rochester Eye and Human Parts Bank Inc.* 519 NYS 2d 928 (Sup. Ct N.Y. 1987); *Lyon* v. *US* 843 F Supp. 531 (D. Minn. 1994); *Schembre* v. *Mid-America Transplant Association* 135 SW 3d 527 (Ct App. Mo. 2004). Compare the dissenting opinion of Judge Johnson in *Virginia Brown* v. *Delaware Valley Transplant Program* 420 Pa. Super. 84, 96–104 (Sup. Ct Pa. 1992), holding that the 'good faith' immunity as enacted applies to a 'person' who is authorized or under obligation to dispose of the body. In his view, while the hospital might be considered a 'person' for this purpose, in the circumstances of that case it had not been proved that the hospital had an obligation to dispose of the body.

[52] *Doodeward*, above n 3, at 412; *O'Connor* v. *City of Victoria* (1913) 4 WWR 4, 11 DLR 577 (Ala. Sup. Ct 1913) [*O'Connor*]. For the question of whether an exclusive right of burial creates an interest in land or a right in contract, see Alan Dowling, 'Exclusive Rights of Burial and the Law of Real Property' (1998) 18 *Legal Studies* 438–52.

to land.[53] Moreover, it was held that the right of the owner of a plot is not absolute, and is perceived as 'a mere privilege or license to make interments in the lot exclusively of others *as long as the burying ground or cemetery remains as such*'.[54] Hence, where a city in the course of constructing a roadway removes human remains from the land where these remains are buried without notice or legal authority, it is liable in trespass to the owner of the land.[55] Any proprietary interest that an executor, administrator or relative may have in the body of the deceased will be defeated by the strong interest of the owner of the land where the body is buried.[56] Similarly, the body of the deceased can be removed and reinterred in another lot for the building of a memorial temple in the cemetery lodge.[57] Under these cases no right to compensation exists for the 'taking of property'. Instead, courts stress the importance of informing the deceased's family in advance so that they can remove the body to another lot. Families are compensated only for their reasonable expenses associated with disinterring and reinterring the body, if at all.[58]

INVESTIGATING THE CAUSE OF DEATH The right to possess the body of the deceased is also defeated in cases where an examination of the cause of a suspicious or unnatural death is required. As long as such an examination is properly performed, the interest of the state in it prevails against any other interests, including religious tenets of relatives.[59] Courts refuse to acknowledge any constitutionally protected right in the body of the deceased that would outweigh the need to perform an autopsy without prior consent from the family.[60]

RETENTION OF BODY PARTS FOR RESEARCH FOLLOWING AN AUTOPSY Even when an autopsy is lawfully carried out, fourteen states in the USA and the District of Columbia allow the retention of organs and body parts removed as a result of autopsies for research purposes without

---

[53] *Doodeward*, above n 3. See also William Blackstone, *Commentaries on the Laws of England* (1766) (Chicago: University of Chicago Press, 1979), vol. II, ch. 28, 429, and *Meagher* v. *Driscoll* 99 Mass. 281, 284 (Sup. Jud. Ct Mass. 1868).

[54] *Grinnan* et al. v. *Fredericksburg Lodge* 88 SE 79, 80 (Sup. Ct App. Va. 1916) [*Grinnan*]; *Smith* v. *Tamworth City Council* et al. [1997] (Sup. Ct Equity Div., NSW, Australia).

[55] *O'Connor*, above n 52.

[56] But see Matthews, who argues that 'if corpses were not before burial properly to be regarded as property, how could the affixation principle be relevant?'. Matthews, above n 3, at 203.

[57] *Grinnan*, above n 54.   [58] *Ibid.*

[59] *Davidson* v. *Garrett* [1899] CCC 200 [*Davidson*]; *Snyder* v. *Holy Cross Hospital* 30 Md. App. 317, 328 (Ct App. Md. 1976) [*Snyder*]

[60] *James Helmer* v. *Daniel D. Middaugh* 191 F Supp. 2d 283 (ND N.Y. Dist. Ct 2002).

consent from families, and seventeen state statutes permit the retention of corneas and/or pituitary glands to be used for research or for manufacturing drugs – also without consent. Moreover, in Minnesota, the brain of a deceased suspected of suffering from Alzheimer's can be removed for the purposes of research unless the coroner knows of any objection to the research.[61] In an English case concerning the removal, retention and subsequent disposal of deceased children's organs following post-mortem without knowledge or consent of their parents, the court held that if the purpose of establishing or confirming the causes of death or of investigating the existence or nature of abnormal conditions properly requires organs to be removed and retained for examination, no further consent is required. On the other hand, if the post-mortem contemplated use of a part or parts of the body for therapeutic, educational or research purposes, consent must be obtained.[62] One may wonder why a property interest in the body, if it exists, enjoys such poor legal protection.[63]

UNAUTHORIZED EXPERIMENTATION ON CORPSES DURING AUTOPSY The property interest in the body of the deceased provides weak protection also when experimentation is performed on the corpse during an autopsy. In one case, the court rejected the claim for the deprivation without due process of constitutional property interests of parents in the body of their deceased infant when a coroner took the corpse 'to the rear of the laboratory, holding the corpse by the feet, dropping the corpse head-first from a predetermined height of one meter onto a surface of virtually smooth concrete ... then X-ray[ed] the skull of the infant and then record[ed] the results'.[64] Moreover, the court held that the right survivors have to possess the body of the deceased in the same condition as the body was at death does not amount to a constitutional liberty or privacy interest and that next-of-kin have adequate remedies to protect their possession in the body of the deceased such as the action to seek recovery for intentional torts or for the tempering of a corpse.[65]

---

[61] See Dorothy Nelkin and Lori Andrews, 'Do the Dead Have Interests? Policy Issues for Research After Life' (1998) 24 *American Journal of Law and Medicine* 261–91, 288 and the references mentioned there.

[62] *AB* et al. v. *Leeds Teaching Hospital NHS Trust* et al. [2004] EWHC 644 (QB).

[63] But compare the English approach where, following the Interim Bristol Inquiry Report, the view was taken that pathologists after post-mortem have no right to retain the tissues no matter what work has been expended on them, and must return them to the person who carries the duty to dispose of the body. David Price, 'From Cosmos and Damian to Van Velzen: The Human Tissue Saga Continues' (2003) 11 *Medical Law Review* 1–47, 36 [Price, 'Cosmos'].

[64] *Dwayne Arnaud* et al. v. *Charles Odom* et al. 870 F 2d 304, 306 (5th Cir. 1989).

[65] *Ibid.*, at 309–10.

In addition to the weak protection of the right to possess the body of the deceased manifested in the above five categories of cases, actions for conversion were unsuccessful when portions of the decedent's tissues and organs were discarded after autopsy,[66] or when an unauthorized autopsy was performed on the deceased.[67] Even when plaintiffs succeeded in arguing for conversion, courts dismissed such actions for evidentiary reasons.[68]

The poor safeguards for the right to possess the body of the deceased under the American jurisprudence may be explained by its historical development. In the USA, deviation from the no property rule, at least rhetorically, could be noticed as early as in 1872. The possessory and custodial interest in the body of the deceased associated with the duty to dispose of the body was classified in America as 'quasi-property'. The first case to discuss such interest was *William G. Pierce and Wife* v. *Proprietors of Swan Point Cemetery and Almira Metcalf.*[69] In this case, the daughter of the deceased brought an action against a widow and cemetery owners following the disinterment of the deceased from a burial plot, bought by him while alive, where he had been interred for thirteen years. The body was removed to another plot purchased by the decedent's widow. The claimant asked to be able to return the remains of her father to the original plot, which at the time of the trial was owned by her as his heir. The order was allowed. The court held:

That there is no right or property in a dead body, using the word in its ordinary sense, may well be admitted. Yet, the burial of the dead is a subject which interests the feelings of mankind to a much greater degree than many matters of actual property. There is a duty imposed by the universal feelings of mankind to be discharged by someone towards the dead; a duty, and we may also say a right, to protect from violation; and a duty on the part of others to abstain from violation; it may therefore be considered as a sort of quasi property, and it would be discreditable to any system of law not to provide a remedy in such a case.[70]

In *Pierce*, the court explained that the person who has quasi-property in the dead 'cannot be considered as the owner of it in any sense whatever;

---

[66] *Shults* v. *US* 995 F Supp. 1270, 1275–6 (D. Kans. 1998).

[67] *Hasselbach* v. *Mount Sinai Hospital* 173 AD 89, 159 NYS 376, 379 (Sup. Ct N.Y., 1916).

[68] *Wint* v. *Alabama Eye and Tissue Bank* 675 So. 2d 383, 384–6 (Ala. 1996); *Spates* v. *Dameron Hospital Association* 114 Cal. App. 4th 208, 7 Cal. Rptr 3d 597, 607–9 (2003) [*Spates*].

[69] *William G. Pierce and Wife* v. *Proprietors of Swan Point Cemetery and Almira Metcalf* 10 RI 227, 14 Am. Rep. 667 (Sup. Ct R.I. 1872) [*Pierce*].

[70] *Ibid.*, at 676–7. The court added: 'Although ... the body is not property in the usually recognized sense of the word, we may consider it as a sort of *quasi* property, to which certain persons may have rights, as they have duties to perform towards it, arising out of our common humanity.' *Ibid.*, at 681.

he holds it only as a sacred trust for the benefit of all who may from family or friendship have an interest in it, and ... a court of equity may well regulate it as such, and change the custody if improperly managed'.[71] The quasi-property right of survivors includes the right to custody of the body; to receive it in the condition in which it was left without mutilation; to have the body treated with respect and without outrage or indignity; and to bury or otherwise dispose of the body without interference.[72] Courts decisively held that any interference with the right to possess or otherwise have custody of the body of the deceased by mutilating or disturbing it is actionable and subject to compensation,[73] although in practice the successful legal actions are ones that are usually not associated with a property right.

Since its establishment, it has been clear that the quasi-property right in the body of the deceased is not classified as the protection of a property interest. Sometimes the right of next-of-kin pertaining to the body of the deceased is classified as a 'personal' right.[74] In other cases such a right is characterized as a 'trust'.[75] It seems obvious, as Prosser noted, 'that such "property" is something evolved out of thin air to meet the occasion, and that in reality the *personal* feelings of the survivors are being protected, under a fiction likely to deceive no one but a lawyer'.[76] Courts have acknowledged that the quasi-property right to possess the body of the deceased is the outcome of a strategic move to overcome the difficulties of suing for damages for emotional distress,[77] and indeed the general belief is that this rule was meant to recognize the continuous dignity owed to the person, even after her death.[78] It follows that 'a cause of action of this nature is not based on the theory of an injury to property rights, nor

---

[71] *Ibid.*, at 681. See also *Larson*, above n 16, at 309, and *Spiegel* v. *Evergreen Cemetery Co.* 117 NJL 90, 93 (1936).

[72] *Whitehair* v. *Highland Memory Gardens Inc.* 327 SE 2d 438, 441 (W.Va. 1985) [*Whitehair*].

[73] *Larson*, above n 16, at 310.

[74] See e.g. *Stewart* v. *Schwartz Bros.–Jeffer Memorial Chapel Inc.* 606 NYS 2d 965, 967 (1993).

[75] *Pettigrew*, above n 28, at 315; *Frost* v. *St Paul's Cemetery Association* 254 NYS 2d 316, 318 (1964).

[76] W. L. Prosser and W. P. Keeton, *On Torts*, 5th edn (St Paul: West, 1984) 63. See also Harry B. Bigelow, 'Damages: Pleading: Property: Who May Recover for Wrongful Disturbance of a Dead Body?' (1933) 19 *Cornell Law Quarterly* 108–12, 110.

[77] *Carney* v. *Knollwood Cemetery Association* 514 NE 2d 430, 434 (Ohio App. 1986) [*Carney*]. See also *Whitehair*, above n 72; *Scarpaci* v. *Milwaukee County* 292 NW 2d 816, 830 (Wis. 1980) [*Scarpaci*].

[78] Mason and Laurie, above n 26, at 714. P. D. G. Skegg, 'Medical Uses of Corpses and the "No Property" Rule' (1992) 32(4) *Medicine, Science and the Law* 311–18, at 314 [Skegg, 'Medical Uses'].

does it involve a negligent injury to the person'.[79] Although some cases considered the interest in the body of the decedent substantial enough to rise to the level of 'legitimate claim of entitlement' in the deceased's body (including her organs) protected under the due process clause,[80] it seems clear that the possessory and custodial right of an executor, administrator or next-of-kin in the body of the deceased is not regarded as property in its true meaning.

The 'work and skill' exception In an Australian Supreme Court decision,[81] affirmed by a recent ruling of the English Court of Appeal,[82] and some public reports in the UK,[83] it was held that:

> when a person has by the lawful exercise of work or skill so dealt with a human body, or part of a human body in his lawful possession that it has acquired some attributes differentiating it from a mere corpse awaiting burial, he acquires right to retain possession of it, at least as against any person not entitled to have it delivered to him for the purpose of burial, but subject, of course, to any positive law which forbids its retention under the particular circumstances.[84]

Although the 'work and skill' principle is presented as an exception to the no property rule, it does not deal with property in the *whole* body of a *buried* (or otherwise disposed of) deceased. Instead, this principle applies to *unburied* dead bodies, and more specifically to organs, body parts or tissues taken from the deceased and preserved by the performance of special work and skill. Regardless of these different classifications, the 'work and skill' principle evokes other difficulties.

The idea that a person may have property in a thing qua producer or labourer can be traced back to John Locke's theory of private property. In what has become an extremely often cited paragraph, Locke writes:

> Though the earth and all inferior creatures be common to all men, yet every man has a property in his own person; this nobody has any right to but himself. *The labour of his body and the work of his hands we may say are properly his. Whatsoever, then, he removes out of the state that nature hath provided and left it in, he hath mixed his labour with, and joined to it something that is his own, and thereby makes it his property.*

---

[79] *Alma Deeg* v. *City of Detroit* 345 Mich. 371, 377–8 (Sup. Ct Mich. 1956).

[80] *Brotherton*, above n 50, at 482 (majority opinion delivered by Judge Boyce). Compare also *Long* v. *Chicago, RI and P Railway Co.* (1905) 86 P 289 (Okla. SC).

[81] *Doodeward*, above n 3.

[82] *R* v. *Kelly and Lindsay* [1999] QB 621, [1998] 3 All ER 741 [*Kelly*]; *In re Organ Retention Group Litigation* [2004] EWHC 644 (QB) para. 148.

[83] Royal College of Pathologists, *Consensus Statement of Recommended Policies for Uses of Human Tissue in Research Education and Quality Control* (1999) 12; Scottish Executive, *Final Report of the Independent Review on the Retention of Organs at Post-Mortem* (2001) para. 70.

[84] *Doodeward*, above n 3, at 414.

It being by him removed from the common state nature placed it in, it hath by this labour something annexed to it that excludes the common right of other men. For this labour being a right to what it is once joined to, at least where there is enough and as good left in common for others.[85]

Presumably, the idea here is one of desert: people who perform useful work deserve to be rewarded with property. As nicely put by Jim Harris, 'My body is the tree; my actions are the branches; and the product of my labouring activities is the fruit.'[86] However, three observations should be made. According to Locke, someone's owning of 'his person' antecedes this person's property in the thing over which he or she performs labour or work. This may entail not only a causal relation but also a conceptual one. The justification of 'work and skill' as a means to gain property over external objects assumes self-ownership in one's 'person', the latter of which is generally interpreted as one's body.[87] In order to own what is outside of me, I need to 'own' (or have property in) my body first. Acknowledging a property interest in body parts of the deceased through 'work and skill' presumes a notion of self-ownership. Specifically, such an idea suggests that the labourer had property in her own person (body) before she gained her rights over the external object, and that this right to self-ownership is related in a constitutive way to the creation of her property right over the object upon which she used her skill and knowledge. Nevertheless, the 'work and skill' exception as developed in legal cases discusses only the property interest of the *labourer* over the body part taken from the deceased. This exception takes for granted the property interest that the labourer has in her own body prior to exercising her labour and skill, and it also does not discuss the relation between the labourer's self-ownership and her property right over that body part.

Second, according to the original Lockean theory, the labourer acquires property over a thing that previously belonged to the 'state of nature', namely an object over which no other proprietary interests exist. Legal decisions applying the 'work and skill' exception to the body of the deceased do not substantiate the argument according to which there exists no proprietary interest in the body of the deceased *prior* to the

---

[85] John Locke, *The Second Treatise of Government*, 3rd edn (Oxford: Basil Blackwell, 1966) 15 (s. 27) [*Locke*].

[86] J. W. Harris, 'Who Owns My Body?' (1996) 16(1) *Oxford Journal of Legal Studies* 55–84, 67 [Jim Harris].

[87] But see Richard Arneson's different interpretation of the Lockean concept of property: 'Owning himself, each person is free to do with *his body* whatever he chooses so long as he does not cause or threaten any harm to non-consenting others. No one is obligated to place herself at the service of others in the slightest degree.' Richard J. Arneson, 'Lockean Self-Ownership: Towards a Demolition' (1991) 39 *Political Studies* 36–54, 40.

labour invested in it, or, put differently, that upon death one's body becomes part of (or returns to) Mother Nature. Such an argument is only, and is as such erroneously, assumed in these decisions. A more general attack on the Lockean idea was made by Jim Harris. He argued that if, according to Locke, an individual is not a slave, and none of us is, then nobody else owns her body, and she therefore must own herself and everything which is produced by her body. But, as Harris correctly argues, just because I am not a slave and nobody owns me, does not mean that I do. It follows, that no-one – including me – owns my body.[88]

A related idea, assumed again by the application of the 'work and skill' exception, is that the labourer gains property over the external object while her first possession of it (prior to the exercise of work and skill) is lawful. But this assumption may sound contradictory, for if the labourer had lawful possession in the object, how did the work and skill put her in a better position to hold the property right than she was previously in? On the other hand, if the labourer did not have lawful possession prior to the work, it seems that any labour or skill invested in the object are irrelevant and immaterial to proposition that she acquired property over it.[89]

Lastly, it is clear from Locke's theory that acquiring property by labour is conditioned upon there being 'enough and as good left in common for others'. The holding of private property over external things can be outweighed by societal concerns, such as equal distribution of (formerly public) property.[90] Other societal constraints may include the prevention of wrong to others.[91] No doubt, the ending of a person's life in a decent and dignified fashion, including the way in which this person's body is appropriated upon death, is a societal interest that should be considered in the discussion of whether one could have property in the body of the deceased. An argument may be made that such a public interest outweighs the recognition of property in the deceased's body or organs.

Moreover, the 'work and skill' exception creates some practical difficulties. Originally, the idea was that by mixing his physical labour with the external object, the labourer joins or annexes to it an attribute which belongs to the person of the labourer, thereby making this object *his* object. In Locke's words, 'The labour put a distinction between them and common; that added something to them more than nature, the

---

[88] Jim Harris, above n 86, at 71.
[89] Paul Matthews, 'The Man of Property' (1995) 3 *Medical Law Review* 251–74, 269 [Matthews, 'Man of Property']. In *Kelly*, above n 82, the question of whether the college was in lawful possession of the body parts at the time they were stolen by the accused was never properly resolved. Nevertheless, this did not prevent the court from upholding the 'work and skill' exception.
[90] Locke, above n 85, at 17 (ss. 31, 32).   [91] Jim Harris, above n 86, at 67.

common mother of all, had done, and so they became his private right.'[92] While discussing the 'work and skill' exception with regard to dead bodies, Clerk and Lindsell refer to the exercise of 'stuffing or embalming'.[93] However, when applied in court, this rule refers to a very thin notion of 'work and skill'. Thus, for example, in *Doodeward*,[94] the whole corpse of a stillborn two-headed child was kept in a bottle with spirits. No dissection or medical examination was made with respect to the body. In *Dobson*,[95] the brain of the deceased was kept in paraffin. The court specifically stated that fixing the body in such a way does *not* constitute property since it was a necessary component in the process of determining the cause of death, and in any event was unnecessary after the cause had been established by the coroner. The court held that the preservation of the brain is not on a par with 'stuffing and embalming a corpse or preserving an anatomical or pathological specimen for a scientific collection or with preserving a human freak'.[96] In *Kelly*,[97] the court acknowledged that the preparation of specimens taken by the prosection involved many hours, sometimes weeks, of skilled work. However, the dissections were performed by a previous generation of anatomists more than twenty years before Kelly and Lindsay were prosecuted for stealing these specimens. It follows from these cases that there exists a considerable uncertainty with respect to how much skill and labour should be performed by the health team so that a property right in the body or body parts be vested in them. This reminds us of Robert Nozick's criticism of the general 'work and skill' Lockean principle: if someone empties a can of tomato juice into the ocean, does she own the ocean?[98]

In addition to the nature of work performed on the body materials, courts also look at the purpose for which the skill and labour are

---

[92] Locke, above n 85, at 16 (s. 28).

[93] Clerk and Lindsell, *On Torts*, 17th edn (London: Sweet & Maxwell, 1995) 653.

[94] *Doodeward*, above n 3.

[95] *Dobson et al.* v. *North Tyneside Health Authority et al.* [1996] 4 All ER 474, [1997] 1 WLR 596, [1997] BMLR 146 [*Dobson*].

[96] *Ibid*. Pawlowski, however, argues that the court's reference to 'stuffing or embalming' is surprising given that most bodies awaiting burial undergo some form of embalming process. Mark Pawlowski, 'The Legal Recognition of Human Body Parts and Genetic Material as Property' (unpublished paper, 2000) 14 [Pawlowski]. Compare, for example, the situation in New Zealand where the Law Commission recommended that the term 'body parts' or 'tissue' should not apply to microscopic samples retained by pathologists as a matter of practice in a post-mortem examination. If this recommendation is accepted, the question of whether there exists any proprietary interest with respect to such samples may not be raised. P. D. G. Skegg, 'The Removal and Retention of Cadaveric Body Parts: Does the Law Require Parental Consent?' (2003) 10(3) *Otago Law Review* 425–43, 433 (note 47).

[97] *Kelly*, above n 82.

[98] Robert Nozick, *Anarchy, State and Utopia* (Oxford: Blackwell, 1980) 175.

exercised. The requirement proposed by courts is that the potential owner will have to show that she had an intention to create a novel item with a use of its own.[99] Thus, in *Dobson*, the court distinguished this case from *Doodeward*, holding that in the latter case the purpose of maintaining the double-headed fetus in the spirit had some value as it was for exhibition purposes or scientific collection.[100]

In *Kelly*, the court went further to establish that body parts taken from the deceased may become property even when work or skill have *not* been expended on them, 'if they have *a use or significance beyond their mere existence*. This may be so if, for example, they are intended for use in an organ transplant operation, for the extraction of DNA or, for that matter, as an exhibit in a trial.'[101] In *Dobson*, the court refused to follow the path initiated in *Kelly*, which would have made the proprietary status of the body become dependent on the funerary rituals and beliefs of executors and mourners,[102] and would have rewritten the 'no property rule' to read 'there is no property in corpses *excluding excised body parts*'.[103] Nevertheless, such an alternative is still open, and in some jurisdictions has already been followed. For example, in *Roche*, the plaintiff sought to perform DNA tests on specimens belonging to the body of the deceased, previously taken during the course of surgery and kept in paraffin. The court ruled that the specimens were subject to property but it did not establish who held the proprietary interest in them.[104]

The 'long-dead' exception[105]   In many cases, human remains and whole dead bodies are preserved for long periods of time, whether embalmed, mummified or in skeletal form. Examples include exhibitions of Egyptian mummies and the preservation of skeletal remains as archaeological resources. The most familiar example of embalmment is that of Jeremy Bentham, whose body is exhibited at University College

---

[99] Andrew Grubb, 'Note: Theft of Body Parts: Property and Dead Bodies' (1998) 6 *Medical Law Review* 247–53, 250; Pawlowski, above n 96, at 13.

[100] *Dobson*, above n 95, at 479.

[101] *Kelly*, above n 82, at 750 (my emphasis).

[102] White, above n 31, at 167.

[103] Andrew Grubb, '"I, Me, Mine": Bodies, Parts and Property' (1998) 3 *Medical Law International* 299–317, 312 [Grubb] (my emphasis).

[104] *Susan Roche v. Ronald Douglas* [2000] WASC 146 [*Roche*]. Compare *AW v. CW* [2002] NSWSC 301 [*AW*], where the New South Wales Supreme Court did not follow *Roche*, and refused to grant an order that a DNA test be done on body materials taken from the deceased.

[105] I choose the term 'long-dead' to describe a person who died long ago in contrast to the term 'newly-dead', namely a person who has just recently died.

London. Remains under these circumstances are merely used for education and have historical and scientific meaning.[106]

It is legally agreeable that there is property – indeed full property – in these long-dead creatures. Hence, a museum owns the mummies exhibited on its premises just as Jeremy Bentham is subject to theft from University College London. The proprietary interest applying to these creatures is explained by one of the two following groups of justifications. According to the first, in order to maintain these creatures for long periods of time, one needs to invest work and material in their preservation. The work and material turn the corpse into something new or different than what it formerly was. In other cases, ethnological collections of skulls or mummies are brought from overseas at considerable expense. Having property over these creatures is thus a sub-type of, and is explained by, the more general 'work and skill' exception discussed above.[107]

The second group of justifications focuses on the specific circumstances in which the corpse is transformed into 'another' object. These circumstances grant property over the long-dead. Judge Higgins in *Doodeward*, for example, provided three justifications for property in mummies. First, the 'clothing of the dead is itself property in English law'. Second, the taking of a buried corpse, which normally constitutes an action of trespass to the land, cannot apply to Egyptian land which is foreign soil. Lastly, property in a mummy is possible as 'there is no one insisting that a mummy shall not be disturbed'.[108]

Yet, all the proposed propositions seem problematic. Judge Higgins does not support his first proposition, according to which property is obtained through the act of clothing the body. If one were to argue against the 'work and skill' exception for requiring too little for a proprietary interest to exist, this first proposition asks even less. The second proposition is not only unpersuasive but also very disturbing. It is suggested that since there could not be an action of trespass in Egyptian land (assumption 'A'), the taking of a buried dead body (assumption 'B') from that land (assumption 'C') is not actionable (assumption 'D'), and hence it can be considered the property of the taker ('conclusion'). Clearly, assumption 'A' may apply to the Egyptian legal system but not necessarily to other systems. Moreover, assumption 'B' assumes that a mummy should be regarded in a similar way to a deceased who is buried in soil.

---

[106] With the help of new DNA technologies, scientists use specimens from the 'long-dead' to uncover knowledge about those individuals, making interesting links to the living. For examples of recent studies, see R. Alta Charo, 'The Speaker: Skin and Bones: Post-Mortem Markets in Human Tissue' (2002) 26 *Nova Law Review* 421–49, 440.

[107] *Doodeward*, above n 3, at 414–15; *Miner*, above n 34, at para. 18.

[108] *Doodeward*, above n 3, at 422–3.

Such an assumption nonetheless needs to be substantiated as one could think of significant differences between the two forms of disposal of the body. On the other hand, assumption 'C' reflects Judge Higgins's narrow perspective on the question of whether there could be property in a mummy. Could museums in Egypt own property over mummies taken from their country? Alternatively, had there been English mummies, would they have been subject to theft if stolen from the British Museum? Under assumption 'D', it is further assumed that an action of trespass to land is the only action suitable for taking the property, and vice versa. Clearly, such an assumption is false in both its directions. Conversion, violation of the due process clause (in the USA), trover and many other actions may substitute the proprietary claim. Consequently and additionally, it does not follow that if there is not an action in trespass to land, there is not property at stake. Finally, even if all Judge Higgins's assumptions were correct, the conclusion suggested by him does not follow from them directly, as it is not necessary that if the taking of property is not actionable in law, then there must be property.

Nor does Judge Higgins's last argument within this group of justifications result in a better outcome than the previous propositions. If no one is insisting that a mummy shall not be disturbed, then, at most, it should not. Property over X is not the only mechanism by which X can be protected from being 'disturbed'. Ethics, criminal law and tort law are examples of other social institutions that can achieve the same goals. Furthermore, even if there were not other institutions to protect X, the fact that no one wants to hurt X does not entail the existence of a proprietary interest with regard to X. At most, it can bring about X's freedom from interference by others.

Not only are the justifications for property over mummies unconvincing, but the rationales for attributing property interests over human skeletons appear deficient as well. Discussion of the matter is once again found in Judge Higgins's decision in the *Doodeward* case.[109] Judge Higgins emphasizes that skeletons are bought and sold for money and that, although such 'traffic as there is in skulls and bones is clandestine', they are regarded as property. It nevertheless seems inappropriate to infer that since there exists commerce in X, X is subject to property, just as it is wrong to assume from the ban of commerce in X that X is not subject to property. As may be implied by Judge Higgins, the commerce in skeletons can be illegal so that reliance on it would be wrong. Alternatively, not everything over which there is commerce should be regarded as property.

[109] *Ibid.*, at 423.

My labour and skill are payable for by my employer although they are not his or her property. My employer cannot 'possess' them, exclude others from using them, transfer or own them in any way.

Other justifications for a property interest in the 'long-dead' are offered by Philippe Ducor.[110] The first justification focuses on the time elapsing from the moment of death. It is argued that an ageing cadaver does not invoke the same sentiments and respect as do the remains of the recently dead. This is because 'as time passes, the shape of the cadaver is less and less reminiscent of the former person'.[111] The second justification involves the issue of anonymity. Society is more inclined to accord property interests to an anonymous anatomical preparation than to remains of identified, let alone well-known, persons. Lastly, it is suggested that it is usually preferable to acknowledge property interests in remains of persons from a dissimilar and remote society than from one's own community.

Of course, Ducor's first justification does not apply to a conserved or embalmed corpse the shape of which remains almost identical to the living person it was, thereby invoking similar sentiments and feelings of respect. Nor does his second justification apply to the embalmed body of Jeremy Bentham or the cryogenically preserved body of Ted Williams who, no doubt, are far from being anonymous. The third justification to confer a proprietary interest in the body of the long-dead suggested by Ducor appears sound, but is applicable to cases where the property holder is distant in time and place from that over which she has property. It does not apply to situations of closer generations.

In sum, although the legal position regarding property in mummies, human skeletons and embalmed bodies is that these 'creatures' are subject to full property (including commerce), a more thorough analysis needs to be made to support such a proposition. It follows from the analysis of this section that the substance of the 'no property' rule has been diminished by its many exceptions to almost total ineffectiveness. Although the theoretical background of these exceptions seems lacking, the rule must be re-examined in light of those evident exceptions.

Undermining the 'no property' outcomes

In addition to its many exceptions, the no property rule has been undermined by the overriding of two of its major outcomes. The first relates to

---

[110] Philippe Ducor, 'The Legal Status of Human Material' (1996) 44 *Drake Law Review* 196, 233–4 [Ducor].
[111] *Ibid.*, at 234.

the proposition according to which a person cannot direct in a will or otherwise the disposal of her body or body parts after death (hereinafter the 'no will' rule). The second concerns the notion that a dead body is not subject to theft (hereinafter the 'no theft' rule).

Undermining the 'no will' rule Statutory provisions in the USA,[112] Canada[113] and the UK[114] allow people to leave directives concerning the use of their body or body parts after death for therapeutic purposes, medical education or scientific research. Although such directives are not compelling, efforts are made to follow them.

In the English case of *Re Matheson*,[115] an order for the disinterment of the body of the deceased and its subsequent cremation was sought eleven years after the deceased had been buried. The widow of the decedent decided that her own remains after death should be cremated and she also wished her dead husband to be disinterred and cremated, so that his ashes would be placed together with hers. The woman died without bringing the action to court, and her son sued for her. Although the court expressed the natural desire of every person that his or her body would not be disturbed after death, and that the 'primary function of the court is to keep faith with the dead', it ruled in favour of the request, thereby holding that it 'must and will have regard to the supposed wishes of the dead', in that case the wishes of the dead widow, even though she did not leave any explicit directive.

A more careful analysis of Canadian cases that allegedly endorsed the no will rule suggests that the expressed wishes of the deceased may have had an important role in these legal decisions. Thus, in *Hunter*,[116] the deceased, who had been a devout Protestant all his life, expressed his wish during his last illness to be buried in a Roman Catholic cemetery where his wife, a devout Roman Catholic, would be buried. A few days before his death, the deceased was baptized by a Roman Catholic priest and was

---

[112] See Uniform Anatomical Gift Act, National Conference of Commissioners on Uniform State Laws, s. 3 (1987).

[113] See Human Tissue Gift Act, RSA 2000, c. H-15; Human Tissue Gift Act, RSBC 1996, c. 211; Trillium Gift of Life Network Act, RSO 1990, c. H-20; Human Tissue Gift Act, SM 1987–8, c. 39; Human Tissue Act, SNB 1986, c. H-12; Human Tissue Donation Act, RSPEI 1988, c. H-12.1; Human Tissue Gift Act, RSY 1986, c. 89; Human Tissue Gift Act, RSNS 1989, c. 215; Human Tissue Act, RSS 1978, c. H-15; Human Tissue Act, RSN 1990, c. H-15; Human Tissue Act, RNWT 1988, c. H-6.

[114] Human Tissue Act 1961, c. 54, ss. 1–4 (Eng.). See also Human Tissue Bill: Explanatory Notes, available at www.publications.parliament.uk/pa/cm200304/cmbills/009/en/04009x–.htm, accessed on 5 May 2007.

[115] *Re Matheson (deceased)* [1958] 1 All ER 202, 1 WLR 246 (Liverpool Consistory Ct).

[116] *Hunter*, above n 2.

received into the Roman Catholic Church. However, there was uncertainty as to the deceased's mental state when he was baptized, and as a result a dispute arose among members of his family regarding the place of burial. One of the deceased's sons, who was named executor in his will, insisted that the deceased be brought to Protestant burial. The widow and her three other children claimed the body for purposes of burial, and asked to bury the deceased in the Roman Catholic cemetery.

Although the court devoted more than eight out of the nine pages of its decision to discussing the deceased's mental condition when he was baptized, and whether he had expressed an earlier intention to be admitted to the Roman Catholic Church, it was held that in principle the executor has a right to possess the body for burial so that the widow and her three children are prevented from interfering with that right. The fact that the court bothered to spend most of its analysis discussing the previous wishes of the deceased raises serious doubts regarding the validity of the no will rule to resolve the dispute at issue.

In *Abeziz* v. *Harris Estate*,[117] the mother of the deceased sought an injunction restraining the cremation of her son, who had expressly asked to be disposed of in that way. The mother, a strict Orthodox Jew, wanted to have her son buried instead. The deceased's executor nonetheless wanted to carry out the wishes of the decedent as expressed in his will. Although it was obvious from the facts of this case that the no will rule, if applied directly, would have provided a clear solution to this legal dispute, the court defined the question at issue as follows: 'Whether either of Ben's wills of May 15th and May 17th are valid'.[118] Indeed, the court's decision is mostly based on an inquiry into whether there was anything wrong with the circumstances in which the decedent's wills were executed, including whether they were made under undue influence. Validating the deceased's wills, the court concluded that 'there is nothing to prevent a valid executor from carrying out a testator's lawful wishes concerning the disposal of the testator's body'.[119] The action was therefore dismissed.

In *Saleh*,[120] which involved similar facts to those in *Abeziz*, the court upheld *in effect* the wishes of the deceased, who had asked to be cremated, despite the opposition of her father, a religious Muslim, who wanted to have her body buried instead. In contrast to *Abeziz*, the deceased in *Saleh* did not leave a will. However, the court was satisfied that prior to her death, the decedent had expressed a wish to be cremated.[121] It was ruled

---

[117] *Abeziz*, above n 34.   [118] *Ibid.*, at para. 2 (per Farley J).
[119] *Ibid.*, at para. 23 (per Farley J).   [120] *Saleh*, above n 2.   [121] *Ibid.*, at para. 7.

that 'the expressed wishes of a person as to the disposition of his or her body cannot be enforced in law'. Nevertheless, the court allowed the administrator of the estate to carry out those wishes, referring to the duty owed by the administrator to dispose of the body of the deceased.

A more explicit deviation from the 'no will' rule is demonstrated in the American jurisprudence. Case law in the USA specifically holds that the 'wishes of the decedent in respect of the disposition of his remains are paramount to all other considerations'.[122] Similar views are reflected in legislation. For example, the law in California provides that 'A right to control the disposition of the remains of the deceased person, the location and condition of interment, and arrangements of funeral goods and services to be provided, *unless other directions have been given by the decedent* ...' vests in next-of-kin.[123] This legal position, which will be discussed in detail in the next chapter, sharply contradicts one of the prominent outcomes of the no property rule, and joins the conclusion previously reached following the analysis of Canadian cases.

Undermining the 'no theft' rule In addition to challenging the no will rule, the proposition that a dead body is not subject to theft was also contested in Scotland in a criminal case that has not been overruled since its holding in 1945.[124] James Dewar, a secretary, resident manager and registrar of a crematorium, was convicted of the theft of two coffins and a large number of coffin lids. The coffins, with the lids fastened, were delivered to the crematorium, and were intended by those who sent them to be destroyed in the furnace along with the bodies they contained. Dewar was sentenced to three years' penal servitude. He appealed against conviction and sentence, and claimed, inter alia, that the property which he was convicted of stealing was abandoned and could not be stolen. Rejecting Dewar's appeal, Lord Moncrieff held that 'a body that has been consigned for burial ceases to be subject of theft only when interment is complete' and that the proper parallel to cremation would be that 'theft should be regarded as having ceased once the body has been enclosed in the furnace'.[125]

Following the *Dewar* decision, scholars argue that it is possible to steal a body which, instead of being buried, has been gifted to laboratory, placed

---

[122] *Eichner's Estate*, above n 40, at 573. See also *Holland* v. *Metalious* 105 NH 290, 198 A 2d 654, 656 (N.H. Sup. Ct 1964).

[123] California Health and Safety Code, Div. 7, Part 1, ch. 3, s. 7100 (West 2005) (my emphasis).

[124] *Dewar* v. *HM Advocate* (1945) SLT Rep. 114 (High Court of Justiciary of Scotland).

[125] *Ibid.*, at 116. Moreover, Lord Moncrieff emphasized that when a body awaits burial, it is most at risk of mishandling and misappropriation.

in a museum or even embalmed and kept in a glass.[126] This line of reasoning joins the recent decision in the matter of *Kelly and Lindsay*,[127] affirming the conviction in theft of body parts extracted from the deceased. Hence, in contrast to previous decisions on the matter which were heavily based on the no property rule, theft could now apply in respect not only to organs or specimens extracted from the dead (*Kelly and Lindsay*) but also to whole bodies.

In conclusion of this part of the chapter, it is more than evident that the historical background of the no property rule is suspicious. Moreover, the many exceptions to the rule as well as the refutation of its outcomes necessitate its re-examination. We must now turn to ask whether a proprietary interest in the body of the deceased *should* be legally recognized.

Should there be a proprietary interest in the body of the deceased?

The question of whether there should be a proprietary interest in the body of the deceased will be addressed through the discussion of four perspectives: the possible theoretical models by which one could gain property in the body of the deceased; the conceptual meaning of a proprietary interest in the body of the deceased as it is understood within the area of property law; the general justifications for the right to private property and their application to the post-mortem context; and the procedural advantages of acknowledging a proprietary interest in the body of the deceased.

Possible theoretical models for acquiring property in the body of the deceased

If one were to have a proprietary interest in the body of the deceased, one would need to accommodate such an interest in a recognizable theoretical model within property law. Four alternatives come to mind: transfer of property, property vesting in the state, abandonment and *res nullius*.

Transfer of property According to the first model, it is assumed that while alive the deceased had a proprietary interest in his or her body, and that upon death such an interest transfers to the executor, next-of-kin or

---

[126] Gerald H. Gordon, *The Criminal Law of Scotland*, Michael G. A. Christie ed., 3rd edn, vol. II (Edinburgh: W. Green, 2001) 27–8.
[127] *Kelly*, above n 82.

other third party. The transfer of property implies that the decedent leaves behind a will and/or has legal heirs.

However, a vast number of cases establish that the body of the deceased does not form part of the estate.[128] Indeed, case law dealing with sperm deposited by the deceased prior to his death suggests that sperm may be transferred by will for use by the deceased's partner, provided that the decedent was competent and not under undue influence when he executed the will.[129] However, these decisions, if they stand at all,[130] provide only for the mere possibility of making such a will, purporting no more than to validate the jurisdiction of probate courts to deal with such wills.[131]

The closer we get to decisions concerning the body of a human being, the clearer is the view that such a 'thing' cannot be part of the estate. Hence, with regard to frozen embryos, we learn from the *Rios* case, which involved two unimplanted embryos of a wealthy dead couple, that the embryos were not included in the Rios estate.[132] Hence, the possibility of transferring a property interest in the body of the deceased by will or by passing it on to legal heirs seems impracticable in light of existing legal doctrine.

Property vests in the state Upon her death, the person may cease to have a property interest in her own body (had she had any while alive), and/or become the property of the state as a residuary owner, namely a 'public' or 'collective' property.[133] Swain and Marusyk hold such a view but apply it only to body parts excised permanently from the human body, e.g. for the production of a cell line.[134] Guido Calabresi considers

---

[128] *Enos*, above n 35, at 69; *Snyder*, above n 59, at 328.

[129] *Deborah Hecht* v. *The Superior Court of Los Angeles County* 16 Cal. App. 4th 836, 850 (Ct App. Calif. 1993) [*Hecht*]; *Hall* v. *Fertility Institute of New Orleans* 647 So. 2d 1348 (Ct App. La. 1994).

[130] For a critique on *Hecht*, see James E. Bailey, 'An Analytical Framework for Resolving the Issues Raised by the Interaction Between Reproductive Technology and the Law of Inheritance' (1998) 47 *DePaul Law Review* 743, 748–56.

[131] *Hecht*, above n 129, at 850.

[132] A Californian trial court ruled that the pre-embryos were neither the heirs nor the property of the estate. Barry Brown, 'Reconciling Property Law with Advances in Reproductive Science' (1995) 6 *Stanford Law and Policy Review* 73, 77.

[133] Although the allocation and use of public property is predicated on an assessment of collective interests, the state possesses power and may enforce it to exclude others. This form of property should be distinguished from 'common property' where there is a shared right to use property and such right is conferred on each member of the public. Hence, in contrast to 'collective property', the state guarantees that each individual will *not* be excluded from the use or benefit of some thing.

[134] Margaret S. Swain and Randy W. Marusyk, 'An Alternative to Property Rights in Human Tissue' (1990) 20(5) *Hastings Center Report* 12–15, 13 [Swain and Marusyk].

the situations of military service and forced participation of soldiers in drugs experiments as other examples where the human body may become the property of the state.[135]

There are some circumstances where an object which is not owned by anyone (*bona vacantia*) becomes, by virtue of the prerogative of the state, a state property.[136] When a person dies intestate, subject to the rights of the decedent's spouse and relatives, his property may fall to the Crown. The same rule may apply to the assets of a dissolved company (subject to the right of shareholders and creditors) or those of a failed trust. In addition, the state may hold property in gold or silver found hidden in ground the owner of which is unknown, in wrecks found on shores or any tidal water, in whales and sturgeon taken from waters forming part of the state's dominion, in wild swans swimming in open and common waters, or in animals found wandering if their owner is unknown. Finally, discarded stolen property before it is recaptured by its true owner can also be claimed by the state.

Two rationales for granting property to the state are offered by Blackstone.[137] First, there is the need to avoid conflicts that would have resulted had the first occupier taken property in the object. Second, the conferral of a property interest to the state guarantees the provision of revenue.

In a significant proportion of cases, it is clear that the state claims property not only over that which *never* had a property holder or indeed *never* was subject to any property interest, but also with regard to that which *temporarily* lost its proprietary characteristic, usually due to the fact that it ceased to exist as a legal entity. In contrast to these cases, it is not unequivocal that the deceased had property in her body before death, and that even if she had such a proprietary interest, she would have lost it temporarily.

Nor do the rationales for collective property apply to the case of property in the body of the deceased. Regardless of its inability to explain all cases of state property,[138] the first rationale may appear to have a weak effect in the post-mortem context. In most cases, there exist no controversies pertaining to ownership of a dead body, and generally the body is disposed of without any conflicts or disagreements. The ban on

---

[135] Guido Calabresi, 'Do We Own Our Bodies?' (1991) 1 *Health-Matrix* 5–18, 7–8.

[136] Andrew Bell, 'Bona Vacantia' in Norman Palmer and Ewan McKendrick eds., *Interests in Goods*, 2nd edn (London: LLP Reference Publishing, 1998) 207–26, 207–10.

[137] 1 *Blackstone's Commentaries* (14th edn) 289.

[138] State ownership following the dissolution of a trust may not be explained by the suggested rationales. In such a situation, the property is already held by the trustees and no conflict over future property is anticipated.

commerciality in dead corpses and organs extracted from the dead is not in harmony with the second rationale either, as no state revenue is expected from these cases.

More generally, it will be argued that members of the human community have elementary interests which must not be sacrificed or overridden for the sake of collective welfare or other goals in society. One such interest is the interest in having one's body left alone unless proper authorization is given. This interest derives from the interest in the recognition of one's symbolic existence discussed in chapter 1. Another interest derived from one's membership in the human moral community is the interest in not being a means to others' well-being. These interests deserve strong protection when the person whose interests they are is incapable of defending herself against violation of the same, especially when she is already dead.

Abandonment Assuming that the deceased had property in her body prior to death, it will now be also assumed that upon death the deceased abandoned her property and that any person or legal entity taking first possession in the body gains title in it. The taking of possession in the object is essential to the transfer of title. The abandonment model is the third alternative way to conceptualize a proprietary interest in the body of the deceased. This model may be appealing since, in some instances, courts have suggested applying the abandonment model to body parts. In *Venner*,[139] the defendant was convicted of possession of marijuana. Venner swallowed a number of balloons containing hashish oil in order to avoid detection. He was admitted to hospital in a semi-conscious state following a hashish overdose as one of the balloons had burst in his body. X-rays revealed that he had a number of balloons in his stomach. After the police were informed, the supervisor of nurses was asked to call the police if any stools containing balloons were detected. Without any search warrant, the police took possession of a total of twenty-one balloons and a fragment of a broken balloon retrieved from Venner's stools in the hospital.

Venner brought an action to suppress the contraband found in his excreta as evidence. The question analysed in court was whether the hospital was entitled to take Venner's stools and examine them, and whether the police were entitled to receive them without a search and seizure warrant. The trial court denied Venner's motion, concluding that the warrantless seizure was reasonable and did not violate Venner's rights

---

[139] *Charles Venner v. State of Maryland* 30 Md. App. 599 (1976) [*Venner*].

118   Posthumous Interests

under the Fourth Amendment. Venner appealed to the Court of Special
Appeals and his appeal was denied. The court ruled that there was no
constitutional protection against a reasonable search and seizure and that
not everything was protected against unreasonable searches and seizures.
Specifically, it was held that the Fourth Amendment did not protect
against police seizure of abandoned property.[140] The court held that
the contraband was not taken from Venner's body, and there was no
intrusion of the body. Rather, the balloons and their contents were
abandoned by Venner:

It could not be said that a person has no property right in wastes or other materials
which were once a part of or contained within his body, but which normally are
discarded after their separation from the body. It is not unknown for a person to
assert a continuing right of ownership, dominion, or control, for good reasons or
for no reason, over such things as excrement, fluid waste, secretions, hair, finger-
nails, toenails, blood, and organs or other parts of the body, whether their
separation from the body is intentional, accidental, or merely the result of normal
body functions. But it is all but universal human custom and human experience
that such things are discarded – in a legal sense, abandoned by the person from
whom they emanate, either 'on the spot', or, if social delicacy requires it, at a
place, or in a manner designed to cause the least offence to others. By the force of
social custom, we hold that when a person does nothing and says nothing to
indicate an intent to assert his right of ownership, possession, or control over such
material, the only rational inference is that he intends to abandon the material.[141]

Since Venner did not attempt to exercise any right of possession or
control over the balloons the court held that they were abandoned by
him, thereby denying Venner's appeal.[142]

The *Venner* decision relates to body waste that may be considered as
being abandoned by Venner. It does not relate to the abandonment of
the body *as a whole* and is inapplicable to other situations in which body
parts are removed for different purposes, e.g. transplantation or medical
research.[143] As Bernard Dickens contends, when a person makes clear
her intention that a body part be transplanted into a designated recipient,
that person asserts a right of ownership and control *until the transplantation takes place*, even though possession may pass to others in the
interim.[144] Even if one does not hold that the donor maintains her
property interest in the excised body part throughout the transplantation

---

[140] *Ibid.*, at 617.   [141] *Ibid.*, at 626–7 (per Judge Powers).
[142] This decision was affirmed by the Court of Appeals of Maryland: 279 Md. 47 (1977).
[143] *John Moore* v. *The Regents of the University of California* et al. 793 P 2d 479, 51 Cal. 3d
120, 153 (Sup. Ct Calif. 1990) [*Moore*].
[144] Bernard M. Dickens, 'Living Tissue and Organ Donors and Property Law: More on
Moore' (1992) 8 *Journal of Contemporary Health Law and Policy* 73–93, 90 [Dickens,
'More on *Moore*'].

process, it still follows from this view that the donor does not abandon her property interest in the part intended for transplantation.[145]

Another case where the abandonment model was raised was in the matter of Moore. John Moore had a condition known as hairy-cell leukemia. A necessary component of his treatment included the removal of his spleen. Since Moore's cells were unique, his spleen was taken to a separate research unit where it was stored and used for research. The medical team developed a cell-line from Moore's cells capable of producing pharmaceutical products of enormous therapeutic and commercial value, estimated to be worth $3 billion. The health team patented the cell-line along with the methods of producing many products therefrom. Additionally, they entered into a series of commercial agreements for rights to the cell-line with pharmaceutical companies, which resulted in payment of hundred of thousands of dollars to the team. Without informing Moore of their real purposes, the medical team continued to monitor his body and extract blood, blood serum, skin, bone marrow aspirate and sperm for almost seven years after the removal of his spleen.

When he found out about the health team's actions, Moore sued the team for damages and declaratory relief, alleging thirteen causes of actions, one of which was conversion. Moore argued that his tissues and all other bodily products were his tangible personal property and that the activities of the medical team constituted a substantial interference with his possession and right thereof. Accordingly, the cell-line and products were obtained exclusively through his property and he alleged damages, including lost profits and punitive damages. Moore's action was denied in the trial court and he appealed. The Court of Appeals of California overruled the lower decision and held in favour of Moore.[146]

At the Supreme Court, Justice Broussard held that Moore had abandoned any interest in the removed organ and was not entitled to demand compensation if it should later be discovered that the organ or cells had some unanticipated value.[147] He explained that the majority opinion that did not acknowledge Moore's claim of conversion 'cannot rest on the broad proposition that a removed body part is not property, but rather rests on the proposition that a *patient* retains no ownership interest in a body part since the body part has been removed from his body'. The court feared that acknowledging property interests in the excised cells would

---

[145] See Nuffield Council on Bioethics Working Party (1995) *Human Tissue: Ethical and Legal Issues* para. 9.14.

[146] *John Moore* v. *The Regents of the University of California* et al., 215 Cal. App. 3d 709, 249 Cal. Rptr 494 (Ct App. Calif. 1988).

[147] *Moore*, above n 143.

compromise the benefits of biomedical research. Nevertheless, the majority stated that it did not purport to hold that excised cells can never be property for any purpose whatsoever. Further to his conclusion, Justice Broussard ruled that if another drug company had stolen all Moore's cells in question and used them for its own benefit, there would be no question, even for the majority, that an action of conversion should lie against the thief. Nevertheless, such an action would be brought by the clinic, and not by Moore.[148]

However, Moore's cell-line (MO) was physically different from Moore's original cells which were removed by the doctors due to the health team expertise. To argue that Moore might have abandoned his cells and left them to be owned by the team ignores this substantial fact. Moreover, Justice Broussard's decision should be read in light of two California Health and Safety Code provisions concerning the disposal of anatomical waste following scientific use, which were present in court. These provisions stated that 'recognizable anatomical parts, human tissues, anatomical human remains, or infectious waste following conclusion of scientific use shall be disposed of by interment, incineration, or any other method determined by the state department [of health services] to protect public health and safety'.[149] Justice Broussard's ruling may not apply to legal systems where such legislation is missing. In addition, and as illuminated by Bernard Dickens, Justice Broussard's decision relates to cells subject to biotechnological processes when traceability of cells is no longer convenient.[150] It may be difficult to apply this decision to other cases where traceability of tissues or organs can be easily made.

Furthermore, there are general obstacles to upholding *Venner* and *Moore*'s observations on the abandonment model. First, it is agreed that abandonment of a proprietary interest has to be *directed* and not just assumed. Indeed, as emphasized by the Kentucky Court of Appeals[151] and the majority opinion in *Moore*, the essential element of abandonment is the intent to abandon.[152] In the *Venner* and *Moore* cases not only was there no such intention, but one can perfectly well argue for the opposite position: had Venner known that his excreta would be searched, or had Moore known that his cells would be used to produce a cell-line worth more than $3 billion, they would have expressed specific intent *not* to abandon their property interests in their body parts/materials. If this rule

[148] *Ibid.*, at 153–4.
[149] California Health and Safety Code s. 7054.4 (West. Supp. 1992).
[150] Dickens, 'More on *Moore*', above n 144, at 92.
[151] *Browning* v. *Norton Children's Hospital* (1974) 504 SW 2d 713 (Ct App. Ky.).
[152] *Moore*, above n 143, at 510. See also Price, 'Cosmos', above n 63, at 32 and Matthews, 'Man of Property', above n 89, at 267.

is applied to the post-mortem context, the deceased would have to mark the abandonment of her proprietary interests in her body by way of communication to others so that the new owner would hold title in it. This seems impracticable if the body is not intended for a specific purpose like transplantation, research or medical education. Finally, and more generally, much doubt surrounds the question of whether – in principle – the theory of abandonment can be extended to body parts, forming part of one's self and identity. At least in the English[153] and Australian law,[154] such theory looks inappropriate.

Res nullius The body of the deceased can be regarded as the property of no one, capable of being titled by the first occupier. An example of such a property model would be the vesting of property in wild animals.[155] The idea behind giving property to the first occupier is one of desert. The law rewards the occupier by granting her interests over that which is capable of being proprietized.

In the literature, there is an attempt to apply the theory of *res nullius* to body parts. Swain and Marusyk argue that body parts excised temporarily from the deceased, for example for transplantation, are the property of no one, and whoever possesses them until the transplantation process is complete holds them in trust ('trust *res nullius*') for the recipient.[156] However, the theory of *res nullius* is heavily criticized,[157] and its application to cases concerning the body of the deceased seems remote.

As a matter of principle, it is difficult to conceive that there could be external objects for which there are no property holders, not even the state or any other body representing collective interests. Specifically, such an objection was held in a case dealing with a dead body where the court established that: 'A man cannot relinquish the property he hath to his goods, *unless they be vested in another.*'[158] This line of ruling was affirmed in more recent cases.[159]

---

[153] Grubb, above n 103, at 305; Pawlowski, above n 96, at 24.
[154] See the example brought by Magnusson of an Australian case where the woman's womb was returned to her at her request following hysterectomy. Robert S. Magnusson, 'Proprietary Rights in Human Tissue' in Norman Palmer and Ewan McKendrick eds., *Interests in Goods*, 2nd edn (London: LLP Reference Publishing, 1998) 52.
[155] Interestingly, if an animal escapes and has no intention to return (*animus revertendi*), the title is lost, whereas if it is a domestic animal the title in it is absolute as it is for other chattels: Bruce Ziff, *Principles of Property Law*, 3rd edn (Scarborough: Carswell, 2000) 122 [Ziff].
[156] Swain and Marusyk, above n 134, at 13.   [157] Matthews, above n 3, at 263.
[158] *Haynes*, above n 1, at 1389.
[159] *Re Wells, Swinburne v. Howard* [1933] 1 Ch. 29, 56 (CA).

Moreover, from a legal perspective there is always someone who owes the duty to dispose of the body of the deceased, and as a consequence has a possessory and custodial interest in the body. The corpse is not free to be titled. One who argues for *res nullius* in a corpse has to acknowledge either that there is no duty to dispose of the body or that there is such duty but no possessory interest following therefrom. This, I argue, will require a substantial revision of the legal position.

Aside from the general difficulty inherent in this model, it follows from the theory of *res nullius* that the identity of the property holder will be arbitrarily determined according to place of death. If a person dies on the street, her finder will acquire property in the body, whereas if she dies at hospital, the first staff member who approaches her will have title in it. If one were to confer proprietary interest in the human body, one would expect to have some substantial criteria for determining the identity of the property holder rather than rely on coincidence or mere luck.

The discussion thus far results in the conclusion that there is no existing model to conceptualize a proprietary interest in the body of the deceased. Perhaps one can establish the understanding of such an interest through the more general concept of property, to the discussion of which I shall now turn.

The conceptual meaning of a proprietary interest in the body of the deceased

This section will examine whether, as a conceptual matter, rights or interests pertaining to the human body in general and the human corpse specifically can be classified as property. This question will be analysed in two stages. First, the idea of property will be subdivided into its different conceptions.[160] Second, the application of each conception to the human corpse will be examined.

One of the difficulties concerning the question of whether there exists any proprietary interest in the body of the deceased involves the more general query regarding the nature of a proprietary interest. It is commonly accepted that the right to property is a bundle of rights/interests, so that property constitutes a legal complex of various normative relations among people with respect to an object.[161] Honore has provided an

---

[160] The methodology used in the following section is inspired by the distinction between concept and conceptions, discussed in Jeremy Waldron, *The Right to Private Property* (Oxford: Clarendon Press, 1988) 51–2 [Waldron].

[161] *Ruckelshaus* v. *Monsanto Co.* 467 US 986, 1003 (1984). For a critique on this view, see J. E. Penner, 'The "Bundle of Rights" Picture of Property' (1996) 43 *UCLA Law Review* 712–820.

exhaustive list of rights/interests comprising the concept of property.[162] There is a consensus that not all components embraced by the concept of property need be present so that a property right/interest is constituted. The next sections will discuss five such components: ownership, possession, use and management, disposal, and transferability and the right to enjoy fruits.

Ownership The right to ownership represents the fullest interest of which a property right may consist. If one legally owns an object, one has an interest the characterization of which is proprietary. However, not every right to property entails ownership. Two questions need to be asked in our context. First, is it possible to own one's own body? By addressing this question, I will assume that a person is the composite of both her body and her mental state, the latter of which is capable in principle of having rights, including property rights. Second, is it possible to own the body of another (dead or alive)?

In order to answer the above questions, I wish to endorse J. E. Penner's separability thesis, which I find highly intuitive. This theory can be expressed as follows: 'only those "things" in the world which are contingently associated with any particular owner may be objects of property; as a function of the nature of this contingency, in theory nothing of normative consequence beyond the fact that the ownership has changed occurs when an object of property is alienated to another'.[163] Penner thus argues that 'inner' characteristics like talents, personalities, eyesight or friendships cannot be regarded as property not because we cannot exploit them or exclude others from them, but because it is difficult to treat these things as separable from us. Hence, it is argued that a necessary criterion of treating something as property subject to ownership is that it is only contingently ours, and that it is possible to show why this thing is ours and not someone else's given that someone else may have property in it.[164] Under this view, to be conceived of as an object of property, a thing must first be considered as separable and distinct from any person who may hold it, and is for that reason rightly regarded as alienable.

Another element in Penner's argument relates to the impersonal relationship between the property holder and the object owned. In order to

---

[162] A. M. Honore, 'Ownership' in A. G. Guest ed., *Oxford Essays in Jurisprudence* (Oxford: Clarendon Press, 1961) 107, at 113 [Honore]. The list includes the right to possess, use, manage, receive income, the right to capital, the right to security, the rights or incidents of transmissibility, the absence of term, the prohibition of harmful use, liability to execution and a residuary right over an object.

[163] J. E. Penner, *The Idea of Property* (Oxford: Clarendon, 1997) 111 [Penner].

[164] *Ibid.*, at 112.

better understand this relationship, we need to ask the following question: Does a different person who takes on the relationship to the thing stand in essentially the same position as the first person? If we give an affirmative answer to this question, the object at issue is a good candidate for property. Can we ask the same question while referring to the relationship between the person and her body? Penner's discussion of the relation one has to one's body provides powerful answers.[165] He argues that both relations involve exclusive use. One has the right to determine exclusively the use of one's body just as one is absolutely free to determine how to utilize that with regard to which one has property.[166]

However, these two relations vary in that an owner is not necessarily connected to, but is separable from, the things he or she holds as property. My body, on the other hand, is not contingently related to me. It is possible to argue that if it was not for my body, it was not for me, for I am me (partly) because of my body.[167] The body, in this regard, constitutes me so that I would have been another person had I had a different body, and that another person who had my body would not have been me. This argument does not necessarily contradict the belief that the conditions for personal identity are psychological, since such a belief merely aims to explore the circumstances by which we should determine whether the *same* person exists in two discrete moments in time. The proposition for personal identity does not expound the criteria for constituting one's self in general. Thus, one can perfectly hold that one of the parameters for constituting a person's identity and self is her body, and yet argue that this parameter is not sufficient to establish the continual existence of a person over time. Moreover, the proprietary relationship dictates the complete control of the owner over the thing and the corresponding absence of any control of the thing over the owner. This entails the ability of the owner to dispose of his or her property or otherwise to alienate it. These capacities are absent in the relation between a person and his or her body.

Not only is Penner's separability thesis grounded in good intuition, but it can also explain many judicial decisions regarding ownership in the human body and body parts. For example, Penner's thesis can help

---

[165] *Ibid.*, at 121.
[166] This is of course subject to fundamental restrictions concerning public safety and accepted moral norms.
[167] Compare Courtney Campbell, who argues that just as one cannot be free to alienate one's own freedom so it is impossible to alienate one's body without doing the same to the person. Courtney S. Campbell, 'Body, Self, and the Property Paradigm' (1992) 22(5) *Hastings Center Report* 34–42, 40.

explain why it is possible to regard body parts[168] and bodily products such as hair,[169] blood[170] and urine[171] as property,[172] and why it is inconceivable to have property over our *whole* body.[173] This is why Margaret Radin argues that body parts not separated from the person should not be considered as objects of rights, but as participating *with* the person herself.[174] Penner's theory can also explain why courts appealed to the theory of informed consent when medical professionals wanted to retrieve an object kept *inside* the body of a patient, regarding its warrantless search and seizure as violating the right to be secure in one's own person,[175] while they upheld the search and possession of bodily waste/products such as saliva[176] or excreta[177] without consent. The application of the separability thesis to the human body also has psychological power. As Philippe Ducor rightly argues, the whole human body retains the shape of the human person for a long time and for this reason it inspires more intuitive and spontaneous respect than any other human material separated from it.[178]

If I did not have property over my body while alive, I could not transfer it to another after my death. However, I can still have property over my body after my death without having it transferred. There is, however, a dramatic difference between having property rights in one's body and being the property of another,[179] as is most evident from the social and legal resistance to slavery but also from the legal deterrence from

---

[168] *Kelly*, above n 82. For the distinction between tissues and organs, see Dickens, 'More on *Moore*', above n 144, at 80–1.

[169] *R* v. *Herbert* [1961] 25 JCL 163 (Wallington magistrates), discussed in Matthews, above n 3, at 224–5. Hair could also have commercial value in making wigs or sentimental or exhibitional value like the locks of Winston Churchill's hair, cut when he was a child and exhibited at Blenheim Palace. *Ibid.*, at 225.

[170] *R* v. *Rothery* [1976] Crim. LR 691 (CA); *Green* v. *Commissioner* 74 TC 1229 (Federal Tax Ct 1980).

[171] *R* v. *Welsh* [1974] RTR 478 (CA).

[172] Compare Dickens, who calls 'to consider the human source as having an inchoate right of property in materials *issuing from his body*'. Bernard M. Dickens, 'The Control of Living Body Materials' (1977) 27 *University of Toronto Law Journal* 142, 183 (my emphasis).

[173] Penner compares this situation to the impossibility of holding a debt against oneself. The one person who cannot hold my legal obligation to pay him a certain sum is *me*. Penner, above n 163, at 125. But compare Dickens, who argues that 'it may seem curious to conclude that an organ from a dead body is legal property when the body itself is not': Dickens, 'Legal and Judicial Aspects', above n 6, at 346.

[174] Margaret J. Radin, 'Property and Personhood' (1982) 34 *Stanford Law Review* 957, 966 [Radin, 'Personhood'].

[175] *Winston* v. *Lee* 470 US 753 (Va. 1985).

[176] *In re Grand Jury Proceedings Involving Vickers* 38 F Supp. 2d 159 (DNH 1998).

[177] *Venner*, above n 139.   [178] Ducor, above n 110, at 227.

[179] *Moore*, above n 143, at 504.

regarding the child as her parent's property, the woman as her husband's asset or even the frozen unimplanted embryo as the property of its biological contributors.[180] I argue that ownership over the body of another has far-reaching implications for the status of a person as an individual, her personality, and the way her life story is being told by others, namely her symbolic existence. To begin with, subjecting a person to being the property of others exploits the fact that she is dead – a situation of the utmost vulnerability. Moreover, it treats her as a mere thing, thereby stripping her humanity. It alters her characterization from a subject holding interests to a mere object with no interests at all. It allows one to ignore the substance of the life she had and the person she was. It thus diminishes her symbolic existence, turning 'her' into 'their'. The idea of owning the whole body of the deceased is thus alien to our understanding of, and the way we perceive, each other.

Possession Although ownership may be the 'full-blooded' property right, possession is the foundation upon which the whole structure of ownership lies.[181] The right to possession makes an interest become 'property' by transforming its relationship with the object into an *in rem* one. To use Carol Rose's language, through the act of possession the holder communicates a text in the form of 'This Is Mine.' This text is a property claim to the world, guaranteed by the exclusion of others from using (and otherwise interfering with) the object. Thus, the idea of exclusion of others, usually regarded as the 'core' element of the bundle of property rights,[182] is inherent in the right to possession. The right to possession has two components: an intention to possess (*animus possidendi*) and physical control (*factum*). The second element is more important than the first[183] for two reasons. The physical act shows to the world a clear act by which property is acquired, and the actual occupation of the object is rewarded by the grant of a property right.[184] When either intention or physical control is absent, a legal fiction described as 'constructive possession' is created. Moreover, the degree of possession that the law will demand will depend on the function that the concept of possession aims to achieve.[185]

[180] Empirical support for such an argument can be found in Russell W. Belk, 'Possessions and the Extended Self' (1988) 15 *Journal of Consumer Research* 139–68, especially 156–7.

[181] Carol Rose, 'Possession as the Origin of Property' (1985) 52 *University of Chicago Law Review* 73 [Rose].

[182] *International News Services* v. *Associated Press* 248 US 215, 250 (1918).

[183] *Pierson* v. *Post* 3 Caines Reports 175 (N.Y. Sup. Ct 1805).   [184] Rose, above n 181.

[185] Ziff, above n 155, at 120–1.

When considered in the post-mortem context, the practicability of the right to possession appears suspicious. If a right to possession of the body of the deceased is related to the legal duty to dispose of the body,[186] then no genuine intention may be qualified. A problem may also occur with regard to the requirement of physical control. In most cases, the actual possession of the body is lacking and next-of-kin, executors or administrators do not have real control over the body of the deceased, which usually lies in a hospital, crematorium or funeral home awaiting disposal. Under these latter circumstances, the body is physically controlled by someone else to whom the law does not wish to grant any proprietary interests, nor is this person or legal entity under any duty to dispose of the body.

Use and management The right to use refers to the owner's personal use and enjoyment of the thing owned.[187] Correlative to the right to use is the disability of others regarding such use. Third parties cannot do anything that represents a rightful use of the thing which will make the property holder lose her right to use it. The right to use is connected to another right mentioned by Honore, namely the right to manage. Under the latter, the property holder has a right to decide, and the legal power to exercise, how and by whom the thing owned should be used.

When applied to the post-mortem context, any proprietary interest deriving from the duty to dispose of the body may infer a right to use and manage the body in respect of this duty only. On the other hand, a proprietary interest in the body of the deceased may also include use of the body for therapeutic, educational or research purposes. In order to use the body for these objectives, the proprietary interest in the body of the deceased, if it exists, must rely on a different conceptual theory than the one extensively argued for in case law, namely the duty to dispose of the corpse.

Disposal The right to dispose of the object over which there exists a proprietary interest reflects the liberty of the property holder to use that object up to its complete and irreversible loss or disposal. It is not forbidden to destroy our body, nor do suicide or self-mutilation constitute criminal offences.[188] On the other hand, assisted suicide is

---

[186] See the court's unwillingness to extend the right to possess the body of the deceased to other situations, such as organ donation (*Robert Colavito v. NY Organ Donor Network Inc.* et al., 356 F Supp. 2d 237, 244 (2005)), or possession of the body for evidentiary purposes (*Dobson*, above n 95).

[187] Honore, above n 162, at 116.

[188] However, this may not necessarily be based on the idea supporting self-ownership. As Munzer writes, in ordinary property-destruction cases the owner of the property

prohibited and punishable, as is any other act of killing or battery per-formed with the consent of the victim. The distinction between acts of self-disposal and acts of disposing of the other may be based on the separability thesis discussed above. It follows that while a person may have a recognized interest in disposing of her body (including after death), she may not have similar interest with regard to the disposal of the body of another, not even a dead one.

Transferability and the right to enjoy fruits A proprietary interest should usually be transferable to others, although both the literature and legal decisions suggest that transferability may not always form part of the bundle of property rights.[189] A well-established legal mechanism allows the donation of bodies for medical education or research, and organ donations from the dead are common. From this perspective it may be assumed that there exist legal mechanisms to provide for the transfer of interests pertaining to the body of the deceased to others in so far as such transfer accords with the purposes of those legal mechanisms.[190]

In addition to the right to transfer, the property holder may have a right to enjoy the fruits of her property, which includes the right to receive benefits from the use and possession of the property or other profits derived from its alienability (either temporary or permanent). Although the transfer of property is generally commercial, it is not necessarily so.[191]

When applied to the human body, the argument for a right to property may have contrasting effects. On the one hand, the property regime may provide a legal means to protect body parts from becoming objects of commerce and exploitation. On the other hand, a system of property can destroy the economic incentive to conduct medical research, thereby

continues to exist and be benefited or harmed after he destroys his property, whereas in suicide the owner *is* his destroyed property. Stephen R. Munzer, *A Theory of Property* (New York: Cambridge University Press, 1990) 54 (note 21). Of course, such criticism can be challenged if one believes that the interest in the body survives the death of the person and is held by the Human Subject.

[189] *The Queen* v. *Toohey* (1982) 158 CLR 327, 342 (Aust. HC); *Dorman* v. *Rodgers* 148 CLR 365, 374 (Aust. HC); Susan Rose-Ackerman, 'Inalienability and the Theory of Property Rights' (1985) 85 *Columbia Law Review* 931–69; Michelle B. Bray, 'Personalizing Personality: Toward a Property Right in Human Bodies' (1990) 69 *Texas Law Review* 209–44 [Bray].

[190] But see Scarmon, who argues that 'although provisions of UAGA have been cited as statutory evidence for the recognition of property rights, the primary goal of the act was to encourage voluntarism by standardising and facilitating organ donation procedures among the states': Michael H. Scarmon, '*Brotherton* v. *Cleveland*: Property Rights in the Human Body – Are the Goods Interred with Their Bones?' (1992) 37 *South Dakota Law Review* 429–49, 444.

[191] Margaret J. Radin, 'Market-Inalienability' (1987) 100(8) *Harvard Law Review* 1849–1937. See also *Andrus* v. *Allard* 444 US 51 (1979); Bray, above n 189, advocating for a market-inalienable property right in the body.

decreasing the monetary significance of biotechnology in general and the value of body parts specifically.[192] Despite extensive literature[193] on the idea of commerciality in the body, the legal position is that: 'It is universally recognized that there is no property in a dead body in a commercial or material sense.'[194] The ban on receiving financial gain from organs used for transplantation is explicit in many statutes[195] and policy statements.[196] The supply of blood is considered a service,[197] and many states in the USA have enacted laws providing immunity to blood banks and healthcare providers from the sale of human blood or its components.[198] In most countries, surrogate motherhood is legally prohibited, especially if it is done for profit.[199] With regard to the dead body, it is also clear that it 'is not commercially transferable, has no monetary value, and therefore, is not property'.[200]

---

[192] *Moore*, above n 143, at 515 and 495 respectively.
[193] See e.g. Danielle Wagner, 'Comment: Property Rights in the Human Body: The Commercialization of Organ Transplantation and Biotechnology' (1995) 33 *Duquesne Law Review* 931.
[194] *Dougherty* v. *Mercantile Safe-Deposit & Trust Co.* 387 A 2d 244, 246 (1978).
[195] See e.g. National Organ Transplant Act, 42 USC s. 274(e) (1994); Uniform Anatomical Gift Act 1968, 8 AULA 63 (1993) s. 10(a); Human Organ Transplants Act 1989 (UK).
[196] Law Reform Commission of Canada, *Procurement and Transfer of Human Tissues and Organs*, working paper 66 (Ministry of Supply and Services, 1992) 184–7 (Recommendation 11) [Law Reform Commission]. The Commission nevertheless did not rule out the possibility of commerciality following research on human bodies or body parts. The Commission recommended that a patient be informed in advance where the development of such research might provide commercial interest, leaving the decision of whether or not to pursue the research to the patient. However, it did not comment on the situation where, having informed the patient, the research provides substantial profit, and more specifically whether this profit 'belongs' to the researcher, the patient or both. See the Commission's Recommendation 13, at 188–9. See also Council of Europe, Convention on Human Rights and Biomedicine (1997), Article 21.
[197] *United Blood Services* v. *Quintana* 827 P 2d 509 (Sup. Ct Colo. 1992) [*United Blood Services*]; *John Gibson* et al. v. *The Methodist Hospital* et al. 822 SW 2d 95 (Ct App. Tex. 1991), rehearing granted, application for writ of error denied, 1992 WL 140842 (Tex.). See also the applicable legislation in Texas: Texas Business and Commerce Code (2007) s. 2.316(e).
[198] Colorado Revised Statutes s. 13-22-104 (Colo. 2007 West). The Colorado provision was enacted to reverse a previous decision which held that the supply of blood can be considered as a sale of goods subject to a strict liability claim. *Belle Bonfils Memorial Blood Bank* v. *Hansen* 665 P 2d 118 (Colo. 1983). For a similar statute in Texas, see Civil Practice and Remedies Code s. 77.003 (Tex. 2005 West). These statutes equate a blood bank's duty of care with the use of 'available and proven scientific safeguards' in acquiring, preparing or transferring human blood or its components for use in medical treatment. *United Blood Services*, above n 197, at 523.
[199] Assisted Human Reproductive Act 2004, c. 2, s. 6(1) (Can.); *A* v. *C* [1985] FLR 445. For a comparative analysis of this subject, see Rachel Cook, Shelley D. Sclater and Felicity Kaganas eds., *Surrogate Motherhood: International Perspectives* (Oxford: Hart Publishing, 2003).
[200] *Culpepper* v. *Pearl St Building Inc.* 877, 880 P 2d 75 (Colo. 1978).

Despite these strong legal statements contra commerce, reference to body parts, tissues and specimens increasingly evokes the language of commerce. Body 'components' are kept in banks, they are the source of financial investment and objects of insurance, and above all they are patented.[201] Additionally, many suggestions have been proposed to commercialize the giving of organs for transplantation through, for example, tax deductions to donors or payments made to the donor in her life or to her relatives or estate after death.[202] Support for commerciality in body parts is also found among groups that use human tissues, fluids and cells for research or development.[203]

The recent trend toward commerce in the body may reflect a change in the moral and social attitudes toward the question of whether the human body should be subject to property. Evidently, the human body's value has been increased dramatically due to advances in medical technologies and scientific knowledge in recent years. Mason and Laurie mention five dimensions of such a phenomenon: public health importance with regard to post-mortem examination; the medical value of human tissues taken from the body; the value of important biotechnological inventions using human material; a broader commercial value of organs and tissues; and an ethical value of the human body more generally.[204] It may be that in a few years the legal position opposing commerce will be reversed. Until then, it is right to conclude that the body of the deceased is not capable of being transferred in a commercial way.

To sum up, it is difficult to conceptualize the application of the right to ownership and the right to possession in the body of the deceased.[205] Moreover, when a proprietary interest is related to the duty to dispose of the body, further difficulties arise with respect to the right to use and manage the corpse. Less clear is the legal position concerning the

---

[201] In *Onyeanusi* v. *Pan Am*. 952 F 2d 788 (3d Cir. 1992) the court held that the plaintiff's deceased mother qualified as 'goods' under the Warsaw Convention so that the plaintiff's delay in giving proper notice precluded him from arguing against the defendant's delay in delivering the corpse according to its destination. See also *US* v. *Garber* 607 F 2d 92, 97 (1979).

[202] See e.g. Andrew C. MacDonald, 'Organ Donation: The Time Has Come to Refocus the Ethical Spotlight' (1997) 8(1) *Stanford Law and Policy Review* 177–84; L. R. Cohen, 'Increasing the Supply of Transplant Organs: The Virtues of a Future Market' (1989) 58 *George Washington Law Review* 1–51; R. D. Blair and D. L. Kaserman 'The Economics and Ethics of Alternative Cadaveric Organ Procurement Policies' (1991) 8 *Yale Journal of Regulation* 403–52.

[203] Lori B. Andrews, 'My Body My Property' (1986) 16(5) *Hastings Center Report* 28–38, 31.

[204] Mason and Laurie, above n 26, at 712.

[205] Compare Erik S. Jaffe, 'She's Got Bette Davis['s] Eyes: Assessing the Nonconsensual Removal of Cadaver Organs Under the Takings and Due Process Clauses' (1990) 90 *Columbia Law Review* 528–74.

requirement of transferability. Existing legal mechanisms for donating the body and its organs after death may indicate that the requirement to transfer the 'property' may be fulfilled. The ban on commerciality in the body and body parts, although heavily criticized in recent years, joins the previous conclusions of this chapter, according to which the basic elements of a right to property may not apply to the body of the deceased.

General rationales for a proprietary interest

This section will analyse the justifications for and the purposes of having a right/interest to private property, and will examine the question of whether the legal rules which would have acknowledged a proprietary interest in the body of the deceased support these justifications or aim to achieve such purposes.

Property as a natural right The idea of private property builds on the concept of 'natural rights', that is rights that are held to be 'natural' in virtue of their historical or moral precedence over legal rights.[206] The idea of property as a natural right, developed by John Locke, is that, when left alone, individuals will gain control over natural resources in a variety of ways, some of which create relationships between the individual and the resources she controls.

Under the Lockean view, it is the person's mix of labour of his own person with common resources that justifies the imposition of duties to respect his private property in them. Moreover, the relationships between the property holder and the natural resources are so important from moral and religious perspectives that they impose duties on others to refrain from interfering with these resources. Corresponding to these duties are natural rights to the exclusive control of those resources, namely natural rights of property.[207] These rights are 'natural' as opposed to 'positive' rights, and their validity does not derive from existing laws. Natural rights partly derive from the nature of human beings. Everyone thus is entitled *but not necessarily obliged* to hold natural rights, depending on the relationship between the individual and the resource.

It is difficult to conceptualize property in the human body based on religious tenets. According to the Judaeo-Christian tradition, the human body is the property of God and any proprietary relationship between the person and her body is thus alien to such line of thinking. On the other hand, it may be possible to validate this relationship on moral grounds. If

---

[206] Alan Ryan, *Property* (Milton Keynes: Open University Press, 1987) 62.
[207] Waldron, above n 160, at 19.

the body represents one's self and is a means by which one communicates to the world, one's relationship with it must receive full moral and legal protection. It may be that the characterization of such relationship as 'property' will provide the fullest protection, but it may also be that means other than property may provide such relationship with the same moral and legal protection.

Property as the advancement of autonomy and freedom Autonomy and the ability to control are at the core of the idea of property. Having a right to property enables one to control some of the resources necessary to fulfil one's own agency. A variation of this argument holds that having property enables one to participate in democracy, to exercise one's freedom of speech, and more generally to fulfil one's own freedom. Property is connected to freedom in two respects. The more property one has, the more choices one can make in and concerning one's life. Moreover, the more property one holds, the less one is reliant on and subordinated to the state.[208] Hence, property draws a boundary between public and private power, thereby providing the owner with greater freedom. The owner may use her property on a whim or capriciously, whereas the state will have to justify its actions purporting to interfere with the owner's property.[209]

To regard property as a means to advance autonomy and freedom assumes that the holding of property necessitates the taking of actions and performing of tasks essential to one's own agency. Under this rationale, a proprietary interest with regard to one's own body may be justified even when applied to the treatment of one's body after death through the direction of wills or advance directives. However, it does not follow that one may have the same interest in the body of another, whether dead or alive. In the post-mortem context, it is a dubious argument that a proprietary interest in the body of the deceased fulfils the freedom and autonomy of next-of-kin, executor or the hospital where the body lies.

Property as constituting personality The notion of property can be regarded as an extension of the idea of a person. Having property enriches some of the person's virtues and characteristics such as responsibility, prudence and a sense of independence. It provides her with a legitimate and legally protected forum to develop and manifest her personal identity and the full expression of her character. More profoundly, the need to

---

[208] Adam Smith, *An Inquiry into the Nature and Causes of the Wealth of Nations*, E. Cannan ed. (New York: Modern Library, 1937) 651.
[209] C. A. Reich, 'The New Property' (1964) 73 *Yale Law Journal* 733, 771.

acquire or possess external objects is a basic need and an innate human quality. Freud, for example, associated this need with early childhood practices of anal retention. The child's longing for possessions such as a security blanket or a pet arises from an uncensored impulse, whether for comfort, reassurance of its expression of aggressive power, or an intuition to possess.[210]

The rationale for property as personhood has been adopted by many great thinkers. Hegel, for example, believed that having property, which requires the projecting of one's will and its subordination over an external object, enables one to shift from being an abstract entity to a sophisticated moral and political person distinct from others. In section 44 of his *Philosophy of Right*, Hegel wrote: 'A person has as his substantive end the right of putting his will into any and every thing and thereby making it his, because it has no such end in itself and derives its destiny and soul from his will. This is the absolute right of appropriation which a man has over all "things."'[211] Hegel believed that imposing one's personality over the external world, including *one's body*, enables transformation of the relationship from *ad personam* to *ad rem*.[212]

Margaret Radin, who follows Hegel's thesis, also argues that 'to achieve proper self-development – to be a person – an individual needs some control over resources in the external environment'.[213] Radin brings to attention the way we treat some items, such as a wedding ring or clothing, as representing facets of ourselves, and other items, such as our home or car, as an extension and manifestation of our character and personality. These items are irreplaceable and no compensation would be high enough to pay off their true value. Radin helps us think of property as personhood by focusing on the way people *feel about* and *regard* their belongings. The strength of the relationship between the person and her belongings will be determined by the pain the person *feels* upon losing the object.[214] Thus, property can be personal or fungible, with a continuum of interests in between, reflecting varying levels of connection between person and object. The stronger such a connection is, the more entitlement there is in respect to it.

It is evident that one's physical integrity and personality is guaranteed through one's ability to control one's body. Controlling one's body enables one to take actions, to be subject to others' actions, or just to refrain from taking actions without being part of another's actions.

---

[210] Ziff, above n 155, at 26–7.
[211] Georg Hegel, *Philosophy of Right*, T. M. Knox trans. (Oxford: Clarendon, 1952), s. 44) [Hegel].
[212] *Ibid.*, at ss. 40, 47.   [213] Radin, 'Personhood', above n 174, at 957.   [214] *Ibid.*, at 959.

However, both Hegel and Radin discuss property in the active meaning of the word, namely as a way to perform positive behaviour reflecting one's own personality. Hegel puts much emphasis on the actual will, holding a monist view according to which the soul is embedded in the body, so that every act of violence to one's body is, in fact, violence to one's personality (soul). It follows from his approach that 'it is only because I am *alive* as a free entity in my body that this *living* existent ought not to be misused by being made a beast of burden'.[215] Reading Hegal conveys the idea that he believed the body could be subject to property only if it is a living body; the person holds a proprietary interest in the body as long as he or she intends to possess it; and the body is not just any body but the body of the person whose property it is. Hence, any inference from Hegel's theory to the argument for property interest in the body of the deceased involves a conceptual misunderstanding of his thesis and should not be upheld.

Radin's powerful argument results in even more rigid conclusions than Hegel's. While advocating an approach that regards property as constituting one's personality, Radin argues that although we are greatly attached to our body, we cannot be separated from it and so cannot have any property in it.[216] Radin's criterion to establish the strength of the relationship between the person and her belongings, namely the feeling of pain upon the loss of an object, is impracticable when one considers one's body as one's belonging.

Nevertheless, upon its biological death the human body becomes separate from the person whose body it was. It may be possible to argue that other persons may gain property in it, and that such a proprietary interest represents and constitutes *their* (rather than *its*) personality. However, much support is needed to substantiate this argument, which, if applied, may be relevant only to family members or close friends of the decedent, whose personal relationships with her (through her body) are significantly strong. Such support cannot be found in either Radin's or Hegel's theories of property.

Property as a system of distributive justice Another justification for the right to private property holds that we have private property so that 'everyone must have property'. Rules of property operate to distribute valuable resources in the society for which there is greater demand than supply. According to Mill, for example, a property interest in a thing involves not only the conferral of ownership over that upon which the labour of the property holder has been performed, but also the materials and the conditions enabling the work to be produced, as well as the

---

[215] Hegel, above n 211, at s. 48.   [216] Radin, 'Personhood', above n 174, at 966.

absence of anyone who may have a better claim to it.[217] A fair and competitive market is a major precondition for the establishment of such an interest.[218] Property establishes but also depends upon equality. A mechanism of property thus provides for the resources in society to be fairly distributed. As suggested by Mill, 'If private property were adopted, we must assume that it would be accompanied by none of the initial inequalities and injustices which obstruct the beneficial operation of the principle in old societies.'[219] Under such theory, without a proprietary regime resources must be possessed and managed by the state which may act inefficiently and unjustly toward producers and other members of the community.[220]

The distributive justice rationale does not have any bearing on the question of whether the whole body of the deceased can be subjected to property, especially when legal rules attributing quasi-possessory interests with regard to the human corpse put those interests in different and sometimes arbitrary categories of legal entities. This is perhaps one of the reasons why Mill himself denied the possibility of having a property interest in the human body.[221]

Property as a form of utilitarianism Without individuals having the right to use, control and dispose of the valued material existing in the outside world, this material will be consumed immediately. The utilitarian justification for the right to property holds that 'the total or average happiness of society will be greater, or the general welfare will be better served, if material resources and in particular the main material means of production are owned and controlled by private individuals and firms rather than by the state or the community as a whole'.[222] It is argued that a system of private property will internalize many of the external costs associated with communal ownership as private owners will be occupied with estimations of costs and benefits, and will have incentives to use resources more efficiently.[223] Another argument from utilitarianism emphasizes that a regime of private property characterized by a system

---

[217] J. S. Mill, *Principles of Political Economy* (New York: Longmans, Green and Co., 1904), bk II, ch. 2, s. 1.
[218] *Ibid.*, at s. 3. [219] *Ibid.*, at ch. 1, s. 2. [220] *Ibid.*, at s. 1. [221] *Ibid.*, at s. 7.
[222] Waldron, above n 160, at 6. But see the decision in the matter of *Moore*, where the Supreme Court of California rejected the claim for conversion on utilitarian grounds, holding that such a claim would compromise the biotechnological and other research and developmental values deriving from Moore's extracted tissues. *Moore*, above n 143.
[223] Harold Demsetz, 'Toward a Theory of Property Rights', mentioned in Waldron, above n 160, at 7–8.

of market prices consists of powerful tendencies to direct efficient resource allocation, thereby promoting overall prosperity.[224]

It is possible to justify a proprietary interest in the body of the deceased on a utilitarian basis. The human corpse has always had, and will have, significant value. Historic[225] and modern[226] scandals throughout the world reflect the permanent tension between the need for human bodies and tissue for diagnostic, research and therapeutic purposes and the societal interest in having the whole body disposed of uneventfully. In principle, conferring a property interest in the body of the deceased enhances the happiness of next-of-kin who care for the deceased as well as that of health teams, museums and medical schools wishing to benefit from utilizing dead bodies on their premises. However, in a system where commerce in dead bodies is banned and where there exists no market or trade in human corpses, the total value derived from a property regime in the body may be undervalued as a result of high demand and low supply, and hence may be inefficient for society at large.

In conclusion of this section, it follows that the application of the general rationales for a right to private property as developed in the literature to the human corpse is very problematic. A proprietary interest in the body of the deceased serves no justified purpose according to most of the theories discussed above, and cannot be argued for convincingly.

Procedural advantages of a proprietary claim with regard to the human corpse

The only advantage that a property claim may have over other claims is that such a claim may bring more certainty in the post-mortem context than in other areas where one needs to take into account the good faith and the motives of the persons acting in a particular way as factors in the decision whether to refuse or to allow a particular cause of action.[227] The following section examines the question of whether there exists such procedural certainty leading to substantial advantages to claimants.

---

[224] Waldron, above n 160, at 9–11.

[225] The famous example is that of the grave-robbers and murderers William Burke and William Hare in the nineteenth century: www.crimelibrary.com/serial_killers/weird/burke/merchandise_3.html, last accessed on 15 October 2007.

[226] Most notably are the retention and storage of deceased children's organs and body parts without parental consent in Alder Hey Hospital (Liverpool, UK) between 1988 and 1995. Similar cases arose in Australia and New Zealand: C. M. Thomas, 'Should the Law Allow Sentiment to Triumph Over Science? The Retention of Body Parts' (2002) (unpublished paper).

[227] Matthews, 'Man of Property', above n 89, at 258.

Specifically, it explores the procedural advantages of the argument for property in the body of the deceased.

Litigants have brought actions arguing for the violation of their possessory and custodial (or quasi-property) interest in the body of the deceased in a variety of cases. Roughly, it is possible to distinguish between four categories of such cases:

(1) Claims to determine the place and manner of the disposition of the body of a decedent, either before[228] or after[229] interment.

(2) Claims for an unlawful or non-consensual action performed on the body of the deceased prior to its interment. Under this category claims were brought for the performance of an unlawful autopsy,[230] unauthorized embalming,[231] and the taking of organs or tissues from the deceased without (and sometimes contrary to) prior consent.[232]

(3) Claims regarding the malicious or negligent performance of actions on the body of the deceased which caused a delay in the disposition of the body[233] or mental distress associated with it,[234] or those regarding failure to inform families of death.[235]

(4) Application of the right to custody and possession of the body for evidentiary purposes such as taking samples from the deceased's body for a medical negligence suit,[236] parentage testing procedures,[237] or testing the decedent's mental capacity when she executed her will.[238]

Reviewing these cases reveals the following conclusions. First, and with regard to the fourth category of cases, this category reflects exploitation

---

[228] *Enos*, above n 35; *Calma* v. *Sesar* (1992) 106 FLR 446.

[229] *Pierce*, above n 69; *Weld*, above n 35; *W. Rufus Sanford* v. *Maude Ware* 191 Va. 43 (Sup. Ct Va. 1950); *Birch* v. *Birch* et al. 123 Misc. 229 (Sup. Ct N.Y. 1924); *Sandra Grisso* v. *Dillard Nolen*, 262 Va. 688, 554 SE 2d 91 (Sup. Ct Va. 2001).

[230] *Phillips*, above n 7; *Edmonds*, above n 48; *Snyder*, above n 59; *Aldreman* v. *Ford* 146 Kan. 698, 72 P 2d 981 (1937).

[231] *Stanley Sworski* et al. v. *B. H. Simons* et al. 208 Minn. 201 (Sup. Ct Minn. 1940); *Mattie Parker* v. *Quinn-McGowen Company Inc.* 262 NC 560 (Sup. Ct N.C. 1964).

[232] *Lynn Ramirez* v. *Health Partners of Southern Arizona* 193 Ariz. 325, 972 P 2d 658 (Ariz. App. Div. 1998); *Brotherton*, above n 50.

[233] *Bastien* v. *Ottawa Hospital (General Campus)* (2001) 56 OR (3d) 397 [*Bastien*].

[234] *Finley* v. *Atlantic Transport Corporation Ltd* 220 NY 249, 115 NE 715 (Ct App. N.Y. 1917); *Wilson* v. *St Louis & SFR Co.* 160 Mo. App. 649 (Ct App. Mo. 1912); *Mary Gadbury* v. *J. J. Bleitz* 133 Wash. 134 (Sup. Ct Wash. 1925); *Gertrude Schmidt* v. *Hugo Schmidt* 49 Misc. 2d 498, 267 NYS 2d 645 (Sup. Ct N.Y. 1966); *Southern Life & Health Ins. Co.* et al. v. *Morgan* 21 Ala. App. 5 (Ct App. Ala. 1925); *Cohen*, above n 35; *Strachan* v. *John F. Kennedy Memorial Hospital* 538 A 2d 346 (Sup. Ct N.J. 1988).

[235] *Finn* v. *City of New York* 335 NYS 2d 516 (N.Y. Civ. Ct 1972); *Crocker* v. *Pleasant* 778 So. 2d 978 (Sup. Ct Fla. 2001).

[236] *Dobson*, above n 95.   [237] *Roche*; *AW*; above n 104.

[238] *Susan D. Camilli* v. *Immaculate Conception Cemetery* 244 NJ Super. 709, 583 A 2d 417 (N.J. Super. Ct 1990).

and misuse of the right to possession and custody in the body of the deceased, since in all these matters litigants do not relate to the original purpose of the right to property as it was thoroughly established in case law, namely the duty to dispose of the body of the deceased. Instead, litigants aim to have an evidentiary advantage over the opposing party and to achieve such an advantage they use the property rhetoric and argumentation. Cases under this category should not have been argued under the right to possession and custody in the body of the deceased in the first place, so that decisions in these cases must not and cannot have any bearing on the question of whether a property claim brings any procedural advantages to claimants.

Second, it seems clear that the first and third categories are closely related to the duty to dispose of the body of the deceased, though in the third category the need to remedy the emotional distress accompanied by the delaying action is more evident. The second category, which accounts for the largest number of cases, is based on the assumption that the duty to dispose of the body of the deceased includes the command to treat the body only with the permission of the duty bearers and without any noticeable disfigurement. Under this category, the right to possess the body includes the right to receive the body of the deceased free from mutilation. This category also reflects accepted and efficient legal means by which the mental distress that families go through under these circumstances can be protected. While in the first category the main remedy includes an injunction ordering interment or disinterment of the body of the deceased following (or not following) the wishes of plaintiffs, in the second and third categories the main remedy is compensatory in the form of damages to claimants.

It will be argued that cases under the first three categories may have a sufficient and complete remedy under the existing legal mechanism, and that a property claim in these categories brings no procedural advantage to plaintiffs. It is sufficient to hold that upon death there is always a legal person *physically* and not necessarily *legally* possessing or controlling the body of the deceased. This legal person, whether a hospital, a funeral home, a crematorium, a museum, etc., can bring actions in tort for the interference with its right to control and possess the body. This right, described minimally as the right to dominion or control, is sufficient for a successful action in conversion for the return of chattel under cases of disinterment (category 1),[239] or trespass to

---

[239] Conversion is a tort involving the *wrongful* interference with the goods of another and dominion wrongfully exerted over them such as taking, using or destroying these goods in a manner inconsistent with the owner's right of possession or control. Originally, the action aimed to remedy against the finder of lost goods who refused to return them to the

chattel (categories 2, 3).[240] Cases involving decisions over the place and manner of disposal prior to burial (category 1) may be brought to courts of equity as part of the common law duty to dispose of the body.[241]

Additionally, and for cases under the second and third categories, a wide variety of actions can be brought to sue damages. Most appropriately are actions for infliction or negligent[242] infliction of mental distress, which do not necessitate any physical injury of survivors.[243] The approach advocated here accords with courts' explicit objection to continue describing such cases in the proprietary discourse.[244] Other legal alternatives may include the action of trespass to person, which has already been used by some courts as a means to award damages for unlawful autopsy on the deceased,[245] actions for the negligent handling of the body of the deceased,[246] and the common law tort of interference with burial that has been raised with regard to bodies awaiting interment.[247]

---

owner but instead 'converted' them to his own use. An action for conversion 'requires neither legal title nor absolute ownership of the property. A party need only allege that "she was entitled to immediate possession at the time of the conversion".' *Spates*, above n 68, at 608. See also Clerk and Lindsell, *On Torts*, 18th edn (London: Sweet & Maxwell, 2000) paras. 14–52.

[240] Trespass to chattel is a tort involving *wrongful* interference with the goods of another who has neither possession nor ownership in them, but merely physical possession. *March v. Kulchar* [1952] 1 SCR 330. The idea that physical control is sufficient for these claims derives from the notion that there exists a sequence in possessing an object rather than a bipolar status of possession, namely a situation according to which the object at stake is either being possessed or not. This first view is represented by the common law doctrine of relative title. Matthews, above n 3, at 215–16.

[241] *Ritter v. Couch* 76 SE 428, 430 (WVa. 1912).

[242] *Lott v. State* 225 NYS 2d 434 (Ct Cl. 1962); *Bastien*, above n 233, at para. 41.

[243] This may be relevant to the American jurisdiction via the tort of interference with dead bodies (below) and through the direct application of case law: *Larson*, above n 16; *Anthony Gotskowski v. The Roman Catholic Church of the Sacred Hearts of Jesus and Mary* et al. 262 NY 320 (1933); *Walser v. Resthaven Memorial Gardens* 633 A 2d 466 (Md. Ct Spec. App. 1993); *Kohn v. US* 591 F Supp. 568 (EDNY 1984). My suggestion may also be applicable to the Canadian jurisdiction: *Mason v. Westside Cemeteries Ltd* [1996] 135 DLR (4th) 361, 380 [*Mason*]. The *Mason* decision overruled the decision in *Miner*, above n 34. But see *Sopinka*, above n 34, where the court refused to grant damages for the tort of *intentional* infliction of mental suffering as there was no evidence for severe mental suffering by the plaintiffs. For a similar legal position in the UK, see *Owens v. Liverpool Corporation* [1939] 1 KB 394 (CA).

[244] *Carney*, above n 77, at 435. See also *Whitehair*, above n 72; *Scarpaci*, above n 77.

[245] *Phillips*, above n 7; Clerk and Lindsell, *On Torts*, 15th edn (London: Sweet & Maxwell, 1982) paras. 21–45. See, however, an earlier case in Canada, where it was ruled that a claim for trespass against the body of an unburied corpse could not lie: *Davidson*, above n 59, at 202.

[246] *Mokry v. University of Texas Health Science Center* 529 SW 2d 802 (Tex. Civ. App. 1975); *Mason*, above n 243.

[247] *Powell*, above n 29.

In the American context, the tort of interference with dead bodies, established by section 868 of the Restatement on Torts, provides a statutory legal mechanism to deal with cases under the second and third categories listed above. The background to this section reflects a statutory effort to abolish the property discourse in such cases, as it was found to be inappropriate.[248]

Section 868 establishes that 'one who intentionally, recklessly or negligently removes, withholds, mutilates or operates upon the body of a dead person or prevents its proper interment or cremation is subject to a member of a family of the deceased who is entitled to the disposition of the body'. The section is very broad, applying to intentional actions but also to reckless and negligent incidents, and to events prior and after interment.[249] Also, damages recoverable under this section include those for the mental distress suffered and the physical harm resulting from the mental distress.

In situations involving criminal actions, such as the stealing of a corpse or body parts previously extracted from the deceased, it is advisable to expand the definition of theft also to include dead bodies and body parts. The reinterpretation of the prohibition against theft will not entail any conclusion concerning the proprietary status of the object stolen, but instead will fill a statutory gap that currently exists in the Anglo-American legal system. This recommendation was made by the Law Reform Commission of Canada in 1992,[250] and it has been suggested in the English literature as well.[251]

Other public offences which may apply in the post-mortem context may include the statutory prohibition against interfering with dead bodies,[252] the common law offence of preventing a lawful burial,[253] obstructing a coroner,[254] offences under the Canadian Human Tissue

---

[248] *Restatement of the Law, Second, Torts*, div. 11, ch. 42, s. 868 (1979).

[249] But see *Williams* v. *City of Minneola* 575 So. 2d 683 (Fla. Dist. Ct App. 1991), where it was held that the tort of interference with dead bodies requires that the action affects the physical body itself, so that publication of a photograph of a body does not amount to an interference with a dead body. Compare the Canadian approach in *R* v. *Moyer* [1994] 2 SCR 899 [*Moyer*], where the court held that physical interference with the dead body is not a necessary element for the parallel criminal offence set in section 182 of the Criminal Code.

[250] Law Reform Commission, above n 196, at 187 (Recommendation 12).

[251] Skegg, 'Medical Uses', above n 78, at 315.

[252] Canadian Criminal Code, RSC c. C-46 (1985), s. 182. For the interpretation given to this section, see *Moyer*, above n 249.

[253] *R* v. *Hunter* [1974] 1 QB 95; *R* v. *Black* [1995] Crim. LR 640. For a discussion of this offence, see Michael Hirst, 'Preventing the Lawful Burial of a Body' (1996) *Criminal Law Review* 96–103.

[254] *R* v. *Stephenson* (1884) 13 QBD 331; *R* v. *Purcy* (1933) 24 Cr. App. R 70.

legislation,[255] offences under public health laws and public nuisance laws,[256] and more generally the crime of acting so as to outrage public decency.[257] The recommendation of the Law Reform Commission of Canada to replace the existing criminal code offence of section 182 with a provision making it a crime 'to abuse a human corpse or human remains' should also be considered.[258]

Finally, and at least with regard to the English jurisdiction, reference to Articles 8 and 9 of the European Convention on Human Rights, providing for respect for private and family life and the right to freedom of thought, conscience and religion respectively, may also be made by next-of-kin in the post-mortem context, as has already been observed.[259]

Conclusion

The question of whether there exists a proprietary interest in the human body in general is difficult to answer. Leon Kass puts it nicely when he writes:

What kind of *property* is my body? Is it mine or is it *me*? Can it be alienated, like my other property, like my car or even my dog? And on what basis do I claim property *rights* in my body? Have I labored to produce it? Less than did my mother, and yet it is not hers. Do I claim it on merit? Doubtful: I had it even before I could be said to be deserving. Do I hold it as a gift – whether or not there be a giver? How does one possess and use a gift? Is it mine to dispose of as I wish – especially if I do not know the answer to these questions?[260]

Moreover, the idea of property in the body is even more difficult when applied to the post-mortem context. This is because:

---

[255] See, for example, Trillium Gift of Life Network Act, RSO 1990, c. H-20, s. 12.

[256] See, for example, Cemeteries Act (Revised), RSO 1990, c. C-4, s. 79. See in England the Public Health (Control of Disease) Act 1984. For US state legislation, see e.g. California Health and Safety Code s. 7052 (West 2005); Massachusetts General Laws Annotated ch. 252 s. 71 (West 1982); Ohio Revised Code Annotated s. 2927.01 (West 2003).

[257] *R* v. *Gibson* [1991] 1 All ER 439 (CA). See also *R* v. *Downey* (1994) 15 Cr. App. R (S) 700, and the case mentioned by White, above n 31, at 159.

[258] The Commission suggested replacing section 182 with the following provision: 'Everyone commits a crime who purposely or recklessly abuses a human corpse or human remains.' Law Reform Commission, above n 196, at 182 (Recommendation 9).

[259] Conway, above n 36, at 442–9; Heather Conway, 'Whose Funeral? Corpses and the Duty to Bury' (2003) 54(2) *Northern Ireland Legal Quarterly* 183–91, 189–91. For an analysis of the American Free Exercise Clause of the First Amendment in the context of post-mortem interventions, see Khalil Jaafar Khalil, 'A Sight of Relief: Invalidating Cadaveric Corneal Donation Laws Via the Free Exercise Clause' (2002) 6 *DePaul Journal of Health Care Law*. 159–78.

[260] Leon R. Kass, 'Thinking About the Body' (1985) 15(1) *Hastings Center Report* 20–30, 21.

Questions which relate to the custody and disposal of the remains of the dead do not depend upon the principles which regulate the possession and ownership of property, but upon the consideration arising partly out of the domestic relations, the duties and obligations which spring from family relationship and the ties of blood; partly out of the sentiment so universal among all civilized nations, ancient and modern, that the dead should repose in some spot where they will be secure from profanation; partly out of what is demanded by society for the preservation of the public health, morality and decency, and partly often out of what is required by proper respect for and observance of the wishes of the departed themselves.[261]

While it may be that overturning the no property rule would, as put by Glanville Williams, 'deprive the common law and statutory exceptions of their *raison d'être* and so make nonsense of them',[262] it is suggested in this chapter that the property discourse be abandoned, especially when one deals with actions performed on the body of the deceased. As shown in this chapter, the question of whether there exists a proprietary interest in the body of the deceased, although frequently addressed in legal decisions, bears much uncertainty. While courts refer to an anachronistic and unsupported rule according to which there is no property in the corpse, exceptions to the rule and negation of its effects diminish its real authority. Rethinking the role of proprietary interest in respect of the corpse leads to the conclusion that there is no recognizable model within property law by which one can conceptualize such an interest. Although some characteristics of a proprietary right like transferability, use, management and disposal are present, many more important characteristics such as ownership, possession and exclusion are absent. Moreover, the general rationales for a right to private property cannot justify a proprietary interest in the body of the deceased. Whatever the case may be, such proprietary interest does not provide any necessary procedural advantage to claimants in the post-mortem context, and cases that deal with interference with dead bodies can be perfectly well decided and remedied without the fictional and unnecessary appeal to the right to property in the body of the deceased.

---

[261] Percival E. Jackson, *The Law of Cadavers and of Burial and Burial Places*, 2nd edn (New York: Prentice-Hall, 1950) at 170.
[262] Glanville Williams, *Textbook of Criminal Law*, 1st edn (London: Stevens & Sons, 1978) 680.

4   Determining the disposal of one's body after death

The interest in determining the disposal of one's body after death applies to situations or states of affairs commencing after one is dead. This is a paradigmatic case of an 'after-life' interest and in that sense its examination is crucial for the general understanding of posthumous interests. In this chapter, it will be examined whether the testamentary interest in the disposal of one's body after death, if it exists, has and should have any legal obligatory power.

By 'the testamentary interest in the disposal of one's body after death' I refer to a legally protected interest in respecting one's prior wishes or directives expressed while alive as to the manner, place and nature of disposal of one's body. There are many ways, indeed unlimited ways, by which a person may ask for disposition of her body once she is dead. A few examples will suffice. In Texas, a man requested that he be buried standing up so that no one would look down on him. Additionally, he requested to be faced west, holding his rifle, with a jug filled and placed at his feet. His wife followed most of his requests except the one concerning the jug. In another case, a rancher named Earl Allen was buried according to his wishes with a telephone in his hand. Allen wanted to be kept in a mausoleum but was afraid of being buried alive. He instructed that if he had not called anyone after three days, the phone could be disconnected. A third example is that of Dr Sophie Hertzog, a physician from Brazoria, Texas, who was buried wearing her twenty-seven slugs necklace. The slugs were bullets she extracted from her patients and there was a gold piece in between each of the bullets. A more famous example for extravagant disposal concerns the case of Sandra Ilene West, a multi-millionaire, who requested that she be buried in a prone position in her blue Ferrari car, wearing a designer gown. According to media reports, a California judge ruled that the request was unusual but not illegal, thereby validating her directive. Sandra was buried in her car which was put in a box and lowered by crane into the grave and covered by concrete.[1]

---

[1] Ross McSwain, 'Cemeteries Provide Unique Look at State's History', *West Texas News and Sport*, 14 April 1997, available at http://web.gosanangelo.com/archive/97/april/14/12.htm, accessed on 10 May 2007.

Aside from the curiosity that these cases evoke, they all raise the question of whether such personal requests are legally binding. Despite the strong intuition, so I presume, that such requests should deserve at least the same legal status as requests concerning the disposal of one's personal property after death, the law in most legal systems in the common law provides a negative answer to this question. However, analysis of this legal situation reveals that such a negative answer is not clear-cut, and in fact not only varies from one system to another, but consists of complex approaches depending on the specific circumstances surrounding the request and the timing in which it is raised, as well as the emotional reaction associated with it.

Unsurprisingly, testaments regarding the disposal of famous or notable personas are usually enforced and mainly evoke a gossiped interest. The most famous example is that of Jeremy Bentham. Bentham, an eminent philosopher and the founding father of utilitarianism, can still be seen 'seated in a large case with his plate-glass front, wearing the clothes he used to put on, and with his stick "Dapple" in his hand'.[2] Bentham's idea of becoming an 'auto-icon', namely a man who is his own image preserved for the benefit of posterity, was realized by his friend, Dr Smith Southwood. Another example is that of Ted Williams, a famous American baseball player, who asked that his body be kept cryogenically, believing that scientists will revive him in due time. Although Ted had previously directed in his will that his body be cremated, his request to remain frozen was pursued by his son.[3] The last example is that of President Dwight D. Eisenhower, who before his death fashioned in great detail the manner in which his funeral was to take place, including the specific casket in which his body was to be laid. Eisenhower's plan was carried out to the letter.[4]

---

[2] C. F. A. Marmoy, 'The "Auto-Icon" of Jeremy Bentham at University College, London' (1958) 2 *Medical History* 77–86, 77.

[3] Lawrence Donegan, 'Frozen in Memory', *Observer*, 14 July 2002; Alexander A. Bove and Melissa Langa, 'Ted Williams: Is He Headed for the Dugout or the Deep Freeze? Property Rights in a Dead Body Resurrected' *Massachusetts Lawyers Weekly*, 19 August 2002.

[4] Richard C. Groll and Donald J. Kerwin, 'The Uniform Anatomical Gift Act: Is the Right to a Decent Burial Obsolete?' (1971) 2 *Loyola University of Chicago Law Journal*. 275–305, 283 [Groll and Kerwin]. There are exceptional cases where the request of a celebrity in respect of the disposal of his body is not fully carried out. Albert Einstein died on 18 April 1955 and his body was cremated per his request. However, the pathologist who conducted the autopsy, Dr Thomas Stoltz Harvey, removed and kept Einstein's brain without any previous consent either from Einstein or from his family, aiming to discover Einstein's brain's unique qualities. When the family learned about Harvey's study, they gave him permission to proceed on condition that he publish the results in scientific journals and that no attempts to sensationalize the findings be made. Dorothy Nelkin and Lori Andrews, 'Do the Dead Have Interests? Policy Issues for Research After Life' (1998) 24 *American Journal of Law and Medicine* 261–91, 266 (note 43).

However, in the majority of cases dealing with non-famous or not otherwise publicly intriguing persons, testamentary provisions regarding the way the body is approached after death, which will be termed in this chapter 'bodily testaments' or BTs, are not compelling unless voluntarily enforced by survivors, executors or administrators outside court. Before analysing the legal situation concerning such testaments, it is necessary to discuss the preliminary theoretical assumption of the question of whether BTs should be binding or not, namely that the testator maintains an autonomy interest in determining how her body is disposed of after death.

Constraints of autonomy interests

Is there an interest in determining the place and manner of disposal of one's body after death, and does this interest survive one's death? These two related questions touch upon two kinds of theoretical issues. According to the first, which focuses on the *subject* of the interest at stake, the difficulty in recognizing such testamentary interest lies in the fact that the potential holder of an autonomy-based interest does not exist after death. However, as argued in chapter 1, interests in the category of 'after-life' interests, should they exist, may be held by the Human Subject, whose existence persists over time. This subject encompasses a broader understanding of the concept of interest than the one associated with the idea of rights held by the 'person'. If one accepts the notion of the Human Subject, one is not necessarily concerned with the problem of the subject discussed in the context of this testamentary interest.

The second and more difficult issue raised in the question above relates to the *content* of the interest at stake. Specifically, it is queried whether an autonomy-based interest in determining how the body is disposed of after death is the kind of interest that should be classified as an 'after-life' interest the effect of which is initiated by the death of the person whose interest it is.[5] In contrast to a welfare-based interest, whose protection advances the welfare of its subject and which, according to some scholars, can still be attributed to insentient, unconscious or dead persons, an autonomy-based interest is a kind of interest the importance of which lies in the freedom of the interest-holder to determine her actions as she finds fit. It is an interest in telling and shaping one's own life story.

---

[5] There may be other after-life interests concerning the treatment of one's body after death. Two obvious examples would be instructions regarding organ donation and the posthumous use of gametes following the death of their contributor. See B. Bennett, 'Posthumous Reproduction and the Meaning of Autonomy' (1999) 23(2) *Melbourne University Law Review* 286–307.

Consequently, serious doubts may arise with regard to such an interest when applied to the dead: does the person retain her freedom to tell the story of her life when no life can be found?

Discussion of this question can be found in the area of advance directives, specifically with regard to the freedom of a competent patient to determine the medical treatment or procedure to be performed on her if rendered incompetent. Rebecca Dresser and John Robertson, for example, argue that autonomy-based interests reflected in a person's prior wishes become empty once the person can no longer appreciate or understand the violation of these interests. Moreover, in their view it is difficult, if not impossible, for competent individuals to predict their interests in future treatment situations when incompetent because their needs and interests will have radically changed.[6] John Harris holds a similar view: 'autonomy involves the capacity to make choices, it involves acts of the will and the dead have no capacities – they have no will, no preferences, wants nor desires, the dead cannot be autonomous and so cannot have their autonomy violated'.[7]

The Dresser–Robertson thesis, if it applies at all to the dead,[8] strips away the autonomy-based interests which the incompetent patient had while competent. However, such a view was in fact rejected in court. Judges recognized that the right to refuse medical treatment derived from a person's constitutional rights to privacy[9] and dignity,[10] both of which promote autonomy-based interests, and these also apply to incompetent patients. Indeed, as demonstrated by these cases, the problem with the Dresser–Robertson formula is that it takes a too-narrow approach to what it means to be autonomous and the significance one attaches to the implementation of one's wishes. Under this approach, the only justification for giving effect to one's prior wishes is one's capacity to make

---

[6] Rebecca S. Dresser and John A. Robertson, 'Quality of Life and Non-Treatment Decisions for Incompetent Patients: A Critique of the Orthodox Approach' (1989) 17(3) *Law, Medicine and Healthcare* 234–44, 236 [Dresser and Robertson].

[7] John Harris, 'Law and Regulation of Retained Organs: The Ethical Issues' (2002) 22 *Legal Studies* 527–49, 531.

[8] Dresser and Robertson specifically distinguish the case of enforcing advance directives and invalidating a will since 'at the time that a will takes effect the testator is dead and no longer has interests that can be harmed by a decision to honor the prior instructions'. Dresser and Robertson, above n 6, at 237. Dresser and Robertson apply their view to situations in which there exists a conflict between past choices and present interests. On its face, the Dresser–Robertson formula would not apply to the dead. However, such formula would still apply to our case under an account acknowledging the interests of the dead held by the Human Subject, as developed in chapter 1.

[9] *In the Matter of Quinlan* 335 A 2d 647, 663–4 (1976).

[10] *Superintendent of Belchertown State School* v. *Joseph Saikewicz* 373 Mass. 728, 745 (Sup. Jud. Ct Mass. 1977).

choices and to reflect on them. But there are other, and indeed broader, understandings of autonomy. Autonomy is first and foremost the moral privilege of a person to cultivate and nurture her particular vision of herself as a human being. It is the prerogative of shaping the images, conceptions and recollections which other persons have or will have of her regardless of whether she will physically witness those images, conceptions or recollections.

It is easy to see how the Dresser–Robertson formula neglects the elementary character of what it means to be an autonomous person. Following Ronald Dworkin, we may think of the person who while alive directed the manner or place of the disposal of her body in one of the two following ways.[11] We may think of her as dead, emphasizing her present situation and (in)capacities, or as a person who has become dead, having an eye to the course of her whole life, including the way she departed life. Choosing between these alternatives draws on a deeper notion of autonomy. What is the rationale for respecting one's autonomy? This question is especially intensified when an autonomous decision is not in the best interests of the person, should she hold any.

There are two main justifications for respecting autonomy. An evidentiary account of autonomy holds that we should respect autonomy even when we regard autonomous decisions as imprudent, because each person usually knows what is best for her rather than anyone else. Endorsing this account in our case will lead to the conclusion that the dead person, who has permanently lost all mental capacities and can no longer appreciate what is best for her, should not be regarded as having autonomy. Still, one can argue that a living person can perfectly anticipate the state of affairs surrounding the disposal of her body after death and in that sense can know – and indeed is the best person to know – what is best for her. However, this first rationale may be problematic. As Ronald Dworkin points out, by respecting people's autonomy we may be required to accept their choices even when they are irrational or against their interest. The point of autonomy is not necessarily (or solely) to respect the person's welfare, thereby fulfilling her overall interests as such.

A more plausible account of autonomy emphasizes the integrity of the autonomous person. In this account, the value of autonomy derives from the capacity to express one's own character and values. Autonomy allows us to 'be responsible for shaping our lives according to our own coherent or incoherent but, in any case, distinctive personality. It allows us to lead our own lives rather than be led along them, so that each of us can be, to

---

[11] Ronald Dworkin, *Life's Dominion* (New York: Alfred Knopf, 1993) 221.

the extent a scheme of rights can make this possible, what we have made of ourselves.'[12] Applying the integrity account of autonomy to the dead will lead to diverse results depending on the specific circumstances. If the person's prior wishes accord to and are continuous with the person's overall character and values, there is no justification in arguing that this person, although dead, does not enjoy autonomy, when certain choices and preferences affect a person's life. On the other hand, when a person's wishes contradict her previous beliefs or are inconsistent with each other, reflecting no sense of a coherent self, then she has presumably lost her capacity for autonomy.[13] It follows that in order to be autonomous, both one's current and one's previous wishes should be protected. The requirement that only a person's present decisions be respected thus shows a partial understanding of the concept of autonomy.

It was Nancy Rhoden who argued that advance directives of a competent person have considerable moral force even if the person fails to understand the dishonour of these prior wishes. In Rhoden's view, moral agency is inherently future directed and 'prior directives are the tools for projecting one's moral and spiritual values into the future'.[14] According to this approach, 'to the extent that you regulate your choices by identifying yourself as the one who is implementing something like a particular plan of life, you need to identify with your future in order to be what you are even now'.[15] Hence, the incompetent patient is essentially the 'shadow of her former self'.[16] It also follows that respect for the previously competent person's wishes derives from his or her moral character. Along this line, it is argued by Norman Cantor that one of the central reasons for directing one's post-competence medical fate is maintenance of one's personal conception of dignity and self-respect, which is important to avoid feelings of embarrassment or humiliation.[17]

There is yet another aspect of our respect for the prior wishes of a previously competent person. We should enjoy prospective autonomy

---

[12] *Ibid.*, at 224. See also, Ronald Dworkin, 'Autonomy and the Demented Self' (1986) 64 *Milbank Quarterly* (Supp. 2) 4–16.

[13] This is not to say that she has lost her right to beneficence. If one takes an objective approach to interests – as I do – one may argue that she has such welfare-based interests, so that respecting her wishes may be in her best interests.

[14] Nancy K. Rhoden, 'The Limits of Legal Objectivity' (1990) 68 *North Carolina Law Review* 845, 858.

[15] *Ibid.*

[16] Nancy K. Rhoden, 'How Should We View the Incompetent?' (1989) 17(3) *Law, Medicine and Healthcare* 264–8, 267.

[17] Norman L. Cantor, *Advance Directives and the Pursuit of Death with Dignity* (Bloomington: Indiana University Press, 1993) 105 [Cantor].

with regard to the manner in which we wish to die or be considered dead because it is a person's effort to shape, and interest in shaping, other people's posthumous recollections of her character and values based on common recognition of the connection between human dignity and a personal image projected to others,[18] in short her interest in the recognition of her symbolic existence. Under this account, which I find highly appealing, 'individual self-fulfillment and self-respect are seen as dependent not just on dominion over important decisions while the person is still competent and acutely aware but on *dominion over a lifetime image*'.[19] Cantor himself applies this notion to situations occurring after death. He comments that the fulfilment of the decedent's wishes gives expression to the decedent's character and that to dishonour his instruction is an offence to his memory.[20]

More generally, provisions coming into effect after a person's death have unique importance. People write testaments to dispose of their personal property in 'ways that are pleasing to them, resisting unavoidable or distasteful appropriation of property they consider uniquely theirs'.[21] If the person gave thought to the way in which her body would be approached after death and she expressed it while alive, it should be presumed that this is one of the things about which she cared much as a living person, and so respect for her wishes is respect for the things that were very important to her while alive.

All of the above reasons suggest that the situation regarding respect for the prior wishes of the deceased as to the place and manner of disposal is more complex than the one offered or implied by Dresser and Robertson, and that in order to determine whether a person should enjoy her autonomy-based interests in a state of full and permanent incompetency like death, one needs to look beyond the limited inquiry of whether this person is able to make conscious decisions or appreciate the dishonour of her previous choices. If one follows the range of accounts for prospective autonomy in the context of bodily testaments, one should conclude that there exists no prima facie reason to object to the proposition that a person's autonomy-based interest in determining her manner or place of disposal after death is an 'after-life' interest, namely one which survives the death of the person whose interest it is.

---

[18] *Ibid.*, at 105.   [19] *Ibid.* (my emphasis).   [20] *Ibid.*, at 196 (note 30).

[21] Abigail J. Sykas, 'Waste Not, Want Not: Can the Public Policy Doctrine Prohibit the Destruction of Property by Testamentary Direction?' (2001) *Vermont Law Review* 911–44, 936 [Sykas].

Legal barriers to enforcing bodily testaments (BTs)

Despite the promising theoretical basis of the interest in determining the disposal of one's body after death, the legal status of BTs is rather weak. While some legal decisions, especially in the American jurisprudence, suggest that a decedent's prior wishes as to disposal of her body are compelling,[22] the general rule is that they are not. Interestingly, in early days the legal view was contrary to the current one. Then, there was a wide spectrum of possibilities by which a person could prescribe the conduct of his funeral and the disposal of his body. Democrates, for example, directed that his body be embalmed in honey, and so it was done. Lycurgus' wishes that his body be cremated and the ashes scattered into the sea were respected. The whole era was governed by Solon's Funeral Law, which held, 'let the dead bodies be laid out in the house according as the deceased gave order'.[23] The variety of disposal possibilities was cut by the rise of Christianity which made its way to the legal system through the ecclesiastical courts and was renewed with the reign of Henry VIII and again at the beginning of the nineteenth century.

The new era has regarded BTs as a voluntary matter and two major explanations have been brought to support the conclusion that a person's directives concerning the manner in which her body be approached after death are not binding and have no obligatory power. The substantial account holds that since the law of succession is occupied only with the transfer of property after death[24] (hereinafter 'Assumption A'), and since the body of the deceased is not subject to property[25] (hereinafter 'Assumption B'), and given that BTs can and should be made only by will ('Assumption C'), a person may not will her body or instruct any power relating to it under the law of succession.[26] The procedural explanation for invalidating testament concerning the treatment of the testator's body after death focuses on the impracticability of enforcing such provision. The argument is that any provision relating to disposal of the body

---

[22] *In re Herskovits* 183 Misc. 411, 412 (1944); *Wood* v. *E. R. Butterworth & Sons* et al. 118 P 212, 65 Wash. 344, 348 (1911) [*Wood*]; *Owen Cooney* v. *George English* et al. 86 Misc. 292, 294 (Sup. Ct NY 1914) [*Cooney*].

[23] Groll and Kerwin, above n 4, at 275.

[24] See e.g. Succession Law Reform Act, RSO 1990, c. S-26, s. 2.

[25] *O'Donnell* v. *Slack* 123 Cal. 285, 55 P 906 (Sup. Ct Calif. 1899) [*O'Donnell*]; *Smart* v. *Moyer* 577 P 2d 108, 110 (Utah 1978) [*Moyer*]; *Fischer's Estate* v. *Fischer* 1 Ill. App. 2d 528, 117 NE 2d 855, 859 (Ct App. Ill. 1954) [*Fischer's Estate*].

[26] Most famously, this proposition was set forth in *Williams* v. *Williams* (1882) 20 Ch. D 659. See also *Enos* et al. v. *Snyder* et al. 131 Cal. 68, 69 (Calif. Sup. Ct 1900) [*Enos*]; *Charles Guerin* v. *Rose Cassidy* 38 NJ Super. 454, 458 (1955)); *Stewart* v. *Schwartz Bros.–Jeffer Memorial Chapel Inc.* 606 NYS 2d 965, 967 (Sup Ct 1993); *Williams on Wills*, 8th edn (London: Butterworths, 2002) 78 [*Williams on Wills*].

after death must be activated, if at all, soon after the person is dead. When such a provision is included in a will, certain procedural requirements must be met to effectuate the will as a whole. Hence, it is usually not practicable, as well as being harmful to public health, to hold the dead body until these requirements are fulfilled. Moreover, in most cases the will is probated long after the body has been disposed of, without next-of-kin being aware of the special provisions concerning disposal.

However, both the substantial and procedural explanations can be disputed. As discussed in the previous chapter, the idea that the human corpse should not be subject to a proprietary interest (Assumption B) is not absolute, although in the view of this author it is desirable. The many exceptions to the no property rule established by case law may support prima facie the argument that the body of the deceased may be subject to property and so included in the estate.

Additionally, it is incorrect to assume that wills contain only provisions relating to the decedent's property (Assumption A). The law states that a person may bequeath, dispose of or devise her property by will, but it does not say that the *only* thing she should bequeath, dispose of or devise must be property. The interpretation according to which the law does not exclude items other than property from being included in a testament can be supported by the mechanism of the law of testaments itself. Although the main purpose of a will is to allow for the disposal of the testator's property after her death, wills occasionally include other instructions or powers of appointment, e.g. provisions concerning the appointment of guardians for the testator's minor children or the appointment of an executor to or a trustee of the will.[27] Moreover, in Oklahoma, Oregon and Texas the testator may delegate her power to determine the disposal of her body to another person by completion of a written statement or affidavit.[28]

Finally, even if one still holds that there is not (and should not be) a proprietary interest in the body of the deceased, validating BT does not necessarily undermine the no property rule. Many states in the USA enacted laws acknowledging BT without overruling the no property rule.[29] As will

---

[27] Parry and Clark, *The Law of Succession*, Roger Kerridge ed., 11th edn (London: Sweet & Maxwell, 2002) 37 [Parry and Clark]; Gareth Miller, *The Machinery of Succession*, 2nd edn (Aldershot: Dartmouth, 1996) 230–4.

[28] 21 Oklahoma Stat. Ann. s. 1151(B) (Thomson/West 2005); Oregon Rev. Stat. s. 97.130(3) (Thomson/West 2005); Vernon's Texas Health and Safety Code Ann. s. 711.002(a) (Thomson/West 2005). For a discussion of these mortal remains proxy provisions, see Tanya K. Hernandez, 'The Property of Death' (1999) 60 *University of Pittsburgh Law Review* 971–1028, 973–4 [Hernandez].

[29] See e.g. Arizona Rev. Stat. Ann. s. 32-1365.01 (1996); Arkansas Code Ann. s. 20-17-102 (West 2005); California Health and Safety Code s. 7100.1 (1997); Minnesota Stat. Ann. s.

be discussed below, such legislation, though now part of the general law, illustrates deficits in the common law, with scarcely any cases supporting similar reasoning.[30] In addition, specific legislation in only one province in Canada states that preferences expressed in writing by the deceased while alive, as stated in a will, a pre-need cemetery services plan or a prearranged funeral services plan respecting the disposal of the remains of that person, are binding on the person who has the right to control such disposal.[31]

As to the procedural explanation, indeed a will is valid only after strict formal requirements are met. These requirements emphasize the importance of making a will, thereby preventing, as far as possible, the execution of a will made imprudently or under duress. Hence, a will must be made in writing, signed and witnessed by others who must also sign it, and the testator must intend by his signature to give it effect upon his death.[32] However, the law may waive the fulfilment of some of these requirements so that urgent testamentary provisions can be carried out. For example, in many states in the USA it is established that, prior to her appointment by probate court, an executor may carry out the decedent's provisions concerning his body and funeral arrangements.[33] Similarly, the Uniform Anatomical Gift Act holds that 'a gift of all or part of the body ... may be made by a will. The gift becomes effective upon the death of the testator without waiting for probate.'[34] In addition, as mentioned above, the testator may leave behind a letter of instruction, specifying where and how he would want his body to be disposed of. The letter would stand as clear evidence without the need to probate the general will.

Above all, the problem with the argument that testamentary provisions regarding one's body do not have legal effect is that it ignores the major justification for the law of testaments, namely respect for the wishes of the ante-mortem person. If by enforcing a will what we care deeply about is respecting the decedent's prior wishes and autonomy, then it is not clear why this principle should be defeated in situations where the decedent's wishes are concerned with the disposal of her own body. On the contrary,

---

149A.80(1) (Thomson/West 2005); Revised Code of Washington Ann. s. 68.50.160(1) (Thomson/West 2006). See also the Uniform Anatomical Gift Act [UAGA], which provides in section 4(a) that 'A gift of all or part of the body ... may be made by will.'

[30] *Pierce* v. *Proprietors of Swan Point Cemetery* 10 RI 227, 239 (1872); *Elizabeth Gilpin Wales* v. *Leonard G. Wales* et al. 21 Del. Ch. 349, 352–3 (1936).

[31] Cemetery and Funeral Services Act, RSBC 1996, c. 45, s. 53.

[32] See e.g. Wills Act 1837, s. 9 (UK); Wills Act, RSA 2000, c. W-12, ss. 4, 5 (Can.).

[33] See e.g. Utah Code Ann. s. 75-3-701 (1953); New York Public Health Act s. 4303(1) (Thomson/West 2005); California Health and Safety Code s. 7100.1(c) (1997).

[34] UAGA, above n 29, at s. 4(a).

it seems unambiguous that a person's body is one of the most precious things about which she cares, certainly more than her real property. In principle, any treatment of her body must be in harmony with her wishes. As Justice Benjamin Cardozo held in *Schloendorff*, every human being of adult years and sound mind has a right to determine what shall be done with her own body.[35] Surely, the fulfilment of such a right should not be defeated when the person is dead while her body still remains subject to mistreatment or exploitation.[36]

Giving much importance to the person's wishes concerning her body appears necessary. As will be discussed below, the formal characterization of a testament as consisting of proprietary items only and its effect on the legal status of BTs seem arbitrary and unjustified in light of the principle of autonomy and the importance of the surviving interests held by the Human Subject.

One way to deal with the problem raised by the objection to validating BTs is to rethink the notion of property in the context of the body of the deceased, in other words to refute Assumption B above.[37] As established in the previous chapter, the body of the deceased cannot and should not be subject to a proprietary interest. It is thus desirable to consider one of the following two alternatives. Under the first, respecting BTs is possible if and only if BTs are not made by a will and as a result are not subject to general doctrines of the law of testaments. This first alternative seeks to undermine Assumption C above. According to the second alternative, BTs could still be made by a will, and should be respected in light of principles other than the idea that in order to be valid, a will must include only property ('Property Classification Criterion' or 'PCC'). Under this second alternative, Assumption A of the general argument against the legal enforcement of BTs must be denied. It follows from such an alternative that there is no prima facie justification to exclude from a testament made by will items which are not property, although there may be compelling reasons to disallow such testament on more substantial grounds.

---

[35] *Schloendorff* v. *Society of New York Hospital* 211 NY 125, 105 NE 92 (1914).

[36] Marvin I. Barish, 'The Law of Testamentary Disposition – A Legal Barrier to Medical Advance!' (1956) 30 *Temple Law Quarterly* 40–6, 46. A similar view is expressed by Groll and Kerwin, above n 4, at 289–90, and Percival E. Jackson, *The Law of Cadavers and of Burial and Burial Places*, 2nd edn (New York: Prentice-Hall, 1950) 42.

[37] See e.g. Jennifer Horan's suggestion to recognize a market-inalienable property right in the body of the deceased vesting in the decedent herself. Such right would allow individuals to determine for themselves what will happen to their body after death, and their prior wishes would be compelling. Jennifer E. Horan, '"When Sleep At Last Has Come": Controlling the Disposition of Dead Bodies for Same-Sex Couples' (1999) 2 *Journal of Gender, Race and Justice* 423–60 [Horan].

Alternatives to the will mechanism

A person may direct the place or manner of disposal of her body by legal means other than a will. The obvious advantage of such an alternative is that it avoids the distinction between the classification of 'property' and 'no property' which is allegedly required under the law of testaments, and yet respects the legal position that there exists no proprietary interest in the body of the deceased. This is a rather conservative alternative, keeping faith with traditional doctrinal understanding of the law of testaments and property law. It is advantageous also because, as a matter of fact, most men and women do not make wills. Accepting the legality of other forms of testaments is thus a more practical solution to the serious problem of unenforced BTs. The next section will discuss six possible legal mechanisms by which BTs can have legal effect.

Human tissue gift laws

Bodily testaments may have legal effect if made under human tissue gift laws. These laws regulate the use of corpses for specific purposes established by the legislator. In Canada, human tissue gift laws exist in all provinces,[38] and in the USA, all states have now adopted the model of the Uniform Anatomical Gift Act.[39]

However, the need for human tissue gift legislation was prompted largely by developments in medical technology that allowed for human organ transplantation,[40] and so unsurprisingly this legislation does not deal with the decedent's and next-of-kin's right to dispose of the body of the deceased for purposes other than therapy, scientific research or medical education. Hence, issues such as burial, cremation, etc. are usually not covered by this legislation[41] and may not fit the rationale behind it.

---

[38] See Human Tissue Gift Act, RSA 2000, c. H-15; Human Tissue Gift Act, RSBC 1996, c. 211; Trillium Gift of Life Network Act, RSO 1990, c. H-20; Human Tissue Gift Act, SM 1987–8, c. 39; Human Tissue Act, SNB 1986, c. H-12; Human Tissue Donation Act, RSPEI 1988, c. H-12.1; Human Tissue Gift Act, RSY 1986, c. 89; Human Tissue Gift Act, RSNS 1989, c. 215; Human Tissue Act, RSS 1978, c. H-15; Human Tissue Act, RSN 1990, c. H-15; Human Tissue Act, RNWT 1988, c. H-6.

[39] The National Conference of Commissioners on Uniform State Laws, *Uniform Anatomical Gift Act* (1987), available at www.law.upenn.edu/bll/ulc/fnact99/uaga87.htm, accessed on 8 January 2006.

[40] Melissa A. W. Stickney, 'Property Interests in Cadaverous Organs: Changes to Ohio Anatomical Gift Law and the Erosion of Family Rights' (2002–3) 17 *Journal of Law and Health* 37–75, 46 [Stickney].

[41] One exception would be with regard to cryonics, namely 'the practice of freezing at extremely low temperature the body or head of a person who has just died in order to preserve it for possible resuscitation at a future time when physical repair and treatment are available'. California's Uniform Anatomical Gift Act regards cryotoriums and the

Although some suggestions in the literature call for the expansion of the human tissue legislation to include also BTs,[42] this view is not dominant.

Donor cards

A direction as to the place and manner of disposal after death may be included on a donor card, namely a card signed by a competent living person indicating her willingness to donate organs or body parts after death or to contribute her whole body to scientific research. Such a direction may be added to an already existing provision regarding donation or it may be an alternative to it. However, donor cards, as such, do not have a peremptory legal status and the health team does not have any legal obligation to carry out the wishes expressed on the card. The non-compulsory nature of donor cards is manifested explicitly in legislation that requires consultation with next-of-kin prior to extraction of organs so that doctors are still free to follow the status quo of deferring to families.[43] The signature on the card symbolizes the deceased's *willingness* to donate her body or organs but the ultimate decision rests with the family. The family may veto an expressed wish of the decedent to donate and the health team may choose to endorse the family's objection.

Even within legal systems where there is no legal requirement to consult the family, e.g. in the USA, doctors do not exclusively follow the directives of the deceased. A survey of organ procurement programmes undertaken in all fifty states and the District of Columbia revealed that in forty-seven states, surgeons still require family approval to remove organs from the deceased despite the fact that the provisions of the Uniform Anatomical Gift Act adopted in all states in the USA do not require this.[44] Hence, the role of donor cards is mainly to provide a channel to signal donation preferences to family members and organ procurement

respective societies as procurement agencies of human body donations. California Health and Safety Code ss. 7150–7156.5, especially s. 7153 (West 2005). See also the law in Alabama where the legislator included the term 'cryogenic storage' in the definition of a cemetery within the Funeral Services Chapter. Alabama Code s. 34-13-1(a)(7) (2007). Still, such practice is regarded as made for research purposes. David M. Baker, 'Cryonic Preservation of Human Bodies – A Call for Legislative Action' (1994) 98 *Dickinson Law Review* 677–711, 677 [Baker].

[42] See Stickney's suggestion to enact a statute that would allow a person complete power to have her body buried, cremated or the like. Stickney, above n 40, at 291.

[43] Ben Berkman, 'Organ Donor Card Effectiveness' in *Case in Health Law* (August 2002: American Medical Association), available at www.ama-assn.org/ama/pub/category/print/8560.html, accessed on 10 May 2007.

[44] T. D. Overcast, R. W. Evans, L. E. Bowen, H. M. Hoe and C. L. Livat, 'Problems in the Identification of Potential Organ Donors: Misconceptions and Fallacies Associated with Donor Cards' (March 1984) 251(12) *Journal of the American Medical Association* 1559–62.

agencies. Even if one includes in them the possibility of making a testament concerning the disposal of one's body after death, this testament may not be binding and its legal force would still be very weak.

Living wills

Living wills are documents that instruct healthcare providers about particular kinds of medical care that an individual would or would not want to have if rendered incompetent. The degree of incompetency under which a living will should operate is debatable. Living wills are part of a larger group, entitled 'advance directives'. An advance directive may also designate a healthcare agent for making health-related decisions for the incompetent patient. Originally, the aim of advance directives was that they would apply when the patient was alive but incapacitated and unable to make reasonable decisions or any other decision concerning his or her health. Yet, in practice the status of advance directives seems much less certain with regard to mandating interventions that are preferred but not required by medical law.

It seems plausible to argue that advance directives can also apply when the patient becomes dead. Under these circumstances, an advance directive functions like a donor card or a will, providing for treatment of the body after death.[45] In New Jersey, for example, the law regards brain-death as legal death, but allows individuals to choose in advance whether they want to be declared brain-dead. Consequently, in its combined advance directive for healthcare, the New Jersey Commission on Legal and Ethical Problems in the Delivery of Health Care endorsed a provision stating that a person may wish in advance that her death be declared solely on the basis of traditional criteria of irreversible cardiopulmonary function. Another provision incorporated in this model allows a person to make an anatomical gift by an advance directive and to provide instructions for any limitations or special uses.[46]

If one accepts the proposition that an advance directive may apply to death or post-death situations, one may argue that an advance directive is an alternative means to a will by which a person may direct the manner and place of disposal of her body after death, and since advance directives

---

[45] Ed Newman, 'Part Four: Patients Have Rights but Doctors Have Rights Too', available at www.cp.duluth.mn.us/~ennyman/DAS-4.html, accessed on 10 May 2007.

[46] The New Jersey Bioethics Commission's Combined Advance Directive for Health Care (March 1991), mentioned in Cantor, above n 17, at 163–4. See also Part III of optional forms at section 4 to the Uniform Health-Care Decisions Act (1994), available at www.law.upenn.edu/bll/ulc/fnact99/1990s/uhcda93.pdf, accessed on 28 November 2005.

have peremptory legal power, BTs included in advance directives may be compelling.[47] However, if one adheres to the distinction between a required and a preferred medical treatment mentioned above, and if one accepts the view that such a distinction should result in different practical outcomes concerning the validation of advance directives, one may argue that when regarded as or included in an advance directive, BTs can only exclude a normal option of disposal, such as cremation, but may not necessarily compel an unorthodox disposal of the body.

In order to examine the applicability of the living wills mechanism to BTs, it is necessary to explore the general purposes of advance directives. In their book, *The Right to Die*, Alan Meisel and Kathy Cerminara identify three such general and interconnected purposes.[48] The first, which they find the most important from the perspective of those who issue the directives, is to provide a means of exercising some degree of control over medical care. As the core concept behind a living will lies in the right to privacy and autonomy in medical decision making, the primary purpose of a living will is to ensure that the individual's wishes are respected.

The second purpose of advance directives according to Meisel and Cerminara is to avoid some of the more serious procedural problems associated with making decisions for patients who lack capacity, primarily by forestalling recourse to the judicial process. In this regard, advance directives motivate health professionals to avoid a judicial resolution to end-of-life decision making for incompetent patients. Advance directives thus anticipate the need for either the clinical designation of a surrogate or the judicial appointment of a guardian.

The third purpose of advance directives, which Meisel and Cerminara see as the most important from the perspective of healthcare providers, is to provide this group of people with immunity from civil or criminal liability. Since most litigated right-to-die cases wind up in court out of fear of liability, the statutory immunity provisions that are secured by advance directives legislation facilitate decision making by providing another reason for keeping cases in the clinical setting.

Advance directives also help lower the costs of providing medical treatment to those who are not likely to benefit from it. Under this rationale, the issuance of health insurance and the premiums for that insurance will depend upon the execution of an advance directive.[49] Finally, advance

---

[47] Of course, the decedent may also provide a durable power of attorney for healthcare and empower an agent to make necessary funeral arrangements. Hernandez, above n 28.

[48] Alan Meisel and Kathy L. Cerminara, *The Right to Die*, 3rd edn (New York: Aspen, 2004) 7-16-7-20.

[49] However, Meisel and Cerminara argue that it is not clear whether it costs less to treat patients at end-of-life with advance directives than those without them.

directives fulfil the need to avoid emotional and financial burdens to attending family during the dying process.

Do the general rationales for advance directives apply to testaments concerning the disposal of the body after death? It appears that all three purposes of advance directives may be relevant here. One can convincingly argue that the interest in respecting one's privacy and dignity with regard to treating one's body in a state of incompetency should be maintained upon death, and that the dead or, more accurately, the Human Subject in its capacity of holding surviving interests of the person may still hold autonomy-based interests validating her past wishes regarding disposal of her body. Moreover, the need to avoid judicial resolution in this regard, especially when disputes between different parties claiming control over remains are not infrequent phenomena, is real. If BTs are made through, and are regarded as, advance directives, and as a result have legal effect, many conflicts will be nullified so that the decedent's prior wishes prevail. Finally, respecting advance directives in the area of disposal of the body may provide civil or criminal immunity to the substitute decision maker. As discussed in the previous chapter, case law firmly establishes the common law duty to dispose of the body of the deceased. This duty is owed by the executor, administrator or next-of-kin depending on the jurisdiction where death occurs. Under some circumstances, violating this duty may result in civil or criminal liability. Classifying BTs as advance directives would not only ensure that the legal duty to dispose of the body of the deceased is fulfilled but also guarantee that any person who would have been held responsible for its violation is now free from such liability.

Trust

A trust is a legally imposed and enforceable conscientious obligation to act in accordance with a moral commitment. A more neutral definition of trust regards it as 'a fiduciary relationship with respect to property in which one person (the trustee) holds property for the benefit of another person (the beneficiary), with specific duties attaching to the manner in which the trustee deals with the property'.[50] Through this legal mechanism a trustee is bound to act in the interests and at the direction of the legally identified beneficiary.[51] Enforcing the trust can be made possible by the beneficiary or, in default, by the Attorney General representing the public interest.

---

[50] Mark Reutlinger, *Wills, Trusts and Estates* (Boston: Little, Brown and Company, 1993) 143.
[51] Bernard M. Dickens, 'Control of Excised Tissues Pending Implantation' (1990) 7 *Transplantation/Implantation Today* 36–41, 40.

When a person instructs another to act on her behalf for the disposal of the former's body after death, and when such an instruction is attached to a bequest, she may construct a legal relationship of trust, specifically in the form of a trust for purpose. Trusts for purpose are divided into three categories.[52] The first group consists of trusts for charitable purposes, namely purposes that serve the public interest. A charity is 'a gift to be applied consistently with existing laws for the benefit of an indefinite number of persons, either by bringing their hearts under the influence of education or religion, by relieving their bodies from disease, suffering or constraint, by assisting them to establish themselves for life, or by erecting or maintaining public buildings or works, or otherwise lessening the burden of government'.[53] These trusts are effective and fully enforceable by the Public Trustee representing society at large, and they exist for as long as the testator wishes, even in perpetuity. The second group of trusts includes trusts for non-charitable purposes accomplishing merely personal ends of the testator. Under these trusts the trustee has power but not duty to carry out the purpose of the trust and she is bound by it only as a matter of honour. Non-charitable trusts have a limited period of duration, usually governed by the Rule against Perpetuities. In the last category of trusts for purpose there exist trusts for purpose deemed by lawmakers to violate public policy. Such trusts are neither enforceable nor permissible for any period of time and they are legally void.

It seems reasonable to regard testamentary direction as to the disposal of one's body after death, including the allocation of funds from the estate for the fulfilment of such purpose, as a bequest for a personal or non-charitable purpose.[54] The purpose at stake is the construction of a memorial for the deceased, whether visible, intelligible or audible. But a bequest for a personal purpose does not benefit survivors at all. One can argue that when the bequest is for a personal purpose, the decedent is consuming resources for her own gratification, and apart from what Adam Hirsch calls 'a secondary multiplier effect' no one other than her benefits from it.[55] One can further argue that as a matter of distributive justice, the welfare of consumption by the living outweighs and should

---

[52] Adam J. Hirsch, 'Trusts for Purposes: Policy, Ambiguity and Anomaly in the Uniform Laws' (1999) 26 *Florida State University Law Review* 913–57, 913–14.

[53] *John J. Detwiller* v. *David Hartman* et al. 37 NJ Eq. 347, 353–4 (N.J. Ct Ch. 1883) [*Detwiller*]. Compare Restatement of Law, Third (Trusts) c. 6 s. 28 (2003). See *Commissioners of Income Tax* v. *Pemsel* (1891) AC 531, 61 LJQB 290.

[54] Hanbury and Martin, *Modern Equity*, Jill E. Martin ed., 7th edn (London: Sweet & Maxwell, 2005) 177.

[55] Adam J. Hirsch, 'Bequests for Purposes: A Unified Theory' (1999) 56 *Washington and Lee Law Review* 33–110, 65 [Hirsch, 'BFP'].

outweigh that of the dead. This view was expressed by courts in the context of a bequest for perpetual care of the decedent's family cemetery lot. It was ruled that: 'Such charities [to care for burial plots] would impoverish the living to decorate the graves of the forgotten dead.'[56]

In line of their theoretical classification, permanent bequests for the maintenance of a place of burial were declared void by court,[57] whereas a temporary trust for this purpose (not offending against the rule against perpetuities) was regarded as lawful but not obligatory.[58] Thus, courts did not approve directions that called for the erection of a base for a flagstaff in a park in memory of the testator's father,[59] nor did they validate a trust made by will for the erection of a fence to keep the burial plot and monument in good repair and for the establishment of a military band playing dirges and performing a funeral march on the testator's birthday and other holidays.[60] Furthermore, a distinction was made between a trust for a graveyard, even though restricted to one denomination, which was regarded as charity,[61] as opposed to a trust for individual tombs in the churchyard.[62] Some cases validated such temporary trusts for a period of twenty-one years following the testator's death,[63] and in some instances this was also achieved by legislation.[64]

Along with these legal decisions there are a few cases upholding trusts for purposes having to do with the disposal of the testator's body. Three examples will suffice. In *In re Henderson's Estate*, the deceased bequeathed one Mr Linforth $20,000 in trust for the purchase of a plot and the building of a vault wherein the remains of her late husband, her son, parents and herself would be placed after the remains of the said relatives were removed from another plot where they had already been buried.[65] The surviving relatives objected to the removal of the deceased and their parents' remains, and the trustee petitioned for further instructions. The trial court ruled that under the previous decision of *Enos*,[66] the

---

[56] *In re Palethorp's Estate* 249 Pa. 389 (Sup. Ct Pa. 1915).
[57] *Re Vaughan* (1886) 33 Ch. D 187; *Hoare* v. *Osborne* (1866) 1 Eq. 585.
[58] *Re Dean* (1889) 41 Ch. D 552, 557.
[59] *Morristown Trust Co.* v. *Mayor and Board of Aldermen of Town of Morristown* et al. 82 NJ Eq. 521 (1913).
[60] *Detwiller*, above n 53.   [61] *Re Manser* [1905] 1 Ch. 68; *Re Eighmie* [1935] Ch. 524.
[62] *Lloyd* v. *Lloyd* (1852) 2 Sim. (NS) 225.
[63] Ronald Atherton, 'Claims on the Deceased: The Corpse as Property' (2000) 7 *Journal of Law and Medicine* 361–75, 370 [Atherton].
[64] See e.g. Perpetuities Act, RSA 2000, c. P-5, s. 20.
[65] *In re Henderson's Estate* 13 Cal. App. 2d 449, 57 P 2d 212 (Dis. Ct App. 1936) [*Henderson's Estate*].
[66] *Enos*, above n 26.

testamentary trust for burial could not be carried out. However, it recommended the trustees to appeal in an attempt to overrule this decision.[67]

On appeal, the Court of Appeals distinguished this case from *Enos*, holding that while in the latter case the deceased's wishes were unknown and the decision regarding the place and manner of burial was completely deferred to Mrs Snyder, this was not the case in *Henderson*. The court held that the deceased's wishes regarding the building of the mausoleum and the removal of her remains and of those who predeceased her should be carried out, and so the trial court decision was overruled.

In *re Shepp's Estate*, the decedent provided $4,000 from his estate for maintenance of his mausoleum and for the placing of flowers in the mausoleum and in the urn on his cemetery lot at specified times and on his parents' cemetery lot yearly on Memorial Day. The court found these provisions legally binding.[68]

Finally, in *Fidelity Union Trust Co. v. Heller*,[69] the decedent requested in his will that his body and the remains of surviving members of his family rest in a mausoleum, for the building of which he provided $25,000 from his estate. Additionally, the decedent set up a trust fund for the care and maintenance of the plot and mausoleum. Seven years after making the will, he bought a plot in another cemetery and secured from that cemetery its approval to erect a mausoleum thereon. Evidence showed that the deceased had started negotiation for the erection of the mausoleum, but he died without completing the building of it. Having not changed his will, the decedent was buried in the receiving vault of the first cemetery, awaiting determination of the place of final burial. The executors and trustees under the will petitioned for instructions as to his burial, the erection of the mausoleum, the removal of bodies of the decedent's family and the trust for the maintenance of the cemetery plot. The court was satisfied that the decedent by his conduct and acts subsequent to the execution of his will changed his mind about interment in the first cemetery and abandoned the plan to build a mausoleum there. Since all but one of the next-of-kin desired that the decedent be buried in the second cemetery, the court relieved executors and trustees from carrying out the directions of the will. As for the direction providing a trust fund for perpetual care and maintenance of a plot in the first cemetery, the court held that such trust was disqualified since the decedent was to be interred

---

[67] *Henderson's Estate*, above n 65, at 213.
[68] *In re Shepp's Estate* 29 Pa. D & C 2d 385 (1962).
[69] *Fidelity Union Trust Co. v. Arthur E. C. Heller* et al. 16 NJ Sup. 285, 84 A 2d 485 (N.J. Sup. Ct 1951).

in another cemetery. The court suggested that the parties apply for the appointment of an appropriate substitute trustee. It did not see any problem appointing a trust for that purpose and did not mention any theoretical difficulties deriving from the law of trusts in this regard.[70]

The idea that a person can create a trust for the management of his or her disposal also has some support in legislation. For example, in California the law explicitly states that a person can make a cemetery care fund, which is regarded as a trust for a 'charitable and eleemosynary purpose', and that such trust does not violate the law against perpetuities.[71] Legislation in Canada also suggests that the Public Trustee may be responsible for the execution of the person's wishes concerning burial and disposal. The Public Guardian and Trustee may be granted letters of probate or letters of administration and may be appointed as a trustee under a will as if he or she were a private trustee.[72] The Public Guardian and Trustee is one of the persons who may take possession of the body of the deceased for the purposes of its burial.[73] The Public Trustee is authorized to arrange the funeral of a person who dies intestate,[74] and he or she may accept and administer any charitable or public trust.[75]

To sum up, the theoretical distinction between charitable and non-charitable trusts leads to the conclusion that if it is possible to create trusts for the management of the disposal of the testator's body, these trusts are limited in their durability by being subject to the rule against perpetuities. Yet, in practice, courts permit the establishment of trusts for disposal even for perpetuity.[76] It was as early as in 1904 that the Supreme Court of Pennsylvania held in *Pettigrew* that 'the law recognizes property in a corpse, but property subject to a trust, and limited in its rights to such exercise as shall be in conformity with the duty out of which the rights arise',[77] namely the duty to dispose of the body of the deceased. This

---

[70] See also *Renga* v. *Spadone* et al. 60 NJ Sup. 353, 159 A 2d 142 (N.J. Sup. Ct 1960).
[71] California Health and Safety Code, s. 8776 (Thomson/West 2006).
[72] Public Guardian and Trustee Act, RSO 1990, c. P-51, s. 7.
[73] Trillium Gift of Life Network Act, RSO 1990, c. H-20, s. 5(5)(b).
[74] Crown Administration of Estates Act, RSO 1990, c. C-47, s. 2(1)(a).
[75] Public Guardian and Trustee Act, RSO 1990, c. P-51, s. 12. But see in England where the Public Trustee cannot accept trusts exclusively for religious or charitable purposes: Public Trustee Act 1906, c. 55, s. 2(5). See also *Calma* v. *Sesar*, where the court ruled that the powers of the Public Trustee extend to the estate of a person but not to the remains. *Calma* v. *Sesar* (1992) 106 FLR 446.
[76] In addition to the common situations of trusts made for the maintaining of the testator's place of burial, there may be trusts made for cryonics. Currently, the cryonics societies fund their operations either by requiring an up-front payment that becomes the property of the society or by establishing a charitable trust fund for cryonic research. Baker, above n 41, at 701.
[77] *Pettigrew* et al. v. *Pettigrew* et al. [1904] 207 Pa. 313, 315.

ruling was affirmed in a later case[78] and is the cornerstone for the idea that
BTs and other directions regarding the management of one's place of
disposal can be regarded as legally valid trusts. As established in this
section, legislation and case law provide additional support for the proposition that matters of disposing one's body after death can be governed
by the law of trusts and are subject, in some jurisdictions, to legal authorities such as the Public Trustee.

Agency

When the deceased nominates a person to act on her behalf with regard to
place and manner of disposal, might there be a relationship of agency
between the two surviving the death of the principal? Agency is 'the
fiduciary relationship which exists between two persons, one of whom
expressly or impliedly consents that the other should act on his behalf so
as to affect his relations with third parties, and the other of whom similarly
consents so to act or so acts'.[79] A broader definition of agency also
includes relations between the principal and the agent when the latter
has no authority or power to affect the principal's relations with third
parties. The agent in such a situation is referred to as 'canvassing' or
'introducing' agent.[80]

However, the actual authority of an agent is usually terminated by the
death of the principal or the agent.[81] This is because the person who
otherwise is liable to third parties, namely the heir or executor, has
become a different person from the giver of the authority.[82] Under this
explanation, the agency relationship is confidential and personal so that
the specific identity of both principal and agent is material to the relationship itself.[83]

A more accepted view, also supported by the American restatement on
agency, is that the authority of an agent may be irrevocable even by
death.[84] Generally, an authority of an agent may be irrevocable in two
types of cases. The first case involves a situation in which the authority
accompanies a security or proprietary interest, or is part of it or a means of
achieving it. Under this scenario, the proposition that an agent's authority

---

[78] *Frost* v. *St Paul's Cemetery Association* 254 NYS 2d 316, 318 (1964).
[79] Restatement of Law, Second, Agency (American Law Institute), s. 1 (1958) [Restatement on Agency].
[80] Bowstead and Reynolds, *On Agency*, 17th edn. (London: Sweet & Maxwell, 2001) 8–9 [Bowstead and Reynolds].
[81] *Drew* v. *Nunn* [1874–80] All ER 1144. See also G. H. L. Fridman, *The Law of Agency*, 6th edn (London: Butterworths, 1990) 367.
[82] *Ibid.*   [83] *Ibid.*   [84] Restatement on Agency, above n 79, at ss. 119(2)(a), 120(3).

is irrevocable upon the death of the principal is premised on the idea that the agency relationship that is at stake involves a proprietary interest that, once granted, is unaffected by loss of capacity of its grantor. However, it is difficult to make such a proposition in regard to the body of a decedent. As argued in chapter 3, the body of the deceased (as a whole) is not and should not be subject to a proprietary interest.[85] Therefore the agent's authority must terminate upon the death of the principal when the agency relationship concerns BTs.

The second situation by which the authority of an agent is irrevocable upon the death of the principal is where authority secures an obligation owed by the principal to her agent.[86] This is a more plausible situation in the post-death context whereby, for example, the principal asks her agent to dispose of the body of the first and in return promises to give the latter some portion of her estate. Hence, it is possible to argue that when such an agreement is constituted whereby a person undertakes to carry out the decedent's prior wishes regarding disposal, and the decedent promises to confer on that person some benefit for her service, an agency relationship may be established.

Contract

It is possible to regard an advance directive concerning the disposal of one's body after death as a contract between the deceased and another person, the effect of which commences after the death of the first. One version of such a contractual model already exists with the acknowledgement of a prepaid funeral contract. In Ontario, for example, the Funeral Directors and Establishments Act establishes the possibility to construct

an agreement whereby a person contracts with a purchaser to provide or make provision for funeral services, funeral supplies, or both, or for the transportation of a dead human body including disbursements, upon the death of a beneficiary, if any payment for the contract is made prior to the death of the beneficiary or the purchaser enters into an insurance contract or plan under which a licensee is to receive directly or indirectly the proceeds of the insurance policy upon the death of the beneficiary.

---

[85] However, this is not to say that organs or tissues extracted from the deceased or the living person may not be subject to property. For example, a direction to cremate the principal's organ or tissues if they are found non-suitable for transplantation may create a proprietary interest.

[86] *Smart* v. *Sandars* (1884) 5 CB 895, 917, [1843–60] All ER 758. See also Bowstead and Reynolds, above n 80, at 556–7.

Under this legislation, the term 'funeral' has a broad definition to include 'a rite or a ceremony in connection with the death of a person where the body is present'.

Although a contractual relationship concerning these matters is legally valid, the law in Ontario, for example, establishes that after the death of the beneficiary the personal representative of the decedent may cancel the contract prior to the delivery of all the services contracted for.[87] The law in Nova Scotia prescribes more rigorous conditions for the cancellation of such a contract. The contract may be cancelled by the personal representative only when 'because of great distance or of some extraordinary circumstance, it is not reasonably feasible to provide or use the goods, merchandise or services contracted for by the purchaser under the purchase agreement'.[88] It is clear, however, that when these conditions are not met, the contract is legally binding, as it is also clear that the contract may not be cancelled even when the conditions set under this statute are met.[89]

In conclusion, this section examined whether Assumption C of the general objection to enforcing BTs, namely that BTs can and should be made only by will and is and should be subject to the law of wills and testaments, is a sound assumption. As demonstrated in this section, there are a few legal institutions by which one can conceptualize the constitution of bodily testaments. While the application of some of these institutions to the context of testaments regarding the disposal of one's body after death raises theoretical and doctrinal difficulties, most of the models suggested in this section seem to offer a reasonable account for the possible legal relationship between the decedent and the addressee of these testaments. It follows that there exist effective legal mechanisms other than the will by which BTs can have legal effect. Assumption C must be overruled.

Alternatives to the property classification criterion (PCC)

In the previous section, it was examined whether it is possible to regard the direction of a decedent as to the manner and place of disposal of her body through the lens of legal institutions other than the will. The current section will analyse the question of whether, regardless of the possibility to explain BTs in legal forms other than a will, BTs could still have legal effect if made under a will. In order to provide an affirmative answer to this question, one needs to challenge Assumption A above, namely that

---

[87] Funeral Directors and Establishments Act, RSO 1990, c. F-36, s. 32(3).
[88] Cemetery and Funeral Services Act, RSNS 1989, c. 62, s. 13.
[89] The legislator uses the word 'may' to imply such legislative intent.

the law of succession is occupied only with the transfer of property after death (the PCC) and that any direction concerning items characterized as non-proprietary cannot be included in it, and therefore does not have peremptory power.

In this section, I will argue that a will can be validated by criteria other than whether the content of it constitutes a proprietary interest or not, and consequently that BTs – even when made by a will – can have legal effect. The motivation to establish criteria other than the PCC derives from the complexities characterizing the circumstances by which BTs are formed and the substantive provisions that they include. It also stems from the understanding that it is legally erroneous necessarily to identify the testamentary relation with one that is focused on the transfer of proprietary interests after death.

One can describe any proprietary interest as the relation between an object and a person (usually the property holder) or as a relation between (at least) two persons over an object. The requirement of the PCC in wills regards the testamentary power as a relation between the testator and an object, the latter of which is part of the scope over which the testator is authorized to exercise her legal power, namely her estate. However, the testamentary relationship should be better seen as a relationship between the testator and (at least) another person over that object. The important component of the testamentary relationship is the *relation* between the different parties derived from the testator's autonomy-based interest in determining the fate of what she cares much about in her life, and not (or not solely) the object itself in which her interest lies.

Moreover, when one examines the general rationales for testamentary power, one finds that there is no sound justification for excluding non-proprietary items from the exercise of such legal power. There are four main rationales for any testamentary power. The first rationale focuses on the objects of the testamentary power themselves. The argument is that since the dead cannot hold property after death, there is a societal concern for the goods previously held by them. According to this rationale, administrating a decedent's estate aims to preserve and protect the estate. Similarly, one can contend that after death the deceased cannot hold an interest in maintaining her reputation or an interest in protecting her body from injury or disfigurement. If society cares about these objects of interest, then under the same reasoning they should also be included in the scope of the testamentary power. There is nothing special in property that should exclude other objects of interest from legal protection.

The second rationale for testamentary power has to do with care for third parties other than the testator. It is argued that one of the purposes of administrating the estate is to satisfy and discharge all debts and claims that are charges or liens on the property. A related motivation focuses on society's concern for the decedent's relatives and surviving legal entities. By administrating an estate the residue of the property is distributed at a proper time to those persons who are entitled to it.[90] Of course, caring for third parties and relatives of the decedent may be secured by means other than the inclusion of property in the estate. For example, the testator may direct in his will that X should teach his daughter piano lessons, accompany his wife on weekly visits to the local church, or make sure that his small brother receives university education. The promotion of cultural, religious or educational aspects of human beings has no less important societal purposes than caring for the material well-being of third parties other than the testator. Focusing solely on the latter aspect misses a wide spectrum of things which society ought to care for.

In addition, there are economic incentives for acknowledging the freedom of testators. It is argued, for example, that owners gain personal satisfaction from bequeathing property. Hence, testamentary freedom adds to the utility owners derive from what they acquire and enhances their incentive both to produce and to save wealth.[91] In addition, the right to bequeath serves as an incentive to industry and saving and, as Jeremy Bentham argued, keeps the younger generation attentive to the care and needs of the ageing generation.[92] The problem with this line of argument is that there are no empirical studies supporting it, and even if there were, one would still need to examine their relevance to the idea that wills should be concerned with property alone. In other words, the proposition that the inclusion of property in wills is efficient does not entail that the inclusion of other items in a will may be inefficient or unnecessary. The economic incentives to testamentary power support the idea that the testamentary power over the property one had while alive should be extended. They do not provide any good explanation, let alone sound justification, for the negative formulation of this argument, namely that the testamentary power should *not* be extended over items which are *not* the testator's property.

A fourth justification for the testamentary power concerns the idea that the law, without conferring positive rights upon the dead, does in some degree take account after a person's death of her desires and wishes as expressed while alive. The argument is that these desires and wishes are

---

[90] See, for example, Succession Law Reform Act, RSO 1990, c. S-26, Part V.
[91] Hirsch, 'BFP', above n 55, at 51.
[92] James E. Bailey, 'An Analytical Framework for Resolving the Issues Raised by the Interaction Between Reproductive Technology and the Law of Inheritance' (1998) 47 *DePaul Law Review* 743, 776–7.

so important to the living person that the meaning attached to them is inter alia conditioned upon their being fulfilled after the person is dead. One explanation for this argument focuses on the nature of the wishes themselves. It is argued that the full value of these wishes may only be determined if they are enforced regardless of the testator's awareness or experience of their enforcement. Another possible explanation originates in the Roman law idea of *hereditas iacens*. This is the notion that after death, the decedent's personality continues to exist for some purposes. Inheritance, in the interval between death and the conferral of property upon heirs, represents the *persona* of the deceased (*personae vice fungitur*).[93] As explained by Holmes, the *persona* which represented the aggregate of the decedent's rights and duties was the aggregate of what had formerly been family rights and duties originally sustained by the deceased as the family head, and so with the death of this person the heir came to be identified with his ancestors for the purposes of the law.[94] The holding of property by the heir was based on a fiction that the heir was the same person as the decedent whose title was not denied. Hence, according to this argument, transferring property through the mechanism of wills or inheritance enables the artificial continuity of the decedent's personality. Nevertheless, respecting the decedent's wishes as to items other than her property may also explain such continuity and it is not clear why it follows from this argument that the inclusion of some items in wills must be invalidated.

Not only do the general justifications for testamentary power not result in the conclusion that a will must not include items other than the testator's property and that these items should not have peremptory power, but there are specific arguments which convincingly justify the inclusion of bodily testaments under the law of wills.

First, people have expectations that their wishes expressed while alive will be respected after they are dead within public policy constraints. Moreover, religious people have expectations that others will not violate their convictions, and a religious community in which the deceased was a member has a legitimate interest in carrying out the religious beliefs of its members to the full. A person's wishes regarding the disposal of her body after death represent this person's most precious cultural or religious beliefs. Overriding the prior wishes of the deceased is an act against one's personal (secular or religious) interest as well as communal interests. A related argument focuses on the institution of keeping promises

---

[93] Glanville Williams, *Salmond on Jurisprudence*, 11th edn (London: Sweet & Maxwell, 1957) 483 [*Salmond*].

[94] O. W. Holmes, *The Common Law* (London: Macmillan, 1882) 343.

and honouring past wishes in general and on the public interest in it. Respecting the decedent's prior wishes as to disposal of her body manifests to survivors that their own provisions for disposal of their bodies will be respected and as such reaffirms the social institution of making promises and builds faith among members of the society. Furthermore, respect for the prior wishes of the deceased as to the place and manner of disposal carries another important societal role. By diminishing familial conflicts and saving legal costs, the enforcement of BTs denies remote relatives or friends any opportunity to challenge the prescribed form of disposal, thereby creating efficiency and promoting the well-being of society and its members at large.[95]

Second, one can argue that people define themselves in terms of their physical selves, and so invasion of the body after death, especially through acts performed contrary to a person' prior wishes regarding disposal of her body, injures the personality of this person and the image she would have wanted to have after death.[96]

Third, regarding BTs as a legally valid form of will accords with the common law duty to dispose of the body of the deceased. Such a duty falls on family or close friends of the deceased with whom the deceased had the most meaningful or personal relationships.[97] The duty is not only moral, but also legal.[98] It is believed that this familial obligation, discussed in the previous chapter, is widely established in the common law as the legal duty to bury the dead. Such a duty has three distinct sources.[99] First, there is a necessity to dispose of the body of the deceased for the prevention of contagion and the protection of the living. The familial duty to bury the dead also involves a humanistic idea that disposal of the body must be carried out in a decent way. This idea reflects an appreciation of the similarity existing between the dead person and the person she was and the relations which are still maintained with the dead person, especially when carrying out her wishes. The second source of the duty to dispose of the body of the deceased stems from the elementary need or

---

[95] Heather Conway, 'Dead, But Not Buried: Bodies, Burial and Family Conflicts' (2003) 23(3) *Legal Studies* 423–52, 434 [Conway].

[96] Horan, above n 37, at 438.

[97] Historically, many functions of the mortuary profession were taken from family members. Before the 1880s, the cleansing, dressing and care of a cadaver until the funeral service and the arrangements for the construction of a coffin were all tasks that fell to a decedent's family. Hernandez, above n 28, at 992.

[98] I discussed the concept of ethics of families elsewhere. See Daniel Sperling, 'From the Dead to the Unborn: Is There an Ethical Duty to Save Life?' (2004) 23(3) *Medical Law* 567–86, 578–81.

[99] Paul M. Quay, 'Utilizing the Bodies of the Dead' (1984) 28 *Saint Louis University Law Journal* 889–927, 901–4.

moral instinct to differentiate humans from animals. Since the act of burial is unique to humans and symbolizes both a person's finality and her purpose in life, treating the body in this context reaffirms the significant values of a human being. Finally, the familial duty to bury the dead derives from piety and fidelity to promises made to the deceased while alive and out of reverence for her and her memory.

As can be seen, the second and third rationales for the duty to dispose of the body of the deceased focus on the dead person herself, specifically her moral status and the expectations she had while alive, and the reflection of her character through the living who cherish her in their memory. It follows that when the deceased leaves an explicit wish as to the manner or place of disposal, the duty to dispose of the body cannot be fully met if such a wish is ignored. The significance one wants to attach to the dead person by disposing of her body is ignored when one does not follow her testamentary wishes.

A fourth specific argument in favour of including BTs in a will concerns the important advances in ideas of death and dying. In recent years there has been a shift from denial of death to acceptance of death, mainly through the following three important changes: the rise of the hospice movement which has empowered the patient to be involved in decisions regarding her care and plans for death; the debate over euthanasia and physician-assisted suicide, which has raised consciousness about the importance of 'death with dignity'; and the focus on the autonomy of the individual to define for herself what that really means.[100] In addition, the Aids pandemic and other terminal illnesses provided a therapeutic value for disposal practices.[101] These developments contributed in two ways to the subject of disposal of one's body after death. They raised its importance to first priority for the dying patient, thereby enhancing its significance among survivors and society at large. Second, they led to ways to institutionalize this new perception of death and its practices and made it permanent and mandatory. It is easy to see how a person's decision as to the final disposal of her body after death facilitates and accords with the process of acceptance of her anticipated death. Only by giving full legal power to BTs does society respect these important developments reflecting changes in the values and beliefs which a person maintains about death.

In conclusion, the general justifications for testamentary power as well as the specific arguments in favour of regarding BTs as a form of will lead

---

[100] Hernandez, above n 28, at 998–1004.
[101] Mark E. Wojcik, 'Aids and Funeral Homes: Common Legal Issues Facing Funeral Directors' (1994) 27 *Journal of Marshall Law Review* 411–34.

to the conclusion that there is no good justification for excluding items other than the testator's property from a will, nor are there convincing arguments to invalidate testaments concerning disposal of the body after death due to their legal characterization, namely that they do not constitute the testator's property. Assumption A of the general argument opposing enforcement of BTs must therefore be denied. Nevertheless, rejecting the formal criterion of the PCC does not entail that BTs must always be validated and respected. The next section will discuss the substantial limitations of enforcing such complex testaments.

Substantial limitations of enforcing bodily testaments

In the previous section it was argued that there is no prima facie justification to object to BTs on the basis of their non-proprietary characteristic, and hence a priori BTs should enjoy peremptory legal power. Indeed, although one can find support in legislation,[102] case law[103] and literature[104] for the view that BTs are legally binding, the question of whether BTs have legal effect does not have a clear-cut answer but is determined on a case-by-case analysis. As will be illuminated shortly, the way courts resolve legal disputes regarding the disposal of the body after death reflects the view that in order to validate or invalidate BTs, their content must be examined and evaluated in light of other conflicting interests.

Traditionally, there are three categories of limitations upon any testamentary power applying to the testator's property.[105] First, there are limitations of *time*. Testamentary power should have legal effect only for a limited period after the testator's death, and any attempt to retain the property beyond that limit makes the testament void. Second, there are limitations of *amount*. The testator can determine the disposition of her property as long as some of it is allotted to those to whom she owes a duty of support, e.g. children or spouse. Lastly, there are limitations of *purpose*. According to Salmond, the power of testamentary disposition is given to 'a man that he may use it for the benefit of other men who survive him and to this end only can it be validly exercised'.[106] Hence, a testament to

---

[102] Above nn 29, 31.
[103] *O'Donnell*, above n 25, at 288; *In re Kaufman's Estate* 158 NYS 2d 376, 378 (Sup. Ct N.Y. 1956) [*Kaufman's Estate*]; *In re Johnson's Estate* 169 Misc. 215, 7 NYS 2d 81 (Sup. Ct N.Y. 1938).
[104] Conway, above n 95.   [105] *Salmond*, above n 93, at 484–5.
[106] Glanville Williams, *Salmond on Jurisprudence*, 12th edn (London: Sweet & Maxwell, 1966) 445.

withdraw or dissolve the testator's property or to bury his money with him must be void.

It is difficult, if at all possible, to apply the above categories to the case of BTs. It is clear that these limitations aim to preserve the property of the decedent, and to promote the interests of those entitled to it upon the death of the testator. More importantly, any limitation of the testamentary power which is called for by these categories assumes that the scope of the testamentary power encompasses items serving parties other than the testator. Bodily testaments for the disposal of the testator's body are different and unique in this respect, since their first and foremost purpose is to serve the testator herself. Carrying out these wishes satisfies the decedent's egoistic and yet justified expectations, and only as a derivative matter does it provide for the living. Rather than apply the general constraints on BTs, it is more desirable to construct an eclectic set of rules, each of which is directly or indirectly established under special circumstances raised by case law or legislation. The general picture formed out of this set of rules will provide much substance for the limitation of the legal effect of BTs.

Limitations directly established under legislation

In Canada, the law in British Columbia provides a statutory test for the invalidation of a testamentary document pertaining to the disposal of the body of a testator. Section 53 of the Cemetery and Funeral Services Act reads that:

Subject to the Human Tissue Gift Act, a written preference by a person as stated in a will, a preneed cemetery services plan or a prearranged funeral services plan respecting the disposition of the human remains of that person is binding on the person who under section 51 has the right to control the disposition of the human remains *unless compliance with that preference would be unreasonable, or impracticable or would cause hardship.*[107]

Although Canadian scholars have suggested adopting this model in other provinces as well,[108] it currently has limited effect and has not been discussed in any of the reported cases since its enactment.

---

[107] Cemetery and Funeral Services Act, RSBC 1996, c. 45, s. 53 (my emphasis). Section 51 specifies the persons who control the disposition of the human remains or cremated remains of the deceased. Interestingly, the legislator regards the nominee in the will as the person with preference to others as to the disposition of the body.

[108] Milton W. Zwicker and M. J. Sweatman, 'Who Has the Right to Choose the Deceased's Final Resting Place?' (2002) 22 *Estates, Trusts and Pensions Journal* 43–54, 48.

Limitations directly established under case law

The legal status of BTs was directly examined in a few cases, mostly within the American jurisprudence. As a result, one can identify two major tests to determine whether BTs are legally valid or not.

Clear and convincing demonstration by competent and credible testimony In *Scheck*,[109] the decedent directed in her will that her body be buried in Palestine and provided $1,200 from her estate for that purpose. However, the children of the decedent buried her in New York with an expenditure of $189. The executor filed an action against the children of the decedent for the settlement of their account and the satisfaction of the will. The respondents argued that during the latter period and up until the time of her death, the decedent frequently expressed a wish to be buried in New York.

The court acknowledged that there is no right to property in a dead body in any commercial sense but merely a personal right primarily of the decedent herself and, if not exercised by her, then of her surviving or nearest relative. It was further held that such a right is not subject to delegation, devolutionary direction or intestate succession.[110] As a result, the court ruled that 'a direction in a will respecting disposal of the body of the testator is not testamentary in character … and is not in any partic-ular, either as to initial insertion, or subsequent revocation, to be gov-erned by the ordinary rules relating to strict testamentary directions'.[111] Instead, the court offered a procedural-evidentiary test to determine whether the expressed wish of the decedent was upheld. The court ruled that reversal of the formally expressed wishes of the decedent regarding disposal of her remains was permissible only upon a clear and convincing demonstration by competent and credible testimony that the latter wish was in fact her desire.[112]

The procedural-evidentiary test set in *Scheck* was affirmed in a recent decision of the District Court of Appeal of the State of Florida where it was held that 'a direction for the disposition of one's body should not be conclusive when contrary and convincing oral or written evidence of a change in intent is present'.[113] It follows that if the parties at stake cannot prove that the recent wishes of the decedent (whether oral or written)

---

[109] *In the Matter of the Estate of Esther Scheck* (1939) 172 Misc. 236, 14 NYS 2d 946.
[110] *Ibid.*, at 239–40.
[111] *Ibid.*, at 240–1. It follows that no formality in the directions is needed.
[112] *Ibid.*, at 242.
[113] *Ivan Cohen* et al. v. *Guardianship of Hilliard Cohen* 896 So. 2d 950, 955 (Fla. 2005).

represent a different approach regarding disposal of her body, BTs should have legal effect.

Reason, decency and accepted customs of mankind In *Smart* v. *Moyer*,[114] the court discussed the situation of whether a body can be exhumed ten months following burial so that it can be cremated according to the decedent's wishes as expressed in his will. It was ruled that 'a person has some interest in his body and organs thereof of such a nature that he should be able to make a disposition thereof, which should be recognized and held to be binding after his death, so long as that is done *within the limits of reason and decency as related to the accepted customs of mankind*'. The court clarified that the right to dispose of one's body is not absolute so that it does not include 'absurd or preposterous directions that would require extravagant waste of useful property or resources, or be offensive to the normal sensibilities of society in respect for the dead'.[115] In the specific circumstances of *Moyer*, the executor knew about the deceased's prior wishes and had the means to carry them out expeditiously but he chose not to do so, and instead permitted the act of burial. It was ruled that because of the executor's failure to act timely thereon, 'the executor should be deemed to have waived any right conferred in the will to direct the disposal of the deceased's remains' and therefore the body should remain buried where it was.[116]

Of course, one has to wonder why the right to direct the disposal of one's body passes to the executor. Under a Hohfeldian right analysis, the executor has only the *power* to make the deceased's wishes come true, and he or she is *immune* from any claims of third parties opposing those wishes. But the executor does not and should not have any rights to direct in advance the disposition of the decedent's body nor can he or she waive such rights or be estopped from exercising them after the death of the testator. In this regard, the court's decision seems to rest on dubious grounds.

Limitations indirectly established under case law

Beside the explicit limitations constituted under case law, there are other parameters which courts consider while discussing conflicts regarding disposal of the body and against which the testator's interest in determining the fate of her disposal is being balanced.

---

[114] *Moyer*, above n 25.   [115] *Ibid.*, at 110 (my emphasis).
[116] There was a similar ruling in *Fischer's Estate*, above n 25.

Timing Both the *Moyer* and *Scheck* cases involved a situation in which the deceased was already buried contrary to his or her explicit directive whose enforcement was sought in court. It is clear, however, that the timing of the request to enforce BTs affects its outcome. Courts are not willing to reinter or otherwise dispose of the body of the deceased once it rests in peace, while in general they enforce disposal requests if rendered possible. In *Gallagher*,[117] for example, the parents of the deceased sought to prevent their son-in-law from cremating the body of their deceased daughter prior to its burial. The husband, who was declared by court as having custody of the corpse, testified that the deceased had asked to be cremated after death, while her parents opposed such action based on their daughter's religious background and beliefs. Validating the daughter's prior wish to be cremated, the court ruled that any such wish should be approved by court as far as possible.

Likewise, in *Kasmer*[118] the decedent expressed in his will that he wanted to be cremated after death, thereby leaving his wife the full discretion regarding the destiny of his ashes. However, the decedent's wife died three months before he did. Upon his death, the probate court ordered cremation pursuant to the will. The parents of the deceased, who were also his personal representatives, appealed, opposing cremation for reasons of conscience. The District Court of Appeal of Florida upheld the lower decision, holding that testamentary directions should be complied with to the fullest extent possible. The court added that if the parents could not act in compliance with the decedent's will because of their religious views they should resign or ask the probate court to appoint another person suitable for carrying out the decedent's wishes.

In another case, the court agreed to disinter the body of the deceased and remove it to another cemetery according to the directions of the decedent even after the passage of a year since original interment. The court ruled that 'it is true that the remains of the deceased person should not be removed from the place of sepulture for light reasons. But compliance with the testator's positive direction is not, in my judgment, a light reason but a controlling one.'[119]

Despite these decisions, it is to be doubted whether the timing of the request to enforce BTs should be very relevant to its validity. If the decedent asked for her body to be disposed of in a specific way and her wish was ignored, it appears that this act is not less disrespectful of the

[117] *Sampson Tkaczyk v. Kenneth Gallagher* 26 Conn. Supp. 290 (1965).
[118] *Rose Kasmer et al. v. Guardianship of Roman Limner* 697 So. 2d 220 (Dist. Ct App. Fla. 1997).
[119] *Cooney*, above n 22, at 286.

decedent than reinterring the body or otherwise treating it in accordance with her previous wishes after it has already been buried. Any action taken with respect to the body once it has already been disposed of also affects the sensitivities of survivors and society overall. If this argument is sound, then what we care about most is not how the decedent would have regarded her disposal, but how it affects the sensitivities of the living.

Not only does the timing of the request to enforce BTs matter, but the timing in which the testament was made also plays an important role in establishing of whether BTs are legally valid. The general rule is that a decedent's preference regarding disposal of her body is entitled to greater weight if it was expressed relatively close to the date of her death. The closer the prior wishes of the decedent to the moment of death, the higher the chances that these wishes will be enforced.[120]

Cost Like any other testament, enforcing BTs will also depend on its cost. It may be that the cost of respecting the wishes of the decedent as to the manner in which her body will be disposed of is disproportionately high in the eyes of court.[121] In *Scheck*, for example, the decedent provided in her will a sum of $1,200 for the transportation of her body and its burial in Palestine. Burying the deceased contrary to her wishes was an expenditure of only $189. The court held that disregarding the formally expressed wish of the deceased would result in a 'material increase in the distributable assets of the estate with consequent financial advantage to those seeking its nullification'. Directing a wish to be preserved cryonically may be very costly and amount to the sum of $150,000.[122] According to the *Scheck* ruling, such a wish may never be enforced. On the other hand, an English case of 1946 upheld the wishes of the deceased who provided £300 for her funeral expenses. The court ruled that the deceased was entitled to spend that sum or any smaller sum she thought proper.[123]

With regard to funeral expenses, the law establishes that as long as these expenses are reasonable, they are payable out of the decedent's estate. The executor of the estate will usually examine the reasonableness of the funeral expenses since these expenses are normally the first charge on the estate. The reasonableness of funeral expenses is usually

---

[120] Frank D. Wagner, 'Enforcement of Preference Expressed by Decedent as to the Disposition of His Body After Death' (1973) 54 *American Law Reports* 3d 1037–67, 1044 [Wagner].

[121] The general rule in this regard holds that 'Dead debtors must not feast to make their living creditors fast.' Atherton, above n 63, at 369.

[122] See www.alcor.org/FAQs/faq01.html#cost, last accessed on 12 May 2007.

[123] *Re Pearce* [1946] SASR 118, mentioned in *Williams on Wills*, above n 26, at 79.

determined by three factors: the insolvency of the deceased's estate, which makes a lower scale of expenses appropriate; the deceased's position in life; and the deceased's religious beliefs and any wishes expressed by her as to her funeral.[124] Any decision examining the cost of enforcing BTs must consider all these factors.

Practicability A large number of cases stipulate the validity of BTs with its practical implications. Courts enforce BTs if they are capable of performance.[125] In *Leschey*,[126] the deceased left a will in which he directed that he be buried in his family lot wherein his mother and sister were interred. Additionally, he directed that the remaining space in the burial lot be reserved and used for the burial of his wife and brother. However, the lot did not permit the burial of more than four persons and the body of the brother of the deceased, who died three months later, was interred in the same lot. The widow of the decedent wanted to remove his body to another lot which she purchased in the same cemetery, but the deceased's children from his former marriage, including the executor of his will, opposed this. Ruling in favour of the testator's widow, the court held that when the deceased's direction in the will is impossible, it is fair to presume that his primary desire was to be buried with his wife. Therefore, the court enforced the deceased's wish to be buried with his wife only, and allowed the body to be removed to the new lot.

Another example of the practicability limitation is demonstrated in the matter of *Kaufman's Estate*.[127] In this case, the decedent appointed in her will one Frank McCarthy to take charge of her ashes and scatter them from an aeroplane proceeding in the direction of a mountainside. The decedent's sister opposed, and Kaufman was buried according to the rites of the Roman Catholic Church. Mr McCarthy filed an action in court, seeking to carry out the decedent's wishes. The court disallowed the action, ruling that since Kaufman had already been buried, regardless of how much time had elapsed since she was buried, it was impossible to comply with her wishes. The court did not relate to the content of these wishes at all but instead invalidated their legal status due to the failure to follow them.

Harm to society Sometimes, BTs involve an additional direction for the destruction of property and as such are regarded as harmful to

---

[124] Parry and Clark, above n 27, at 510.
[125] *In the Matter of the Estate of Benjamin B. Eichner* 173 Misc. 644, 18 NYS 2d 573 (N.Y. Surr. Ct 1940).
[126] *Leschey* v. *Leschey* et al. 374 Pa. 350, 97 A 2d 784 (Sup. Ct Pa. 1953).
[127] *Kaufman's Estate*, above n 103.

society. The *Meksras* case provides a good example. Eva Meksras directed in her will that her executor take possession of her jewellery and pictures and deliver them to the funeral director with instructions that these items be placed with her remains and interred in her mausoleum.[128] Since the decedent had already been buried without her valued items, the court's decision was theoretical yet guiding for cases similar to *Meksras*. The court emphasized that a testator may dispose of her property in any manner which is not contrary to law or public policy. It was held that permitting the decedent to be buried with her jewellery would create a great potential for public harm, since such practice would result in the ravaging and violation of cemeteries and tombs. Hence, the court found that implementing the deceased's wishes was contrary to public policy and void.[129]

The *Meksras* case is particularly interesting since the provision of the will which discussed property belonging to the deceased was intertwined with an instruction concerning the disposal of the testator's body. In this case there was no doubt that the items included in the will were classified as property, yet the court negated the effect of the testamentary provision for societal reasons. Of course, Meksras could have anticipated that implementing her directive would lead to the violation of her tomb. Still, she cared much about her personal items, and this is why she wanted to be buried with them. Despite her attachment to her belongings, the court ignored her specific wishes and took the position to decide what was best for her and for others wishing to be buried with their precious items.[130] By doing so, the court regarded her case as an example of a general phenomenon the occurrence of which is harmful to society. The public interest in the protection of burial sites is in conflict with and

---

[128] *Meksras Estate* 63 Pa. D & C 2d 371 (Pa. Com. Pl. 1974). Meksras' wish to be buried with her personal items is not unusual, as in ancient times people were buried with items of personal property, mainly because they believed they could continue to use them in the after-life. Sykas, above n 21, at 911.

[129] The court could have reasoned its decision by holding that the will called for the destruction of property and as such was against public policy. See *Eyerman* v. *Mercantile Trust Co.* 524 SW 2d 210, 217 (Miss. Ct App. 1975); Teresa Wear, 'Wills – Direction in Will to Destroy Estate Property Violates Public Policy' (1976) 41 *Missouri Law Review* 309. But see *National City Bank* v. *Case Western Reserve University* 369 NE 2d 814 (Ohio 1976); *In the Matter of the Estate of Anna M. Beck* 177 Misc. 2d 203, 676 NYS 2d 838, 841 (1998). Another example of disposal of a body against public policy is the request that the decedent be buried in an unauthorized place: *In the Matter of the Estate of James Walker* 64 NY 2d 354, 359 (1985).

[130] It remains doubtful whether the court would have ruled differently had Meksras directed, like Sandra West, that her burial plot be covered by concrete. See text accompanying above n 1.

prevails against the interest of individuals in shaping their own burial sites.[131]

Another case where harm to society was relevant in the context of BTs was in the matter of Sandra West.[132] As described by Sykas, in that case a multi-millionaire bequeathed her estate to her brother-in-law on the condition that he bury her in her baby-blue Ferrari, dressed in a lace negligee and seated in the driver's seat. According to media reports, the case came to court, and the judge upheld her directive, observing that it was 'unusual but not illegal'.[133] Although West's place of burial could be of no less interest to robbers or vandals than that of Eva Meksras, unlike the court in *Meksras*, this court did not share any concern for grave robbery. It is suggested that the reason for the different results in these cases lies in the nature of the items which were disposed of with the testator's body, specifically how close or remote these items were from reflecting the testator's personality. Thus, in the matter of Sandra West the court acknowledged that the car and her style of dressing in it were part of her character. These latter elements were found substantial enough to enforce her directive.[134] No similar observation was found in the case of Meksras.

It seems appropriate to infer from these cases that any form of disposal of a body after death that is clearly linked to the person's character, personality or 'story of life' may carry considerable weight when in conflict with the public interest in preventing harm to society. It is correct to argue that BTs fulfil unique personal objectives and so the argument that the public good is severed by such directions underestimates the importance of these testaments to personhood and their personal role in the relation between the testator and her body.

Public mores and vulnerabilities of other groups Bodily testaments may include practices contrary to public mores and decency that may offend certain groups in the society to which the testator belongs. In *Mitty v. Oliviera*, it was held that: 'From the act of joining a voluntary society there is implied an agreement to abide by the society's rules and regulations, to the extent at least that they are not in contravention of law or against public policy.'[135] It is likely that a provision in a will that the testator be cremated may hurt public feelings and be against public mores

---

[131] The fear of grave robbery is not unrealistic as is most manifested by the destruction and violation of ancient Egyptian graves.

[132] Text accompanying above n 1.

[133] Sykas, above n 21, at 926. The case could not be found in legal databases or on the internet.

[134] *Ibid.*, at 938.   [135] *Mitty* v. *Oliveira* 111 Cal. App. 2d 452, 459 (1952).

if the testator lives in an orthodox Jewish society, is a member of the
Roman Catholic church, or is part of a family of Holocaust survivors who
may associate cremation with the evils of the Nazis.[136]

Also, the practice of disinterment of a body is so socially and emotionally disfavoured, even when it is done to carry out the decedent's wishes
regarding burial, that courts use a presumption against removal of
remains to decline such requests. Courts hold that, once interred, the
body must not be removed, unless emergency or compelling private rights
are concerned.[137] Therefore, BTs may not be legally valid if their enforcement is delayed after the body is interred.

A more general opposition to public policy There may be other cases
in which general directions in a will are contrary to public policy and
therefore may not be valid. Destroying the testator's pet,[138] devising
property to the Devil, leaving property to a surviving relative on condition
that she wear nothing but white linen clothing every day of the year,
including winter, or on condition that the beneficiary not marry a domestic servant are only a few examples.[139] More relevant examples include
Lord Avebury's donor card expressing his wish that after his death parts
of his body should be used for transplantation and the rest given to the
inmates of the Battersea Dogs Home, and a huntsman's wishes for his
corpse to be fed to the hounds with which he hunted by cremating it first
and mixing his ashes with the dog food.[140]

The practice of cryogenic suspension of bodies may also be contrary to
public policy, at least in some jurisdictions, and any directions relating to
it may not be enforced. British Columbia, for example, explicitly states in
its legislation that 'a person must not offer for sale or sell any arrangement
for the preservation or storage of human remains based on cryonics,
irradiation or any other means of preservation or storage by whatever
name called, that is offered or sold on the expectation of the resuscitation

---

[136] The legality of the first crematorium in Israel, imported by Aley Shalechet, remains to be
seen. See www.aleyshalechet.co.il/english/eng_index.php, accessed on 12 May 2007.

[137] Wagner, above n 120, at 1049.

[138] *In re Capers' Estate* 34 Pa. D & C 2d 121 (1964); *In the Matter of the Estate of Clive Wishart*
(1992) ACWSJ Lexis 34836, 129 NBR (2d) 397. These directions usually aim to
prevent the testator's animals from mistreatment or abuse. This is especially true
when the decedent does not have family or friends to take care of the animal. Pubic
policy considerations may result in the argument that it is cruel to kill animals. Sykas,
above n 21, at 939.

[139] Sykas, above n 21, at 912 (note 11).

[140] Vanetia J. Newall, 'Folklore and Cremation' (1983) 49 *Pharos International* 18, 24;
Stephen White, 'The Law Relating to Dealing with Dead Bodies' (2000) 4 *Medical
Law International* 145–81, 177 (note 66).

of human remains at a future time'.[141] In a Californian case, the plaintiff, a mathematician and computer software scientist who suffered from a malignant brain tumour, desired to be cryogenically suspended pre-mortem with the assistance of an operator of a cryogenic preservation facility.[142] In order not to destroy the plaintiff's chance of reanimation, he also sought an injunction against a coroner performing an autopsy on his body after death. The court disallowed the plaintiff's action since it was regarded as calling for the assistance of a third party actually to kill him, and thereby refused to enjoin the coroner from carrying out his inquiry should the plaintiff commit suicide.

Procedural obstacles Occasionally, courts deal with the question of whether or not to enforce BTs by validating or invaliding their form. Procedural obstacles for enforcing BTs established by case law hold that, in order to be valid, BTs must be sufficiently detailed, clear and complete and must be in the form of instruction rather than a mere request. Thus, in *Bartlett*,[143] prior to his death the deceased selected and noted on a diagram one of his plots as a burial site ('Rex wants this for himself'). As the deceased was buried in another plot, his second spouse asked for permission to disinter his remains and remove them to his preferred plot. The California Court of Appeals refused to infer from the note on the diagram and from the purchase contract that the decedent had left an instruction as to place of burial. Instead, it was held that the statement written on the map was a mere preference and therefore was not binding.

Protection from harm to third parties There are rare circumstances in which BTs are invalidated to protect third parties from possible harm. In *Herold* v. *Herold*,[144] a dispute arose as to the possession of the deceased's body for the purpose of its interment. While the widow of the decedent wanted to bury the body in Lakeview cemetery in Cleveland, the father of the decedent, who was appointed by the deceased in a paper he wrote the day before he died, sought to have absolute control and disposition of the body and have it buried in Greenwood cemetery, Hamilton. In addition, the deceased's sister testified in court that the deceased had expressed his wish to be buried in Hamilton several times before his death. Despite clear evidence of the deceased's wishes to be buried in Hamilton, the

[141] Cemetery and Funeral Services Act, RSBC 1996, c. 45, s. 57. See also Cremation, Interment and Funeral Services Act, SBC 2004, c. 35, ss. 14, 61(2)(f).
[142] *Thomas Donaldson* et al. v. *Daniel Lungren as Attorney General* et al. 4 Cal. Rptr 2d 59 (Ct App. 1992).
[143] *Beverly Bartlett* v. *Annie Roberts Bartlett* WL 1161586 (Cal. App. 4 Dist. 2002).
[144] *Sarah Herold* v. *Henry Herold* et al. 3 Ohio NP (NS) 405 (Ct Com. Pl. 1905).

court ruled that since there was no clear proof that the decedent's family would approve the future interment of the decedent's widow in the family lot at Hamilton or that it would also include a place for the burial of the deceased's child, it was best that the widow should have custody over the body. Another reason for invalidating the decedent's BTs was the fact that the deceased had a child living in Cleveland so that if the body was interred in Hamilton the child could not go to visit it and pay the tributes of respect and affection that she would like to pay him.

Even if the court's decision in *Herold* is not free from criticism for the court's paternalism, it reflects the idea that when deciding whether BTs have legal effect, courts may also balance the interests of all parties involved as against the testator's interest in determining the fate of disposal of her body. The testator's prior wishes do not have peremptory power if they conflict the interests of others.

Quality of familial relationship At times, the decision of whether or not to enforce BTs is dependent upon the quality of familial relationship between the testator and the next-of-kin objecting to carry out BTs. In *Feller* v. *Universal Funeral Chapel Inc.*,[145] the deceased directed in his will that his body be put in a family mausoleum in Salem Falls cemetery. His widow and daughter, however, wanted to bury him elsewhere and the court had to decide whether to invalidate his wish. In deciding this question, the court examined the quality of the relationship between the deceased and his widow and daughter. It was held that the Feller couple lived separately for three years prior to Mr Feller's death and that there had been a strained relationship between the deceased and his daughter. The court ruled that when a normal filial relationship does not exist between father and daughter, the child does not have the right to dictate the place and manner of her father's burial. It follows that if the relationship between the deceased and his daughter was a positive one, the court was prepared to overrule the decedent's prior wishes, thereby adhering to the daughter's preference as to the place and manner of burial.[146]

When taken seriously, the *Feller* decision is very problematic. It suggests that a person's prior wishes regarding disposal of her body may be overridden by her loving next-of-kin only because of the positive relationship they had when the deceased was alive. This decision ignores the

---

[145] *Feller* v. *Universal Chapel Inc.* 124 NY Supp. 2d 546 (1953), discussed in Stickney, above n 40, at 286–7.

[146] See also *Burnett* v. *Surratt* et al. 67 SW 2d 1041, 1042 (Tex. Civ. App. 1934). The idea that the familial relationship must be given preference over the testator's wishes may also find support in the English Wills Act holding that a will shall be revoked by the testator's marriage. Wills Act 1837, c. 26, s. 18 (Eng.)

implication of the next-of-kin's objection to BTs on the relationship itself when no other problems pertain to the making of the testaments, such as duress or incompetency. The court assumes that the relationship between the testator and her next-of-kin ends upon the death of the first, and that this relationship cannot be changed or re-evaluated thereafter. Clearly, this is a wrong assumption, especially when the deceased leaves behind an explicit bodily testament.

Conditioned bodily testaments Sometimes, BTs include provisions according to which the disposal of the body is conditioned upon the occurrence of an event or state of affairs. *Holland* v. *Metalious* is one such case. Grace Metalious directed in her will that 'no funeral services be held for me, and that my body be given to the Dartmouth School of Medicine, for the purpose of experimentation in the interest of medical science. If Dartmouth does not accept then to Harvard Medical School.'[147] The surviving spouse of the decedent and her children objected to carrying out this provision and both medical schools declined to accept the body of the deceased. Although it was held that in the ordinary case, instructions by a decedent in a will or otherwise with respect to disposition of her body should be followed in preference to opposing wishes of survivors, the court interpreted the direction that no funeral services be held for the deceased in association with the decedent's attempted donation of her body for scientific uses. Since the primary purpose of the deceased failed, it was ruled that the wishes of her surviving spouse and children should prevail.

However, it is possible to challenge the court's interpretation of the specific provision, and arrive at the conclusion that the woman's wish not to have funeral services should be respected by all means. The *Holland* case represents the court's willingness to use the reasoning of conditioned BTs to invalidate their effect, and consequently to reach an outcome supportive of next-of-kin. Of course, regarding a direction concerning the disposal of the body as dependent upon the occurrence of a specific condition may jeopardize the importance someone accords to her BTs and may defeat her interest in determining her fate in matters about which she cares much.

Quality of relationship to place of disposal When the issue at stake concerns the place where the body is to be disposed of, the quality of the relationship between the deceased and the specific place of interment can

---

[147] *John S. Holland* v. *George Metalious* et al. 105 NH 290, 198 A 2d 654 (N.H Sup. Ct 1964).

sometimes play an important role in favouring or disfavouring her prior expressed wishes with regard to that place. In *Wood* v. *E. R. Butterworth & Sons* et al.,[148] the second wife and widow of the deceased brought a suit against the decedent's surviving sons, seeking to bury the deceased where she resided some time before her husband's death. The appellant's request was contrary to the decedent's prior wishes to be buried in South Dakota, where he had lived for many years and where his former wife and two children by his second wife were buried. One of the parameters examined by the court was the nature of the relationship that the decedent had with his home city in South Dakota. It was found that the deceased was prominent in the social, political and business life of the city and a factor in its development. Hence, given the deceased's overall relation to the state of South Dakota, the court held that his will should prevail over his widow's preference as to place of interment.

Conclusion

This chapter examined whether a person has and should have a legally protected interest in determining the place and manner of the disposal of her body held by the Human Subject after her death. As this interest focuses on the autonomy of a person who no longer exists, a preliminary question regarding the nature of such interest, specifically whether an autonomy-based interest is and should be the kind of interest the classification of which is 'after-life', was analysed. Following this analysis, the main argument against validating bodily testaments was presented, and two of its major assumptions were challenged in subsequent sections.

The assumption examined in this chapter according to which bodily testaments must be made in the form of a will was proved false with the exploration of substitute legal mechanisms which can explain and regulate such directions. The proposition that a will must only include proprietary items was proved insufficient by the discussion of the general rationales for testamentary power and the specific justifications for the inclusion of bodily testaments under the law of wills. As a result, it was argued in this chapter that there is no prima facie justification, let alone any formal reason, to invalidate the legal effect of bodily testaments even when made by a will. However, it was further questioned whether there are substantial and procedural limitations to the power of such testament. Three categories of limitations were discussed: limitations directly introduced by legislation; limitations directly established under case law; and

---

[148] *Wood*, above n 22.

limitations indirectly constituted by judicial decisions. With regard to the latter and larger group, eleven types of parameters were examined. The richness of legal cases in this respect suggests not only that the right of a person to make a testamentary disposition of her body after death is 'more honoured in the breach than in the observance',[149] but also that judges look for ways to resolve these legal disputes because they feel obligated in some sense to give weight to the prior wishes of the deceased, although they are legally restrained from doing so. The analysis in this chapter also reveals that although prior wishes of the decedent concerning disposal of her body are balanced with the interests of third parties and society at large, they are not immediately overruled, despite well-informed doctrines in the law of wills and testaments and property law. This limbo whereby judges make new law can be fixed and reorganized by making serious revisions to the major assumptions objecting to the legality of BTs. As shown in this chapter, this move is more than plausible.

---

[149] B. C. Ricketts, 'Validity and Effect of Testamentary Direction as to Disposition of Testator's Body' (1966) 7 *American Law Reports* 3d 747–54, 748.

5   Medical confidentiality after death

The previous two chapters examined two categories of interests: the proprietary interest in one's body and the testamentary interest in determining the disposal of one's body after death. Analysis of these interests resulted in the conclusion that if these two interests exist, the first should be characterized as a life interest whereas the second must be classified as an after-life interest. In this chapter, the discussion of a third category of interest, the privacy interest with regard to one's personal health information, will be discussed. This chapter will examine whether such a privacy interest exists, and, if so, whether it should be classified as a 'far-lifelong interest' so that the duty of confidentiality still exists after death.

Introduction

What kind of interest is the privacy interest in regard to one's personal health information? 'Health information' refers to any information relating to one's medical condition which is 'personal', namely 'those facts, communications or opinions which relate to the individual and which it would be reasonable for him to regard as intimate and sensitive and therefore to want to withhold or at least to restrict their collection, use and circulation'.[1] Before examining the question, a distinction between 'privacy' and 'confidentiality' is needed. Privacy, and more specifically health information privacy, is 'an individual's *claim to control* the circumstances in which personal health information is collected, used, stored and transmitted'.[2] Privacy therefore involves the right to limit access to one's health information derived from the more general entitlement to

---

[1] Raymond Wacks, *Personal Information Privacy and the Law* (London: Bodley Head, 1989) 26.
[2] Lawrence O. Gostin, *Public Health Law: Power, Duty and Restraint* (Berkeley: University of California Press, 2000) 128. See also Barbara Von Tigerstrom, 'Protection of Health Information Privacy: The Challenges and Possibilities of Technology' (1998) 4 *Appeal* 44–59, 46 (author's emphasis) [Von Tigerstrom].

determine the fate of one's personal belongings, treatment and the like. Confidentiality is a branch or subset of informational privacy. It 'prevents re-disclosure of information that was originally disclosed within a confidential relationship'.[3] It follows that confidentiality comes into effect only after the information has been obtained by another person or by an agency.[4] By definition, confidentiality is voluntary. The patient may waive her right to confidentiality and allow the custodian of the health information to pass it on to a third party. In such case no violation of privacy or confidentiality arises. The distinction between privacy and confidentiality must result in the proposition that if a privacy interest exists after death, so does the duty of confidentiality, whereas the duty of confidentiality may still be owed post-mortem even when no privacy interest survives the death of the confider.

The question of whether there exists a privacy interest in one's personal health information after death is not only theoretical but also has important practical implications. Indeed, there are many uses of information related to dead patients. Some of these uses are for therapeutic purposes, e.g. providing treatment for relatives of the deceased or other parties in need, yet others are for research purposes involving the cause of death or disease from which death occurred. These uses become more central as development of electronic health records and increased risk of unauthorized access to them, as well as the rising significance of genetic information, become more dominant. Other uses of patients' information after death are required for evidentiary purposes. In the criminal context, for example, an accused would want to present the decedent's medical records (usually the autopsy report) to show that he or she was not responsible for the death of the victim. Likewise, defendants in tort actions such as in wrongful death or medical malpractice suits would want to show that their actions did not result in the death of the claimant's relative. Medical data concerning a decedent who dies testate can also be sought by parties aiming to show that the decedent was in unsound mind when she made her will and they may also be required by insurers in relation to death benefits claims.[5]

---

[3] Tom L. Beauchamp and James F. Childress, *Principles of Biomedical Ethics*, 5th edn. (New York: Oxford University Press, 2001) 304 [Beauchamp and Childress].

[4] Bernard M. Dickens, 'The Doctor's Duty of Confidentiality: Separating the Rule from the Exceptions' (1999) 77(1) *University of Toronto Medical Journal* 40–3, 42 [Dickens, 'The Doctor's Duty'].

[5] *Palmer* et al. v. *Order of United Commercial Travelers of America* 191 Minn. 204, 253 NW 543 (Minn. 1934).

Post-mortem confidentiality in ethics and law

Ethics of post-mortem confidentiality

In the medical context, the duty of confidentiality is one aspect of the primary and transcending medical ethic of non-malfeasance ('do no harm').[6] As early as in the Hippocratic oath, it was stated that: 'What I may see or hear in the course of the treatment or even outside of the treatment in regard to the life of a man, which on no account one must spread abroad, I will keep to myself, holding such things shameful to be spoken about.'[7] Ever since the oath, many ethical codes and professional guidelines[8] have established widely the patient's general right to confidentiality, and some of these guidelines also provide for a post-mortem duty of confidentiality. For example, in Article 30 to its 2004 report, entitled *Confidentiality: Protecting and Providing Information*, the UK General Medical Council instructs physicians as follows:

You still have an obligation to keep personal information confidential after a patient dies. The extent to which confidential information may be disclosed after a patient's death will depend on the circumstances. If the patient had asked for information to remain confidential, his or her views should be respected. Where you are unaware of any directions from the patient, you should consider requests for information taking into account: (1) whether the disclosure of information may cause distress to, or be of benefit to, the patient's partner or family; (2) whether disclosure of information about the patient will in effect disclose information about the patient's family or other people; (3) whether the information is already public knowledge or can be anonymised; (4) and the purpose of the disclosure.[9]

Another example of ethical and professional regulation of post-mortem confidentiality is the report on *Confidentiality of Medical Information Postmortem*, issued in December 2000 by the American Medical Association. In this report, it was held that 'all medical related confidences disclosed by a patient to a physician and information contained within a deceased patient's medical record, including information entered

---

[6] B. M. Dickens and R. J. Cook, 'Law and Ethics in Conflict Over Confidentiality?' (2000) 70 *International Journal of Gynaecology and Obstetrics* 385–91, 386.

[7] Hippocratic oath, available at www.pbs.org/wgbh/nova/doctors/oath_classical.html, accessed on 12 May 2007.

[8] See e.g. United Nations Educational, Scientific and Cultural Organization, Universal Declaration on Bioethics and Human Rights, 19 October 2005, Article 9; Canadian Medical Association, Code of Ethics, 1996, ss. 31–7.

[9] General Medical Council, *Confidentiality: Protecting and Providing Information* (April 2004), available at www.gmc-uk.org/guidance/library/confidentiality.asp, accessed on 1 April 2006.

postmortem, should be kept confidential to the greatest possible degree'.[10] The report states that, at their strongest, confidentiality protections after death would be equal to those in force during a patient's life. Posthumous disclosure of medical information for research or education is permissible under the report as long as confidentiality is maintained to the greatest possible degree by removing any individual identifiers. Moreover, when a family member of the deceased gives her consent to the performance of an autopsy, the autopsy results may be disclosed to her. Disclosure for other purposes will be conditioned upon consideration of the following factors: (1) the imminence of harm to identifiable individuals or public health; (2) the potential benefit to at-risk individuals or public health (e.g. if a communicable or inherited disease is preventable or treatable); (3) any statement or directive made by the patient regarding post-mortem disclosure; (4) the impact disclosure may have on the reputation of the deceased patient; (5) personal gain for the physician that may unduly influence professional obligations of confidentiality.[11]

It follows from these guidelines that an interest in post-mortem confidentiality is ethically acknowledged at least within the UK and American medical professions and that although this interest is not absolute and may be balanced with competing interests, it must be protected by the health team as much as possible. As will be shown in the next section, the existing legal opinion with regard to post-mortem confidentiality differs from its ethical companion by being less assertive in its recognition of a posthumous right to confidentiality and more restrictive in its extent.

The legal position

International law Many international conventions, treaties and guidelines affirm the legal right to confidentiality in the medical context.

---

[10] American Medical Association: Council on Ethical and Judicial Affairs, *Report E-5.051: Confidentiality of Medical Information Postmortem* (December 2000), available at www.ama-assn.org/ama/pub/category/8354.html, accessed on 12 May 2007. For a discussion of this report, see Andrew H. Maixner and Karine Morin, 'Confidentiality of Health Information Postmortem' (2001) 125 *Archives of Pathology and Laboratory Medicine* 1189–92 [Maixner and Morin]. In another report, the AMA acknowledged that although from a legal perspective the patient's privacy rights may terminate upon death, from an ethical perspective physicians have an ethical obligation to maintain the patient's confidentiality even after his death. American Medical Association: Council on Ethical and Judicial Affairs, *Report C-A-92: Confidentiality of HIV Status on Autopsy Report* (AMA: June 1992) at 3, available at www.ama-assn.org/ama1/pub/upload/mm/369/ceja_ca92.pdf, last accessed on 12 May 2007 [*Confidentiality of HIV Status*].

[11] *Confidentiality of HIV Status*, ibid.

They include, for example, the Convention on Human Rights and Biomedicine,[12] OECD Guidelines on the Protection of Privacy and Transborder Flows of Personal Data[13] and the Charter of Fundamental Rights of the European Union.[14] In addition, Article 4.1 of the Declaration on the Promotion of Patients' Rights in Europe specifically addresses the issue of post-mortem confidentiality, providing that: 'All information about a patient's health status, medical condition, diagnosis, prognosis and treatment and all other information of a personal kind must be kept confidential *even after death*.'[15] Although these legal documents recognize the right to confidentiality, they do not specify the conditions upon which a breach of confidence may be justified, nor do they provide substitute decision-making processes in case of confidentiality after death. However, more concrete guidelines may be found at the national level.

Canada In Canada, personal health information is defined in federal[16] and provincial legislation[17] as information with respect to an individual, whether living or deceased. Provincial legislation allows the custodian of health information to disclose to family members or close friends of the deceased without the consent of the individual when she is dead, provided that the disclosure in not contrary to the express request of the individual and that the information relates to circumstances of death or health services recently received by the individual.[18] The rights of an individual with regard to the duty of confidentiality include giving,

[12] Council of Europe, Convention on Human Rights and Biomedicine, 4 April 1997, Article 10, available at http://conventions.coe.int/treaty/en/treaties/html/164.htm, accessed on 12 May 2007; Council of Europe, European Convention on Human Rights, 4 November 1950, Article 8.

[13] Organization for Economic Co-operation and Development, Guidelines on the Protection of Privacy and Transborder Flows of Personal Data, 23 September 1980, Articles 9, 10, available at www.oecd.org/document/18/0,2340,en_2649_34255_1815186_1_1_1_1,00.html, accessed on 20 April 2006.

[14] European Parliament, Charter of Fundamental Rights of the European Union, 18 December 2000, Article 8, available at www.europarl.eu.int/charter/pdf/text_en.pdf, accessed on 12 May 2007.

[15] European Consultation on the Rights of Patients, *A Declaration on the Promotion of Patients' Rights in Europe* (Amsterdam: World Health Organization, 30 March 1994) Article 4.1.

[16] Personal Information Protection and Electronic Documents Act, SC 2000, c. 5, s. 2.

[17] Personal Health Information Act, SM 1997, c. 51; Health Information Protection Act, SS 1999, c. H-0.021; Health Information Act, RSA 2000, c. H-5; Personal Health Information Protection Act, SO 2004, c. 3. For a general discussion of the Quebec informational privacy law, see P. A. Comeau and A. Ouimet, 'Freedom of Information and Privacy: Quebec's Innovative Role in North America' (1995) 80 *Iowa Law Review* 651.

[18] See e.g. Health Information Act, RSA 2000, c. H-5, ss. 35(1)(d), 35(1)(d.1).

withdrawing or withholding consent in respect to the health information. When the patient is dead, these rights may be exercised by her personal representative,[19] estate trustee or administrator.[20] Some provinces restrict the power of the decedent's representatives by providing the requirement that the exercise of these rights be made only for the administration of the decedent's estate.[21]

Although very rarely, the legal recognition of confidentiality after death is also acknowledged by case law. The Court of Queen's Bench of Alberta recently ruled that the duty of confidentiality owed by a doctor to a patient survives the death of the patient and is, after death, within the management of *both* the deceased's executor *and* his heirs, so that it may be waived by either.[22] In *Petrowski*, the decedent's daughter, Joan, was the executor of the estate and its sole beneficiary. Joan's brother brought an action against Joan, claiming that their deceased father was not mentally competent while executing the will and was unduly influenced by his sister. He sought an order permitting his counsel to conduct ex parte interviews with the decedent's treating physicians. Joan agreed to her brother's request on the condition that her counsel would attend these interviews. The court explained that if an executor has exclusive authority in relation to a doctor's duty of confidentiality owed to the decedent, it would constitute an abuse of that authority for the executor to use her authority to advance her own personal position in litigation when such position is distinct from, and in conflict with, her duties to the estate.[23] Therefore, in the circumstances of that case, the court declined Joan's request to insist that her counsel be present in the interviews. The court reached its decision regardless of the specific legislation in the province of Alberta supporting it.

The USA Post-mortem confidentiality is legally regulated in the USA. While the general rule is that physician–patient privilege may be waived by personal representative, surviving spouse or next-of-kin,[24] the law in some states grants every interested party the power to waive the privilege when the interests of personal representatives conflict with those of the estate.[25]

---

[19] *See* Personal Health Information Act, SM 1997, c. 51, s. 60(f); Health Information Protection Act, SS 1999, c. H-0.021, s. 56(a).

[20] Personal Health Information Protection Act, SO 2004, c. 3, Sched. A, s. 23(1)(4).

[21] Health Information Protection Act, SS 1999, c. H-0.021, s. 56(a).

[22] *Peter Petrowski* v. *Joan Petrowski* [2005] CarswellAlta 1823, 1 December 2005 (Alta. Ct Queen's Bench) para. 7 [*Petrowski*].

[23] *Ibid.*, at para. 9.

[24] *In re Application of D'Agostino, MD* 181 Misc. 2d 710, 695 NYS 2d 473 (1999).

[25] See e.g. Consolidated Laws of New York Annotated, s. 4504 (c)(2) (Thomson/West 2006).

The US Department of Health and Human Services recommended in its proposed rule, entitled 'Standards for Privacy of Individually Identifiable Health Information', that the privacy of deceased patients be protected for up to two years following death so that the right to control one's health information within that time be held by an executor, administrator, next-of-kin determined by legislation, or the holder of the health information. The idea was that a two-year period of confidential treatment with provisions for authorization by specific persons would preserve dignity and respect but still permit disclosure for proper purposes during this period.[26] However, such a recommendation was not followed, and currently there is no time limit by which the privacy of the dead is protected. Instead, the federal rule establishes as a general principle that its requirement in respect to the protection of health information also applies to the dead, and that if under applicable law an executor, administrator or other person has authority to act on behalf of a deceased individual or the individual's estate, such person will be regarded as a personal representative and will be treated the same as the individual patient.[27]

The UK In the UK, an application for access to health records may be submitted to the holder of the records by the decedent's personal representative and by 'any person who may have a claim arising out of the patient's death'.[28] However, access to the decedent's health records may not be permitted if in the opinion of their holder they would 'disclose information which is not relevant to any claim which may arise out of the patient's death'.[29] Of course, this is a very broad definition and may encompass almost any situation involving the personal health information of the deceased. It is to be noted that the law does not elaborate on the persons eligible to make an application for access to health records of a deceased patient, nor does it specify the criteria which the holder of these records should consider when deciding whether to accept the application. The English law further establishes a right to have access to any medical report relating to an individual which is to be, or has been,

---

[26] Health and Human Services, *Recommendations of the Secretary of Health and Human Services: Confidentiality of Individually-Identifiable Health Information*, 11 September 1997, Article F(1), available at: www.epic.org/privacy/medical/hhs_recommendations_1997.html, accessed on 12 May 2007.

[27] US Department of Health and Human Services, *Standards for Privacy of Individually Identifiable Health Information*, 45 CFR ss. 164.502(f), 164.502(g)(4), available at www.hhs.gov/ocr/combinedregtext.pdf, accessed on 3 March 2006 [*Standards for Privacy*].

[28] Access to Health Records Act 1990, c. 23, s. 1(1) (Eng.).

[29] *Ibid.*, ss. 3(1)(f), 5(4); Access to Medical Reports Act 1988, c. 28 (Eng.).

supplied by a medical practitioner for employment purposes or insurance purposes. The law, however, does not define the term 'individual' and no specific provision refers to dead patients.

The ethical and legal positions in regard to post-mortem confidentiality raise some difficulties. First, there is a tension between the ways the post-mortem duty of confidentiality is represented in ethics and in law. While ethical and professional guidelines tend to acknowledge and so declare such duty without compromising it by means of waiver, the legal framework seeks to find ways to permit the consensual disclosure of private health information. In some instances, the legal position is in an ethical void, like in Canada where no ethical or professional guidelines as to confidentiality after death exist.

Second, in some cases there is inconsistency within the same legal system with regard to the requirement to waive the duty of confidentiality. Provinces in Canada vary substantially in this very issue, empowering next-of-kin, executors and/or close persons to the decedent to permit disclosure of information. In one province, such power can only be exercised for the administration of the decedent's estate. The different approaches expressed in legislation are not supported by any theoretical understanding of the notion of confidentiality. This is extremely problematic when no ethical guidelines address the issue of post-mortem confidentiality throughout the whole country, and where not even all provinces have specific legislation regulating it.

Third, even if in principle one can justify the waiver of confidentiality after death by relatives or executors following a specific legal provision, it is not clear why inability to obtain consent for disclosure from the deceased should influence the extent to which medical confidentiality should be protected. Why not, for example, continue to enforce confidentiality after death unless otherwise expressed by the deceased herself or by a person appointed by the deceased while alive as a designated proxy? The solution opted for by the legislator is partial and far from being optimal. It does not distinguish between different disclosure situations, thereby failing to take into account the various purposes of disclosure, the nature of information at stake and the personal characteristics of the patient the information on whom is to be disclosed. Moreover, the legal response to post-mortem confidentiality ignores the duty not to disclose to family members and other related parties information concerning a former living patient. The law merely assumes that disclosure to family or other parties in order to exercise power of waiver is legitimate. In any event, existing legal solutions to the problem of post-mortem confidentiality do not make the theoretical examination of it unnecessary.

General justifications for confidentiality

In order to establish a proper understanding of the question of whether the duty of confidentiality should extend after the death of the patient, it is essential to examine the general justifications for such a duty. There are four main categories by which one can justify the patient's right (and the corresponding physician's duty) to confidentiality: consequentialism, rights-based justifications, fidelity (equity) and the duty to keep promises.[30]

Consequentialism

By reference to its consequences, consequentialism, and in the particular case utilitarianism, focuses on the outcomes of a system respecting the right to confidentiality. The utilitarian justification for physician–patient privilege was enunciated by John Wigmore.[31] He postulated four conditions for the establishment of such privilege: the communications must originate in a confidence that they will not be disclosed; the element of confidentiality must be essential to the full and satisfactory maintenance of the relation between the parties; the relation must be one which, in the opinion of the community, ought to be sedulously fostered; and the injury that would inure to the relation by the disclosure of the communications must be greater than the benefit thereby gained for the correct disposal of litigation.

Under the consequentialist justification, acknowledgement of the right to confidentiality provides trust in the medical team, and so encourages patients to disclose full personal health information. It is argued that much information leads patients to seek treatment even for certain diseases with social stigma, and enables physicians to perform more accurate diagnoses and prognoses, thereby providing the best treatment for their patients.[32]

In the post-mortem context, it is possible to hold that respecting confidentiality after death assures living patients that their health information will not be disclosed after death. However, under this rationale, disclosing facts from the autopsy report or providing a copy of the patient's death certificate without the decedent's prior wishes does not constitute a breach of her right to confidentiality for such action may not impede

---

[30] Beauchamp and Childress, above n 3, at 306–8.
[31] John Wigmore, *Evidence in Trials at Common Law*, J. McNaughton ed. (1961), mentioned in 'Developments in Law: Privileged Communications' (1985) 98(2) *Harvard Law Review* 1450–1666, 1472 ['Privileged Communications'].
[32] *Elizabeth McInerney* v. *Margaret MacDonald* [1992] 2 SCR 138 at para. 27 [*McInerney*].

treatment, nor can it harm the physician–patient relationship which allegedly terminates upon the death of the patient. Such disclosure may
amount to a violation of the patient's right to privacy, if she retains such
right after death, but cannot be inexcusable by the utilitarian justification
for medical confidentiality.

Moreover, the utilitarian justification for the right to confidentiality
may be more relevant to illnesses that are particularly sensitive, such as
HIV/Aids or mental diseases, so that if health information related to these
illnesses is known to others, patients may be deterred from seeking treatment. Its appeal to disclosure of information following the death of a
patient from any other illness is less obvious. Above all, the utilitarian
justification rests on the dubious assumption that patients are actively
involved with their right to confidentiality. In fact, people know very little
or nothing about their privilege and, even if they knew about it, they
would hardly ever change their communicative behaviour.[33] As argued by
Beauchamp and Childress, not only does no substantial evidence support
the proposition that exceptions to the right to confidentiality reduce
prospective patients' willingness to seek treatment and cooperate with
their physicians or significantly impair the physician–patient relationship,[34] but there are at least two studies in Canada showing that there is
very little difference in the behaviour of patients in seeking treatment both
with and without medical privilege.[35] Empirical studies examining
patients' understandings and awareness of confidentiality reveal that a
significant proportion of patients cannot even provide a definition of the
word 'confidentiality'.[36] Studies also show that many of those who are
able to define confidentiality are unfamiliar with physicians' ethical obligations and their own legal right to medical confidentiality. It is further
found that patients sign release-of-information statements because they
believe they have no choice, and sometimes they are not even aware of
having done so. For example, a 1997 study found that 35 per cent of 490
Massachusetts adolescent subjects did not believe or know that HIV test
results were kept confidential, and 90 per cent falsely believed that
automatic partner notification followed a positive test result.[37]

---

[33] Edward W. Cleary, *McCormick on Evidence*, 3rd edn (St Paul: West, 1984) 184, 201, 244.
[34] Beauchamp and Childress, above n 3, at 307. For a possible response to this critique, see
'Privileged Communications', above n 31, at 1475–9. For some empirical support,
see C. Jones, 'The Utilitarian Argument for Medical Confidentiality: A Pilot Study of
Patients' Views' (2003) 29 *Journal of Medical Ethics* 348–52.
[35] See D. W. Shuman, W. F. Weiner and G. I. Pinnard, 'The Privilege Study'' (1986) 9
International Journal of Law and Psychology 393.
[36] Pamela Sankar, Susan Moran, Jon F. Merz and Nora L. Jones, 'Patient Perspectives on
Medical Confidentiality' (2003) 18 *Journal of General Internal Medicine* 659–69, 660.
[37] *Ibid.*

It is therefore difficult to justify the right to confidentiality on a consequentialist basis and much empirical work needs to be done to support its primary premises. In any event, the application of such a justification to confidentiality after death appears less compelling.

Rights-based justifications

An alternative group of justifications for the right to confidentiality focuses on arguments for respect of the patient's rights. This group of justifications suggests that there is something intrinsically wrong in disclosing information relating to the patient's health. The wrong that is at stake is a clear violation of the patient's elementary rights: privacy, autonomy and property.

Privacy Respecting the patient's confidentiality secures her right to privacy. There are a few areas in which the argument for privacy may arise.[38] First, patients depend on their physicians and they need 'a zone of privacy' to seek this help. This 'zone of privacy' is secured by protecting, inter alia, the patient's health information. Second, one aspect of privacy is control over personal information about oneself and it is this aspect that medical confidentiality aims to protect.[39] Third, because medicine involves intimate facts about the patient's body, health and mind, a 'privacy zone' surrounding these facts must be protected.[40] Fourth, confidentiality prevents the disclosure of stigmatized or personal issues about which the patient does not feel comfortable. In order to protect such matters, one needs to secure the information freely given by the patient. Fifth, one's right to be secure against unreasonable search and seizure, which is an aspect of one's right to privacy, may also apply to the therapeutic context where the patient holds expectations of privacy in her medical records.[41]

---

[38] Generally, the right to privacy consists of four categories: intrusion upon the person's seclusion or solitude or into her private affairs; public disclosure of embarrassing facts; publicity which places the person in a false light; and appropriation of the person's name or likeness. William L. Prosser, 'Privacy' (1960) 48 *California Law Review* 383–423, 389 [Prosser].

[39] Mary Marshall and Barbara Von Tigerstrom, 'Health Information' in J. Downie, T. Caulfield and C. Flood eds., *Canadian Health Law and Policy*, 2nd edn (Toronto: Butterworths, 2002) 157–203, 158.

[40] Stephen A. Salzburg, 'Privileges and Professionals: Lawyers and Psychiatrists' (1980) 66 *Virginia Law Review* 597–652, 619; L. O. Gostin, J. Turek-Brezina, M. Powers, R. Kozloff, R. Faden and D. D. Steinauer, 'Privacy and Security of Personal Information in a New Health Care System' (1993) 270 *Journal of the American Medical Association* 2487–93.

[41] See e.g. *R* v. *Mills* [1999] 3 SCR 668 at para. 82.

The privacy justification for the duty of confidentiality in the medical context is acknowledged by case law. For example, in the matter of *Hammonds* the court remarked:

When the patient seeks out a doctor and retains him, he must admit him to the most private part of the material domain of man. Nothing material is more important or more intimate to man than the health of his mind and body.[42]

However, the idea of privacy evokes some difficulties. First, it is argued that there is no coherent interest in privacy as such since the interests promoted by privacy are not unique, but common to and protected by other areas of law, e.g. anti-discriminatory law, torts and criminal law. In addition, there is no universal philosophical definition of 'privacy'. This phenomenon can be attributed to three factors: variation in the use and denotational and connotational meanings of 'privacy'; variation in the purposes for which the definition of 'privacy' is undertaken; and variation in approaches taken to the task of definition itself.[43] As a result, privacy is related to many fundamental human relations and as such is a diffuse concept.[44]

Moreover, with the rise of new methods of recording, storing and transmitting data the sanctity of the right to privacy has been challenged. Medical developments and new technologies have now raised the claim that the idea of privacy is obsolete so that technology should drive society and social values, not the other way round. Sceptics have argued that rather than keep the futile exercise of trying to protect privacy, we should dispense with that concept altogether and turn to other more appropriate paradigms of management of information by directing our attention to preventing the harm that may be caused as a result of the disclosure and improper use of the information. Along this line, Mark Siegler has argued that medical confidentiality is a principle which has become old, worn out and useless, and that this principle is compromised systematically in the course of routine medical care.[45] A more moderate approach advocates retaining a high standard of security and privacy only for certain kinds of extremely sensitive data, e.g. data on HIV/Aids.[46]

---

[42] *Hammonds v. Aetna Casualty & Surety Company*, 243 F Supp. 793, 801–2 (ND Ohio 1965) [*Hammonds*].
[43] Anita L. Allen, 'Privacy as Data-Control: Conceptual, Practical and Moral Limits of the Paradigm' (2000) 32(3) *Connecticut Law Review* 861–75, 864 [Allen].
[44] Charles Fried, 'Privacy' (1968) 77 *Yale Law Journal* 475–93, 477–8 [Fried].
[45] Mark Siegler, 'Confidentiality in Medicine: A Decrepit Concept' (1982) 307(24) *New England Journal of Medicine* 1518–21 [Siegler].
[46] Von Tigerstrom, above n 2, at 55–6.

Specific difficulties also arise with regard to the dead. Legislation,[47] case law[48] and literature[49] establish the proposition that there is no right of action for the publication of information concerning one who is already dead, and more generally that the dead do not retain their privacy interests.[50] If this proposition adequately reflects the current legal position, then the argument for respecting confidentiality after death as a way of securing the patient's privacy rights rests on shaky grounds.

Autonomy Another right discussed under the rights-based group of justifications for medical confidentiality concerns the patient's right to autonomy. The idea of autonomy as a form of control may be attached to the concept of privacy by definition,[51] and it may have originated in Alan Westin's description of privacy as 'the claim of individuals, groups, or institutions to determine for themselves when, how and to what extent information about them is communicated to others'.[52] Anita Allen identifies three distinguishable notions in the privacy-control paradigm: first, the notion that the term 'privacy' means control over the use of personal data or information; second, the notion that the expression 'right to privacy' means the right or claim to control the use of personal data or information; and third, the notion that the central aim of privacy regulation should be promoting individuals' control over personal data or information.[53]

In a system of confidentiality, the patient retains her power to control the distribution of any information related to her. Disclosing information without the patient's consent thus 'destroys the claimant's control over the breadth of the audience receiving personal information as well as his control over the timing and conditions of its release'.[54] The privacy-control paradigm puts the individual at the centre of decision making

---

[47] See e.g. Restatement of the Law, Second, Torts s. 652I (1977); Ontario Trustee Act, RSO 1990, c. T-23, s. 38.

[48] *National Archives and Records Administration* v. *Favish* 541 US 157 (2004) [*National Archives*]; *Austin and Janie Smith* v. *City of Artesia* et al. 108 NM 339, 772 P 2d 373 (N.Mex. Ct App. 1989) [*City of Artesia*].

[49] Prosser, above n 38, at 408; Samuel A. Terilli and Sigman L. Splichal, 'Public Access to Autopsy and Death-Scene Photographs: Relational Privacy, Public Records and Avoidable Collisions' (2005) 10 *Communication Law and Policy* 313–48 [Terilli and Splichal].

[50] *Alma Tillman* v. *Detroit Receiving Hospital* et al. 138 Mich. App. 683, 687 (Ct App. Mich. 1984).

[51] Fried, above n 44, at 482.

[52] Alan F. Westin, *Privacy and Freedom* (New York: Athenaeum, 1967) 7.

[53] Allen, above n 43, at 863.

[54] Thomas G. Krattenmaker, 'Testimonial Privileges in Federal Courts: An Alternative to the Proposed Federal Rules of Evidence' (1973–4) 62 *Georgia Law Journal*. 61–124, 86.

about personal information use. This paradigm has much appeal since it complements our focus on the interests of individual persons as moral agents. It thus provides them with respect by regarding them first as persons and only after as patients.

However, the privacy-control (autonomy) paradigm suffers from some problems. First, the idea that privacy represents one's control over one's personal information is too narrow. Privacy is about not just controlling one's information but also preventing unwanted interventions, e.g. in the case of abortions and other medical procedures performed on pregnant women. As illuminated by Prosser, the complexity of the notion of privacy requires us to regard it not only as an expression of one's autonomy, but also as a means to secure the conditions for one's solitude and need for repose, as well as the respect for one's interest in seclusion needed for intimacy.[55]

Second, it follows from the autonomy paradigm that a person may have her right to confidentiality only in regard to that over which she may have control. Once the person loses her control over the information, she may not be justified in protecting her informational privacy. The control condition is limited when one deals with the confidentiality of patients who cannot retain their capacity to control personal information, whether living or dead patients. One may further hold that control over personal information is neither necessary nor sufficient for privacy to occur. A person may still be regarded as not having a right to privacy even when she has full control over her personal information. She may also enjoy her privacy without ever controlling her personal information.

Third, with regard to protection of health information it is claimed that the idea of control is conceptually inappropriate. Anita Allen, for example, argues that the interests we have in medical privacy are best addressed by focusing less on the misleading ideal of controlling medical information, and more on the wider concern of some social norms like civility, respect and responsibility and on fair information practices such as informed consent, patient access to records, etc.[56] The importance of our social norms and information practices receives more weight as the capacities of patients to control their personal health information becomes more limited, such as when after the patient dies. Allen's arguments may have powerful effect in the post-mortem context.

Fourth, reliance on the patient's capacities to control her health information may turn out to be illusionary. A person's exercise of control may be irrational, unreasonable and sometimes foolish so that we would still

---

[55] Prosser, above n 38, at 389.   [56] Allen, above n 43, at 873.

want to protect this person's privacy or informational privacy. Should a patient be allowed to broadcast her mastectomy live on the internet for educational purposes?[57] Should the first recipient of facial transplantation be free (or forced by her treating physician) to waive her right to privacy and share her medical condition with others?[58] These somewhat rhetorical questions suggest that there is more in the patient's privacy than the power to control her own health information represented by the autonomy paradigm. More generally, can someone be free to waive her own privacy? There is some good reason to believe that a right to privacy in its true meaning is one the alienability of which is theoretically impossible. It follows that when objectively required, privacy may be forced on individuals.[59]

From a practical perspective, it is difficult to control personal information since there are other people (and, at times, too many of them) using the information or having some access to it, and demands of bureaucratic efficiency such as those of insurers override individuals' expectations of privacy. Support for such difficulty is found in the context of health law. The requirements of disclosure to and by health providers and the obligation of accountability to insurers manifest that the individual cannot fully and successfully control her health information. Controlling health information encounters additional problems in light of the difficulty of concealing such sensitive information from family members, close friends, co-workers, etc., and given the very fact that many medical conditions are easy to spot.[60]

Property Another right discussed under the rights-based group of justifications for medical confidentiality involves the patient's proprietary right in her health information. If such right exists, it would be in the form of intellectual property.[61] A general justification for property in personal information holds that information for the obtaining and creation of which time, money and effort are expended is a valuable entity that

---

[57] Sam Matthews, 'BBC Three Brings Flashmob Opera to Railway Station' Brand Republic (25 August 2004), available at www.brandrepublic.com/bulletins/media/article/220252/bbc-three-brings-flashmob-opera-railway-stations/, accessed on 13 March 2006.

[58] George J. Agich and Maria Siemionow, 'Facing the Ethical Questions in Facial Transplantation' (2004) 4(3) *American Journal of Bioethics* 25–7.

[59] Anita L. Allen, 'Coerced Privacy' (1999) 40(3) *William and Mary Law Review* 723–57.

[60] Allen, above n 43, at 870–3.

[61] Compare *McInerney*, above n 32, where the Supreme Court of Canada held that while the doctor, institution or clinic compiling the medical records owns the physical record, the patient has 'a vital interest' in the information contained in her medical records which is an equitable interest arising from the physician's fiduciary obligation to disclose the records upon request.

should be protected under property law.[62] This justification focuses on the nature of the information at stake.[63] It is argued that personal health information is so central to the person that it should be regarded as the patient's property or quasi-property. Hence, as part of her general right to control her own property, the patient has a right that the information provided by her to her physician be kept confidential.[64]

A complementary support for the proprietary model of medical confidentiality originates in the literature on law and economics. The argument is that under a system of no property rights in personal information, a company which acquires such information gains the full benefit of using it in its own marketing efforts or in the fee received from the selling of that information to a third party. However, the company does not suffer losses from disclosing the information, and usually is not disciplined by customers, who are unlikely to learn about the disclosure. The company internalizes the gains from using the information, but can also externalize some of the losses, and therefore has a systematic incentive to overuse it. This scenario creates a market failure which is intensified by the costs of bargaining for the desired level of privacy depending on time, effort and expertise. In order to overcome such market failure, a property right in one's personal data should be recognized so that individuals would be able to bargain more efficiently. Thus individuals should be allowed to sell their personal data and so capture some of their value, and make companies internalize certain social costs of the widespread collection and use of personal data which are now borne by others.[65]

However, even from an economic perspective one can seriously doubt whether patients are able and willing at all to comprehend and accurately assess the risks of revealing personal health information to others or the risks involved in the selling of their property rights akin to their personal health information. In addition, a system of property rights in information has its own costs, mainly concerning the establishment of new procedures to collect and use private information and the implementation of them. These costs should also be taken into account.

---

[62] D. F. Libling, 'The Concept of Property: Property in Intangibles' (1978) 94 *Law Quarterly Review* 103.

[63] In most cases, the property justification serves as a metaphor to describe the rights which a patient has in relation to her communications with her health provider. In this section, I will not focus on this aspect, rather I will discuss the independent property justification which arises in the context of medical law.

[64] M. S. Faigus, '*Moore* v. *Regents of the University of California* – A Breach of Confidence Within the Physician–Patient Relationship: Should Unique Genetic Information be Considered a Trade Secret?' (1993) 24 *University of West Los Angeles Law Review* 299.

[65] Pamela Samuelson, 'Privacy and Intellectual Property' (2000) 52(5) *Stanford Law Review* 1125–74, 1127–9 [Samuelson].

Other problems may occur with regard to the alienability of the property right in personal information. Since the information at stake is personal, it is likely that its holder may want to alienate it to X but prevent the latter from further transferring it to another party, Y. The holder of information may also want to stipulate some conditions for the alienability of the property right to X, creating practical and economic hardship for X.[66] In addition, data collectors may compel the property holder to transfer all of her right, title and interest in the information. The property holder may further be foreclosed from exercising her control over the information in the hands of the transferee or in the hands of third parties to whom the information is transferred.[67] All these possible scenarios challenge the standard understanding of alienability of property rights and call in question the suitability of the property model to deal with legitimate requests concerning personal 'items', including personal health information.

Additionally, a property right in personal information aims to make the information scarcer than it was, to exclude it from others, and hence to control its exclusive use. The idea of property in information is to restrict the personal health information rather than share it with others. Establishing a property right for that purpose goes against one of the major justifications for the right to private property, namely to enable market allocations of scarce resources. Peculiarly, the property model is counterintuitive to its more common purposes.

Indeed, the property model of medical information suffers from serious theoretical and motivational problems. In contrast to the typical situation of property or intellectual property, a particular use of information by one person or group of persons does not preclude others from engaging in other uses of the information, since no (at least) two uses are mutually exclusive.[68] Recognizing an intellectual property right in personal information may therefore lead to greater incoherence in intellectual property law.[69] Furthermore, unlike any other right to intellectual property, acknowledging a property right in health information does not aim to promote the progress of science, art or technological innovation. Quite the contrary, the purpose of such property right is to suppress the widespread misuse of personal information to better protect individuals' privacy.

---

[66] *Ibid.*, at 1137–8.

[67] *Ibid.*, at 1145. See also Paul M. Schwartz, 'Privacy and the Economics of Personal Health Care Information' (1997) 76(1) *Texas Law Review* 1–76.

[68] Graeme Laurie, *Genetic Privacy: A Challenge to Medico-Legal Norms* (Cambridge: Cambridge University Press, 2002) 302.

[69] Samuelson, above n 65, at 1140–1.

If accepted, the property model for medical confidentiality may lead to the proposition that when the patient dies, the right to control her information forms part of her estate and transfers upon death to her heirs. Under this view, the right to waive confidentiality or to continue to hold it after the death of the patient should vest solely in legal heirs. Such an analysis is disputable,[70] and it does not enjoy full legal support under existing laws in Canada, the USA and the UK where confidentiality after death is viewed as a personal right that can be waived by relatives or close members of the deceased as well. In Canada, the property model was applied, although hesitantly, to medical records of a deceased patient by the Ontario Supreme Court.[71] The Court held that the personal representative of the deceased might hold something akin to a property interest in the content of the medical records. It did not explain what that 'something' really was and how, if the interest at stake was proprietary, it did not vest in legal heirs. A more general decision of the Supreme Court of Canada in *McInerney* v. *MacDonald* refused to hold that a doctor is merely a 'custodian' of medical information.[72] In addition to the theoretical and economic difficulties inherent in the property model, it follows from the above cases and the existing health legislation that the application of the proprietary model to justify the duty of medical confidentiality after death may still need significant support.

Fidelity (equity)

A physician's duty of confidentiality can also be justified by the physician's more general obligation to treat her patient in fidelity and to be faithful to her. This is the obligation to act in good faith and not to take advantage of the confidential information from the moment it is communicated.[73] More generally, the physician's duty to act in fidelity derives from the nature of the physician–patient relationship.[74] Such a relationship will generally consist of the physician's duty to act with utmost good faith and loyalty, hold information received from or about a patient in confidence, and provide the patient with access to the information which the physician uses in

---

[70] See Gareth Jones, 'Restitution of Benefits Obtained in Breach of Another's Confidence' (1970) 86 *Law Quarterly Review* 463–92, 464–5 [Gareth Jones].
[71] *Mitchell* v. *St Michael's Hospital* 29 OR (2d) 185, 112 DLR (3d) 360 (1980) at para. 11.
[72] *McInerney*, above n 32, at para. 25.   [73] Gareth Jones, above n 70, at 477.
[74] *McInerney*, above n 32, at para. 19; *Henderson* v. *Johnston* [1956] OR 789, 5 DLR (2d) 524 (HC). But see *Sidaway* v. *Board of Governors of the Bethlem Royal Hospital and the Maudsley Hospital* [1985] 1 All ER 643 (disavowing the notion of a fiduciary relationship in the medical context).

administering treatment.[75] The idea of fidelity in medicine was developed by Paul Ramsey, who wrote that the practice of medicine must include within it the principles of justice, fairness, righteousness, faithfulness, etc.[76]

A similar approach to Ramsey's is taken by Toulson and Phipps.[77] The authors argue that physicians owe a duty of confidence to their patients and a duty in conscience toward other persons (whether or not their own patients) with regard to the information communicated to them by their patients. Toulson and Phipps contend that considerations of equity operating upon the conscience of physicians would disallow them to disclose information to other parties upon the death of their patient. Hence, the physician's obligation of confidentiality survives the death of the patient.[78] The next three sub-sections will examine whether Toulson and Phipps are right to argue for a post-mortem duty of confidentiality.

The durability of the obligation to act in confidence In general, a confidant will continue to be bound by an obligation of confidence until he is released by an agreement for consideration, the express or implied consent of the confider, or the expiration of the confidentiality of the information which is the subject of that obligation. Such expiration usually occurs when the confidential information loses its confidential character, namely when it becomes completely accessible to the public in its pristine form.[79] It follows that if there is no express provision to terminate the duty of confidentiality upon death or if the proposed health information has not become public, the fiduciary duty of a physician may continue after the death of her patient.

Survivability of the physician–patient relationship The extension of the duty of confidentiality after death also depends on the question of whether the physician–patient relationship continues after a patient's death. Although this question was raised in a few legal cases, it did not receive a satisfactory answer. In an Australian case, a doctor was charged with making a false statement in Medicare assignment forms where he declared that he had provided a particular 'medical service' to a named patient who at the time was dead.[80] Dr Pawsey inspected the dead bodies

---

[75] *McInerney*, above n 32, at paras. 20–1.
[76] Paul Ramsey, *The Patient as Person* (New Haven: Yale University Press, 1970) xii–xiii.
[77] Toulson and Phipps, mentioned in Ian Kennedy and Andrew Grubb, *Medical Law*, 3rd edn (London: Butterworths, 2000) 1082–3 [Kennedy and Grubb].
[78] R. G. Toulson and C. M. Phipps, *Confidentiality* (London: Sweet & Maxwell, 1996) para. 6–04 [Toulson and Phipps].
[79] Francis Gurry, *Breach of Confidence* (Oxford: Clarendon, 1984) 245–53 [Gurry].
[80] *R* v. *Pawsey* [1991] 3 Med. LR 39 (Ct Crim. App. Tasmania).

of his former patients and charged the national health insurance for that. The question analysed in court was whether Pawsey's examination of the dead patients constituted medical treatment for which he should have been reimbursed. In order to answer this question, the court had to decide whether the dead subjects examined by Pawsey continued to be Pawsey's patients for the purposes of the Medicare report.

Pawsey was acquitted by the trial judge, who ruled that the physician–patient relationship, like the solicitor–client relationship, continues to have some obligations arising out of the living relationship. The trial judge saw no reason why the term 'patient' should not be read for the purposes of the Health Insurance Act and its regulations as being confined to living patients capable of receiving treatment. On appeal, it was held that in the absence of a specific provision indicating that the expression 'patient' should be given a meaning other than the ordinary one, the trial judge erred in holding that the body of a dead patient could still fit the description of 'patient' in the regulations. The court based its ruling on 'well-known dictionaries' which define a patient as a living person under medical treatment, although it did not refer to any such dictionaries specifically.

Another holding that a deceased patient is no longer a patient was given by the Ontario Court of General Division in a case from 1994.[81] In *Re Thompson*, a woman died while in the custody of a mental health centre in circumstances which necessitated an inquest. At a pre-inquest hearing, the Ministry of Health argued that the woman was still a patient under section 35 of the Mental Health Act, which required that information about her be obtained by court permission. The court rejected this argument, holding that the woman ceased to be a patient for the purposes of the Act. However, the court did not substantiate its decision but instead only mentioned that an amendment to the Act permitting the personal representative of the deceased patient to obtain information otherwise unavailable to that representative did not change the definition of 'patient' to also include the deceased.

A third case in which the question of whether the physician–patient relationship continues after death was raised was in the matter of *Powell*, where the English Court of Appeal suggested that, upon the death of a patient, her relatives may become 'patients', depending on whether they undertake to be treated by the physician especially with regard to procedures or situations occurring after the death of the former patient. In that case, informing relatives of the cause of death was not regarded as an

---

[81] *Re Thompson* 18 OR (3d) 291 (Ont. Ct Gen. Div. 1994).

action constituting a physician–patient relationship between the health team and relatives.[82] Nevertheless, the court did not directly discuss the possibility of violating the physician's relationship with the deceased, and this may reflect the court's opinion that such a relationship no longer existed. Moreover, the court's query of whether relatives of a decedent maintain a doctor–patient relationship with the treating physician suggests, in line with the two other cases mentioned above, that a physician–patient relationship terminates upon the death of a patient.

An analogy from posthumous attorney–client privilege The question of whether the duty of confidentiality survives the death of a patient can also be addressed in comparison to other areas of fiduciary duties and the examination of whether these duties survive the death of the confider. One such area is the attorney–client privilege.

A decision of the US Supreme Court held that the attorney–client privilege continues after the death of the client. In *Swidler*, an attorney made three pages of notes of an initial interview with his client nine days before the latter committed suicide. The US government sought the notes for a criminal investigation and the question discussed in the Supreme Court was whether the attorney–client privilege continues after the client's death.[83] Having no explicit law to address, the court admitted that its interpretation of the privilege's scope was guided by the principles of common law in the light of reason and experience. The majority found many reasons in favour of posthumous application of the attorney–client privilege. It held that upholding confidentiality after death encourages the client to communicate fully and frankly with the counsel.[84] The dissenting opinion also found that the attorney–client privilege will ordinarily survive the death of the client, but it did not agree with the majority that the interest in confidentiality inevitably precludes disclosure of a deceased client's communications in criminal proceedings.[85]

The view expressed by the majority in *Swidler* has some support in the literature,[86] and its application was also extended to the medical context. The New Jersey Supreme Court affirmed *Swidler*, holding that the psychologist–patient privilege also survives the death of the patient.[87] It

---

[82] *Powell* et al. v. *Boldaz* et al. 39 BMLR 35 [1998] (CA).
[83] *Swidler & Berlin and James Hamilton* v. *US* 524 US 399 (1998).
[84] *Ibid.*, at 407.   [85] *Ibid.*, at 412.
[86] Simon J. Frankel, 'Attorney–Client Privilege After the Death of the Client' (1992–3) 6 *Georgia Journal of Legal Ethics* 45–9.
[87] *Constance E. Correia* v. *Kenneth V. Sherry* et al. 760 A 2d 1156, 335 N.J. Sup. 60, 66 (2000) [*Correia*].

remains to be seen whether courts will follow this path and apply post-mortem medical confidentiality to other practices of medicine. There is no prima facie reason to distinguish between medical privilege in other areas of practice and the one relating to the psychologist–patient relationship. The tension between the ruling in *Swidler* and the decisions dealing with survivability of the physician–patient relationship discussed in the previous section also needs to be addressed in future case law.

The discussion thus far reveals that, according to the more general rules concerning the durability of the duty of confidence and the specific ruling pertaining to posthumous attorney–client privilege, which has also been applied to some areas of medicine, a duty of confidentiality may not cease upon the death of a patient. However, this latter proposition needs much support in light of the fact that there are few legal cases, suggesting an opposite view according to which the physician–patient relationship may not extend after the patient's death.

The duty to keep promises: a contractual justification

A fourth justification for medical confidentiality holds that the duty to keep health information confidential derives from an implicit or explicit promise made to the patient that her personal health information would be secured.[88] The characterization of the physician–patient relationship as a promise is well established in medical ethics.[89] A legal expression of this characterization regards the physician–patient privilege as an expressed or implied provision in contract made between the two. The contract may provide that the physician should not pass on to third parties confidential information acquired from her patient. Confidentiality thus protects the patient's expectations evolving out of this contract.[90] In *Hammonds* v. *Aetna Casualty & Surety Company*, the court endorsed the contractual model of medical confidentiality, holding that:

Anytime a doctor undertakes the treatment of a patient, and the consensual relationship of physician and patient is established, two jural obligations are simultaneously assumed by the doctor. Doctor and patient enter into a simple

---

[88] But see the English Court of Appeal decision in *Attorney General* v. *Guardian Newspapers (No. 2)* [1990] AC 109, suggesting that the duty of confidence may be discerned objectively.

[89] Raanan Gillon, 'Medical Ethics: Four Principles Plus Attention to Scope' (1994) 309 *British Medical Journal* 184–8, 185.

[90] See generally Eugene Volokh, 'Freedom of Speech and Information Privacy: The Troubling Implications of a Right to Stop People from Speaking About You' (2000) 52(5) *Stanford Law Review* 1049–1124, 1058–9.

contract, the patient hoping that he will be cured and the doctor optimistically assuming that he will be compensated. As an implied condition of that contract, this court is of the opinion that the doctor warrants that any confidential information gained through the relationship will not be released without the patient's permission ... Consequently when a doctor breaches his duty of secrecy, he is in violation of part of his obligations under the contract.[91]

However, the contractual model of medical confidentiality is limited at least in two aspects. First, the parties to the contract are the patient and her physician and possibly also the institution where treatment is provided. The contract may not be binding upon other health professionals, who may nevertheless learn about the health information.[92] Nor is the contract applicable to other physicians who are not paid on a fee-for-service basis or to other institutions (and their members) than the one where treatment is provided, the latter of which may physically hold part of the patient's medical information.

Second, the contractual model of the physician–patient relationship looks back to an early era when independent medical professionals were the main deliverers of health services, and when most patients paid for these services out of their own pockets. In the modern era, on the other hand, there are more parties participating in the process of providing medical treatment.[93] Three reasons are mentioned by Siegler to support the shift described. First, modern high-technology healthcare is mostly provided in hospitals, and requires many trained and specialized workers. Second, healthcare services are usually expensive and few patients can afford to pay for them directly. As a result, it is essential to grant access to the patient's health information to persons who are responsible for obtaining payment for these services. Third, with the expansion of medicine from a narrow, diseased-based model to a model encompassing psychological, social and economic problems, the size of the health team has increased and more sensitive information, such as the patient's personal habits and financial condition, is now included in her medical record.

It follows from this shift that a variety of healthcare providers, insurers and other administrators all act responsibly in providing care to patients. Modern healthcare is characterized by a permanent tension between the patient's interest in maintaining confidentiality and her personal interest

[91] *Hammonds*, above n 42, at 801. See also *Jane Doe* v. *Joan Roe* et al. 93 Misc. 2d 201, 210–11 (N.Y Sup. 1977); *Paul MacDonald* v. *O. W. Clinger* 84 AD 2d 482, 485–6 (NYAD 1982).
[92] See e.g. *Darnell* v. *Indiana* 674 NE 2d 19 (Ind. 1996); *Evans* v. *Rite Aid Corp.* 478 SE 2d 846 (S.C. 1996) and *Suarez* v. *Pierard* 663 NE 2d 1039 (Ill. App. 1996).
[93] Siegler, above n 45, at 1519.

in receiving the best possible healthcare. It is therefore difficult to infer the patient's expectations of privacy in her records because these expectations are complex, varied and aimed at persons other than the physician herself.[94] Alan Westin explores three zones where medical information is used: zone one is direct patient care (doctors, clinics, nursing homes); zone two includes supporting and administrative activities (service payers, third party administrators, quality of care reviewers); and zone three consists of 'secondary uses', namely credential and evaluation decisions, public health reporting, social welfare programmes and direct marketing.[95] Moreover, the patient's expectations for privacy and confidentiality are significantly shaped by the possible uses of the health information. For example, a patient's expectations of confidentiality with regard to her genetic information will differ greatly from those in respect of the medical checks she undergoes periodically.[96]

Another argument against the application of a contractual model to the medical context holds that such a model imports rules of private law into an area which has become dominated by public law. The argument is that because medical services are significantly important to the well-being of society in general, and because the government is greatly involved in financing, supplying and regulating health services, modern healthcare is increasingly becoming an area of public law.[97] As a result, freedom of contract is severely limited, and the traditional idea of forming a contract for medical treatment between parties who are free to negotiate with each other and who stand in equal bargaining positions is illusionary and out of place.[98] A paternalistic approach substitutes the *laissez faire* perspective, according to which the state has many reasons not to allow private negotiation over these personal and sensitive data, and so the state is being justified in interfering with what was previously held to be 'freedom of contract'.

In conclusion of the second part of this chapter, none of the justifications for the right to medical confidentiality is solid and sufficient enough to establish sound rationales for acting in accordance with that right. This becomes more apparent when one considers the ethical and legal obligation to maintain the patient's confidentiality after death. In this context, the problems attached to the patient's (loss of the) right to privacy and

---

[94] Paul M. Schwartz, 'The Protection of Privacy in Health Care Reform' (1995) 48(2) *Vanderbilt Law Review* 295–347, 301–4 [Schwartz, 'Protection of Privacy'].

[95] Alan Westin, 'Interpretive Essay' in Health Information Privacy Study 7, discussed in Schwartz, 'Protection of Privacy', *ibid.*, at 301.

[96] Paul M. Schwartz, 'Free Speech vs. Information Privacy: Eugene Volokh's First Amendment Jurisprudence' (2000) 52(5) *Stanford Law Review* 1559–72, 1565–6.

[97] *Ibid.*, at 1566.   [98] *Ibid.*, at 1567.

autonomy, the different powers of heirs versus relatives, the extent to which the physician–patient relationship is established after death, the continuance of a fiduciary duty of confidence and the inherent limits of a contractual model all come into play, adding much complexity to the already difficult concept of keeping one's health information confidential.

The theoretical difficulties associated with the justifications for medical confidentiality nevertheless do not impede courts from deciding complicated issues which they are called upon to consider. Courts are not concerned with classifying the breach of confidence into an existing conceptual category, but instead use existing legal disputes to enforce the more fundamental notion of confidentiality, making the action of breach of confidentiality *sui generis*.[99] More generally, the law shows a flexible approach, providing that the right to medical confidentiality is not absolute.[100] A wide variety of exceptions to the right to confidentiality has been developed by case law and legislation, including the obligation to warn third parties of the patient's threatened violence,[101] the requirement to report genetic risks,[102] the duty to disclose contagious disease (including HIV)[103] and child abuse,[104] disclosure for the investigation of a crime, or disclosure of information necessary to 'a proper administration of justice'.[105] In addition,

[99] Gurry, above n 79, at 25–6.
[100] *Whalen* v. *Roe* 429 US 589, 602 (1977). For an alternative approach, see Michael H. Kottow, 'Medical Confidentiality: An Intransigent and Absolute Obligation' (1986) 12 *Journal of Medical Ethics* 117–22.
[101] *Tarasoff* v. *Regents of the University of California* 188 Cal. Rptr 129, 529 P 2d 533 (1974). But see *Bellah* v. *Greenson* 146 Cal. Rptr 535, 81 Cal. App. 3d 614 (1978), where the court rejected the parents' claim that under *Tarasoff* their daughter's physician owed a duty to warn them of her suicidal inclinations. The court did not extend *Tarasoff* to situations involving self-harm, and ruled that *Tarasoff* required a 'duty to protect' and not a 'duty to warn'.
[102] See Institute of Medicine, Report of the Committee on Assessing Genetic Risks, *Assessing Genetic Risks: Implications for Health and Social Policy* (Washington: National Academy Press, 1994) 264–73, mentioned in Beauchamp and Childress, above n 3, at 312.
[103] Beauchamp and Childress, above n 3, at 309–11; Bernard Dickens, 'Confidentiality and the Duty to Warn' in L. O. Gostin ed., *Aids and the Health Care System* (New Haven: Yale University Press, 1990) 98; Health Protection and Promotion Act, RSO 1990, c. H-7, s. 26(Can.).
[104] See Child Family Services Act, RSO 1990, c. C-11, s. 72.5(a)(Can.).
[105] *Juanita Sims* v. *Charlotte Liberty Mutual Insurance Company* 257 NC 32, 125 SE 2d 326, 331 (1962). Other exceptions include the reporting of potential dangerous drivers: Highway Traffic Act, RSO 1990, c. H-8, s. 203(Can.), and the reporting of air traffic controllers, pilots and other aviation licence holders suffering from a condition which is likely to be a hazard to aviation safety: Aeronautics Act, RSC 1985, c. A-3, s. 6.5(1)(Can.). For another suggested exception to the rule of confidentiality compelling parents to make their medical histories available to their children, see Bernard Friedland, 'Physician–Patient Confidentiality: Time to Reexamine a Venerable Concept in Light of Contemporary Society and Advances in Medicine' (1994) 15 *Journal of Legal Medicine* 249–77.

case law establishes that a patient might lose her right to medical confidentiality when she affirmatively places her physical condition at issue in a judicial proceeding in either a complaint or an answer.[106] However, it was ruled that the waiver of medical privilege would not take place when the issue at stake did not directly relate to the patient's medical condition,[107] unless established differently by specific legislation.[108]

Although the vast number of legal rules established in the area of medical confidentiality do not necessarily reflect a coherent and settled understanding of confidentiality, they still provide some guidelines for dealing with questions related to disclosure of health information after death. These questions are characterized by the following attributes: (1) the health information to be disclosed relates to a former patient who has recently died; (2) the health information was something the patient shared with her physician prior to her death while seeking treatment from her physician, or was obtained following medical procedures performed on the deceased after death, e.g. during the production of the death certificate or the performance of medical examination of the body; (3) an interested party seeking to disclose information may have had a personal relationship with the deceased while alive so that she may also be legally empowered to control the patient's surviving right to medical confidentiality: in case she does have such power, she may be in conflict of interests when, aside from her interest in protecting the confidentiality of the deceased, she may have a personal interest which can only be advanced by disclosure and waiver of the same confidentiality.

In the discussion above, the application of the general justifications for medical confidentiality, especially the rights-based justifications concerning the privacy and autonomy models, to the post-mortem context was found to be very problematic and substantially deficient. The analysis above also demonstrated that the fiduciary duty of confidentiality might not survive the death of the patient, and that the idea of keeping promises made to the patient while alive or enforcing a contract for treatment to which she was a party involves some theoretical problems. As with confidentiality of health information relating to living patients, it is argued in

---

[106] *Valentin Koump* v. *James E. Smith* 25 NY 2d 287, 294, 250 NE 2d 857, 864 (1969); *Carolyn D. Luce* v. *State of New York* 266 AD 2d 877, 697 NYS 2d 806 (1999). See, in Canada, *La Métropolitaine, Compagnie D'assurance-Vie* c. *Raymond Frenette et Hôpital* 89 DLR (4th) 653, [1992] 1 SCR 647, 677.

[107] *Charles J. Simek* v. *Superior Court of the County of San Mateo* 117 Cal. App. 3d 169 (1981).

[108] Some states in the USA have legislation abrogating the patient's privilege in cases of workmen's compensation and medical malpractice. See 'Privileged Communications', above n 31, at 1537 and the references mentioned in notes 44 and 45 therein.

this chapter that a better approach to resolving disputes concerning the disclosure of information related to dead patients would be to establish a case-by-case analysis without the exclusive commitment to any of the theoretical understandings of the notion of confidentiality mentioned earlier. After such a case-by-case analysis has been provided, it will be possible to suggest the more general principles to guide policy makers in future such situations.

Practical solutions to breach of confidentiality

One can address the question of whether – and if so how – medical confidentiality can be maintained after death by providing general principles applying to all disclosure requests taking place after the death of the patient or by discussing specific cases of such requests and providing ad hoc guidelines for these cases. The first alternative guarantees some degree of certainty and coherency in addressing similar cases, while the second alternative gives sufficient weight to the substantial differences between the various cases and sub-categories of disclosure requests resulting in different – and sometimes more just – legal outcomes. In the next two sections both proposals will be examined.

General solutions to post-mortem confidentiality

More weight to confidentiality during life There are three possibilities to solve the dilemma of whether to disclose health information after the death of a patient. Under the first possibility, the right to confidentiality should be given less weight after death than in life. This may be explained by the termination of the physician–patient relationship and the physician's duty to maintain confidentiality thereon,[109] the proposition that the confidence is prima facie a personal matter ending with the death of the patient,[110] or the fact that the decedent is not aware of the breach of confidentiality. If confidentiality during life deserves more protection than post-mortem confidentiality, then one of the following results may be brought about. When the patient is dead:

(1) The medical information becomes public;
(2) The information can be disclosed at the discretion of the physician;

---

[109] *Re Freeman* 46 Hun 458, 12 NYSR 175 (1887), mentioned in Jean V. McHale, *Medical Confidentiality and Legal Privilege* (New York: Routledge, 1993) 114 [McHale].
[110] J. K. Mason, R. A. McCall Smith and G. T. Laurie, *Law and Medical Ethics*, 5th edn (London: Butterworths, 1999) 213 [Mason *et al.*].

(3) The information can be disclosed with the permission of the decedent's representatives (executor/administrator/next-of-kin) or legal heir. Under this suggestion, two additional alternatives are possible: the decision of whether to disclose the health information is examined by the deceased's representative or heir in light of the patient's 'best interests', if she retains any such interests; alternatively, the deceased's representative or heir acts as the patient's surrogate decision maker, purporting to ascertain the decedent's hypothetical wishes as to the question of whether health information should be disclosed. An appeal to the patient's surrogate decision-making procedure is usually problematic, for it is frequently difficult to find an appropriate decision maker for the deceased who will be able genuinely to elucidate the decedent's wishes. This is especially troubling when the substitute decision maker may have a personal interest in disclosing the information;

(4) The information can be disclosed only when it is shown that the patient herself would have decided to waive the privilege had she still been alive;[111]

(5) The information can be disclosed only following a court order and only if application of the privilege would lead to a substantially different view of the evidence being taken in court.[112] Of course, this solution is applicable only when the application for disclosure of health information is brought to court and is dependent upon other evidence being in existence with regard to that application;

(6) The decision whether to disclose the information depends on the purpose for which disclosure is sought. When the information is of a proprietary nature, such as information relating to the experience and skills acquired during life ('know-how'), it can be regarded as the decedent's estate so that the personal representative of the deceased would be empowered to give her consent to using or disclosing it. On the other hand, the personal representative would not be able to bring action for breach of confidentiality to protect the relations or friends of the deceased from mere distress resulting from the disclosure.[113]

Arguing for the proposition that post-mortem confidentiality may be waived under some circumstances and by certain people, and that it should be less stringent than confidentiality during life, has obvious

---

[111] C. Ploem, 'Medical Confidentiality after a Patient's Death, with Particular Reference to the Netherlands' (2001) 20 *Medicine and Law* 215–20, 218 [Ploem].

[112] McHale, above n 109, at 115.

[113] See the English Law Commission, *Breach of Confidence: Report No. 110* (1981), discussed in Kennedy and Grubb, above n 77, at 1082.

practical advantages. For this one may find support in the area of the law of defamation, which also protects one's privacy rights and personal reputation.[114] The general rule in this area of law is that the decedent's representatives or heirs cannot bring action for the violation of the deceased's right to privacy or a good name, unless they can also show that they were personally hurt by the publication.[115] However, in contrast to defamation after death, which is an event happening after the person is dead and not originating in any act of the deceased while she was alive, in the typical confidentiality cases the living patient has entrusted her personal health information to her physician. Confidentiality may survive the death of the patient even if her privacy right may not. The analogy from the law of defamation provides only partial justification for not protecting the patient's health information to the full.

The 'no-difference' approach Under the second approach, although the physician–patient relationship does not survive the patient's death, the duty to keep medical information confidential still exists.[116] Hence, just as while alive only the patient could waive her right to confidentiality, if the patient did not waive her right to confidentiality before she died, the health information could not be disclosed. Case law provides support for this approach,[117] but creates far-reaching practical difficulties. Most of all, this alternative does not determine any time limit or substantial criteria to control the decedent's right to confidentiality extending after death. There are serious doubts whether this view represents, and should represent, the current legal opinion.[118]

More weight to post-mortem confidentiality Under the third possible approach, the right to confidentiality has, and should be given, more weight after death than in life, since the patient is in her most vulnerable position by not being able to control the use of her health information.

---

[114] *Ibid.*
[115] *Lambert* et al. v. *Garlo* et al. 19 Ohio App. 3d 295, 484 NE 2d 260, 263 (1985) [*Lambert*].
[116] McHale, above n 109, at 113.
[117] *Westover* v. *Atena Life Insurance Co.* 1 NE 104 (N.Y. 1885); *Reinhan* v. *Dennin* 9 NE 320 (N.Y. 1886); *In re Flint's Estate* 34 P 863, 100 Cal. 391 (Sup. Ct Calif. 1893) [*Flint*]; *Bullivant* et al. v. *Attorney General for Victoria* [1900–3] All ER 812.
[118] See *Reianne Mayorga* v. *Robert Tate* 752 NYS 2d 353 (N.Y. 2002), distinguishing the *Westover* decision to apply only when no opposite statutory provision which allows executors, among others, to waive the physician–patient privilege on behalf of their decedents exists.

Support for this approach may be found in the writings of Toulson and Phipps,[119] and in some court decisions in the USA.[120]

Even if this approach is descriptively correct, it has serious practical implications: What does the fact of the patient's being in her most vulnerable condition entail for the practical protection of the decedent's right to confidentiality? Specifically, can heirs or relatives of the deceased bring an action on behalf of the deceased? And if this is not the kind of protection aimed for under this category, what is it then? One can think of three levels of such protection: a patient may have a right to inspect (ahead or simultaneously) his or her medical information; a patient may have a right to give consent before any use or transfer of that information is being made; and a patient may have a right to receive (ex post) an accounting of instances in which her personal health information has been disclosed. The protection of medical confidentiality advanced by this approach does not distinguish between these three levels of protection. Moreover, it is not clear how long after death the patient will still be considered to be in a vulnerable condition. Nor is it apparent what this approach would hold in respect of patients who left clear instructions about the use of health information after death. It seems unreasonable to argue that these patients are in the same vulnerable position as those who did not direct the use of their personal information.

A better approach than choosing between one of the three general principles discussed above is to examine specific cases and categories of informational requests and to analyse each of these cases according to the unique interests at issue. The next section will follow this route.

Casuistical case analysis of post-mortem confidentiality

Disclosure to protect at-risk third parties Sometimes, health information concerning a deceased patient will be needed to prevent the emergence of infectious disease among people with whom the deceased had physical contact, or control genetic diseases that may show up among blood relatives of the decedent. Disclosure of information for such purposes constitutes a special exception to the duty of confidentiality in the nature of the 'duty to warn' – not by future actions of the patient herself but in respect of a health condition that may be relevant to others. However, as contended by Maixner and Morin, 'in nearly all instances, a deceased patient's medical information cannot lead to the diagnosis of a

---

[119] Toulson and Phipps, above n 78.
[120] *Flint*, above n 117; *McCaw* v. *Turner* 126 Miss. 260, 88 So. 705 (1921); *Auld* v. *Cathro* 20 ND 461, 128 NW 1025 (1910); *Correia*, above n 87, at 66–7.

living individual, only to a probability of developing a specific health problem'.[121] Much thought is needed when one considers whether or not to disclose information for such purposes.

Disclosure in the best interests of another patient There are cases in which disclosure of medical information pertaining to the decedent may be of great assistance to another patient, for example the decedent's child,[122] mainly in determining her prognosis.[123] Such disclosure may indirectly benefit society as well, since without disclosure the child will need to go through expensive tests, the costs of which will be borne by society. In these cases, the concern is not with preventing immediate harm from another patient but with accruing some good for her.[124] Ethically, the physician should benefit her patient no less than she is obligated not to harm her. The principle of beneficence is an important component of the physician–patient relationship. However, from a legal perspective and at least in the common law juridical system, a patient does not have any duty to assist or even rescue the life of another patient.[125] There are few states in the USA where disclosure of medical information pertaining to a deceased patient is allowed, especially when such disclosure may assist in the medical diagnosis of another patient.[126] Nevertheless, due to the tension between the ethical duty of physicians to care for all their patients and the legal privilege of patients not to assist other patients, such disclosure should not be taken for granted and more discussion is needed in this regard.

Disclosure in death certificates Death certificates are documents which contain the date of death, identity of the decedent, age at death,

---

[121] Maixner and Morin, above n 10, at 1191.

[122] The more common cases would include disclosure to provide help to the natural child of the decedent. But there could be situations in which a person fears genetic inheritance from the decedent who is not his or her biological father (e.g. the mother's husband). These situations are more complex and I will not discuss them here.

[123] A more complex question would be whether a physician owes a duty to disclose medical information to benefit another person who is not his patient. One can hold that the physician owes a duty of equity ('duty in conscience') to other parties – whether the physician's other patients or not – in regard to the information communicated to him unless the patient did not want to reveal facts concerning third parties. See Kennedy and Grubb, above n 77, at 1083.

[124] An intermediate situation would include the disclosure of medical information with regard to some genetic diseases so that early treatment of those diseases halts the course of the disease.

[125] *McFall* v. *Shimp* 10 PD & C 3d 90, 91 (Allegheny County Ct 1978).

[126] See e.g. S.C. Code Ann. s. 38-93-30(4) (2005) discussing disclosure of genetic information.

home address, place of death and cause of death. The cause of death is determined by the physician signing the certificate, and is usually the most troubling piece of information revealed by the death certificate. The advantage of a central registry of deaths was first realized by Edwin Chadwick, who pressed the English government for a cause of death to be included in the death register, mainly because of interest in infant mortality which was a sensitive indicator of social conditions.[127]

Death certificates are public documents. The information disclosed in them is usually available to interested parties. In some states in the USA, death certificates are made public only after the elapse of some years since death.[128] Undoubtedly, the inclusion of detailed diagnoses on death certificates is valuable for producing high-quality mortality statistics.[129] In addition, death certificates are the most widely available and commonly used data for global policies and programmes to combat diseases and injuries.[130] When the patient dies of a stigmatized disease her physician may substitute other causes of death or omit the underlying diagnosis of such disease in order to spare her mourning family the added psychological stress caused by the stigmatization. For example, before 1984 chronic alcoholism was considered in England and Wales to be within the broad remit of unnatural death, and was subject to public inquest. To avoid embarrassment to relatives, pathologists proposed more acceptable causes of death such as myocardial ischaemia, thereby avoiding the need to inform the coroner. Another example is suicide. In addition to avoiding embarrassment to families, a threat of reduction or loss of life insurance benefits for the victim's dependants was a reason to alter the cause of death as suicide. As a result, many death certificates were and still are inaccurate and statistical data are frequently useless.[131]

The problem of inaccurate death certificates was aggravated with the spread of HIV/Aids. Relatives of the deceased were obliged to present the death certificate to the Registrar of Births and Deaths whose office was

---

[127] Michael B. King, 'Aids on the Death Certificate: The Final Stigma' (1989) 298 *British Medical Journal* 731–6, 731 [King].

[128] See e.g. Del. Code Ann. s. 3110(f) (2005) (death certificates become public forty years after death).

[129] See World Health Organization, *Medical Certification of Cause of Death* (Geneva: WHO, 1968).

[130] Colin D. Mathers, Doris Ma Fat, Mie Inoue, Chalapati Rao and Alan D. Lopez, 'Counting the Dead and What They Died From: An Assessment of the Global Status of Cause of Death Data' (2005) 83(3) *Bulletin of the World Health Organization* 171–7.

[131] For a study on the subject, see B. Swift and K. West, 'Death Certification: An Audit of Practice entering the 21st Century' (2002) 55 *Journal of Clinical Pathology* 275–9; D. S. James and A. D. Bull, 'Information on Death Certificates: Cause for Concern' (1996) 49 *Journal Clinical Pathology* 213–16 [James and Bull]. See also *Confidentiality of HIV Status*, above n 10, at 2.

sometimes located in the neighbourhood where they were well known. Moreover, death certificates are usually reproduced for the decedent's former employer, insurance company, mortgage company, bank, solicitor and others. In some cases where the decedent's sexual orientation was unknown to her family, publication of the death certificate creates further difficulties and embarrassment. As a result, some suggestions to restrict access and use of information expressed in the certificates have been made. A British government publication suggested, for example, that death certificates relating to recent deaths should be available only to those who might legitimately want them. According to this proposal, applicants to view the certificate would now be asked to provide details that could not be derived from public indexes, e.g. full name of the deceased, age or year of birth and occupation.[132] Another suggestion in the USA recommended the use of a two-part death certificate: one part for disposal and immediate legal purposes containing evidence of death without stating cause of death, and a more detailed part for medical certification.[133] A third proposal in Finland suggested requiring a review of all death certificates by a regional screener prior to registration, thereby ensuring adequate inquiry into deaths and providing that certificates were correctly completed, and adequate and screened information was supplied.[134]

Along with these professional initiatives, there exists specific legislation providing for the disclosure of information in death certificates or in documents written soon after the patient dies in a health institution. In the USA, for example, some state legislation provides that when a patient who has been diagnosed as having an infectious or communicable disease, e.g. infectious hepatitis, tuberculosis, syphilis, gonorrhoea, chancroid or Aids, dies in a hospital or other healthcare facility, the attending physician will prepare a written notification describing such disease to accompany the body when it is picked up for disposition. Any person who picks up the body must present such notification to any embalmer, funeral home or other person 'in possession' of the body. The information in the note is confidential and may be disclosed only if some conditions are met.[135]

---

[132] HMSO, *Registration: A Modern Service* (Cm 531), published on 1 December 1988, discussed in Mason, *et al.*, above n 110, at 213.
[133] King, above n 127, at 735.   [134] James and Bull, above n 131, at 216.
[135] Ga. Stat. Ann. s. 31-21-3 (Thomson/West 2006); Kans. Stat. Ann. s. 65-2438 (2004). Other legislation provides only that information concerning such disease is confidential and may be disclosed under the specified conditions: Ind. Code Ann. s. 16-41-13-3 (Thomson/West 2005).

In Canada, provincial legislation provides for disclosure of the certified cause of death. Under this legislation, a copy of the death certificate may be issued to the nearest living relative of the decedent, a medical practitioner who requires the copy for use in the life-saving treatment of a member of the decedent's immediate family, a person authorized by court to order that copy, or an officer of any provincial or federal government requiring the copy for use in the discharge of official duties. If more than twenty years have passed since the death of the decedent, the law also permits any person to order a copy of the certificate, and in addition the chief executive officer has the discretion to give a copy to any person requiring it with no time limit following the death of the decedent.[136] While the law in Ontario and British Columbia, for example, does not specifically address the issue of whether publication of cause of death to third parties should be limited, in Manitoba, Northwest Territories and Nunavut the law establishes that a certificate of death should not disclose a cause of death unless the certificate was issued with regard to a death that occurred seventy or more years prior to the request, or a member of the executive council or an order of court permitted disclosure.[137] In Prince Edward Island, publication of the death certificate is permissible to close relatives of the decedent and to a public officer requiring the information for use in the discharge of official duties.[138]

The varied regulation of disclosure of information included in death certificates reflects an effort to protect the confidentiality of the deceased and her family on one hand, and to provide information to parties who need it on the other hand. Nevertheless, the regulation in this area has many gaps and creates some inconsistencies between one province or state and another, leading to different legal outcomes. Some of the issues to be further considered include the disclosure of cause of death to family, the effect of the time since death on the extent of disclosure, the criteria by which remote parties may have access to the health information, and the degree to which the information included in the death certificate should be specified.

Autopsy disclosures Disclosure in the course of an autopsy consists of the three following types: disclosure prior to the performance of an

---

[136] See e.g. Vital Statistics Act, RSBC 1996, c. 479, s. 38(3); Vital Statistics Act, RSO 1990, c. V-4, s. 21.

[137] Vital Statistics Act, RSM 1987, c. V-60, s. 32(12); Vital Statistics Act, RSNWT 1988, c. V-3, s. 33(3).

[138] Vital Statistics Act, SPEI 1996, c. 48, s. 32(6).

220 Posthumous Interests

autopsy, disclosure from the autopsy procedure itself and disclosure of autopsy results.

DISCLOSURE PRIOR TO PERFORMING AN AUTOPSY Before a coroner is appointed, the law in the USA and Canada establishes that the disclosure of health information relating to a person who has died, when there is a suspicion that the death resulted from a criminal offence, is not only allowed but is also necessary.[139] The rationale for this rule accords with the more general justification for the institution of autopsies, namely the promotion of the public interest in investigating sudden, suspicious or unexplained deaths.[140]

More controversial situations involve the performance of autopsies for research and educational purposes. Autopsies play a critical role in quality control in medical care. They are used to evaluate the accuracy of pre-mortem diagnoses, the efficacy of new drugs, new diagnostic and surgical technologies, and to develop technology such as gene therapy. Autopsies may also assist in epidemiological and medical research, for example to identify and help control previously unrecognized diseases, and more significantly to identify and help in finding effective therapy for diseases like Aids. Finally, autopsies may help in evaluating the accuracy of cause-of-death information on death certificates.[141] It is reasonable to hold that disclosure for the performance of autopsy for these purposes need not be extensive and should only be for people authorized to make the decision of whether or not to commence the examination.

DISCLOSURE FROM THE AUTOPSY PROCEDURE ITSELF When disclosure of the very autopsy procedure is being sought, it is less an issue of confidentiality and more one of privacy. The common scenario would be the publication of photographs taken in the post-mortem examination.[142] Another example concerns the release of a recording of the decedent's voice prior to and during the death event.[143] Legislation and

---

[139] *Standards for Privacy*, above n 27, at ss. 164.512(f)(4), 164.512(g)(1). For the law in Canada, see e.g. Coroners Act, RSO 1990, c. C-37, s. 10(1).
[140] For a study on the level of information available before necropsy, see H. Sampson, A. Johnson, N. Carter and G. Rutty, 'Information Before Coronial Necropsy: How Much Should Be Available?' (1999) 52 *Journal of Clinical Pathology* 856–9.
[141] *Confidentiality of HIV Status*, above n 10, at 1.
[142] See also the application to seal autopsy photographs in the murder case of fashion designer Gianni Versace. Terilli and Splichal, above n 49, at 328–9.
[143] See the *New York Times's* application to release tapes of conversations between ground controllers and astronauts during the time between liftoff and the explosion of the NASA space shuttle and its immediate aftermath on 28 January 1986. *New York Times Co. v. NASA* 782 F Supp. 628 (DCC 1991).

ethical guidelines do not address this issue, but some guiding principles may be extracted from case law. In *Reid v. Pierce County*,[144] relatives of decedents sued Pierce County at Washington on allegations that county employees appropriated and displayed photographs taken at autopsies of the bodies, showing them at cocktail parties, using them to create personal scrapbooks, and showing them to co-workers, friends and other co-workers at a new job. In some of the instances the photographs also indicated on them the decedent's name and identification. The action in court was brought when disclosure was already made, and relatives sought compensation based on several legal claims.

The court held that the relatives' tort action of outrage and negligent infliction of emotional distress was unsuccessful, because relatives were not present when county employees appropriated and displayed the photographs. The court, however, accepted the relatives' claim that the county was liable for common law invasion of privacy. It was held that photographs of the deceased constitute intimate details of *the relatives'* lives and are facts *they* do not wish to expose to the public. As a result, it was ruled that the *immediate relatives* of the decedent have a protectable relational privacy interest in the autopsy records of the decedent. The court emphasized that such interest is grounded in maintaining the dignity of the deceased, not the relatives, but in any event it does not amount to constitutional protection.[145] However, the court did not clarify why this is so, nor did it explore the theoretical background leading to its holding.

Moreover, the court did not explain how its decision goes hand in hand with other decisions holding that relatives do *not* have such a privacy interest.[146] The court merely stated: 'We agree with the plaintiff's interpretation of the common law right of privacy and recognize that the cases relied upon by plaintiffs are more consistent with our own jurisprudence on this issue than those relied upon by the county.'[147] Perhaps the motivation to hold for the relatives was merely intuitive,[148] and is the result of serious difficulties grounded in current legal doctrines,[149] but it may still be unconvincing. Furthermore, the court relied on Washington's legislation providing that autopsy records remain

---

[144] *Reid v. Pierce County* 136 Wash. 2d 195, 961 P 2d 333 (Sup. Ct Wash. 1998) [*Reid*].
[145] *Ibid.*, at 212.
[146] *City of Artesia*, above n 48, at 375 and the other cases mentioned there.
[147] *Reid*, above n 144, at 210.
[148] 'To hold, as the county would suggest, that the relatives of a decedent have no cause of action, no matter how egregious the act is, is counter intuitive.' *Reid*, above n 144, at 212.
[149] *Loft v. Fuller* 408 So. 2d 619, 624 (Fla. App. 1981).

confidential and are distributed only to a select few.[150] However, this legislation refers to records and reports, and it is not clear whether photographs from autopsy procedures fall into the characterization of these items as they appear in Washington's legislation.[151] The court did not discuss this question and its failure to do so adds to the dubious grounds upon which its overall decision rests.

PUBLICATION OF AUTOPSY REPORTS Autopsy reports are 'investigating records compiled for law enforcement purposes'.[152] These reports contain the findings and conclusions of medical examinations performed on dead bodies. Unlike death certificates, they are not records protected under the vital statistics acts,[153] and therefore are not considered 'public'. This section will examine whether there is and should be any limit to the publication of autopsy reports.[154] In this case, we are dealing with the relational or derivative relative's right to privacy based on their status and relationship with the decedent and regardless of their own right to privacy, protecting them from trauma, mental suffering, etc. On the one hand, this is a relational right to privacy because it reflects a violation of the values that privacy usually protects in relation to another person, namely the deceased. On the other hand, the subjects of this right are relatives of the deceased but not the deceased herself. Actions brought under such a right are not suits made on behalf of the deceased. Rather, they are claims for breach of the relatives' own right to privacy.

The American Medical Association (AMA) set up a committee to discuss the problem of disclosing autopsy reports. Based on that committee's findings, the AMA issued their guidelines, establishing that autopsy reports are part of the decedents' medical records and should not be regarded as public property. The guidelines state that autopsy reports should be held confidential, unless one of the following two conditions are met: state laws prescribe disclosure to public health authorities and at-risk third parties, or, when such laws are absent, disclosure would fulfil

---

[150] Revised Code Wash. Ann. s. 68.50.105 (Thomson/West 2006).

[151] In a similar situation, the court did not find the photographs and x-rays of President Kennedy's autopsy to be 'agency records' under the Freedom of Information Act. *Katz v. National Archives and Records Administration* 862 F Supp. 476 (DDC 1994).

[152] *Joe Swickard v. Wayne County Medical Examiner* 475 NW 2d 304, 438 Mich. 536, 580 (per Justice Levin) (Sup. Ct Mich. 1991) [*Swickard*].

[153] *Lisa A. Lawson* et al. v. *Vincent Meconi* et al. 2005 WL 1323123 (Del. Ch. 2005) [*Lawson*].

[154] A similar question may apply to the publication of photographs from the scene of death. See *National Archives*, above n 48.

ethical obligations to notify endangered third parties.[155] The guidelines also establish that if state laws mandate that autopsy information be accessible to the public, physicians should comply with these laws provided that HIV status should be recorded only when it would be relevant to determine cause of death. It is emphasized that it would still be unethical for a physician to disclose in public an individual patient's HIV status independent of the legal requirement governing the filing or processing of autopsy records.[156]

Additional guiding principles may scarcely be found in legislation. Statutes providing for the preparation of autopsy reports do not address the issue of their publication to parties other than ones immediately related to the inquest. The law in Ontario, for example, states that 'the person who performs the post-mortem examination shall forthwith report his or her findings in writing only to the coroner who issued the warrant, the Crown Attorney, the regional coroner and the Chief Coroner'.[157] When the report is introduced in court, the coroner has authority to limit further cross-examination of the witness where he or she is satisfied that the cross-examination of the witness has been sufficient to disclose fully and fairly the facts in relation to which the witness has given evidence.[158]

In the USA, some states hold in their legislation that autopsy reports become part of the public record, and are available to anyone interested in them unless an exception applies. Many other states, on the other hand, have statutes establishing that autopsy reports are confidential, and case law interpreting such legislation establishes that while these statutes relate to the report being confidential in the hands of the coroner, as a secondary matter the report obtained by virtue of the statutes would still remain confidential in the hands of the prosecuting attorney.[159]

A better handling of autopsy disclosures is observed in case law. Courts in Canada reject the view that the minute an inquest is called, all the personal medical information of the deceased automatically becomes public. Courts emphasize that it is a matter of individual judgement in each case and in respect of each part of the private health record whether the relevance of that information and the public interest in its disclosure outweigh the general public and individual interest in privacy. In making that judgement the coroner would have regard to many factors, including

---

[155] This includes a report to the organ or tissue procurement agency if any part of the decedent's body was taken for use in transplantation. American Medical Association, E-5.057: *Confidentiality of HIV Status on Autopsy Reports* (June 1994), available at www.ama-assn.org/ama/pub/category/8358.html, accessed on 16 May 2007.
[156] *Ibid.*   [157] Coroners Act, RSO 1990, c. C-37, s. 28(2).   [158] *Ibid.*, at s. 50(2).
[159] *The State of Washington* v. *Armida D. Petersen and Harold Petersen* 47 Wash. 2d 836, 838 (Sup. Ct Wash. 1956).

the extent of the interest of the party seeking disclosure, the factual issues vitally relevant to the interest of that party, the extent to which disclosure is in fact necessary for the proper representation of that party and any consent or opposition by those connected with the records, such as relatives. Moreover, notice should be made not of whether disclosure might help a party in advancing its interest but of whether the need of that party for the medical records is so acute, essential and superordinate in the particular circumstances that it outweighs the very *strong presumption in favour of non-disclosure* to strangers of private medical information.[160]

In the American case law, the general rule is that autopsy reports are confidential, but the following persons may examine and obtain copies of reports: the personal representative of the deceased, any family member, the attending physician, public health officials, or the Department of Labor and Industry in case of an unknown industrial death. In addition, a trial court retains the discretion to admit a report.[161] On the other hand, courts declined an action of a decedent's relatives against a coroner who stated that the deceased was 'a pusher', and against a reporter and publisher who made this statement public.[162]

In 1991, the Supreme Court of Michigan rejected the claim for invasion of relatives' privacy with regard to the disclosure of an autopsy report following the suicide of a Chief Judge of the District Court of Michigan.[163] Referring to case law on this issue, the court held that the right to privacy perishes with the death of the person. It ruled that since the finding of the medical examiner in his report relates only to the deceased and not to the family, the material in the autopsy report is not personal, intimate or embarrassing to the family of the deceased.[164] The court further refused to extend the physician–patient privilege to autopsy reports. It explained that because the purpose of such privilege is to protect the doctor–patient relationship and ensure that communications between the two are confidential, and given that 'there is no communication in an autopsy', applying the privilege to the autopsy situation serves no purpose. In addition, it held that when a doctor performs an autopsy, she is not prescribing treatment for the deceased nor is she

---

[160] *People First of Ontario* v. *Porter, Regional Coroner Niagara* 5 OR (3d) 609, 632–3 (Ont. Ct Gen. Div. 1991) [*People First of Ontario*].

[161] *Mark A. Zueger* et al. v. *Public Hospital District No. 2 of Snohomish County* et al. 57 Wash. App. 584, 789 P 2d 326, 328 (Wash. App. 1990) [*Zueger*].

[162] *Lambert*, above n 115.   [163] *Swickard*, above n 152 (majority opinion by Justice Riley).

[164] Furthermore, the court added that even if the toxicology results were to disclose an illegal narcotic in the bloodstream of the deceased at the time of his or her death, the disclosure would not reveal any information personal to the family of the deceased. *Ibid.*, at 558.

performing surgery. Hence, 'information acquired in the performance of an autopsy falls outside the scope of the privilege'.[165]

But the majority proposition according to which publication of the autopsy report would not harm the deceased's relatives was correctly challenged by Justice Levin, who held that any embarrassing information provided by disclosure of the autopsy and test results might detract from the good name of the deceased, and might cause harm to individual members of the deceased's family, who similarly are 'heirs to that respected name'.[166] Moreover, the court's decision in *Swickard* is inconsistent with other decisions in this area. For example, in *Globe Newspaper Co.* v. *Chief Medical Examiner*,[167] the Supreme Judicial Court of Massachusetts held that 'autopsies performed by physicians are diagnostic in nature and yield detailed, intimate information about the subject's body and medical condition. They are medical records and their disclosure may constitute an unwarranted invasion of personal privacy'.[168] Finally, the *Swickard* decision was held to apply only with regard to information concerning a public figure.[169] Its application to disclosure of autopsy reports concerning non-public figures remains in doubt.

When reports are required to resolve a legal dispute, the rule established in case law is that the coroner is authorized to give counsel for the parties access to medical records obtained under the Coroners Act if it is essential for the representation of the interest *of the parties*.[170] Furthermore, special rules apply when the purpose of the publication of autopsy reports is to benefit the deceased or her relatives/dependants, for example when disclosure is sought to refute false and misleading coverage concerning death, or to provide to insurance companies an alternative cause of death than the fault of the decedent or another party. For example, in *Lawson* v. *Meconi*,[171] the decedent's wife sought to prevent publication of a report, arguing for her relational right to privacy with regard to information about the deceased. Dismissing the widow's action, the court held that the deceased's relative does not have any common law or statutory right to privacy and so she cannot protect the confidentiality of the autopsy information. In line with this decision, courts ruled that when the relative of a deceased files an action against a health practitioner, e.g. a malpractice suit, he or she is deemed to waive the

---

[165] *Ibid.*, at 561.   [166] *Ibid.*, at 583.

[167] *Globe Newspaper Co.* et al. v. *Chief Medical Examiner* 404 Mass. 132, 533 NE 2d 1356 (1989).

[168] *Ibid.*, at 134. See also *Confidentiality of HIV Status*, above n 10, at 2.

[169] *Larry S. Baker* v. *City of Westland* 245 Mich. App. 90, 627 NW 2d 27 (Ct App. Mich. 2001) [*Baker*].

[170] *People First of Ontario*, above n 160, at 631.   [171] *Lawson*, above n 153.

physician–patient privilege applying also to information included in the autopsy report, and therefore is estopped from raising any objections to disclosure of the report.[172]

Disclosure to providers of disposal services and organ procurement organizations Breach of confidentiality after death may also occur as a result of disclosure of health information to providers of disposal services and organ procurement organizations. The protection against such disclosure is mainly guaranteed by legislation. Under American federal rules, protected health information may be disclosed to funeral directors as necessary to enable them to carry out their duties with respect to the body. The rules also allow for the disclosure of health information prior to, and in reasonable anticipation of, the patient's death, if required.[173] Similar rules are also provided by some state legislation in the USA in case of death resulting from a known contagious disease.[174] American federal rules also establish that disclosure of protected health information to any entity responsible for transplantation or banking of cadaveric organs, eyes or tissue is permissible for these purposes only.[175]

In contrast to the American legal system, health law legislation in Canada dealing with disclosure of information concerning a deceased patient does not specifically address the issue of disclosure to providers of disposal services or organ procurement agencies. This lacuna must be filled in accordance with the general principles established under American legislation.

Disclosure of research outcomes concerning dead subjects There are many instances in which research on human subjects is performed for the advancement of medicine and science. Of course, some of these subjects may die during research. In addition, there are cases where medical research is performed on dead subjects. When disclosure of research results is being sought, the confidentiality owed to these subjects may be at risk.[176] Mark Wicclair and Michael DeVita mention four reasons to protect the confidentiality of information about the deceased obtained

---

[172] *Zueger*, above n 161, at 328.
[173] *Standards for Privacy*, above n 27, at s. 164.512(g)(2).
[174] See e.g. Va. Code Ann. s. 32.1-37.1 (2005); Ala. Code s. 22-11A-38(b) (2007); Kans. Ann. Stat. ss. 65-2438(a), 65-2438(b) (2004).
[175] *Standards for Privacy*, above n 27, at s. 164.512(h).
[176] The fear of breach of confidentiality is substantially reduced if individual identifiers are removed from these results, or if living subjects who participated in the research specifically addressed the situation of publishing the results after they die.

from post-mortem research.[177] First, and more generally, the authors argue that it is incompatible with the principle of respect for persons to give no moral weight to confidentiality after an individual dies. Second, respecting post-mortem confidentiality can contribute to the well-being of people while they are still alive. Third, it is assumed that people who give their consent to post-mortem research may have legitimate expectations that confidentiality protections will extend after their death. These expectations may give rise to a duty to protect confidentiality after the person is dead. Lastly, breach of post-mortem confidentiality may constitute posthumous harm to the person's image and reputation.

The authors argue that the duty of confidentiality is also owed to the family of the deceased. From a practical point of view, in some cases information acquired during post-mortem research may be disturbing to family members if it is disclosed to them, e.g. genetic information implying a medical risk to next-of-kin. In order to prevent possible breach of confidentiality and distress to families, the authors suggest that research protocols should make appropriate provisions for families to indicate their preferences in this regard when investigators think such information may be discovered.[178] Additionally, protocols should indicate whether media coverage is anticipated, and what measures are planned to ensure that there will be no inappropriate breaches of privacy or confidentiality by the disclosure to other parties as well, such as insurers or employers. Due attention should be paid to potential conflicts between disclosure of information about the deceased to family members and the confidentiality interests of the decedent, for example when the disclosure of genetic information relates to a paternity claim.[179]

In the USA, a multidisciplinary expert consensus panel on research with the recently dead (CPRRD) crafted ethical guidelines for research with the newly-dead.[180] The major principle expressed in these guidelines is that cadavers should be treated in a manner that is consistent with

---

[177] Mark R. Wicclair and Michael DeVita, 'Oversight of Research Involving the Dead' (2004) 14(2) *Kennedy Institute of Ethics Journal.* 143–64, 145–6 [Wicclair and DeVita].

[178] *Ibid.*, at 157. If the proposed research includes genetic testing, the authors recommend that family members should be offered genetic counselling prior to deciding whether and when to receive the results. These rules may also be balanced with the more general disclosure policy regarding disclosure in the best interests of another person (or patient) discussed above.

[179] *Ibid.*, at 158. Wicclair and DeVita propose the setting up of a special committee for oversight of research involving the dead (CORID) because, in their view, the feasibility and desirability of assigning oversight responsibilities to either an IRB or a hospital ethics committee is doubtful. *Ibid.*, at 153.

[180] Rebecca D. Pentz *et al.*, 'Ethics Guidelines for Research with the Recently Dead' (2005) 11 *Nature Medicine* 1145–9.

respect for the value and dignity of the person so that research on the deceased person should abide by his life goals and treat his body in a dignified way. Such research must be, at a minimum, 'not mocking, indiscreet, crude or careless, avoiding commodification of the deceased's body'. More specifically, the panel recommended that review boards approve proposals for research with the recently dead 'only if confidentiality protections are satisfactory', and that the provisions of the Healthcare Insurance Portability and Accountability Act, which is the comprehensive federal protection for the privacy of personal health information, should be met when applicable. As to disclosure of research results, the panel concluded that if the research may produce information that is medically useful to next-of-kin, they should be offered results after appropriate counselling about the risks and benefits of disclosure, whereas if disclosure conflicts with confidentiality to the deceased, protocols should establish how the conflicts will be resolved.

In Canada, there are no specific rules or guidelines pertaining to post-mortem disclosure of research outcomes. According to the general rule, any research concerning human subjects with which the National Research Council (NRC) is involved must be carried out with the approval of one of the NRC's research ethics boards. According to NRC policy, research involving human subjects includes, inter alia, the situation where human biological materials that are obtained from cadavers are being studied or where personal or private materials that have not been placed in the public domain with the consent of the person directly affected are studied.[181] This suggests that the confidentiality of any such research concerning the dead should be considered and dealt with by research ethics boards. However, since the definition cited is very narrow, it may exclude many forms of post-mortem research from being reviewed by the research ethics boards.

When medical or scientific research is supervised by research ethics boards the Tri-Council Policy Statement may apply.[182] The general guiding principle of this policy is that 'information that is disclosed in the context of a professional or research relationship must be held

---

[181] National Research Council Canada, *Policy for Research Involving Human Subjects*, available at www.nrc-cnrc.gc.ca/randd/ethics/policy_e.html#def, last accessed on 16 May 2007.

[182] Canadian Institutes of Health Research, Natural Sciences and Engineering Research Council of Canada, Social Sciences and Humanities Research Council of Canada, *Tri-Council Policy Statement: Ethical Conduct for Research Involving Humans*, 1998 (with 2000, 2002, 2005 amendments), available at http://pre.ethics.gc.ca/english/pdf/ TCPS%20October%202005_E.pdf, accessed on 16 October 2007. But see the statement according to which the term 'research subjects' refers to living individuals. *Ibid.*, at 1.2.

confidential'.[183] When the subject of research has died after contributing her data to research, their disclosure or use by the researcher is regulated under Article 3.4, which discusses the researcher's general access to secondary data involving identifying information. The article requires that such access be dependent on consultation with, among others, representatives of those who contributed data. The consultation may be relevant when the subject of research died so that it is not possible to obtain informed consent.[184]

The Tri-Council Policy protects the privacy of the individual in relation to research involving human tissue as well, and such protection is also extended to situations where the tissue is obtained from the deceased. For example, with regard to post-mortem acquisition of brain-tissue from a person suffering from dementia, the Policy states in its section on privacy and confidentiality that such acquisition 'would require the free and informed consent of an authorized third party if there were no prior directive of the deceased'.[185]

In the USA, federal rules establish that a covered entity may use or disclose protected health information for research regardless of the source of funding of the research on condition that the IRB or private research board provide a statement determining the alteration or waiver under specified conditions mentioned there.[186] It seems proper to regard post-mortem research as being covered by these rules as well.

Disclosure for teaching purposes Sometimes, photographs or videos of real patients are required for training new generations of medical professionals. In clinical medicine this would include videos taken of a laparoscopy, images taken of internal organs and unlabelled x-rays.[187] Usually, such items do not contain any identifying characteristics of their subjects, and any accompanying data such as the patient's name, date of birth or death and treating hospital is removed. However, two issues remain to be addressed: consent to participating in the teaching endeavour and publication of the teaching resources.

Despite their anonymity, the production of such images requires that the patient's consent to being photographed or filmed be obtained. Can a pathologist take pictures of specimens found during an autopsy without the patient's prior consent or that of her family? It is suggested in the

[183] *Ibid.*, at 3.1.   [184] *Ibid.*, at 3.5–3.6.   [185] *Ibid.*, at 10.2.
[186] *Standards for Privacy*, above n 27, at s. 164.512(i), pp. 27–8.
[187] H. A. Tranberg, B. A. Rous and J. Rashbass, 'Legal and Ethical Issues in the Use of Anonymous Images in Pathology Teaching and Research' (2003) 42 *Histopathology* 104–9 [Tranberg *et al.*].

literature that acting in this way is not tortious, since there is no unauthorized touching of the patient or invasion of her property, and taking the photograph does not actually harm the patient.[188] Ethically, this may receive some support in the UK, where the General Medical Council recently exempted health professionals from requiring patients' permission in regard to images taken from pathology slides, x-rays, laparoscopic images, images of internal organs and ultrasound images, and waived patients' consent to using them for any purpose provided that before use the recordings are effectively anonymized by the removal of any identifying marks.[189] However, no other guidelines exist in Canada or the USA to manage this medical practice, and this may be very disturbing because, even if the images are used anonymously, it is still questionable whether principles of medical ethics justify using the body and image of a deceased patient for teaching purposes without due notification.[190]

Should photographs or videos of a decedent's body be unlimitedly published? No direct ruling may reflect on this question. However, in a recent case, the English Court of Appeal was called upon to discuss the duty of confidentiality with regard to disclosing for commercial purposes the information contained on prescription forms. The information at stake contained the names of general practitioners and the identity and quantity of drugs prescribed but not the names of patients. The court held that in a case involving personal confidences, the disclosure of information by the confidant would not constitute a breach of confidence provided that the confider's identity was protected.[191] According to this line of reasoning, scholars found it appropriate to hold that using anonymous images for education does not amount to breach of confidentiality.[192] Nevertheless, there may still be substantial differences between the disclosure of an image which by itself is very telling and the disclosure of health data on prescriptions which, without identifiers, seems indeed less problematic. Further discussion on this issue is needed.

Disclosure for contesting a will or supporting an insurance claim
Occasionally, the disclosure of health information concerning a dead

---

[188] *Ibid.*, at 105.
[189] General Medical Council, *Making and Using Visual and Audio Recording of Patients* (2002) para. 5, available at www.gmc-uk.org/guidance/library/making_audiovisual.asp, accessed on 26 March 2006.
[190] Daniel Sperling, 'Breaking Through the Silence: The Illegality of Performing Resuscitation Procedures on the Newly-Dead' (2004) 13(2) *Annals of Health Law* 393–426.
[191] *R* v. *Department of Health, ex parte Source Informatics Ltd* [2000] 1 All ER 786, [2000] 2 WLR 940.
[192] Tranberg *et al.*, above n 187, at 107–8.

patient is sought to support the argument that the decedent was of unsound mind when she executed or changed the existing provisions of her will. In such cases, a litigant would want to disclose the medical facts supporting her argument, whereas the other party might use the medical privilege to oppose disclosure. A recent case in Alberta indicated that a person who usually has the power to control and protect the confidentiality of the decedent might not be allowed to misuse such power in pursuing her own interests.[193] This ruling accords with the more general exception to medical confidentiality, according to which a patient might lose her right to medical confidentiality when she affirmatively places her physical condition in a judicial proceeding in either a complaint or an answer,[194] and may also find support in other jurisdictions.[195]

The medical information concerning a deceased patient may be of additional interest to insurance companies wishing to reject claims. A New Jersey court was called to rule upon the disclosure of health information concerning a deceased child to an insurer. The court held that when a relative makes a claim involving the health of a deceased patient, they lose any right to non-disclosure that they may have had, so that the physician is justified in providing the relevant information to the insurance company.[196] The medical privilege exception discussed above is therefore extended to disputes occurring outside court when no judicial proceeding has been filed. However, when a third party other than relatives or the executor seeks disclosure of information for personal use when there is no public interest in disclosure, it is probable that such an application would be rejected.[197]

Disclosure of the medical history of public figures This final section deals with disclosure of health information relating to public figures. Most famously, this category of cases includes the disclosure of Winston Churchill's medical history by his physician, Lord Moran, in a book he wrote in 1966,[198] the publication of autopsy reports in the matter of President Kennedy following his assassination,[199] the publication of a book written by President François Mitterand's general practitioner

---

[193] *Petrowski*, above n 22.
[194] Above n 109 and accompanying text.   [195] Ploem, above n 111, at 218.
[196] *George J. Hague v. William E. Williams* 37 NJ 328, 181 A 2d 345 (N.J. 1962).
[197] *Baker*, above n 169.
[198] The information included Churchill's series of strokes, his gradual deterioration and his attempt to maintain his prestige and power in the early 1950s. Jonas B. Robitscher, 'Doctors' Privileged Communications, Public Life and History's Rights' (1968) 17 *Cleveland-Marshall Law Review* 199–212, 202 [Robitscher].
[199] John Latimer, 'Factors in the Death of President Kennedy' (October 1966) 198 *Journal of the American Medical Association* 327.

revealing a secret medical condition,[200] the releasing of tapes of Anne Sexton's therapy sessions to a biographer,[201] the releasing of contents of therapy sessions of Nicole Simpson, O. J. Simpson's decedent wife, in his murder trials,[202] and more recently the publication of Slobodan Milošević's autopsy report and post-mortem toxicological tests.[203] The question raised in these cases is whether by being a 'public figure' a person deserves less or more protection of her confidentiality after death.

Some have argued that public figures are deemed to have lost, to some extent, their privacy for the following three reasons. First, they have sought publicity and consented to it, and so cannot complain of it; second, their personalities and affairs have already become public and can no longer be regarded as their own private business; and third, the press or biographers have a privilege guaranteed by the constitutional freedom of speech to inform the public about those who have become legitimate matters of public interest.[204] However, one can hold that having a public personality ends at death so that there is no reason why public figures should enjoy their right to confidentiality less than other dead persons.

The issue of post-mortem confidentiality of public figures has hardly been raised in case law. In *Swickard*, the court discussed the publication of an autopsy report and toxicological tests on a former Chief Judge who was found shot dead. The question briefly discussed in court was whether the deceased had a lower expectation of personal privacy than a private citizen would have. Justice Levin analysed other cases concerning privacy interests of public officials, and concluded that the general rule is in favour of disclosure when a government official's actions constitute a violation of public trust.[205] Since in the specific case there was no claim of misconduct in office (the judge was already retired and the paraphernalia were found at the judge's mother's home and not in his chambers), the court held that the deceased's and his family's personal privacy interest in nondisclosure outweighed the public interest in disclosure.[206]

---

[200] News: 'Mitterand Book provokes Storm in France' (1996) 312 *British Medical Journal* 201.
[201] Sharon Carton, 'The Poet, the Biographer and the Shrink: Psychiatrist–Patient Confidentiality and the Anne Sexton Biography' (1993) 10 *University of Miami Entertainment and Sports Law Review* 117–64.
[202] Nicole's therapist received disciplinary sanctions from the California Licensing Board for the violation of medical confidentiality. James L. Werth, 'Confidentiality in End-of-Life and After-Death Situations' (2002) 12(3) *Ethics and Behavior* 205–22, 215 (note 3).
[203] See http://news.bbc.co.uk/2/hi/europe/4801292.stm, accessed on 16 May 2007.
[204] Prosser, above n 38, at 411.
[205] See e.g. *Fund for Constitutional Government* v. *National Archives and Records Services* 656 F 2d 856, 865 (CADC 1981).
[206] *Swickard*, above n 152, at 595.

But the court's ruling in *Swickard* raises serious concerns: should it ethically and legally matter whether the disclosure sought is required to support violation of trust rather than sustain other public interests? It seems somehow arbitrary to construct a disclosure policy which is based on the question of whether the public trust in the public figure may be undermined. Although physicians may owe general duties to the public,[207] it still remains questionable whether they owe any positive obligation to inform the public or promote knowledge of historical events by disclosing personal health information to the media or biographers.[208] On the other hand, it appears unfair to disadvantage medically qualified historians compared with their colleagues who are non-medical,[209] as much as it is problematic to create areas of knowledge for which the public could not have access. An intermediate approach might suggest that doctors do not owe any duty to aid historians or biographers, but they should be allowed to give details in public about the medical conditions of a dead person where this would serve to correct a serious error and rehabilitate this person's reputation.[210] Alternatively, one can propose to specify a time limit from the moment of death after which publication of information relating to a deceased public figure may not contradict doctors' obligation of confidentiality.[211]

Ethical and professional guidelines may provide further help. The American Medical Association establishes that in instances where disclosure in biographical studies is being considered, an effort must be made to ascertain the decedent's prior wishes as to the impact of disclosure, and if no express concern is found, the impact which the disclosure may have on the reputation of the deceased should be considered.[212] However, in most of the disputed cases, disclosure of personal health information

---

[207] *W* v. *Egdell* [1990] 1 All ER 835, 852–3.

[208] See Dr Willard Gaylin's interview in the *New York Times*, where he specifically stated that 'doctors have no obligation to history and should not act as a research assistant to a biographer'. Alessandra Stanley, 'Poet Told All; Therapist Provides the Record', *New York Times*, 15 July 1991, at A1, available at http://query.nytimes.com/gst/fullpage.html?sec=health&res=9D0CE2DE1730F936A25754C0A967958260, accessed on 16 May 2007. Compare this view with that of Robitscher, who argues that not only is the physician a doctor to his patient but he also fulfils a public role, that of giving reassurance to the public concerning the health of its elected officials, so that 'during the lifetime of the patient his doctors should not reveal information without consent. *After his death* it would seem appropriate to set the record straight in the hopes that history's lessons can be useful in the evaluation of similar situations which inevitably arise.' Robitscher, above n 198, at 206–7 (my emphasis).

[209] Irvine Loudon, 'How it Strikes a Historian' (1984) 288 *British Medical Journal* 125–6, 126 [Loudon].

[210] Stephen Lock, 'A Question of Confidence' (1984) 288 *British Medical Journal* 123–5, 125.

[211] Loudon, above n 209, at 126.   [212] Maixner and Morin, above n 10, at 1191–2.

concerning public figures would have a serious impact on the reputation of these figures, and yet we would still want to challenge the proposition that such information should not be disclosed. Unfortunately, the AMA guidelines do not go that far and their assistance would be appreciated in only a few of the cases.

Conclusion

This chapter examined the question of whether the interest in medical confidentiality survives the death of the person whose interest it is. As shown in this chapter, some legislation in Canada and the USA supports an affirmative answer to this question. The medical confidentiality of a dead patient is controlled by a relative or the executor, who may waive the physician's duty of confidentiality for reasons which are not fully explored in the law. Problems arise with gaps in legislation and case law, and with many issues under-regulated by the medical profession as well. Inconsistent legal rulings within the same national legal system also make it difficult to construct a coherent and convincing approach to post-mortem confidentiality. This is aggravated by conceptual difficulties in applying the general justifications for medical confidentiality to the post-mortem context, should they hold at all.

It is argued by Bernard Dickens that 'the duty to maintain strict confidentiality is so clear in medical ethics and law that modern cases add little to its emphatic nature'.[213] This may be true, but the analysis brought in this chapter proves that at least in the post-mortem context no theoretical understanding of the concept of medical confidentiality can tell why this is so. However, at this stage it is possible to propose the basic principles upon which any fundamental theory of post-mortem medical confidentiality should be built. These principles should serve as guidelines for striking any balance between competing interests in protecting and disclosing health information after death. The principles derive from the casuistical case analysis suggested in this chapter and they can be summarized as follows:

(1) When a patient provides specific instructions as to use of her health information after death, one should follow them unless they are unreasonable, impractical or may cause harm to third parties. If a patient provides instructions as to use of her health information while alive, efforts should be made to follow these instructions after the patient dies as well and under the conditions set out above.

[213] Dickens, 'The Doctor's Duty', above n 4, at 41.

(2) Any information obtained by the physician in attending a living patient which is necessary to prescribe for or treat the patient must remain confidential after the patient dies, and may not be disclosed unless there are exceptional circumstances. If the information at stake consists of impressions or knowledge obtained by the physician as a result of the physician's observation, examination and treatment of the patient, and was not part of the patient's communication with her physician, such information may be disclosed at the discretion of the physician on condition that individual identifiers are removed from it.

(3) Information obtained during and as a result of medical procedures performed on the deceased's body or organs to investigate her cause of death, previous illness, etc., and which may have a negative or stigmatized effect on the perception of the deceased by others, including family members, should not be disclosed unless it is necessary to protect third parties (including family members), or it is necessary for the administration of justice.

(4) Any other health information relating to a deceased patient which may not fall into one of the three categories above may be disclosed with the discretion of close family members of the deceased. In considering whether to waive confidentiality, family members will take into account the following criteria: the patient's general attitude concerning her privacy and reputation; the relevancy and importance of the information to the purposes for which its disclosure is sought; whether disclosure of the information is proportional to its purposes; whether there are any other means by which such purposes may be achieved; and whether disclosure may harm third parties other than family members.

Conclusions

The previous chapters explored the legal status of posthumous interests, namely interests whose application or fulfilment occurs after a person's death. Chapter 1 discussed the survivability of interests held by the Human Subject despite the death of the person whose interests they are. In that chapter it was argued that the scope of human interests is, and must be, broader than the scope of a person's legal rights, and that the concept of 'person' which usually captures the entitlement of holding rights is not legally sufficient to protect other categories of interests existing either prior to the person's birth or after her death. Thus, if one acknowledges these categories of interests and their possible holding by the Human Subject, their defeat or setback by posthumous events may constitute harm to that subject.

It was further argued in this chapter for the legal acknowledgement of the interest in the recognition of one's symbolic existence representing another form of human existence occurring throughout and beyond one's life. The chapter concluded that such an interest, which closely accords with the concept of the Human Subject whose existence persists over time, may strongly apply to situations after death, so that it could explain and also justify some, if not most, of our attitudes to the dead and to practices performed on them.

In chapter 2 the proposition according to which there exist interests surviving or coming into effect after a person's death was taken further, and it was examined whether all or some of these interests also amount to the protection of legal rights. The analysis provided in that chapter resulted in the argument that if the Human Subject can hold interests the existence of which extends the lifespan of the person whose interests they are, then it can also be a potential right-holder. As to the question of whether such subject is also an actual right-holder, it was further established that the Human Subject may hold rights whose content relates mostly to the past experiences and cognitive capacities of the person whose interests they are or to her continuous membership in the human moral community and her ongoing identification as 'human' by living people. These rights may exist for at least as long as the deceased is still 'present' (symbolically existent) among the living, but they may also exist for longer or shorter periods of time depending on the content of the interests whose protection and promotion is sought.

The examination of the theoretical concepts relating to posthumous interests was followed by a practical analysis of posthumous interests. Chapters 3–5 were specifically concerned with three categories of posthumous interests arising in the medico-legal context: the proprietary interest in the body of the deceased, the testamentary interest in disposal of the body after death and the interest in post-mortem medical confidentiality. The analysis suggested in these chapters identified three levels of problems concerning the concept of posthumous interests in the medical context: practical, theoretical and normative.

On the practical level, legal disputes arise between next-of-kin, executors, administrators and health practitioners in relation to various procedures performed on the newly-dead. Examples of such problems include the taking of organs from the decedent or the performance of an autopsy, embalmment, medical research or training, etc., without consent and sometimes contra the decedent's or relatives' prior objection. Other cases involve the overriding of the decedent's express wishes as to disposal of her body after death, and the disclosure of sensitive medical information pertaining to a dead patient. These cases are decided on an ad hoc basis, usually without any doctrinal or theoretical understanding of the questions related to the legal disputes at stake.

On the theoretical level, the traditional legal theories of property law, law of wills and testaments and privacy law cannot entirely accommodate the legal disputes arising under these situations. The difficulties of applying the above theories to the post-mortem context are twofold. First, these theories provide strict terminological and theoretical distinctions that fail to portray the exact legal status of the issues at stake. For example, the body of the deceased is regarded as either a 'person' or 'property'. A theory of property law cannot conceptualize the holding of an interim category consisting of both classifications and/or none at the same time. This difficulty is sometimes resolved by an attempt to regard the creature at stake as *sui juris*, like in the case of unimplanted pre-embryos.[1] Such an attempt is far from being convincing. Second, the various justifications for the existence of legal institutions offered by these theories cannot successfully defend claims raised in these complex situations. Thus, for example, a rights-based justification for post-mortem medical confidentiality may not be applicable to the deceased, who, according to some traditional theories of rights, do not hold rights at all. Similarly, the law of wills and testaments will lack

---

[1] See e.g. *Davis* v. *Davis* 842 SW 2d 588 (Tenn. 1992).

explanatory and justificatory power in its effort to conceptualize testaments concerning items not classified as property, including testaments concerning the disposal of the body after death.

Finally, on the normative level the law encounters serious difficulties in categorizing the legal dilemmas which death situations provoke. The conflicting values arising out of these disputes are difficult to frame. At times, these values protect society's interest in the protection of the dead reflected by its commitment to humanity, dignity and sensibility of its human members. At other times, it is the living person, mostly surviving families, whose obscure interests 'in' the deceased are protected. The property, privacy and occasionally also liberty interests of these latter parties are at the core of this legal protection. However, along with these two groups of interest-holders, the analysis suggested in these chapters also shows that a major concern occupying judges and legislators focuses on the deceased herself. Such focus is, nevertheless, difficult to articulate.

In an attempt to resolve these difficulties, the application of the interest in the recognition of one's symbolic existence to post-death practices has been advocated. As discussed in chapter 1, symbolic existence is a form of human existence which usually takes place in the minds, thoughts and language of other existing creatures or in the actions, possessions and the like of materially existing creatures. Symbolic existence represents the real or abstract existence of the person whose existence it is/was. Such an interest is held by the Human Subject and it survives the death of the person whose interest in symbolic existence it is.

I wish to argue that if we acknowledge the interest in our symbolic existence and if we legally protect it, we should enjoy the power to shape our symbolic existence and such power should have prima facie peremptory legal status. Hence, any interference with the way we choose to dispose of our body after death is prima facie a violation of our freedom to shape our own symbolic existence, and therefore must not be allowed. Similarly, subjecting our bodies to the proprietary interest of another or the disclosure of sensitive information concerning our health condition after death diminishes our symbolic existence and portrays it in a distorted fashion which we cannot defend successfully.

The application of the interest in the recognition of one's symbolic existence

The proprietary interest in the body of the deceased

The human body, wrote Richard Gold, is 'the means through which each of us experiences the external world and the means through which each of us recognizes each other. It is also inherently valuable as a source of our identities and, on some view, as a representation of God.' Thus, concluded Gold, for both instrumental and inherent reasons, society values the body deeply and heterogeneously.[2] In our culture, we attach great importance to the embodiment of our beings. As argued by Murray, 'we only know of ourselves and each other in and through our bodies'.[3] One's interest in the dominion of one's image and self-recognition has its application in the way one's body is treated within life but also after death. The interest in the recognition of one's symbolic existence implies that one's whole body – dead or alive – must never be subject to property. A general objection to the recognition of a proprietary interest in the body of the deceased therefore holds that the very same thing which enables one's characterization and recollection by others must never be subject to the dominion of others.

But the interest relatives may have with regard to the body of the deceased may be so strong and meaningful that it may constitute part of their very selves. One can hold that in order to protect that interest, family members, and perhaps even close friends of the deceased, should be vested with a proprietary interest in the body. This question was analysed in chapter 3. Unlike the common view extensively expressed in that chapter, according to which such interest may derive from the relatives' duty to dispose of the body of the deceased, the proposition examined here is that the proprietary interest relatives may have with regard to the body of the deceased can serve and enhance an important component of *their* identities and selves, thereby manifesting their interest in the recognition of their own symbolic existence.

Indeed, applying the idea of one's interest in symbolic existence to property law results in a richer and a more diverse understanding of the purposes which property over external objects may fulfil. If by holding property one symbolically exists in the world, then the purpose of the property is to project a desirable image of the property holder to others, to express her social status, and to make visible her personal characteristics.

Many great thinkers like Fromm and Sartre have analysed the relationship between having and being, suggesting that we can know who we are by observing what we have.[4] By analysing extensive empirical data on

---

[2] E. Richard Gold, *Body Parts: Property Rights and the Ownership of Human Biological Material* (Washington: Georgetown University Press, 1996) 12.
[3] Thomas H. Murray, 'Are We Morally Obligated to Make Gifts of Our Bodies?' (1991) 1 *Health Matrix* 19, 24.
[4] Erich Fromm, *To Have or To Be?* (New York: Harper & Row, 1976); Jean-Paul Sartre, *Being and Nothingness: A Phenomenological Essay on Ontology* (New York: Philosophical Library, 1943).

consumers' behavior, Russell Belk developed the idea of the extended self.[5] This is the idea that, knowingly or unknowingly, intentionally or unintentionally, we regard our possessions as part of ourselves.[6] The self in this definition is perceptual and shaped by culture.[7] Likewise, Helga Dittmar has argued that people express their personal and social characteristics, both to themselves and to others, through material possessions.[8] In the modern era, this phenomenon may be evidenced in the way people represent themselves by creating personal websites as new forums which they own as property on the one hand, and which allow them to share their identities with others on the other hand.[9]

Beside the dubious grounds discussed in chapter 3 upon which a proprietary interest in the body of the deceased may vest, there are good reasons to object to the idea of property in the body of another by an appeal to the interest in a person's symbolic existence. The strong association between a person's identity and an external object she owns continues to exist after her death. For example, the custom of burying the decedent with her personal belongings and society's deterrence from wearing the decedent's clothes are evidence of society's avoidance of controlling the deceased's personal property representing her extended identity. The existence of the deceased through her belongings, most notably through her body, is symbolic and should receive full legal protection.

On the other hand, the symbolic existence of relatives through the body of the deceased is only one form of their symbolic existence as living persons, and must receive a weaker protection. This is because acknowledgement of the relatives' proprietary interest in the body of the deceased ignores the decedent's symbolic existence through her body and its recollections in the minds of others. The subordination of one's sole form of existence as a member of the human community to relatives' control and property amounts to slavery, whereby the identity and symbolic existence of the slave is extinguished and alienated to his master. The law is reluctant to regard situations such as slavery, the dominion of men over 'their' wives, the ownership of children by their parents and

---

[5] Russell W. Belk, 'Possessions and the Extended Self' (1988) 15 *Journal of Consumer Research* 139–68.

[6] For a critique of this idea, see Joel B. Cohen, 'An Over-Extended Self?' (1989) 16 *Journal of Consumer Research* 125–8.

[7] Russell W. Belk, 'Extended Self and Extending Paradigmatic Perspective' (1989) 16 *Journal of Consumer Research* 129–32.

[8] Helga Dittmar, *The Social Psychology of Material Possessions: To Have is To Be* (New York: St Martin's Press, 1992) 11.

[9] See e.g. Hope J. Schau and Mary C. Gilly, 'We Are What We Post? Self-Presentation in Personal Web Sites' (2003) 30 *Journal of Consumer Research* 385–404.

even the classification of unimplanted pre-embryos as 'property' as ones deserving any legal recognition. The interest in the recognition of one's symbolic existence helps us articulate such reluctance, and in so doing better explains why a proprietary interest in the body of the deceased is inapposite.

The testamentary interest in determining the disposal of one's body after death

The interest in the recognition of one's symbolic existence can also be identified in cases dealing with the question of whether there exists a testamentary interest in determining the place and manner of disposal of one's body. These cases were discussed in great detail in chapter 4. Empirical studies show that before they die, people interpret and apportion cues to their personal identities for those who will survive them. Researchers identify three strategies of such identity preservation: solidifying identities, accumulating artifacts and distributing artifacts.[10] In this section I wish to focus on the first strategy, according to which dying people begin to make sense of their lives by accentuating portions of their personal histories for which they wish to be remembered. One way to supply survivors with information about what should be preserved is to plan for the disposal of one's body.[11] The need to avoid emotional and financial burdens to attending family and friends may be grounded, in Norman Cantor's view, in one's efforts to perpetuate a relationship which one sought to cultivate as part of a lifetime character.[12] In addition, making funeral arrangements assures the testator that 'everybody won't

---

[10] David R. Unruh, 'Death and Personal History: Strategies of Identity Preservation' (1983) 30(3) *Social Problems* 340–51.

[11] Recognizing an interest in symbolic existence and its application to the human body and body parts has implications for organ donations as well. Belk, for example, cites empirical data showing that of all the tangible manifestations of self, body and body parts are consistently found to be the most central to identity. Studies also found that organs which are more central to the extended self, like eyes or heart, were likely to be donated because of their centrality. Russell W. Belk, 'Me and Thee Versus Mine and Thine: How Perceptions of the Body Influence Organ Donation and Transplantation' in James Shanteau and Richard Jackson Harris eds., *Organ Donation and Transplantation: Psychological and Behavioral Factors* (Washington, D.C.: American Psychological Association, 1990) 139–49. Belk's conclusions find support in more recent empirical studies. See e.g. John J. Skowronski, 'On the Psychology of Organ Donation: Attitudinal and Situational Factors Related to the Willingness to be an Organ Donor' (1997) 19(4) *Basic and Applied Social Psychology* 427–56.

[12] Norman L. Cantor, *Advance Directives and the Pursuit of Death with Dignity* (Bloomington: Indiana University Press, 1993) 106.

be up in the air and not know what they're going to do'.[13] This is an act by which the testator continues to control and be present in a situation after she no longer exists in reality. The decedent is both the subject in and the object of the testamentary disposal. Moreover, providing directions regarding disposal of the body represents a final act of foresight which will be the first act to be publicly acknowledged after death. This is an act the enforcement of which is symbolically important because it is the first showing of respect to the person who has just passed away.

Testamentary wishes pertaining to disposal of the body after death allow the testator to exist symbolically by, inter alia, being physically close to her loved ones. Testaments including, for example, burial in a family lot or the keeping of urns by family members purport to situate the decedent close to survivors. The physical closeness to family members both enables and symbolizes the continuance of the decedent's existence in their lives. Respecting these testaments and enforcing them serves first and foremost the decedent's interest in the recognition of her symbolic existence. Case law discussing this issue struggles to articulate the exact nature of this very interest. For example, in *Thompson* v. *Deeds* the court held that:

It has always been and will ever continue to be the duty of courts to see to it that the expressed wish of one as to his final resting place shall, so far as possible, be carried out. In one view, it is true it may not matter much where we rest after we are dead, and yet there has always existed in every person a feeling that leads him to wish that after his death his body shall repose beside those he loved in life. Call it sentiment, yet it is a sentiment and belief which the living should know will be respected after they are gone.[14]

More generally, the power to make wills and testaments is the most obvious device used by the dying to dispense objects storing information and cues concerning their identities and characters. Such power enables the dying not only to distribute their belongings, but also to signal to survivors which parts or aspects of their identities, represented in the inherited items, should be preserved. Conditional testaments, under which the dying bequeath certain items on the condition that a specific result be brought about, and disinheritance, where the dying exclude legal heirs from gaining title in their personal property, are other forms of identity preservation by which the dying continue to exist symbolically after death.

---

[13] An interview with one widow mentioned in Ira O. Glick, Robert Weiss and C. Murray Parkes, *The First Year of Bereavement* (New York: Columbia University Press, 1974) 41.
[14] *Thompson* v. *Deeds* 93 Iowa 228, 61 NW 842 (1895).

Chapter 4 discusses many cases of bodily testaments which are conditioned upon the occurrence of a specific outcome and where the testator's wishes are in conflict with those of her legal heirs or relatives. When these cases are analysed by traditional property law and the law of wills and testaments, they cannot be convincingly justified. It was therefore argued in that chapter for the development of a broader understanding of the testamentary interest, most importantly by expanding the items included in the testament to non-proprietary items as well. The idea of identity preservation and symbolic existence offers an original perspective to the testamentary interest, and can better explain the legal analysis brought in that chapter.

The interest in post-mortem confidentiality

The discussion in chapter 5 revealed that the application of the general justifications for the right to medical confidentiality to the post-mortem context raises many practical problems and conceptual difficulties. However, it is possible to argue that one of the sources for the idea of confidentiality lies in the notion that there exists an interest in fashioning one's own identity and its appearance among others. This interest includes the interest in controlling how much information about oneself is concealed or disclosed to others. Hence, 'protecting confidentiality after death functions to respect the former interest of the deceased in controlling personal health information'.[15] Along this line, Jessica Berg prefers the view that medical confidentiality after death 'defends' the decedent's reputation or identity.[16] Berg writes:

It may be necessary to have stronger confidentiality protections in the postmortem context because the individual in question is no longer available either to consent to the disclosure or to 'defend' his or her reputation or identity. Individual control over identity rests upon two related factors: the individual's ability to control what information other people know (confidentiality), as well as that individual's ability to shape his or her own personality and public image (which includes what private information is disclosed in the first place).[17]

But Berg misses an important factor which also forms part of the individual's more general interest in having her own identity and reputation preserved. This is the Human Subject's interest in having her image

---

[15] Andrew H. Maixner and Karine Morin, 'Confidentiality of Health Information Postmortem' (2001) 125 *Archives of Pathology and Laboratory Medicine* 1189–92, 1190.

[16] Jessica Berg, 'Grave Secrets: Legal and Ethical Analysis of Postmortem Confidentiality' (2001) 34(1) *Connecticut Law Review* 81–122 [Berg].

[17] *Ibid.*, at 93–4.

and symbolic existence, as expressed through her personal information, protected as such and regardless of her previous or present control of such protection. If one acknowledges the interest in the recognition of a person's symbolic existence and accepts that such recognition does not necessarily depend upon the subject's awareness, experience or control with regard to it,[18] one is not led to conclude that 'the interest in maintaining identity is protected only to the extent that the deceased can "control" the dissemination of confidential information postmortem'.[19] The interest in the recognition of a person's symbolic existence provides a broader protection in cases where the control of the decedent or her family is impossible or not in place, including many of the situations dealt with in chapter 5, such as autopsy disclosures, disclosure in death certificates, disclosure during research and for teaching purposes, and most notably disclosure of sensitive information about the decedent to her surviving family.

Possible objections to the idea of symbolic existence

Subject of interest

One can argue that the interest in the recognition of one's symbolic existence does not belong to the dead but to the living person, usually the decedent's relative who cherishes the memory and character of the deceased. Along this line, the New York Court of Appeals held that: 'A privilege may be given the surviving relatives of a deceased person to protect his memory, but the privilege exists for the benefit of the living, to protect their feelings, and to prevent a violation of their own rights in the character and memory of the deceased.'[20]

In reply, it will be argued that this objection suffers from serious conceptual difficulties. To start with, the interest in the recognition of a person's symbolic existence does not belong to the dead person. It is held by the Human Subject and is the interest of the person she was while alive. As explained in chapter 1, such an interest survives the death of the person and is continuously held by the Human Subject. It is true that the interest 'belongs' to the living. It is not true that it belongs to living persons or Human Subjects *other* than the person for whom the Human Subject holds the surviving interests.

---

[18] For an objective perspective of interest, see the discussion in chapter 1 at pp. 11–13.
[19] Berg, above n 16, at 94.
[20] *Schuyler v. Curtis* et al. 42 NE 22, 147 NY 434, 447 (Ct App. N.Y. 1895).

Second, if, as held by the court, the relatives' privilege to protect the deceased's memory contributes to their emotional and otherwise general well-being, it is unclear why the court characterizes the entitlement relatives have as mere 'privilege'. Under the reasoning offered by the court, it should have been expected that relatives have a *right* to protect and promote their emotional and otherwise general well-being akin to acts performed on the deceased. On the other hand, if relatives do not have such a right but only a 'privilege', and if this privilege aims to protect their right 'in the character and memory of the deceased', it is again unclear why the recognition of that right is not sufficient for the court to decide this case. It follows that the idea of the relatives' 'privilege' does not add anything to their already holding a right 'in' the memory and character of the deceased.

Third, it is not clear at all what the right 'in' the character and memory of the deceased really is. Specifically, it is difficult to understand what the preposition 'in' aims to stand for and what legal weight it enjoys, if any. Fourth, one can seriously question why relatives have rights in the memory and character of dead people only. Why not declare a more general right in the memory and character of a beloved one (dead or alive)? It appears reasonable that when focusing on the benefit and feelings of relatives, there should be no difference between actions hurting the memory and character of the decedent and ones degrading the memory and character of loved ones who are still alive. If there is such a difference, and if that difference stems from the fact that those living people can bring actions by themselves to protect their memory and character, then by making an application to court relatives of the deceased do not seek to remedy the wrong done to *their* feelings, but they act on behalf of the dead person who can no longer defend her interests. Such an outcome nevertheless is in sharp contradiction to the court's previous holding on this issue.

Duration of symbolic existence

One can argue that the notion of symbolic existence is vague and obscure and brings much uncertainty. For example, it is not clear how long the subject exists symbolically and whether her interest in recognition of her symbolic existence should be legally protected for its entire possible duration.

In response to such concern, it should be emphasized that it is not an uncommon phenomenon that the law consists of abstract ideas. A few examples of these ideas would include the concepts of right, negligence, bona fide and reasonableness, all of which play central roles in structuring the legal thinking of almost all legal systems. Moreover, some of these abstract ideas, such as personhood, human being, citizenship, etc., already construct various forms of symbolic existence, so that without the explicit legal acknowledgement of such forms of existence, more disputes and controversies would be encouraged.

An interest in symbolic existence may sound a bit obscure. Still, the advantages of its recognition outweigh this possible disadvantage. As shown in chapters 3–5, the law dealing with posthumous interests in the medical context is poorly regulated, inconsistent and occasionally unjust to decedents and families. Recognition of a person's symbolic existence allows law and policy makers to extend and enrich their discussion of the competing interests at stake, and directly focus on the decedent who is misrepresented in these cases.

There are two possible views regarding the duration of symbolic existence. According to the first, an arbitrary fixed period of time for symbolic existence should be determined. For example, one could hold that symbolic existence should begin from conception or week twelve of pregnancy and last until twenty-one or seventy years after the death of the person whose interest it is. A second approach, which I find more appealing, would hold that the duration of symbolic existence would depend upon the purposes for which, and the different forms by which, such existence is argued for. Hence, the subject's symbolic existence in thoughts, language and memories of others would last and expire each time anew depending upon her occurrences and their durability in the minds of others. On the other hand, a subject existing symbolically through her deeds from the past or through her personal belongings held by others would be limited by the general rules controlling these deeds or items, e.g. limitation periods, expectation interests of third parties, the rule against perpetuity, etc. Opting for this latter approach provides more certainty than the first alternative and maintains some harmony with existing legal doctrines governing the issues at stake.

Balancing the interest in the recognition of one's symbolic existence with other interests

Critics may argue that since the content and scope of the interest in the recognition of one's symbolic existence are unclear, it is difficult to balance such an interest with other competing interests. An abstract recognition of one's symbolic existence, so it will be argued, cannot provide practical guidelines to resolve the legal disputes discussed in chapters 3–5, and therefore has no evident advantage over the current legal regulation of posthumous interests.

The difficulties associated with balancing the interest in the recognition of one's symbolic existence with other competing interests are not unique to that interest but are inherent in the act of balancing itself. The acknowledgement of such an interest nevertheless enables one to regard the cases discussed in chapters 3–5 in the following way:

(1) Any disputes concerning an alleged proprietary interest in the body of the deceased should be rephrased to capture the protection of the body as a forum whereby the deceased exists symbolically after death. Standing may be given to any party who may represent the deceased's interest regardless of her proprietary or familial status. As shown in chapter 3, legal disputes regarding control over the body can be remedied by an appeal to tort, criminal or constitutional law. The relation between one's property and one's extended identity (*cathexis*) may also provide a possible hierarchy for the proprietary interests at stake. In general, the more an item is identified with a person's or the deceased's self or identity, the stronger is the proprietary interest held in regard to this item.

(2) Bodily testaments containing specific provisions regarding the disposal of the body after death should be seen as legal mechanisms to extend the deceased's symbolic existence through and following the act of disposal. These testaments should bind survivors and outweigh any competing interests, unless they are impracticable, unreasonably expensive or they intolerably hurt public sensitivities.

(3) Because disclosure of personal health information may affect the deceased's symbolic existence in her family or other third parties, and depict her in a way which she may not have wished, the decision of whether to disclose such information should hinge upon a hypothetical examination of her attitudes toward the disclosure of such information. The focus of that examination should be on the deceased patient's subjective values and beliefs, specifically on her views concerning the representation of her persona (through her medical information) in the minds, thoughts and memories of others. However, when disclosure of health information is required to save the immediate life of another or prevent the occurrence of an acute disease, other interests may prevail.

A right to the recognition of symbolic existence

Applying the analysis provided in chapter 2 to the idea of the interest in recognition of one's symbolic existence may result in the proposition that such an interest should also be protected as a legal right. This is an interest whose content relates to the deceased's actions in the past, the life-story written by her while competent and to her being part of the human moral community. It will further be suggested that this right should be regarded under the umbrella of the 'right to security of the person' constituted under section 7 of the Canadian Charter of Rights and Freedoms. Use of that right has been proven successful in the context of disclosing medical information[21] and in relation to decisions concerning treatment of the body.[22] Moreover, the right to 'security of the person' was also extended to apply to a person's *mental* integrity and control over it.[23] In *Mills*, Justice Lamer emphasized that:

Security of the person is not restricted to physical integrity; rather, it encompasses protection against 'overlong subjection to vexations and vicissitudes of a pending criminal accusation' ... these include stigmatization of the accused, loss of privacy, stress and anxiety resulting from a multitude of factors, including possible disruption of family, social life and work, legal costs, uncertainty as to the outcome and sanction.[24]

Expansion of the application of the right to security of the person to cases from areas of law other than the criminal should be encouraged, and it should be regarded as a right to protect one's sense and appearance as a complete and inviolable persona, namely to defend the idea of wholeness embedded in the interest of symbolic existence. In *Rodriguez*, the court explained that 'security of the person has an element of personal autonomy, protecting the dignity and privacy of individuals with respect to decisions concerning their own bodies. It is part of the *persona* and dignity of the human being that he or she have the autonomy to decide what is best for his or her body.'[25] If one accepts the view that the right to the recognition of one's symbolic existence can enjoy support under section 7 of the Charter, then in order for the state to interfere with that right, such interference must conform to the principles of fundamental justice.

The analysis suggested in this book, and the argument for the interest in the recognition of one's symbolic existence, may have important implications for several other issues. The discussion in chapter 3 and the relation between one's property and one's extended self or identity may contribute to questions concerning the proprietary status of gametes, unimplanted embryos and genetic information. The exploration of the testamentary interest pertaining to one's body and its significant role in

---

[21] *Canadian AIDS Society* v. *Ontario* (1995) 25 OR (3d) 388 (Gen. Div.).
[22] *R* v. *Morgentaler* [1988] 1 SCR 30.   [23] *R* v. *Videoflicks Ltd* (1984) 48 OR (2d) 395, 433.
[24] *R* v. *Mills* [1986] 1 SCR 863, 919–20.
[25] *Sue Rodriguez* v. *Attorney General of Canada* et al. [1993] 7 WWR 641, 107 DLR (4th) 342 at para. 91.

one's symbolic existence expands our general understanding of the institutions of testaments and advance directives, and may also have practical implications in regard to policies concerning organ and gamete donations. Finally, the expansion of medical confidentiality in the postmortem context opens up the possibility to bring actions for breach of the privacy interest relating to the deceased, and paves the way to examine other privileges in that context, particularly the attorney–client privilege. More general implications of the discussion of previous chapters may include revisions of legal actions concerning the defamation of the dead, a better protection of moral rights, the resolving of the question regarding the alienability of the right to publicity and the interpretation of criminal offences concerning actions performed on dead bodies or human remains. Revising our understanding of the concepts of interest and right and making better decisions in issues such as harm to offspring and our duties to future generations are additional areas to which the analysis provided in these chapters may contribute.

If the above conclusions are sound, and if the analysis provided in the previous chapters is convincing, then a substantial change in the way we think about and conceptualize the idea of posthumous interests is necessary. It is hoped that the investigation of this subject will result in a fruitful understanding of the legal issues described, and more importantly in better knowledge of what we really are.

Select bibliography

Monographs

Alexander, Ronald G., *The Self, Supervenience and Personal Identity* (Aldershot: Ashgate, 1997)

Aristotle, *Nicomachean Ethics*, trans. J. A. K. Thomson (Baltimore: Penguin Books, 1953)

Beauchamp, Tom L. and Childress, James F., *Principles of Biomedical Ethics*, 5th edn (New York: Oxford University Press, 2001)

Blackstone, William, *Commentaries on the Laws of England* (1766) (Chicago: University of Chicago Press, 1979), vol. II

Bowstead and Reynolds, *On Agency*, 17th edn (London: Sweet & Maxwell, 2001)

Broome, John, *Weighing Lives* (New York: Oxford University Press, 2004)

Cantor, Norman L., *Advance Directives and the Pursuit of Death with Dignity* (Bloomington: Indiana University Press, 1993)

Cleary, Edward W., *McCormick on Evidence*, 3rd edn (St Paul: West, 1984)

Clerk and Lindsell, *On Torts*, 18th edn (London: Sweet & Maxwell, 2000)

Coke, Edward, *Institutes of the Laws of England*, Part 3 (1797)

Cook, Rachel, Sclater, Shelley D. and Kaganas, Felicity eds., *Surrogate Motherhood: International Perspectives* (Oxford: Hart Publishing, 2003)

Cooley, Charles Horton, *Human Nature and the Social Order* (New York: Charles Scribner's Sons, 1922)

De-Shalit, Avner, *Why Posterity Matters* (London: Routledge, 1995)

Dittmar, Helga, *The Social Psychology of Material Possessions: To Have is To Be* (New York: St Martin's Press, 1992)

Dworkin, Ronald, *Life's Dominion* (New York: Alfred Knopf, 1993)

Feinberg, Joel, *Social Philosophy* (Englewood Cliffs, N.J.: Prentice-Hall, 1973)
   Harm to Others (New York: Oxford University Press, 1984)

Feldman, Fred, *Confrontations with the Reaper – A Philosophical Study of the Nature and Value of Death* (New York: Oxford University Press, 1992)

Frey, R. G., *Interests and Rights – The Case Against Animals* (Oxford: Clarendon Press, 1980)

Fridman, G. H. L., *The Law of Agency*, 6th edn (London: Butterworths, 1990)

Fromm, Erich, *To Have or To Be?* (New York: Harper & Row, 1976)

Geach, P. T., *God and the Soul* (Indiana: St Augustine's Press, 1969)

Gold, E. Richard, *Body Parts: Property Rights and the Ownership of Human Biological Material* (Washington: Georgetown University Press, 1996)

Gordon, Gerald H., *The Criminal Law of Scotland*, Michael G. A. Christie ed., 3rd edn, vol. II (Edinburgh: W. Green, 2001)

Gostin, Lawrence O., *Public Health Law: Power, Duty and Restraint* (Berkeley: University of California Press, 2000)

Gurry, Francis, *Breach of Confidence* (Oxford: Clarendon, 1984)

Hanbury and Martin, *Modern Equity*, Jill E. Martin ed., 7th edn (London: Sweet & Maxwell, 2005)

Harris, John, *Wonderwoman and Superman: The Ethics of Human Biotechnology* (Oxford: Oxford University Press, 1992)

Hegel, Georg, *Philosophy of Right*, T. M. Knox trans. (Oxford: Clarendon, 1952)

Hillel-Ruben, David, *Action and its Explanation* (New York: Oxford University Press, 2003)

Holmes, O. W., *The Common Law* (London: Macmillan, 1882)

Jackson, Percival E., *The Law of Cadavers and of Burial and Burial Places*, 2nd edn (New York: Prentice-Hall, 1950)

Kamm, Frances A., *Morality, Mortality – Death and Whom to Save from It*, vol. I (New York: Oxford University Press, 1993)

Kant, Immanuel, *The Metaphysics of Morals*, Mary Gregor ed. and trans. (Cambridge: Cambridge University Press, 1996)

Kennedy, Ian and Grubb, Andrew, *Medical Law*, 3rd edn (London: Butterworths, 2000)

Laurie, Graeme, *Genetic Privacy: A Challenge to Medico-Legal Norms* (Cambridge: Cambridge University Press, 2002)

Lewis, David, *On the Plurality of Worlds* (Oxford: Blackwell, 1986)

Locke, John, *The Second Treatise of Government*, 3rd edn (Oxford: Basil Blackwell, 1966)

Lomasky, Loren E., *Persons, Rights and the Moral Community* (New York: Oxford University Press, 1987)

Mason, J. K., Smith, R. A. McCall and Laurie, G. T., *Law and Medical Ethics*, 5th edn (London: Butterworths, 1999)

McHale, Jean V., *Medical Confidentiality and Legal Privilege* (New York: Routledge, 1993)

McMahan, Jeff, *The Ethics of Killing: Problems at the Margins of Life* (New York: Oxford University Press, 2002)

Mead, George H., *Mind, Self and Society* (Chicago: University of Chicago Press, 1934)

Meisel, Alan and Cerminara, Kathy L., *The Right to Die*, 3rd edn (New York: Aspen, 2004)

Mill, J. S., *Principles of Political Economy* (New York: Longmans, Green and Co., 1904)

Munzer, Stephen R., *A Theory of Property* (New York: Cambridge University Press, 1990)

Nelson, Leonard, *System of Ethics*, H. J. Paton trans. (New Haven: Yale University Press, 1956)

Nozick, Robert, *Anarchy, State and Utopia* (Oxford: Blackwell, 1980)

Parfit, Derek, *Reasons and Persons* (New York: Oxford University Press, 1984)

Parry and Clark, *The Law of Succession*, Roger Kerridge ed., 11th edn (London: Sweet & Maxwell, 2002)

Penner, J. E., *The Idea of Property* (Oxford: Clarendon, 1997)

Prosser, W. L. and Keeton, W. P., *On Torts*, 5th edn (St Paul: West, 1984)

Ramsey, Paul, *The Patient as Person* (New Haven: Yale University Press, 1970)

Raz, Joseph, *The Morality of Freedom* (Oxford: Clarendon Press, 1986)

Reutlinger, Mark, *Wills, Trusts and Estates* (Boston: Little, Brown and Company, 1993)

Richardson, Ruth, *Death, Dissection and the Destitute* (London: Routledge & Kegan Paul, 1987)

Ryan, Alan, *Property* (Milton Keynes: Open University Press, 1987)

Salmond on Jurisprudence, 12th edn (London: Sweet & Maxwell, 1966)

Sartre, Jean-Paul, *Being and Nothingness: A Phenomenological Essay on Ontology* (New York: Philosophical Library, 1943)

Smith, Adam, *An Inquiry into the Nature and Causes of the Wealth of Nations*, E. Cannan ed. (New York: Modern Library, 1937)

Sperling, Daniel, *Management of Post-Mortem Pregnancy: Legal and Philosophical Aspects* (Aldershot: Ashgate, 2006)

Steinbock, Bonnie, *Life Before Birth – The Moral and Legal Status of Embryos and Fetuses* (New York: Oxford University Press, 1992)

Steiner, Hillel, *An Essay on Rights* (Oxford: Blackwell, 1994)

Sumner, L. W., *The Moral Foundation of Rights* (Oxford: Clarendon Press, 1987)

Toulson, R. G. and Phipps, C. M., *Confidentiality* (London: Sweet & Maxwell, 1996)

Wacks, Raymond, *Personal Information Privacy and the Law* (London: Bodley Head, 1989)

Waldron, Jeremy, *The Right to Private Property* (Oxford: Clarendon Press, 1988)

Wellman, Carl, *Real Rights* (New York: Oxford University Press, 1995)

Westin, Alan F., *Privacy and Freedom* (New York: Athenaeum, 1967)

White, Alan R., *Rights* (Oxford: Clarendon, 1984)

Williams on Wills, 8th edn (London: Butterworths, 2002)

Williams, Glanville, *Textbook of Criminal Law*, 1st edn (London: Stevens & Sons, 1978)

Ziff, Bruce, *Principles of Property Law*, 3rd edn (Scarborough: Carswell, 2000)

Articles

Agich, George J. and Siemionow, Maria, 'Facing the Ethical Questions in Facial Transplantation' (2004) 4(3) *American Journal of Bioethics* 25–7

Allen, Anita L., 'Coerced Privacy' (1999) 40(3) *William and Mary Law Review* 723–57

  'Privacy as Data-Control: Conceptual, Practical and Moral Limits of the Paradigm' (2000) 32(3) *Connecticut Law Review* 861–75

Andrews, Lori B., 'My Body My Property' (1986) 16(5) *Hastings Center Report* 28–38

Arneson, Richard J., 'Lockean Self-Ownership: Towards a Demolition' (1991) 39 *Political Studies* 36–54

Atherton, Ronald, 'Claims on the Deceased: The Corpse as Property' (2000) 7 *Journal of Law and Medicine* 361–75

Augustine, Keith, 'The Case Against Immortality' (unpublished draft), available at www.infidels.org/library/modern/keith_augustine/immortality.html, last visited on 13 February 2007

Baier, Annette C., 'The Rights of Past and Future Persons' in Partridge, Ernest ed., *Responsibilities to Future Generations* (Buffalo, N.Y.: Prometheus Books, 1980) 177

Bailey, James E., 'An Analytical Framework for Resolving the Issues Raised by the Interaction Between Reproductive Technology and the Law of Inheritance' (1998) 47 *DePaul Law Review* 743

Baker, David M., 'Cryonic Preservation of Human Bodies – A Call for Legislative Action' (1994) 98 *Dickinson Law Review* 677–711

Barish, Marvin I., 'The Law of Testamentary Disposition – A Legal Barrier to Medical Advance!' (1956) 30 *Temple Law Quarterly* 40–6

Bayne, Tim, 'On Death and Being Dead' (unpublished), available at www.phil.mq.edu.au/staff/tbayne/death.doc, last visited on 12 December 2007

Belk, Russell W., 'Possessions and the Extended Self' (1988) 15 *Journal of Consumer Research* 139–68

'Extended Self and Extending Paradigmatic Perspective' (1989) 16 *Journal of Consumer Research* 129–32

'Me and Thee Versus Mine and Thine: How Perceptions of the Body Influence Organ Donation and Transplantation' in Shanteau, James and Jackson Harris, Richard eds., *Organ Donation and Transplantation: Psychological and Behavioral Factors* (Washington, D.C.: American Psychological Association, 1990) 139–49

Bell, Andrew, 'Bona Vacantia' in Palmer, Norman and McKendrick, Ewan eds., *Interests in Goods*, 2nd edn (London: LLP Reference Publishing, 1998) 207–26

Belliotti, Raymond A., 'Do Dead Human Beings Have Rights?' (1979) *The Personalist* 201–10

Bennett, B., 'Posthumous Reproduction and the Meaning of Autonomy' (1999) 23(2) *Melbourne University Law Review* 286–307

Bentham, Jeremy, 'Pennomial Fragments' in Bowring, John ed., *The Works of Jeremy Bentham* (Edinburgh: W. Tait, 1843–59, vol. III)

Berg, Jessica, 'Grave Secrets: Legal and Ethical Analysis of Postmortem Confidentiality' (2001) 34(1) *Connecticut Law Review* 81–122

Berkman, Ben, 'Organ Donor Card Effectiveness' in *Case in Health Law* (August 2002: American Medical Association), available at www.ama-assn.org/ama/pub/category/print/8560.html, accessed on 10 May 2007

Bigelow, Harry B., 'Damages: Pleading: Property: Who May Recover for Wrongful Disturbance of a Dead Body?' (1933) 19 *Cornell Law Quarterly* 108–12

Blair, R. D. and Kaserman, D. L., 'The Economics and Ethics of Alternative Cadaveric Organ Procurement Policies' (1991) 8 *Yale Journal of Regulation* 403–52

Bove, Alexander A. and Langa, Melissa, 'Ted Williams: Is He Headed for the Dugout or the Deep Freeze? Property Rights in a Dead Body Resurrected' *Massachusetts Lawyers Weekly*, 19 August 2002

Bradley, Ben, 'When Is Death Bad for the One Who Dies?' (2004) 38(1) *Nous* 1

Bray, Michelle B., 'Personalizing Personality: Toward a Property Right in Human Bodies' (1990) 69 *Texas Law Review* 209–44

Brazier, Margaret, 'Retained Organs: Ethics and Humanity' (2002) 22 *Legal Studies* 550

Brecher, Bob, 'Our Obligation to the Dead' (2002) 19(2) *Journal of Applied Philosophy* 109–19

Brown, Barry, 'Reconciling Property Law with Advances in Reproductive Science' (1995) 6 *Stanford Law and Policy Review* 73

Brueckner, Anthony L. and Fischer, John Martin, 'Why is Death Bad?' (1986) 50 *Philosophical Studies* 213

Calabresi, Guido, 'Do We Own Our Bodies?' (1991) 1 *Health-Matrix* 5–18

Callahan Joan C., 'On Harming the Dead' (1987) 97 *Ethics* 341

Campbell, Courtney S., 'Body, Self, and the Property Paradigm' (1992) 22(5) *Hastings Center Report* 34–42

Carton, Sharon, 'The Poet, the Biographer and the Shrink: Psychiatrist–Patient Confidentiality and the Anne Sexton Biography' (1993) 10 *University of Miami Entertainment and Sports Law Review* 117–64

Charo, R. Alta, 'The Speaker: Skin and Bones: Post-Mortem Markets in Human Tissue' (2002) 26 *Nova Law Review* 421–49

Chisholm, Roderick M., 'Coming into Being and Passing Away: Can the Metaphysician Help?' in Donnelly, John ed., *Language, Metaphysics and Death* (New York: Fordham University Press, 1978) 13

Cohen, Joel B., 'An Over-Extended Self?' (1989) 16 *Journal of Consumer Research* 125–8

Cohen, L. R., 'Increasing the Supply of Transplant Organs: The Virtues of a Future Market' (1989) 58 *George Washington Law Review* 1–51

Comeau, P. A. and Ouimet, A., 'Freedom of Information and Privacy: Quebec's Innovative Role in North America' (1995) 80 *Iowa Law Review* 651

Conway, Heather, 'Dead, But Not Buried: Bodies, Burial and Family Conflicts' (2003) 23(3) *Legal Studies* 423–52

  'Whose Funeral? Corpses and the Duty to Bury' (2003) 54(2) *Northern Ireland Legal Quarterly* 183–91

Dickens, Bernard M., 'The Control of Living Body Materials' (1977) 27 *University of Toronto Law Journal* 142

  'Confidentiality and the Duty to Warn' in Gostin, L. O. ed., *Aids and the Health Care System* (New Haven: Yale University Press, 1990) 98

  'Control of Excised Tissues Pending Implantation' (1990) 7 *Transplantation/ Implantation Today* 36–41

  'Living Tissue and Organ Donors and Property Law: More on *Moore*' (1992) 8 *Journal of Contemporary Health Law and Policy* 73–93

  'Legal and Judicial Aspects of Post-Mortem Organ Donation' in Collins, G. M., Dubernard, J. M., Land, W. and Persijn, G. G. eds., *Procurement, Preservation and Allocation of Vascularized Organs* (Dordrecht: Kluwer, 1997) 343–57

  'The Doctor's Duty of Confidentiality: Separating the Rule from the Exceptions' (1999) 77(1) *University of Toronto Medical Journal* 40–3

Dickens, B. M. and Cook, R. J., 'Law and Ethics in Conflict Over Confidentiality?' (2000) 70 *International Journal of Gynaecology and Obstetrics* 385–91

Dowling, Alan, 'Exclusive Rights of Burial and the Law of Real Property' (1998) 18 *Legal Studies* 438–52

Dresser, Rebecca S. and Robertson, John A., 'Quality of Life and Non-Treatment Decisions for Incompetent Patients: A Critique of the Orthodox Approach' (1989) 17(3) *Law, Medicine and Healthcare* 234–44.

Ducor, Philippe, 'The Legal Status of Human Material' (1996) 44 *Drake Law Review* 196

Dworkin, Ronald, 'Rights as Trumps' in Waldron, J. ed., *Theories of Rights* (Oxford: Oxford University Press, 1984) 153–67

   'Autonomy and the Demented Self' (1986) 64 *Milbank Quarterly* (Supp. 2) 4–16

Fabre, Cecile, 'The Choice-Based Right to Bequeath' (2001) 61(1) *Analysis* 60–5

Faigus, M. S., '*Moore v. Regents of the University of California* – A Breach of Confidence Within the Physician–Patient Relationship: Should Unique Genetic Information be Considered a Trade Secret?' (1993) 24 *University of West Los Angeles Law Review* 299

Feinberg, Joel, 'Duties, Rights and Claims' (1966) 4 *American Philosophical Quarterly* 137–44

   'Harm and Self-Interest' in Hacker, P. M. S. and Raz, J. eds., *Law, Morality and Society* (Oxford: Clarendon Press, 1977) 308

   'The Nature and Value of Right' in Feinberg, Joel ed., *Rights, Justice and the Bounds of Liberty* (Princeton: Princeton University Press, 1980) 143–58

   'The Rights of Animals and Unborn Generations' in Feinberg, Joel ed., *Rights, Justice and the Bounds of Liberty* (Princeton: Princeton University Press, 1980) 159

Feldman, Fred, 'Some Puzzles About the Evil of Death' (1991) 100(2) *Philosophical Review* 205

   'The Termination Thesis' (2000) 24 *Midwest Studies in Philosophy* 98

Fischer, John Martin, 'Introduction: Death, Metaphysics, and Morality' in Fischer, John Martin ed., *The Metaphysics of Death* (Stanford: Stanford University Press, 1993) 17

Frankel, Simon J., 'Attorney–Client Privilege After the Death of the Client' (1992–3) 6 *Georgia Journal of Legal Ethics* 45–9

Fried, Charles, 'Privacy' (1968) 77 *Yale Law Journal* 475–93

Friedland, Bernard, 'Physician–Patient Confidentiality: Time to Reexamine a Venerable Concept in Light of Contemporary Society and Advances in Medicine' (1994) 15 *Journal of Legal Medicine* 249–77

Gillon, Raanan, 'Medical Ethics: Four Principles Plus Attention to Scope' (1994) 309 *British Medical Journal* 184–8

Glannon, Walter, 'Persons, Lives and Posthumous Harms' (2001) 32(2) *Journal of Social Philosophy* 127

Golding, Martin, 'Obligations to Future Generations' (1972) 56(1) *The Monist* 85–99

Gostin, L. O., Turek-Brezina, J., Powers, M., Kozloff, R., Faden, R. and Steinauer, D. D., 'Privacy and Security of Personal Information in a New Health Care System' (1993) 270 *Journal of the American Medical Association* 2487–93

Grey, William, 'Epicurus and the Harm of Death' (1999) 77(3) *Australian Journal of Philosophy* 358

Groll, Richard C. and Kerwin, Donald J., 'The Uniform Anatomical Gift Act: Is the Right to a Decent Burial Obsolete?' (1971) 2 *Loyola University of Chicago Law Journal* 275–305

Grover, Dorothy, 'Posthumous Harm' (1989) 39 *Philosophical Quarterly* 334

Grubb, Andrew, '"I, Me, Mine": Bodies, Parts and Property' (1998) 3 *Medical Law International* 299–317

'Note: Theft of Body Parts: Property and Dead Bodies' (1998) 6 *Medical Law Review* 247–53

Harel, Alon, 'Theories of Rights' in Golding, Martin P. and Edmundson, William eds., *Blackwell's Guide to the Philosophy of Law and Legal Theory* (2005) 191–206

Harris, J. W., 'Who Owns My Body?' (1996) 16(1) *Oxford Journal of Legal Studies* 55–84

Harris, John, 'Law and Regulation of Retained Organs: The Ethical Issues' (2002) 22 *Legal Studies* 527–49

'Organ Procurement: Dead Interests, Living Needs' (2003) 29(3) *Journal of Medical Ethics* 130

Hart, H. L. A., 'Legal Rights' in Hart, H. L. A., *Essays on Bentham* (Oxford: Clarendon Press, 1982) 162–93

'Are There Any Natural Rights?' in Waldron, Jeremy ed., *Theories of Rights* (Oxford: Oxford University Press, 1984) 77–90

Hernandez, Tanya K., 'The Property of Death' (1999) 60 *University of Pittsburgh Law Review* 971–1028

Hirsch, Adam J., 'Bequests for Purposes: A Unified Theory' (1999) 56 *Washington and Lee Law Review* 33–110

'Trusts for Purposes: Policy, Ambiguity and Anomaly in the Uniform Laws' (1999) 26 *Florida State University Law Review* 913–57

Hirst, Michael, 'Preventing the Lawful Burial of a Body' (1996) *Criminal Law Review* 96–103

Hoffman, Brian F., 'Importance and Limits of Medical Confidentiality' (1997) 17 *Health Law Canada* 94

Hohfeld, Wesley, 'Some Fundamental Legal Conceptions as Applied in Juridical Reasoning' in Cook, W. ed., *Fundamental Legal Conceptions as Applied in Juridical Reasoning* (New Haven: Yale University Press, 1923) 23–64

Honore, A. M., 'Ownership' in Guest, A. G. ed., *Oxford Essays in Jurisprudence* (Oxford: Clarendon Press, 1961) 107

Horan, Jennifer E., '"When Sleep At Last Has Come": Controlling the Disposition of Dead Bodies for Same-Sex Couples' (1999) 2 *Journal of Gender, Race and Justice* 423–60

Ishiguro, Hide, 'Possibility' (1980) 54 *Proceedings of the Aristotelian Society* 73

Jaffe, Erik S., 'She's Got Bette Davis['s] Eyes: Assessing the Nonconsensual Removal of Cadaver Organs Under the Takings and Due Process Clauses' (1990) 90 *Columbia Law Review* 528–74

James, D. S. and Bull, A. D., 'Information on Death Certificates: Cause for Concern' (1996) 49 *Journal of Clinical Pathology* 213–16

Jones, C., 'The Utilitarian Argument for Medical Confidentiality: A Pilot Study of Patients' Views' (2003) 29 *Journal of Medical Ethics* 348–52

Jones, Gareth, 'Restitution of Benefits Obtained in Breach of Another's Confidence' (1970) 86 *Law Quarterly Review* 463–92

Kass, Leon R., 'Thinking About the Body' (1985) 15(1) *Hastings Center Report* 20–30

Kennedy, Ian, 'Negligence: Interference with Right to Possession of a Body' (1995) 3 *Medical Law Review* 233

Khalil, Khalil Jaafar, 'A Sight of Relief: Invalidating Cadaveric Corneal Donation Laws Via the Free Exercise Clause' (2002) 6 *DePaul Journal of Health Care Law* 159–78

King, Michael B., 'Aids on the Death Certificate: The Final Stigma' (1989) 298 *British Medical Journal* 731–6

Kottow, Michael H., 'Medical Confidentiality: An Intransigent and Absolute Obligation' (1986) 12 *Journal of Medical Ethics* 117–22

Kramer, Matthew H., 'Rights Without Trimmings' in Kramer, Matthew H., Simmonds, N. E. and Steiner, Hillel eds., *A Debate Over Rights* (Oxford: Clarendon Press, 1998) 7–111

'Do Animals and Dead People Have Legal Rights?' (2001) 14 *Canadian Journal of Law and Jurisprudence* 29–54

'Getting Rights Right' in Kramer, Matthew ed., *Rights, Wrongs and Responsibilities* (Cambridge: Palgrave, 2001) 28–95

Krattenmaker, Thomas G., 'Testimonial Privileges in Federal Courts: An Alternative to the Proposed Federal Rules of Evidence' (1973–4) 62 *Georgia Law Journal* 61–124

Lamont, Julian, 'A Solution to the Puzzle When Death Harms Its Victims' (1998) 76(2) *Australian Journal of Philosophy* 198

Latimer, John, 'Factors in the Death of President Kennedy' (October 1966) 198 *Journal of the American Medical Association* 327

Levenbook, Barbara Baum, 'Harming Someone After His Death' (1984) 94 *Ethics* 407

'Harming the Dead, Once Again' (1985) 96 *Ethics* 162

Lewis, David, 'Extrinsic Properties' (1983) 44 *Philosophical Studies* 197

Lock, Stephen, 'A Question of Confidence' (1984) 288 *British Medical Journal* 123–5

Loudon, Irvine, 'How it Strikes a Historian' (1984) 288 *British Medical Journal* 125–6

Luper, Steven, 'Posthumous Harm' (2004) 41(1) *American Philosophical Quarterly* 63

Luper-Foy, Steven, 'Annihilation' (1987) 37 *Philosophical Quarterly* 233

MacCormick, D. N., 'Rights in Legislation' in Hacker, P. M. S. and Raz, J. eds., *Law, Morality and Society – Essays in Honour of H. L. A. Hart* (Oxford: Clarendon, 1977) 189–209

MacCormick, Neil, 'Children's Rights: A Test-Case for Theories of Right' in MacCormick, Neil, *Legal Right and Social Democracy – Essays in Legal and Political Philosophy* (Oxford: Clarendon Press, 1982) 154–66

MacDonald, Andrew C., 'Organ Donation: The Time Has Come to Refocus the Ethical Spotlight' (1997) 8(1) *Stanford Law and Policy Review* 177–84

Magnusson, Robert S., 'Proprietary Rights in Human Tissue' in Palmer, Norman and McKendrick, Ewan eds., *Interests in Goods*, 2nd edn (London: LLP Reference Publishing, 1998) 52

Maixner, Andrew H. and Morin, Karine, 'Confidentiality of Health Information Postmortem' (2001) 125 *Archives of Pathology and Laboratory Medicine* 1189–92

Marmoy, C. F. A., 'The "Auto-Icon" of Jeremy Bentham at University College, London' (1958) 2 *Medical History* 77–86

Marshall, Mary and Von Tigerstrom, Barbara, 'Health Information' in Downie, J., Caulfield, T. and Flood, C. eds., *Canadian Health Law and Policy*, 2nd edn (Toronto: Butterworths, 2002) 157–203

Mason, J. K. and Laurie, G. T., 'Consent or Property? Dealing with the Body and its Parts in the Shadow of Bristol and Alder Hey' (2001) 64(5) *Modern Law Review* 710–29

Mathers, Colin D., Fat, Doris Ma, Inoue, Mie, Rao, Chalapati and Lopez, Alan D., 'Counting the Dead and What They Died From: An Assessment of the Global Status of Cause of Death Data' (2005) 83(3) *Bulletin of the World Health Organization* 171–7

Matthews, Paul, 'Whose Body? People as Property' (1983) 36 *Current Legal Problems* 193–239

'The Man of Property' (1995) 3 *Medical Law Review* 251–74

McMahan, Jeff, 'Death and the Value of Life' (1988) 99 *Ethics* 32

Montague, Philip, 'Two Concepts of Rights' (1980) 9(3) *Philosophy and Public Affairs* 372–84

Mulgan, Tim, 'The Place of the Dead in Liberal Political Philosophy' (1999) 7(1) *Journal of Political Philosophy* 52

Murray, Thomas H., 'Are We Morally Obligated to Make Gifts of Our Bodies?' (1991) 1 *Health Matrix* 19

Nagel, Thomas, 'Death' in Nagel, Thomas ed., *Mortal Questions* (New York: Cambridge University Press, 1979) 1

Nelkin, Dorothy and Andrews, Lori, 'Do the Dead Have Interests? Policy Issues for Research After Life' (1998) 24 *American Journal of Law and Medicine* 261–91

'*Homo Economicus*: Commercialization of the Body Tissue in the Age of Biotechnology' (1998) 28(5) *Hastings Center Report* 30–9

Netanel, Neil, 'Alienability Restrictions and the Enhancement of Author Autonomy in United States and Continental Copyright Law' (1994) 12 *Cardozo Arts and Entertainment Law Journal* 1

Newall, Vanetia J., 'Folklore and Cremation' (1983) 49 *Pharos International* 18

Overcast, T. D., Evans, R. W., Bowen, L. E., Hoe, H. M. and Livat, C. L., 'Problems in the Identification of Potential Organ Donors: Misconceptions and Fallacies Associated with Donor Cards' (March 1984) 251(12) *Journal of the American Medical Association* 1559–62

Partridge, Ernest, 'Posthumous Interests and Posthumous Respect' (1981) 91 *Ethics* 243

Pawlowski, Mark, 'The Legal Recognition of Human Body Parts and Genetic Material as Property' (unpublished paper, 2000)

Penner, J. E., 'The "Bundle of Rights" Picture of Property' (1996) 43 *UCLA Law Review* 712–820

Pentz, Rebecca D. *et al.*, 'Ethics Guidelines for Research with the Recently Dead' (2005) 11 *Nature Medicine* 1145–9

Pitcher, George, 'The Misfortunes of the Dead' (1984) 21(2) *American Philosophical Quarterly* 183

Ploem, C., 'Medical Confidentiality after a Patient's Death, with Particular Reference to the Netherlands' (2001) 20 *Medicine and Law* 215–20

Portmore, Douglas W., 'Desire Fulfillment and Posthumous Harm' (2007) 44(1) *American Philosophical Quarterly* 27

Price, David, 'From Cosmos and Damian to Van Velzen: The Human Tissue Saga Continues' (2003) 11 *Medical Law Review* 1–47

Prosser, William L., 'Privacy' (1960) 48 *California Law Review* 383–423

Quay, Paul M., 'Utilizing the Bodies of the Dead' (1984) 28 *Saint Louis University Law Journal* 889–927

Radin, Margaret J., 'Property and Personhood' (1982) 34 *Stanford Law Review* 957

'Market-Inalienability' (1987) 100(8) *Harvard Law Review* 1849–1937

'The Liberal Conception of Property: Cross Currents in the Jurisprudence of Takings' (1988) 88 *Columbia Law Review* 1667

Raz, Joseph, 'Legal Rights' (1984) 4(1) *Oxford Journal of Legal Studies* 1–21

'Right-Based Moralities' in Waldron, J. ed., *Theories of Rights* (Oxford, Oxford University Press, 1984) 182–200

'Rights and Individual Well-Being' in Raz, Joseph, *Ethics in the Public Domain* (Oxford, Clarendon, 1994) 44–59

Regan, Tom, 'The Moral Basis of Vegetarianism' (1975) 5(2) *Canadian Journal of Philosophy* 181–214

'Feinberg on What Sorts of Beings Can Have Rights?' (1976) 14(4) *Southern Journal of Philosophy* 584–98

Reich, C. A., 'The New Property' (1964) 73 *Yale Law Journal* 733

Rhoden, Nancy K., 'How Should We View the Incompetent?' (1989) 17(3) *Law, Medicine and Healthcare* 264–8.

'The Limits of Legal Objectivity' (1990) 68 *North Carolina Law Review* 845

Ricketts, B. C., 'Validity and Effect of Testamentary Direction as to Disposition of Testator's Body' (1966) 7 *American Law Reports* 3d 747–54

Robitscher, Jonas B., 'Doctors' Privileged Communications, Public Life and History's Rights' (1968) 17 *Cleveland-Marshall Law Review* 199–212

Roeder, Martin A., 'The Doctrine of Moral Rights: A Study in the Law of Artists, Authors and Creators' (1940) 53 *Harvard Law Review* 554

Rose, Carol, 'Possession as the Origin of Property' (1985) 52 *University of Chicago Law Review* 73

Rose-Ackerman, Susan, 'Inalienability and the Theory of Property Rights' (1985) 85 *Columbia Law Review* 931–69

Rosenbaum Stephen, 'How to Be Dead and Not Care: A Defense of Epicurus' (1986) 23(2) *American Philosophical Quarterly* 217

'Epicurus and Annihilation' (1989) 39 *Philosophical Quarterly* 81

Salzburg, Stephen A., 'Privileges and Professionals: Lawyers and Psychiatrists' (1980) 66 *Virginia Law Review* 597–652

Sampson, H., Johnson, A., Carter, N. and Rutty, G., 'Information Before Coronial Necropsy: How Much Should Be Available?' (1999) 52 *Journal of Clinical Pathology* 856–9

Samuelson, Pamela, 'Privacy and Intellectual Property' (2000) 52(5) *Stanford Law Review* 1125–74

Sankar, Pamela, Moran, Susan, Merz, Jon F. and Jones, Nora L., 'Patient Perspectives on Medical Confidentiality' (2003) 18 *Journal of General Internal Medicine* 659–69

Scarmon, Michael H., '*Brotherton v. Cleveland*: Property Rights in the Human Body – Are the Goods Interred with Their Bones?' (1992) 37 *South Dakota Law Review* 429–49

Scarre, Geoffrey, 'Should We Fear Death?' (1997) 5(3) *European Journal of Philosophy* 269

'Archaeology and Respect for the Dead' (2003) 20(3) *Journal of Applied Philosophy* 237

Schau, Hope J. and Gilly, Mary C., 'We Are What We Post? Self-Presentation in Personal Web Sites' (2003) 30 *Journal of Consumer Research* 385–404

Schwartz, Paul M., 'The Protection of Privacy in Health Care Reform' (1995) 48(2) *Vanderbilt Law Review* 295–347

'Privacy and the Economics of Personal Health Care Information' (1997) 76(1) *Texas Law Review* 1–76

'Free Speech vs. Information Privacy: Eugene Volokh's First Amendment Jurisprudence' (2000) 52(5) *Stanford Law Review* 1559–72

Shuman, D. W., Weiner, W. F. and Pinnard, G. I., 'The Privilege Study' (1986) 9 *International Journal of Law and Psychology* 393

Siegler, Mark, 'Confidentiality in Medicine: A Decrepit Concept' (1982) 307(24) *New England Journal of Medicine* 1518–21

Silverstein, Harry S., 'The Evil of Death' (1980) 77(7) *Journal of Philosophy* 401

Simmonds, Nigel E., 'Rights at the Cutting Edge' in Kramer, Matthew H., Simmonds, N. E. and Steiner, Hillel eds., *A Debate Over Rights* (Oxford: Clarendon Press, 1998) 113–232

Skegg, P. D. G., 'Human Corpses, Medical Specimens and the Law of Property' (1975) *Anglo-American Law Review* 412

'Medical Uses of Corpses and the "No Property" Rule' (1992) 32(4) *Medicine, Science and the Law* 311–18

'The Removal and Retention of Cadaveric Body Parts: Does the Law Require Parental Consent?' (2003) 10(3) *Otago Law Review* 425–43

Skene, Loane, 'Proprietary Rights in Human Bodies, Body Parts and Tissue: Regulatory Context and Proposals for New Laws' (2002) 22 *Legal Studies* 102–27

Skowronski, John J., 'On the Psychology of Organ Donation: Attitudinal and Situational Factors Related to the Willingness to be an Organ Donor' (1997) 19(4) *Basic and Applied Social Psychology* 427–56

Sperling, Daniel, 'Breaking Through the Silence: The Illegality of Performing
  Resuscitation Procedures on the Newly-Dead' (2004) 13(2) *Annals of Health
  Law* 393–426
'From the Dead to the Unborn: Is There an Ethical Duty to Save Life?' (2004)
  23(3) *Medicine and Law* 567–86
Sreenivasan, Gopal, 'A Hybrid Theory of Claim-Rights' (2005) 25(2) *Oxford
  Journal of Legal Studies* 257–74
Stickney, Melissa A. W., 'Property Interests in Cadaverous Organs: Changes to
  Ohio Anatomical Gift Law and the Erosion of Family Rights' (2002–3) 17
  Journal of Law and Health 37–75
Sumner, L. W., 'A Matter of Life and Death' (1976) 10 *Nous* 145
Swain, Margaret S. and Marusyk, Randy W., 'An Alternative to Property Rights
  in Human Tissue' (1990) 20(5) *Hastings Center Report* 12–15
Swift, B. and West, K., 'Death Certification: An Audit of Practice entering the
  21st Century' (2002) 55 *Journal of Clinical Pathology* 275–9
Sykas, Abigail J., 'Waste Not, Want Not: Can the Public Policy Doctrine Prohibit
  the Destruction of Property by Testamentary Direction?' (2001) *Vermont
  Law Review* 911–44
Terilli, Samuel A. and Splichal, Sigman L., 'Public Access to Autopsy and Death-
  Scene Photographs: Relational Privacy, Public Records and Avoidable
  Collisions' (2005) 10 *Communication Law and Policy* 313–48
Thomas, C. M., 'Should the Law Allow Sentiment to Triumph Over Science?
  The Retention of Body Parts' (2002) (unpublished paper)
Tranberg, H. A., Rous, B. A. and Rashbass, J., 'Legal and Ethical Issues in the
  Use of Anonymous Images in Pathology Teaching and Research' (2003) 42
  Histopathology 104–9
Unruh, David R., 'Death and Personal History: Strategies of Identity
  Preservation' (1983) 30(3) *Social Problems* 340–51
Veale, Kylie, 'Online Memorialisation: The Web as a Collective Memorial
  Landscape for Remembering the Dead' (2004) 3 *Fibreculture*, available at
  http://journal.fibreculture.org/issue3/issue3_veale.html, accessed on 6
  March 2006
Volokh, Eugene, 'Freedom of Speech and Information Privacy: The Troubling
  Implications of a Right to Stop People from Speaking About You' (2000)
  52(5) *Stanford Law Review* 1049–1124
Von Tigerstrom, Barbara, 'Protection of Health Information Privacy: The
  Challenges and Possibilities of Technology' (1998) 4 *Appeal* 44–59
Wagner, Danielle, 'Comment: Property Rights in the Human Body: The
  Commercialization of Organ Transplantation and Biotechnology' (1995)
  33 *Duquesne Law Review* 931
Wagner, Frank D., 'Enforcement of Preference Expressed by Decedent as to the
  Disposition of His Body After Death' (1973) 54 *American Law Reports* 3d
  1037–67
Waluchow, W. J., 'Feinberg's Theory of "Preposthumous" Harm' (1986) 25
  Dialogue 727
Warren, Mary Anne, 'Do Potential People Have Moral Rights?' (1977) 7(2)
  Canadian Journal of Philosophy 275–89

Wear, Teresa, 'Wills – Direction in Will to Destroy Estate Property Violates Public Policy' (1976) 41 *Missouri Law Review* 309

Werth, James L., 'Confidentiality in End-of-Life and After-Death Situations' (2002) 12(3) *Ethics and Behavior* 205–22

White, Stephen, 'The Law Relating to Dealing with Dead Bodies' (2000) 4 *Medical Law International* 145–81

Wicclair, Mark R. and DeVita, Michael, 'Oversight of Research Involving the Dead' (2004) 14(2) *Kennedy Institute of Ethics Journal* 143–64

Wilkinson, T. M., 'Last Rights: The Ethics of Research on the Dead' (2002) 19(1) *Journal of Applied Philosophy* 31

Williams, Bernard, 'The *Makropulos* Case: Reflections on the Tedium of Immortality' in Williams, Bernard ed., *Problems of the Self* (Cambridge: Cambridge University Press, 1973)

Wojcik, Mark E., 'Aids and Funeral Homes: Common Legal Issues Facing Funeral Directors' (1994) 27 *Journal of Marshall Law Review* 411–34

Yourgrau, Palle, 'The Dead' (1987) 86(2) *Journal of Philosophy* 84

Zwicker, Milton W. and Sweatman, M. J., 'Who Has the Right to Choose the Deceased's Final Resting Place?' (2002) 22 *Estates, Trusts and Pensions Journal* 43–54

Other bibliographical resources

American Medical Association, *E-5.057: Confidentiality of HIV Status on Autopsy Reports* (June 1994), available at www.ama-assn.org/ama/pub/category/8358.html, accessed on 16 May 2007

American Medical Association: Council on Ethical and Judicial Affairs, *Report C-A-92: Confidentiality of HIV Status on Autopsy Report* (June 1992), available at www.ama-assn.org/ama1/pub/upload/mm/369/ceja_ca92.pdf, accessed on 12 May 2007

   Report E-5.051: Confidentiality of Medical Information Postmortem (December 2000), available at www.ama-assn.org/ama/pub/category/8354.html, accessed on 12 May 2007

Canadian Institutes of Health Research, Natural Sciences and Engineering Research Council of Canada, Social Sciences and Humanities Research Council of Canada, *Tri-Council Policy Statement: Ethical Conduct for Research Involving Humans*, 1998 (with 2000, 2002, 2005 amendments), available at http://pre.ethics.gc.ca/english/pdf/TCPS%20October%202005_E.pdf, accessed on 16 October 2007

Canadian Medical Association, Code of Ethics, 1996

Council of Europe, European Convention on Human Rights, 4 November 1950
   Convention on Human Rights and Biomedicine, 4 April 1997, available at http://conventions.coe.int/ treaty/en/treaties/html/164.htm, accessed on 12 May 2007

Donegan, Lawrence, 'Frozen in Memory', *Observer*, 14 July 2002

European Consultation on the Rights of Patients, *A Declaration on the Promotion of Patients' Rights in Europe* (Amsterdam: World Health Organization, 30 March 1994)

European Parliament, Charter of Fundamental Rights of the European Union, 18 December 2000, available at www.europarl.eu.int/charter/pdf/text_en.pdf, accessed on 12 May 2007

General Medical Council, *Making and Using Visual and Audio Recording of Patients* (2002), available at www.gmc-uk.org/guidance/library/ making_ audiovisual.asp, accessed on 26 March 2006

Confidentiality: Protecting and Providing Information (April 2004), available at www.gmc-uk.org/guidance/library/confidentiality.asp, accessed on 1 April 2006

Health and Human Services, *Recommendations of the Secretary of Health and Human Services: Confidentiality of Individually-Identifiable Health Information*, 11 September 1997, available at www.epic.org/privacy/medical/hhs_ recommendations_1997.html, accessed on 12 May 2007

Law Reform Commission of Canada, *Procurement and Transfer of Human Tissues and Organs*, working paper 66 (Ministry of Supply and Services, 1992)

Matthews, Sam, 'BBC Three Brings Flashmob Opera to Railway Station' Brand Republic (25 August 2004), available at www.brandrepublic.com/ bulletins/media/article/220252/bbc-three-brings-flashmob-opera-railway-stations/, accessed on 13 March 2006

McSwain, Ross, 'Cemeteries Provide Unique Look at State's History', *West Texas News and Sport*, 14 April 1997, available at http://web.gosanangelo.com/ archive/97/april/14/12.htm, accessed on 10 May 2007

National Research Council Canada, *Policy for Research Involving Human Subjects*, available at www.nrc-cnrc.gc.ca/randd/ethics/policy_e.html#def, last accessed on 16 May 2007

Newman, Ed, 'Part Four: Patients Have Rights but Doctors Have Rights Too', available at www.cp.duluth.mn.us/~ennyman/DAS-4.html, accessed on 10 May 2007

Nuffield Council on Bioethics Working Party, *Human Tissue: Ethical and Legal Issues* (England, 1995)

Organization for Economic Co-operation and Development, Guidelines on the Protection of Privacy and Transborder Flows of Personal Data, 23 September 1980, available at www.oecd.org/document/18/0,2340,en_ 2649_34255_1815186_1_1_1_1,00.html, accessed on 20 April 2006

Royal College of Pathologists, *Consensus Statement of Recommended Policies for Uses of Human Tissue in Research Education and Quality Control* (England, 1999)

Scottish Executive, *Final Report of the Independent Review on the Retention of Organs at Post-Mortem* (Scotland, 2001)

Stanley, Alessandra, 'Poet Told All; Therapist Provides the Record', *New York Times*, 15 July 1991, at A1, available at http://query.nytimes.com/gst/ fullpage.html?sec=health&res= 9D0CE2DE1730F936A25754C0A967958260, accessed on 16 May 2007

United Nations Educational, Scientific and Cultural Organization, Universal Declaration on Bioethics and Human Rights, 19 October 2005

US Department of Health and Human Services, *Standards for Privacy of Individually Identifiable Health Information*, available at www.hhs.gov/ocr/combinedregtext.pdf, accessed on 3 March 2006

World Health Organization, *Medical Certification of Cause of Death* (Geneva: WHO, 1968).

Internet websites

http://news.bbc.co.uk/2/hi/europe/4801292.stm, accessed on 12 March 2006

www.alcor.org/FAQs/faq01.html#cost, accessed on 12 May 2007

www.aleyshalechet.co.il/english/eng_index.php, accessed on 12 May 2007

www.crimelibrary.com/serial_killers/weird/burke/merchandise_3.html, accessed on 15 October 2007

Index

death certificates, 217, 218
disposal of one's body
 cryonics, 154–5
 delegation, 151
 examples, 143
 Feller case, 182–3
 Herold case, 181–2
 Holland case, 183
 local links, 183–4
 organ donations, 155
 procedural obstacles, 181
 respect for wishes, 111, 113, 150
 Scheck case, 173–4
 statutes, 151, 162
 trusts, 162–3
 Uniform Anatomical Gift Act, 152, 154
 urgency, 152
duty to bury, 95
interference with dead bodies, 140
mental incapacity and consent, 71
Moore case, 119–21, 135
NASA shuttle explosion, 220
organ donations
 corneas, 46, 98
 liabilities, 98
post-mortem confidentiality
 case law, 215
 contractual model, 207–8
 empirical studies, 195
 guidelines, 188–9
 insurance companies, 231
 interests of other patients, 216
 regulation, 191–2
 research data, 229
 teaching data, 230
posthumous lawyer–client privilege, 206
quasi-property, 101–2
urine, 125
utilitarianism
 Bentham, 73, 144
 bequests, 53
 corpses and property, 51
 post-mortem confidentiality and, 194
 property as form of, 135–6

Versace, Gianni, 220

Waldron, Jeremy, 135
Waluchow. W.J., 25
waste matter, proprietary rights, 117–21, 125
Wellman, Carl, 58
West, Sandra Ilene, 143, 179
Westin, Alan, 198, 209
whales, 116
White, Alan, 80–1
Wicclair, Mark, 226–7
Wigmore, John, 194
Wilkinson, T.M., 22
will theory. *See* choice theory
Williams, Bernard, 27
Williams, Glanville, 142
Williams, Ted, 110, 144
wills
 autonomy, 149
 bodily testaments
  alternatives, 154–65
  enforceability, 144–5, 150–3
  examples, 143, 144
  limitations on enforcement, 171–84
  Property Classification Criterion, 153, 165–71
 contesting, 146, 230–1
 contractual rights, 56
 Fabre, 56
 formal requirements, 152
 legal fiction, 55, 57
 living wills. *See* advance directives
 posthumous rights, 53–7
 Steiner, 53–7
 testamentary power, rationales, 166–8
 transfer of property only, 89, 150–2, 153, 165–71
witchcraft, 89, 90
work and skill exception, 102, 103–7, 108

Yourgrau, Palle, 17

CPSIA information can be obtained at www.ICGtesting.com
Printed in the USA
LVOW130012210512

282461LV00005BA/13/P